Access to Library Collections

An inquiry into the validity of the
direct shelf approach, with special
reference to browsing

by

Richard Joseph Hyman

The Scarecrow Press, Inc.
Metuchen, N. J.   1972

IN MEMORY OF MY PARENTS AND BROTHER

CONTENTS

PART II.   QUESTIONNAIRE ANALYSIS

ix

LIST OF TABLES

PREFACE

Shelf classification with relative location is a standard practice in American libraries. In recent years, questions have arisen about its expense and its theoretical problems and practical difficulties.

Shelf classification has been defended constantly on the basis of its value to the reader who, when he has direct access, is able to "browse." Although used freely in library parlance, "browsing" was not thoroughly described nor its theory rigorously examined until this far-ranging study by Richard J. Hyman of the direct shelf approach.

This study assumed that an additional use study held less promise than an analytical consideration of concepts. The basic approach was a survey comparing traditional and current professional ideas on direct access. Principal data-gathering instruments were documentary analysis and opinion questionnaire.

Findings of the documentary analysis included the following:

Research from 1890 to 1970 on the direct shelf approach and browsing left the problems largely unresolved and evidently resistant to established methods of use and user research. The need for an exhaustive study of concepts was confirmed.

Open-shelf libraries--organized through shelf classification and relative location--were meant to arouse the intellectual, social, and political interest of the average citizen and affect his democratic self-realization.

Definitions of "browsing" varied greatly: self-indulgence by the untutored in objectionable works; beneficial self-education for the general reader; valuable guidance for the scholar in his research.

Ambivalence and inconsistency were expressed by

classification experts who joined practical ends to seemingly impractical means. Similar attitudes were shown towards close classification, linearity, subject cataloging, and notation. Faith in shelf classification raised the danger of expecting the shelving scheme to offset or restore collection inadequacies.

The questionnaire, presenting hypotheses derived from the documentary analysis, obtained responses from 152 practitioners and teachers of librarianship in the United States and Canada. The questionnaire measured the level of acceptance for statements whose implications or assumptions could directly influence shelf policies incorporating systematic classification.

Respondents, confirming attitudes in the literature, were ambivalent towards the function of classification in direct access. The validity of the direct shelf approach was not given a convincing theoretical justification. The American librarian and patron unmistakably preferred to continue direct access, though how to implement it remained moot.

Dr. Hyman has specific suggestions for policy changes in connection with library school curricula and library management. Roles for the Library of Congress and the Dewey Decimal Classifications, close and broad classification, reclassification, and centralized processing are indicated. His book should be of value to teachers, students, administrators, and practitioners.

Maurice F. Tauber
Melvil Dewey Professor of Library Service
Columbia University

PREFATORY QUOTATIONS

It is clearly the duty of a librarian so to conduct
his library that everything it contains shall be accessible to every reader, and that with as little inconvenience as possible.... What means have you
adopted to make your books most useful? Until this
question is answered the working power of no library can be correctly estimated.

Otis H. Robinson, "On Indexing Periodical and Miscel-
laneous Literature," in U.S., Bureau of Education, Public
Libraries in the United States of America. 1876.

In thinking out classification thoroughly, we find
ourselves reminded of nearly every other library
question.... The open access question--very important, whatever be our particular views--abso-
lutely depends on classification.

T. W. Lyster, "Observations on Shelf Classification,"
Library Association Record. 1900.

The most highly philosophical treatment that can be
given to its [library science] problems has important bearing on progress in the most practical
details of the art.

Ernest Cushing Richardson, Classification: Theoretical
and Practical. 1901.

Subject-classification has been established in library
economy and its value is generally recognized. The
question now is, what shall we do to improve and
develop library classifications and to adapt and
economize them?

A problem arises in any undertaking to solve or

xv

control a complex situation of facts and events, forces, motives and relations. A valid answer is a theory. An adequate answer is a solution. A difficult problem seldom has a solution without a theory. A theory is a generalized statement of basic facts, relations and principles. The problem should usually be stated first, and then the theory may be derived from the applicable principles involved. An unsolved problem of importance needs an applicable theory.

Henry Evelyn Bliss, The Organization of Knowledge in Libraries; and the Subject-Approach to Books. 1939.

We cannot revert to arrangement of reading materials in accession order and deny open-access-- the greatest human contribution of the library profession.

S. R. Ranganathan, "Colon Classification and Its Approach to Documentation," in Chicago, University, Graduate Library School, Library Conference, Bibliographic Organization. 1951.

Now he would prowl the stacks of the library at night, pulling books out of a thousand shelves and reading in them like a madman. The thought of these vast stacks of books would drive him mad: the more he read, the less he seemed to know ....

He read insanely .... He read no more from pleasure--the thought that other books were waiting for him tore at his heart forever. He pictured himself as tearing the entrails from a book as from a fowl. At first, hovering over book stalls, or walking at night among the vast piled shelves of the library, he would read, watch in hand, muttering to himself in triumph or anger at the timing of each page: 'Fifty seconds to do that one. Damn you, we'll see! You will, will you?'--and he would tear through the next page in twenty seconds.

Thomas Wolfe, Of Time and the River. 1935.

Stood in the Library overwhelmed by titles: Green
Mansions, The Jungle Book, Droll Tales, Boswell's
Journal, One Life One Kopek, Anna Karenina, The
Moth and the Flame, Silas Marner, Penguin Island,
and A Tale of Two Cities. My eyes got stuck. I
couldn't choose one. The librarian offered to help,
but there was no helping me; I didn't want to read,
I wanted to sense the overwhelming mystery of
shelved creation.

Rosalyn Drexler, I Am the Beautiful Stranger. 1965.

When I was growing up in Newark in the forties we
were taught, or perhaps just assumed, that the
books in the public library belonged to the public.
Since my family did not own many books, or have
very much money for a child to buy them, it was
good to know that solely by virtue of my citizen-
ship, I had the use of any of the books I
wanted. . . .

And then there was the lesson in order. The institution itself was the instructor. What trust it
inspired--in oneself and in systems--to decode the
message on the catalogue cards; then to make it
through the network of corridors and staircases into the stacks; and there to find exactly where it
was supposed to be, the right book. For a ten-
year-old to be able to steer himself through thousands of books to the very one he wants is not
without its civilizing influence, either.

Philip Roth, "Topics: Reflections on the Death of a
Library." New York Times, March 1, 1969.

PROLEGOMENA

Chapter I

INTRODUCTION

An investigation of any aspect of the direct shelf approach involves one immediately in a central problem which ramifies, often unexpectedly, into almost every major concern, theoretical and practical, of librarianship. Thus, one may easily become entangled in: selection and acquisition policy (which may well require consideration of such controversial matters as censorship, community pressures, cooperative collecting agreements, standardized booklists); the function of cataloging, particularly of subject headings, vis-à-vis classification; general versus special classification schemes; documentation as related to librarianship; the utility of mnemonic and of expressive notation; bibliothecal as against bibliographical classification; the differing interpretations of the browsing concept (and of browsability) for research and for non-scholarly library use; how to determine and store less-used or obsolescent materials; the divergent philosophies on the desirable extent of readers' services and reference assistance; the worth and form of independent study in the library; the suitability of the Library of Congress Classification (LC) or of the Dewey Decimal Classification (DC) for various types and sizes of libraries--an issue often complicated by concomitant problems of reclassification; the encroachments on direct access resulting from increased use of microforms and from possible mechanized information storage and retrieval; the proper educational, social, or scholarly functions of libraries. Nor is this by any means a full listing of the threatening entanglements.

Many other questions, once considered safely interred, reemerge: printed or card catalogs; broad or close classification; relative or fixed location; regional or union catalogs; classified or dictionary catalogs; librarians as generalists or as subject specialists?

Furthermore, there are disciplines which might offer insights for the fundamental understanding of direct access:

2

the psychology of learning, the philosophy of knowledge and of perception, the sociology of institutions, even the neurological or biochemical study of the human brain. [1] For the investigator the perils of diffused aims and fragmented effort are all too evident; but equally evident must be the import of so protean a problem.

This study has endeavored to skirt these dangers by attempting to maintain the functional principle of usefulness as the criterion for the problems under investigation: what is the stated purpose of this library policy or practice in terms of its intended usefulness to the reader (and the librarian), and how does the evidence demonstrate the success with which that purpose has been fulfilled?

Such an approach may not assure valid answers, but it seems a prudent methodological precaution. The criterion of usefulness, moreover, has the sanction of every considerable library authority since the generation of Panizzi and Jewett; it has been given many formulations, e.g., Cutter's classic statement in Rules for a Dictionary Catalog[2] and Ranganathan's "Five Laws of Library Science."[3] That this criterion, however, is not the philosophers' stone for success in research is abundantly shown in the literature where librarians constantly invoke it to install their own and demolish opponents' schemes. Metcalfe's campaign against Ranganathan's ideas, [4] a striking example, will in part be discussed.

The particular problems--and the reasons for their choice--will, one hopes, be elucidated below. Here, a few general comments on the pretensions of this project seem in order. The inquiry does not pretend to aim at final solutions to the many perplexing difficulties attendant on direct access. Thus, it does not presume to "justify" or "refute" the role of classification in American libraries, nor to deliver definitive judgment on open versus closed-shelf policies, nor to prescribe any one classification scheme.

This study does advance a series of hypotheses so that various apparently heterogeneous problems associated with direct access may be tested by accepted research methods within a unifying framework. Such hypotheses, by juxtaposing hitherto separately regarded factors, may sharpen the focus on those problems and lead to a more balanced view of what might seem irreconcilable polarities of opinion. If the study succeeds in some reasonable degree, the parameters of the central problem may be more clearly drawn, the numerous scattered topics of debate more convincingly subsumed within a recognizable universe of discourse.

In the preliminary research for this study it became clear that the professional literature presented dilemmas and paradoxes in regard to open-shelf access and shelf classification which, after almost a century, would hardly be resolved by one more investigator almost completely dependent on the contributions of his predecessors. Equally puzzling, and apparently as unyielding of solution, was the frequently disconcerting contrast between the theory and practice of leading librarians and classificationists. It thus seemed discreet to essay a somewhat less frontal attack on the problems. Accordingly, instead of attempting, for example, another user study, or of working to accumulate and weigh evidence which might contribute to a "conclusive" verdict on close shelf classification, this study tries to test hypotheses which would accommodate factors possibly inherent in the basic concept of the direct shelf approach. Such factors might, perhaps unwittingly, create those situations wherein apparently contradictory opinions could be maintained and practice could frequently diverge, evidently, from declared theory. Some of the hypotheses are quite broadly based, having been suggested by the literature of sociology, of psychology, or of philosophy. These generalizing hypotheses, it is hoped, are no less governed by the criterion of usefulness. For example, in certain respects Durkheim or Lovejoy or Piaget might provide just as helpful insight into the nature and limits of practical library classification as Cutter or Dewey or Sayers or Bliss.

The chief method of attack in this study is that of the normative survey. Two major data-gathering tools, documentary analysis and opinion questionnaire, were employed in the formulation and testing of "structural" hypotheses. The first part of the study reports on the documentary analysis, the second on the opinion questionnaire. During the documentary analysis most hypotheses are both formulated and--as far as possible--tested. However, some hypotheses were formulated and tested only in the questionnaire. Although in the first part occasional reference may be made to evidence detailed in the second, most of the questionnaire results are reserved for discussion in the latter. Thus, the reader may follow the hypotheses from their origin in the documentary analysis on to their testing against both additional documentary evidence, historical and current, and against the opinions of today's library profession as expressed

in the questionnaire.   Further data are presented, when
necessary, from the investigator's experience in technical
and reader services, and from consultation and correspon-
dence with recognized authorities.

The next three chapters delimit the problems to be
investigated and explain why certain aspects were emphasized.   In search of definition, the "browsing" concept is
studied linguistically.   In order to circumscribe the problem
and to clarify the study's methodology, attention is given to
significant past research.   Such records suggest what former
researchers assumed was the "real" problem and why, therefore, they developed and applied their particular methodology.
This "state-of-the-art" report is of especial importance for
this study because of its intentionally different approach. It
is no less important for illuminating the underlying beliefs
of past researchers.

There follows a history of open access, insofar as
relevant to modern American library practice, with stress
on its social and educational implications.   A functional
definition of "browsing"--a central factor in open access--
is then attempted.   Next to be studied in the literature are
the influences on the direct shelf approach of acquisition
policy and of classification theory and application.   Again,
those aspects are emphasized which seem most significant
for current American library practice.

The second major part concerns the extent to which
the hypotheses have been supported by the opinions of present-day American library practitioners and teachers.   As
indicated, not all the hypotheses were suitable for this double testing.   For some, documentary analysis had to suf-
fice, while for others only the questionnaire was appropriate.

The study ends with an attempt at a synthesis of the
data and of conclusions to be derived therefrom.   Some possible developments in practice and research are suggested.

On the threshold of this project, the apprehensive
researcher must needs draw assurance from Broadfield's
comment introducing his study of the philosophy of classification: "If the state of being educated is not a condition of
this type of work, that of being more educated than before
certainly seems to be a result of it."[5]

Notes

1. Phyllis A. Richmond, Transformation and Organization
    of Information Content: Aspects of Recent Research
    in the Art and Science of Classification (Copenhagen:
    Danish Centre for Documentation, 1965), p. 36.
    (Pamphlet)

2. Charles Ammi Cutter, Rules for a Dictionary Catalog
    (4th ed., rewritten; Washington: Govt. Print. Off.,
    1904), p. 6.   ("The convenience of the public is al-
    ways to be set before the ease of the cataloger.")

3. S. R. Ranganathan, Prolegomena to Library Classifica-
    tion (3rd ed.; New York: Asia Publishing House,
    1967), p. 7.

4. John Metcalfe, Information Indexing and Subject Cata-
    loging: Alphabetical, Classified, Coordinate, Me-
    chanical (New York: Scarecrow Press, 1957), pp. 116-
    21, 134-35, 166-68; Subject Classifying and Indexing
    of Libraries and Literature (New York: Scarecrow
    Press, 1959), pp. 240-48.

5. A. Broadfield, The Philosophy of Classification (London:
    Grafton, 1946), p. vii.

Chapter II

DEFINITIONS OF PROBLEMS AND TERMS

Shelf classification with relative location has been a dominant feature of American public and academic libraries since the last quarter of the nineteenth century:

> Under this system, books on a given subject can be located without knowledge of their titles or authors simply by inspecting the shelves in the stack area for that subject, and the searcher will also find related materials on nearby shelves in ever-widening circles of subject matter.[1]

Some obvious limitations have, however, from time to time been noted in the literature: (1) even in a non-circulating library, all books cannot be on the shelves at all times;[2] (2) bibliothecal classification (governing the shelf arrangement) is restricted by (a) systematic inadequacies and (b) linearity;[3] (3) all readers may not have an awareness of the classification system; and (4) many collections, especially in large academic and research libraries, may not be available for open-stack use to all patrons.

Recently concern has increased, particularly in larger libraries, with respect to the expense and the theoretical and practical difficulties of maintaining shelf classification.[4] Rapidly changing, merging, overlapping, and developing subject fields, as well as the concurrent emphasis of documentalists on non-book information storage and retrieval, have supported doubts concerning the efficacy of traditional book classification.[5] Too, as collections grow astronomically, the availability and cost of shelf space become critical considerations. Shelf classification "requires that space be left on the shelves for the addition of new books on the same subject and, eventually, that whole sections be shifted at great expense to acquire still more space for expansion."[6] A few libraries have weighed a return to pre-Dewey fixed location schemes because books shelved by size can save much space.[7] Another space-saving expedient, cooperative and

7

centralized storage, has met with strong objections from researchers who demand immediate access to all relevant materials. [8]

A recurrent defense of shelf classification (which in
modern American libraries also almost always means relative location) stresses the value of permitting the reader direct access to the shelves and stimulating him to "browse"
--an opportunity afforded by the "browsability" of a collection
so organized. An A. L. A. Classification Committee has reported: "DC has the advantage of providing browsability. In
open-stack libraries, this is important. It is practically impossible to browse with LC although people try it all the
time. "[9] (This conclusion will be discussed below and tested
by the questionnaire.)

Thus it is clear that the issues of direct access and
of shelf classification (with relative location) are inextricable;
any serious investigation of one inevitably involves the other.
Cutter held that "in a library where the public have access
to the shelves, ... the books are their own classed catalog,
better than any that the librarian can make. "[10]

An inquiry into the validity of the direct shelf approach as a concept for the organization of library materials
subsumes the problems of "browsing" and "browsability. "
This study does not claim that "browsing" and the "direct
shelf approach" are necessarily interchangeable terms, but
they seem so intimately related that a meaningful investigation must frequently treat them simultaneously. They almost
always share common characteristics and are, as will be
seen, often combined in librarians' thought. The problem to
be investigated might, indeed, be described as follows: to
what extent and under what conditions do the concepts of the
"direct shelf approach" and of "browsability" justify organizing library materials by an allegedly complicated and expensive system of shelf classification involving relative location?
(This study often uses the phrase, "relative shelf classification, " to describe the above system.) The study attempts to
examine and define the concepts of the "direct shelf approach"
and "browsability" in all their important verbal variants, and
to assess their validity as a basis for shelf classification of
library collections.

Though common in library discourse, "browsing" has
not been definitively described, nor has the theory supporting
the concept been rigorously examined. [11] The word appears

in many contexts and with apparently varying meaning. The
public library patron is said to be browsing for a mystery
novel; a student is assumed to be educating himself when he
browses in the college library. In the research library, the
scholar seeking subject relationships or relevant facts or in-
spiration may resort to browsing and be blessed by an occurrence of "serendipity." Shelf classification with relative
location, by making browsing possible, is evidently presumed
to realize these ends.

     The numerous library use and user studies have al-
most all been concerned with what happens before and after
the patron utilizes the collection. Such studies have sought
to learn, through interview, questionnaire, or diary, what the
patron did at the card catalog; or, by circulation record
analysis, what the reader took out of the library; or, by citation analysis and reference counting, what sources the researcher apparently needed. State-of-the-art reviews have
expressed general dissatisfaction with the methods and results. Frarey and Dunkin[12] did not think more catalog use
studies necessarily desirable. Taube,[13] though confining his
comments to scientific information, questioned the overall
value of user studies. Brodman[14] criticized assumptions of
citation analysis.

     Very few studies have investigated the movements of
patrons within the stacks, or have attempted to relate users'
handling of books to the "intellectual" act of browsing.
Tauber surveyed faculty members on their attitude towards
classification.[15] The ambitious 1956 Jackson Catalog Use
Study recommended investigating the effectiveness of card
catalog use as compared with the direct shelf approach.[16]
A 1960 pilot study of stack use at the Library of Congress
evoked the comment that "the questionnaires were not designed to show whether these individuals could have obtained
the needed information if access to the stacks had been denied them."[17] The Davis and Bailey Bibliography of Use
Studies lists 438 entries, from 1902 to 1963, but only one,
a 1961 Master's dissertation, has "browsing" in its title, and
only one other[18] has the word in the editors' annotation.
The former is annotated: "There are no conclusive findings
... although there are some interesting facts." A 1962 survey of library usage at Johns Hopkins asked patrons to record "browsing" but did not define it; nor did Fussler and
Simon[19] who sampled "browsing," though their study set levels of specificity and value, and emphasized handling.

Some of these research efforts, as indicated in the Introduction, will be considered in some detail because of their contributions to definition of problems and also to this study's methodology.

Also, the need for this study has been heightened by: interlibrary loan, photographic copying and microreproduction, plans for computerized central stores of library materials and catalog information--all of which reduce or possibly eliminate "browsing" or direct access in one's own library. If it can be suggested under what conditions and to what extent the direct shelf approach and "browsability" are valid concepts for the organization of library materials, the implications for shelf arrangement, perhaps generally for book classification theory, could be considerable. Also of some account is the possible economic and administrative significance for national bibliographic organization and control.

Whatever research proposals may result from this study, it seems most desirable to try to define with greater exactitude the concepts of the "direct shelf approach" and of "browsing."

Basic Assumptions

The basic assumptions of this study, and also of the criterion of usefulness described in the Introduction, are as follows:

1. (a) Physical, as well as bibliographical, organization of materials is an important function of libraries and affects a collection's usefulness, so that (b) such organization should aim at maximum effectiveness in meeting patron needs.

2. (a) Optimum organization should be based on sound theoretical principles, because (b) adherence to faulty or untested theory can result in lack of usefulness to clientele as well as in wasted time, effort, and money in library operations. Accordingly, (c) it is important to investigate possible error, inconsistency, misunderstanding, or confusion in formulating, interpreting, and applying theoretical principles for the physical, as well as bibliographical, organization of library materials.

Definitions and Delimitations

"Validity" is defined as conformance with generally accepted rules of inductive reasoning, from which logical consistency emerges as a major criterion.

Although the study intends to pursue intensively the meanings of "browsing" and its verbal variants, a working definition might here be given: a patron's random examination of library materials as arranged for use. "Materials" are books or serials; other types will be considered when necessary. A goal of this project is to examine the possible connotations of "random examination" subsumed under the "browsing" concept. Here the phrase can be further defined only through the synonymous "casual inspection."

"Concept" is meant to include the cluster of ideas and intellectual assumptions embodied in "direct shelf approach," "browsing," and their verbal variants.

The study is designed for American libraries primarily, although necessary historical and systematic comparisons will be made with non-American, chiefly British, institutions. Though this study may emphasize the larger academic and research libraries--which present extreme instances of the problem--such libraries, as will be explained by the hypotheses, must be placed within a national setting of smaller academic and research libraries and public libraries of all sizes.

Outline of the Methodology

This study's methodology is based on the belief that additional use studies--as indicated by Frarey, Taube, and Dunkin[20]--are not promising, and that the problem, as here posed, invites a theoretical investigation. Among others, Richmond[21] has called for fundamental research into the psychology of classification.

As explained in the Introduction, the chief method of attack is that of the normative survey; the main data-gathering means, documentary analysis and opinion questionnaire.

Pertinent library and related literature are surveyed for evidence which suggests or tests the hypotheses. Although the words are methodologically imprecise, the approach may be described as "inductive" and "theoretically

oriented. " The study, as it proceeds, may make these
words more tenable. Sources include: representative monographs, textbooks, and articles on librarianship, cataloging,
classification, documentation, and information storage and
retrieval--particularly as reflecting the criterion of usefulness; also pertinent library surveys, technical reports, dissertations, and use studies. Classic works on the history
and philosophy of American librarianship have been reviewed.
Some attention has been given to pertinent statements on
American education, to current psychological theories of
learning, and to promising sources in sociology and philosophy. Representative works were sought for the various periods of American library development, principally since
1870, with necessary reference to earlier and/or non-American data.

Many relevant sources are not necessarily indexed or
described as "direct shelf approach" or "browsing. " This
does not mean a "random" literature search. The concepts
can be found under such rubrics as "books and reading, "
"non-specific book search, " and in well-known texts concerned with open-shelf access, e.g., Branscomb's Teaching
with Books. [22] Also, later works related to the subject usually provide literature review and retrospective citations.

The second major data-gathering tool, the opinion
questionnaire, was sent to a group of authorities on library
classification and reader services. Names were selected
from the professional literature, directories, personal knowledge, and consultation with experts, so as to represent practitioners in various types and sizes of libraries throughout
the United States and Canada, as well as teachers of classification and reader services in the accredited library
schools. (The statistical basis for selection is discussed in
Chapter Nine.) Over 150 responses were received, representing almost a two-thirds return. The content of the questionnaire was determined after literature search and questionnaire pretesting. Format, though basically check-off,
provided also for respondents to comment differently or at
length. Many of these comments proved significant for testing the hypotheses.

The questionnaire was planned to arouse interest. It
posed theoretical and practical questions in the form largely
of opinions paraphrased from the professional literature. Its
statements concerned the nature of the direct shelf approach,
"browsing, " and their connection with relative location and

shelf classification. It asked for the respondents' opinions
on the opinions as listed in the questionnaire. It thus aimed
to elicit from practitioners and teachers in the technical and
reader services their assumptions and beliefs concerning the
"direct shelf approach" and "browsing" as concepts for organizing library collections. The "Questionnaire Analysis"
not only summarizes these responses but attempts to relate
them to significant respondent characteristics, e.g., teacher
or practitioner, public or academic librarian. As indicated
in the Introduction, responses are compared with the findings
of the "Documentary Analysis"; special attention is paid to
seeming contradictions between published theory and prevalent
assumptions among practitioners and teachers. The opinions
expressed (directly or by implication) thus further test hypotheses on the variant meanings of the "direct shelf approach" and "browsing" and their possible significance for
shelf classification in different library situations.

Notes

1. "Analysis of Book-Stack Use, " U.S. Library of Congress Information Bulletin, XIX (July 25, 1960),
   436.

2. Verner Clapp, The Future of the Research Library
   (Urbana: University of Illinois Press, 1964), p. 98-
   99. ("Program 14. Improvement of Record Control of Circulation. ")

3. Grace Osgood Kelley, The Classification of Books: An
   Inquiry into Its Usefulness to the Reader (New York:
   Wilson, 1937), p. 68.

4. Maurice F. Tauber and Edith Wise, Classification Sys-
   tems, in The State of the Library Art, ed. by
   Ralph R. Shaw, Vol. I, Pt. 3 (New Brunswick,
   N.J.: Graduate School of Library Service, Rutgers
   University, 1961), p. 3.

5. Richard S. Angell, "On the Future of the Library of
   Congress Classification, " in International Study Conference on Classification Research, 2d, Elsinore,
   Denmark, Classification Research: Proceedings, ed.
   by Pauline Atherton (Copenhagen: Munksgaard,
   1965), p. 101-12.

6. U.S., Library of Congress, Annual Report of the Li-
    brarian of Congress for the Fiscal Year Ending June
    30, 1961 (Washington, 1962), p. xiv.

7. The Reference Department of the New York Public Li-
    brary now uses this arrangement for part of its col-
    lection. See also Tauber and Wise, Classification
    Systems, p. 3.

8. Clapp, The Future of the Research Library, p. 1-17.

9. American Library Association, Classification Committee,
    "Report, May 15, 1964: Statement on Types of
    Classification Available to New Academic Libraries, "
    Library Resources and Technical Services, IX (Win-
    ter, 1965), 104-11.

10. Charles Ammi Cutter, "Library Catalogues, " in U.S.,
    Bureau of Education, Public Libraries in the United
    States of America; Their History, Condition, and
    Management; Special Report; Part I (Washington:
    Govt. Print. Off., 1876), p. 548.

11. Information scientists have generally shown more theo-
    retical awareness, e.g., Malcolm Rigby, "Brows-
    ability in Modern Information Retrieval Systems: The
    Quest for Information, " in Symposium on Education
    for Information Science, Airlie House, 1965, Pro-
    ceedings, ed. by Laurence B. Heilprin, Barbara E.
    Markuson, and Frederick L. Goodman (Washington:
    Spartan Books, 1965), p. 47-52.

12. Carlyle J. Frarey, "Subject Headings, in The State of the
    Library Art, " Library Quarterly Vol. 1, Pt. 2 (1960),
    p. 64; Paul S. Dunkin, "Catalog Use Study by Sidney L.
    Jackson, " Library Quarterly. XXIX (April, 1959), 142.

13. Mortimer Taube, "An Evaluation of 'Use Studies' of
    Scientific Information, " in Emerging Solutions for
    Mechanizing the Storage and Retrieval of Information,
    Vol. V of his Studies in Coordinate Indexing (Wash-
    ington: Documentation, Inc., 1959), p. 46-71.

14. Estelle Brodman, "Choosing Physiology Journals, " Bul-
    letin of the Medical Library Association, XXXII
    (October, 1944), 479-83.

15. Tauber, "Reclassification and Recataloging in College
     and University Libraries" (unpublished Ph. D. dis-
     sertation, University of Chicago, 1941), p. 208-56,
     286-335.

16. American Library Association, Cataloging and Classifi-
     cation Section, Catalog Use Study: Director's Re-
     port by Sidney L. Jackson, ed. by Vaclav Mostecky
     (Chicago: American Library Assn., 1956), p. 42.

17. Saul Herner, "A Pilot Study of the Use of the Stacks of
     the Library of Congress," Washington: Herner,
     1960 (Typewritten); Henry J. Dubester, "Stack Use
     of a Research Library," American Library Associa-
     tion Bulletin, LV (November, 1961), 893.

18. Richard A. Davis and Catherine A. Bailey, Bibliography
     of Use Studies (Philadelphia: Graduate School of Li-
     brary Science, Drexel Institute of Technology, 1964);
     Alice Bowen, "Non-recorded Use of Books and
     Browsing in the Stacks of a Research Library" (un-
     published Master's dissertation, University of Chi-
     cago, 1961) (Davis and Bailey: No. 043); Herman
     H. Fussler and Julian L. Simon, Patterns in the
     Use of Books in Large Research Libraries (Chicago:
     University of Chicago Library, 1961) (Davis and
     Bailey: No. 139) (A reedited version with unchanged
     conclusions appeared in 1969.)

19. Johns Hopkins University, Progress Report on an Opera-
     tions Research and Systems Engineering Study of a
     University Library (Baltimore, 1963), p. 53-108;
     Fussler and Simon, Patterns in the Use of Books.

20. Frarey, Subject Headings, p. 64; Taube, "An Evalua-
     tion of 'Use Studies' "; Dunkin, "Catalog Use Study
     by Sidney L. Jackson," p. 142.

21. Phyllis A. Richmond, Transformation and Organization
     of Information Content: Aspects of Recent Research
     in the Art and Science of Classification (Copenhagen:
     Danish Centre for Documentation, 1965) (Pamphlet.)

22. Harvie B. Branscomb, Teaching with Books: A Study of
     College Libraries (Chicago: Assn. of American Col-
     leges and American Library Assn., 1940).

PART I

DOCUMENTARY ANALYSIS

Chapter III

A LINGUISTIC APPROACH TO THE BROWSING CONCEPT

The desirability of "browsing" is usually invoked by librarians against those opposed to shelf classification and open access. Hypotheses, derived chiefly from the professional literature, were included in the questionnaire to test the opinions of librarians and teachers on the various aspects of this protracted debate. But what does the concept mean literally? What can linguistic analysis reveal of the underlying theory? This chapter attempts to "place" "browsing" etymologically, the better to understand its later attributive usage. The findings may surprise many for whom "browsing" is a commonplace word or activity. The findings also seem to bear theoretically and practically on the concept as understood in librarianship.

As another step in the linguistic analysis, documentary frequency analysis was applied to "browsing" as recorded in library literature, specifically in indexes and bibliographies.

Etymology

The etymology of "browse" (or "browze") as noun and verb has not been definitively ascribed by all scholarly sources. Skeat[1] gives the word a French-Middle High German origin. Cassell's English Dictionary follows Skeat: "French brouster, brouter (Middle High German broz, a bud, Old Saxon brustian, to bud, cp. brēotan, to break)."[2] Wyld also traces the Old French form to Teutonic beginnings, but cites different cognates: "The word is of Germanic origin, cp. O.S. brustian, 'sprout, bud', connected with O.E. bryst q.v. under bristle, and with the base meaning 'spike', etc. there discussed."[3] Partridge shows some caution:

> To browse comes from MF brouster (OF bruster; F brouter), from MF broust (OF brost), a sprout, a shoot, of Gmc origin; of OS brustian, to sprout:

basic meaning, 'to swell' (IE *bhreus-), therefore
of BREAST. Browse, young shoots, hence such
fodder, prob comes from MF broust; but browse,
an act of browsing, clearly derives from 'to
browse. '4

Webster's Third New International Dictionary is even
more cautious: "Perhaps from (assumed) Middle French
brouser (whence obsolete French brouser), probably from
brouts, plural of brout, sprout, shoot."5   Onions gives a
reason for the uncertainty: "Both sb. and vb ... are ult.
-early modF. broust (earlier brost, now brout) bud, young
shoot, brouster (now brouter) crop; prob. of Germ. origin;
but loss of t is difficult to account for. "6   Klein, like Partridge, indicates by an asterisk an assumed or hypothetical
form:

> From the obsolete noun browse, 'shoots, twigs'
> (often used as cattle food), fr. MF. broust
> (whence F. brout), 'sprout, shoot' (whence MF.
> brouster, F. brouter, 'to browse'), fr. OF. brost,
> of same meaning, fr. Teut. *brustjan, 'to bud, '
> lit. 'to swell, ' fr. I. -E. base *bhreus-, 'to swell. '
> See breast. 7

No source, though, disputes the primary meaning.
Onions defines: "sb. young shoots and twigs, cattle-fodder;
vb. crop and eat, feed on leaves, etc." He places the origin of both noun and verb in the fifteenth century and says
they "are first recorded from Fitzherbert's 'Husbandry, '
1523. "8   Funk and Wagnalls New Standard Dictionary of the
English Language states: "To eat the twigs, etc. of growing
vegetation. "9   Cassell's English Dictionary says: "To nibble
and eat off (twigs, young shoots, etc.). "10   Oxford English
Dictionary defines:

> To feed on the leaves and shoots of trees and
> bushes; to crop the shoots or tender parts of rough
> plants for food; said of goats, deer, cattle. (Some-
> times carelessly used for graze, but properly im-
> plying the cropping of scanty vegetation.)11

Wyld gives as the primary meaning: "To feed as
animals do, nibble off grass and young shoots, etc., to
graze. "12

Oxford English Dictionary cites usage in a figurative

sense from 1542, but only in 1823 finds an example of its application to reading: "and browsed at will upon that fair and
wholesome pasturage [a good library].   (Lamb)"[13]   The derived meaning, "To read passages here and there in a book
or a collection of books," is given by Webster's New International Dictionary (Second Edition) with a quotation from
Browning: "To go and browse on Paul's Epistles,"[14] which
dates from 1850.   Oxford English Dictionary cites an 1870
passage from Lowell: "We thus get a glimpse of his brows-
ing--for ... he was always a random reader--in his father's
library."[15]

Slang and colloquial derivations began to appear in
documentable form only as the nineteenth century progressed.
Perhaps the original agricultural sense was still too strong
to encourage widespread metaphorical use.   Partridge lists
the meaning "to idle, to take things easily" as coming from
the "19th-20th century."[16]   Mathews cites an American use,
"to eat here and there, now and then," as an expression of
Abraham Lincoln and labels this meaning rare.[17]   Indeed,
Thornton does not list "browsing."[18]

Already in the original denotation, however, the idea
of unhurried casualness or of an informal search pattern is
evident.   What is not so evident to the modern reader (and
perhaps to the modern librarian)--unless he pursues the logical implications of the etymology--is that pastoral browsing
is possible only where and when browse is available.
Browse is by no means as certain or as plentiful as pasture.
Animals resort to browse for lack of pasture.   Actually,
what is meant by "browse" applied to books and reading is
"graze."   Although, as just indicated, Oxford English Dictionary warns against confusing the two words, modern usage
and the dictionaries based on it present the words as syno-
nyms.   (See Wyld, Cassell's English Dictionary, American
College Dictionary, and Webster's Collegiate Dictionary.)[19]

In fact, Morris and Morris rationalize the use of
"browse" for "graze" and further extend its figurative use:

> The original meaning of browse had nothing to do
> with browsing in stores, for it came from the Old
> French word brouz, meaning the twigs and leaves
> an animal could feed on.   There is still a very
> nice distinction between browsing and 'grazing' in
> that an animal who browses eats only foliage from
> trees and bushes, while a grazing animal eats

grass from the ground.

So to browse literally means to nibble at. It also
has the related meaning of glancing in casual fashion through a book or the various books in a li-
brary--nibbling, so to speak, at learning.   Many
of our bookstores today carry signs in the window
inviting passers-by to 'come in and browse around. '
Quite possibly this is where some get the idea that
the use of browse should be limited to places like
libraries and bookstores.

However, this seems to me an unwarranted limitation on the word's use and, providing that it's used
in the sense of making a leisurely tour of inspection, I don't see why one can't browse through a
department store just as well as through a bookstore. 20

Nevertheless, it is important to note that the difference between "browse" and "graze" lies in the degree of pur-
posiveness, shown especially in the transitive verb meaning
of "graze": "To feed or supply (cattle, sheep, etc.) with
grass or pasture. "21 With no intention of drawing invidious
comparisons between humans and animals, one might infer
an analogy between such physical conditions and those of the
recreational "browsing collection" or "browsing room" provided by the library. The etymology suggests, moreover,
that "browse" and its verbal variants, as employed in library
discourse, should more accurately read "graze. "

A hypothesis, included in the questionnaire, restated
such possible physical conditions of "grazing" alias "browsing. " The hypothesis was worded at a high level of generalization: "The greater limits imposed on browsing by acquisition policy and by classification, the more valuable browsing will be. " (V:5)22 The following related hypothesis was
worded more specifically: "The value of open-shelf access
is primarily conditioned by the quality and appropriateness
of the library's collection. " (IV:4)

"Browse" in the sense of casual inspection of books
is clearly of quite recent origin. Cutter was born four
years after Lamb's 1823 use of the metaphor. Whatever the
rigorously systematic definition of the word should be in librarianship, modern dictionaries present a seemingly clear
layman's explanation. Wyld gives as its extended, figurative

use: "To read or study in a desultory way. "[23] Webster's
Third New International Dictionary gives similar definitions:

> To look over casually (as a book): SKIM / he
> lazily browsed the headlines / to make (one's way)
> by browsing / I browsed my way through the agony
> column / to skim through a book reading at ran-
> dom passages that catch the eye; to look over books
> (as in a store or library) especially in order to
> decide what one wants to buy, borrow, or read; to
> casually inspect goods offered for sale usually with-
> out prior or serious intention of buying; to make
> an examination without real knowledge or purpose.
> ... browsing room: a room or section in a li-
> brary designed to allow patrons an opportunity to
> freely examine and browse in a collection of
> books. [24]

None of these definitions indicates any strong intellectual motivation or serious research purpose. Indeed, the
derived meaning of "skim" as an equivalent for "browse" is
"to read or examine superficially and rapidly; as, to skim
a book" or "to go over in reading, treatment, etc., in a
superficial manner. "[25]

Vocabularium Bibliothecarii links English equivalents
of "to browse": "to skim (through); to turn over the
pages. "[26]

The ambiguities of language may be seen in the contrary use of "skim" to indicate removing the best part of a
mixture, as to skim the cream from the surface of the milk.
In this sense a reader might "skim" a book for its most
valuable information. This meaning seems implied by those
who consider "skimming through books" a rapid means of
finding what is significant in them. Mathews in 1876 proposed that college students be taught a variety of what might
now be called "speed reading":

> At this day, the art of reading, or at least one of
> the arts, is to skip judiciously--to omit all that
> does not concern us, while missing nothing that
> we really need .... It is a miserable bondage to be
> compelled to read all the words in a book to learn
> what is in it. [27]

The popular definitions of "browsing" seem to exclude the scholarly ambitions of shelf classification of which a goal, according to library literature, is also to effectuate "browsing." A hypothesis was framed to test the extent to which librarians accepted the layman's connotation of "browsing" as a largely superficial or non-serious activity: " 'Browsing' is not a sufficiently precise term to characterize serious research, so its use should be limited to describing recreational, non-research activities in 'browsing' collections or their equivalent." (V:14)

Documentary Frequency Analysis: Indexes and Bibliographies

Though even a cursory examination of the literature reveals frequent occurrence of "browsing" and its verbal variants, the "official" recording of the word in catalogs, indexes, and bibliographies is disproportionately rare. For the earlier period, an explanation may lie in the hesitance to accept a fairly recent "literary" metaphor as a formal term of entry or reference. For later years, the explanation is less clear. (These comments are confined to the bibliographic record of traditional librarianship, excluding documentation.) Older feelings about the word's propriety or dignity may have survived. The discussion below of Hosmer's article will illustrate this residual embarrassment. It is also possible, however, that the term quickly assumed a generic familiarity whose lack of precision and whose apparent self-explanatory homely meaning made its use in library discourse as natural as its official recording undesirable.

As of July 1, 1969, neither BROWSING nor any verbal variant appeared in the "Topical Subject" division of the Public Card Catalog for the Columbia University Butler Library. Nor was the term included in the seventh edition of Subject Headings Used in the Dictionary Catalogs of the Library of Congress. [28]

"Browsing" does not appear in: Poole's Index to Periodical Literature (1802-1906); Cannons' Bibliography of Library Economy ... 1876 to 1920; Nineteenth Century Readers' Guide to Periodical Literature, 1890-1899; or Subject Index to Periodicals (1915-68), now British Humanities Index. [29]

When the word does occur in indexes to periodicals,

it is usually a "refer from" or in "browsing room." So, in the Readers' Guide to Periodical Literature,[30] the word first appears in the 1935-1937 cumulation: "BROWSING--See Books and Reading." This "refer from" continues in the cumulated biennial volumes from 1937 to 1943. In the cumulation for 1943-1945 even this "refer from" disappears, to be replaced by "BROWSING rooms. See Libraries--Browsing rooms." This last entry also appears in the 1945-1947 cumulation. In the 1947-1949 volume reappears "BROWSING. See Books and reading." From then to the issue of May 15, 1969, the word had not recurred.

"Browsing" appeared only once in the International Index (1907-), now Social Sciences and Humanities Index,[31] in the 1928-1931 cumulation: "BROWSING--See Books and Reading." The word had not reappeared as of June, 1969. In an index directly oriented to librarianship, Library Literature[32] (1921-), "BROWSING rooms" appears in eleven cumulated volumes from 1921 to 1968. "Browsing" appeared for the first time in the February, 1969 fascicle in reference to a British article of a non-technical nature by a non-librarian.

In the Library Journal Index[33] (1876-), "Browsing rooms" or its equivalent has appeared as of December 31, 1968 in the annual indexes for 1925, 1927, 1929 through 1932, 1936, 1937, 1941, 1943, 1946, 1952. The relative frequency and subsequent disappearance of "Browsing rooms" in the periodical indexes present an interesting instance of the history of a particular library development, perhaps "fad." The documentary evidence seems to confirm the evident lack of interest in the idea, particularly on the part of academic library directors, administrators, and architects.

"Browsing" appeared once in the 1890 Library Journal Index. The article indexed, "On Browsing by a Book-Worm" by Professor James K. Hosmer, deserves more than cursory mention. (It will also be discussed in a later chapter.) The text is an address given at the 1890 A.L.A. White Mountains Conference by a Professor of History at Washington University. Hosmer, like many humanist scholars since--including the author of the article indexed in the February, 1969 fascicle of Library Literature[34]--tried to explain to librarians how best a library through its collection, staff, and physical layout could serve the needs of the academic researcher. Hosmer's self-consciousness is evident in using the metaphor "browsing" in tandem with still

another: "book-worm. " He can not forget the literal meaning of "browsing" and attempts at least a semantic reconcil-
iation between bovine and invertebrate:

> The moderate demand of the present worm for him-
> self, and the great fraternity he represents, is
> that they may have the privilege of browsing.   The
> book-worms, like cattle in general (surely, with
> horns, and tail, and a genius for humping not sur-
> passed even by the bison, we are cattle), find their
> chief felicity in browsing.   What terms shall I use
> in order to magnify duly before my audience this
> great matter of browsing?[35]

Hosmer's elaborate effort to make his metaphor respectable shows that the derived sense of the agricultural
term was still fresh.   Probably for most Americans of 1890,
"browsing"--read "grazing"--was still a farming word.   Today, the popular understanding seems the opposite: the derived sense is more likely to be the "natural" one.

In spite of the word's wide use in library conversa-
tion and writing, "browsing" is rare in the titles of library
research studies and dissertations.   As indicated in the preceding chapter, the Davis and Bailey Bibliography of Use
Studies, which lists 438 items from 1902 to 1963, has only
one title including the word and only one of 438 annotations
containing it. [36]   Both studies are discussed in the next chapter.

In 1963 the United States Office of Education published a bibliography of library science dissertations from
1925 to 1960. [37]   "Browsing" does not appear in any of the
titles nor in the bibliography's "Subject Index. "   "Browsing
collection" is used incidentally in one of the abstracts.

Even in indexes where greater specificity is needed
(and expected) by the reader, "browsing" is most often missing.   Thus, the 1961 Annual Report of the Librarian of Congress includes significant paragraphs on the role of browsing in a shelf-classified collection of enormous size and
complexity, [38] but "browsing" does not appear in the index
to the report.

How, then, can an investigator of "browsing" locate
relevant research studies or printed sources?   The difficulties are not as fearsome as they appear at first glance.   A

brief general answer has already been given in the "Outline
of the Methodology" section of Chapter Two. More specifically, the following points can be made: First, the browsing
"concept" (see the "Definitions and Delimitations" section of
Chapter Two) relates inevitably to certain standard problems
of library organization and use: open-shelf versus closed-
shelf policies; relative effectiveness of various kinds of catalogs; diverse library-use aids and instructional programs for
different types of libraries, collections, and clienteles. All
such problems are treated to some extent in the numerous
"use studies" prepared as monographs, reports, dissertations, conference and symposium proceedings, and journal
articles. Enough annotated bibliographies and "state-of-the-
art" reviews seem available to facilitate a representative selection of those studies significant for the theoretical investigation of direct access and of the browsing concept. The
discussion in the next chapter should confirm this.

Secondly, even though "browsing" may not occur in
the index or even in the text, it is usually quite clear to the
librarian when the concept itself is implied. Thus, such index entries as "Books and Reading, " "Library Usage, " and
"Stack Use in Research Libraries" obviously belong to the
cluster of ideas subsuming the browsing concept. Such index entries, together with any available abstract, annotation,
or citation, help narrow the search for relevant sources.
Citation is of extreme methodological importance: previous
important contributions are often analyzed and evaluated.
Rigby and Rigby[39] have described this as the "entropy" of
the bibliographic system. Retrospective bibliography in research reports and in the professional literature thus makes
practicable the search for materials on an "invisible" subject like browsing.

Finally, there is the very valuable and strangely un-
acknowledged aid to selection of materials: personal communication with colleagues and expert advisers.

Because in the professional literature "browsing" is
a widely used but "officially" a largely unrecognized term
within the broader area of the "direct shelf approach" and of
"open-shelf access, " the questionnaire employs all three
terms. The intent is to signify the "direct shelf approach"
and "open-shelf access" as generally synonymous terms, and
to present "browsing" as a possible component in library situations involving the direct shelf approach and open-shelf access, but not necessarily as interchangeable nor cotermin-

ous with them.   Analogous questionnaire statements could
thus be tested both under rubrics of "direct shelf approach
(open-shelf access)" and of "browsing."

The first statement in Section IV, "Direct Shelf Approach (Open-Shelf Access): Its Suitability in Various Libraries," is: "Open-shelf access is generally desirable in all libraries."   Analogously, the first statement in Section V,
"Direct Shelf Approach (Open-Shelf Access): The Role of
'Browsing' and Related Activities," is: "All readers should
be encouraged to browse."   Again, the second statement in
Section IV is: "Maintaining open-shelf access is a significant educational responsibility of libraries."   The second
statement in Section V is: "Browsing provides a valuable
learning experience."   (This technique was applied only to
some statements and not necessarily in strict sequence.)

Analysis of the questionnaire data aims to assess the
correlation between the responses to these analogous statements placed in a frame of "direct access--open-shelf" vis-
à-vis "browsing."   Some light may be expected, therefore,
on the relative willingness of librarians and teachers to accept the "browsing" concept as a legitimate term to connote
particular conditions of access to library collections.   Conversely, the influence of the term's literal meaning on librarians' opinions may to some extent be gauged.

Notes

1.   Walter William Skeat, An Etymological Dictionary of
      the English Language (new ed. rev. and enl.; 1879-
      82), p. 76.

2.   Cassell's English Dictionary (1962), p. 144.

3.   Henry Cecil Wyld, ed., The Universal Dictionary of the
      English Language (1932), p. 131-32.

4.   Eric Partridge, Origins: A Short Etymological Diction-
      ary of Modern English (4th ed.; 1966), p. 61.

5.   Webster's Third New International Dictionary of the Eng-
      lish Language, Unabridged (1961), p. 285.

6.   Oxford Dictionary of English Etymology, ed. by C.T.
      Onions with the assistance of G.W.S. Friedrichsen

and R. W. Burchfield (1966), p. 121.

7. Ernest Klein, A Comprehensive Etymological Dictionary of the English Language ... (2 vols.; 1966-67), I, 204.

8. Oxford Dictionary of English Etymology, p. 121.

9. Funk and Wagnalls New Standard Dictionary of the English Language (1963), p. 342.

10. Cassell's English Dictionary, p. 144.

11. Sir James Augustus Henry Murray, Oxford English Dictionary ... (12 vols. and suppl.; 1933), I, 1137.

12. Wyld, The Universal Dictionary of the English Language, p. 132.

13. Murray, Oxford English Dictionary, I, 1137.

14. Webster's New International Dictionary of the English Language (2d ed., unabridged; 1959), p. 344.

15. Murray, Oxford English Dictionary, I, 1137.

16. Partridge, A Dictionary of Slang and Unconventional English (5th ed. in one vol.; 1961), p. 97.

17. Mitford M. Mathews, A Dictionary of Americanisms on Historical Principles (2 vols.; 1951), I, 196.

18. Richard H. Thornton, An American Glossary ... (3 vols.; 1931-39).

19. Wyld, The Universal Dictionary of the English Language, p. 132; Cassell's English Dictionary, p. 144; American College Dictionary, ed. by Clarence L. Barnhart (1965), p. 153; Webster's Seventh New Collegiate Dictionary (1963), p. 107.

20. William Morris and Mary Morris, Dictionary of Word and Phrase Origins (2 vols.; 1962-67), I, 52-53.

21. Webster's Seventh New Collegiate Dictionary, p. 107.

22. The Roman and Arabic numerals in parentheses after a

questionnaire statement locate that statement in the questionnaire by section (Roman numeral) and by statement (Arabic numeral) within that section. Thus, the quoted statement here is the fifth statement in the fifth section of the questionnaire.

23. Wyld, The Universal Dictionary of the English Language, p. 132.

24. Webster's Third New International Dictionary, p. 285.

25. Webster's Seventh New Collegiate Dictionary, p. 107; American College Dictionary, p. 153.

26. Anthony Thompson, Vocabularium Bibliothecarii (2d ed.; 1962), p. 295.

27. William Mathews, "Professorships of Books and Reading," in U.S., Bureau of Education, Public Libraries in the United States of America; Their History, Condition, and Management; Special Report; Part I (Washington: Govt. Print. Off., 1876), p. 250-51.

28. U.S., Library of Congress, Subject Cataloging Division, Subject Headings Used in the Dictionary Catalogs of the Library of Congress (7th ed.; Washington: Govt. Print. Off., 1966).

29. Poole's Index to Periodical Literature, 1802-1906 (7 vols., rev. ed.; Boston: Houghton, 1891-1908); Harry George Turner Cannons, Bibliography of Library Economy, 1876 to 1920 (Chicago: American Library Assn., 1927); Nineteenth Century Readers' Guide to Periodical Literature, 1890-1899, with Supplementary Indexing, 1900-1922, ed. by Helen Grant Cushing and Adah V. Morris (2 vols.; New York: Wilson, 1944); Subject Index to Periodicals, 1915-61 (London: Library Assn., 1919-62); British Humanities Index, 1962-   (London: Library Assn., 1963-   ).

30. Readers' Guide to Periodical Literature, 1900-   (New York: Wilson, 1905-   ).

31. International Index to Periodicals ..., 1907-65 (New York: Wilson, 1916-65); Social Sciences and Humanities Index, 1965-   (New York: Wilson, 1965-   ).

32. *Library Literature*, 1931/32-   (New York: Wilson,
     1934-).

33. *Library Journal Index*, 1876-   (New York: Bowker,
     1876-).

34. Francis Celoria, "The Archaeology of Serendip," *Li-
     brary Journal*, XCIV (May 1, 1969), 1846-48.

35. James K. Hosmer, "On Browsing by a Book-Worm,"
     Library Journal, XV (December, 1890), 34.

36. Richard A. Davis and Catherine A. Bailey, *Bibliography
     of Use Studies* (Philadelphia: Graduate School of Li-
     brary Science, Drexel Institute of Technology, 1964);
     Alice Bowen, "Non-recorded Use of Books and
     Browsing in the Stacks of a Research Library" (un-
     published Master's dissertation, University of Chi-
     cago, 1961) (Davis and Bailey: No. 043); Herman
     H. Fussler and Julian L. Simon, *Patterns in the
     Use of Books in Large Research Libraries* (Chicago:
     University of Chicago Library, 1961) (Davis and
     Bailey: No. 139).

37. U.S., Office of Education, Library Services Branch,
     *Library Science Dissertations: 1925-60; An Anno-
     tated Bibliography of Doctoral Studies*, comp. by
     Nathan M. Cohen, Barbara Denison, and Jessie C.
     Boehlert (Washington: Govt. Print. Off., 1963).

38. U.S., Library of Congress, *Annual Report of the Li-
     brarian of Congress for the Fiscal Year Ending
     June 30, 1961* (Washington, 1962), p. xiv.

39. Malcolm Rigby and Marian K. Rigby, "Cost Analysis of
     Bibliographies or Bibliographic Services," in Inter-
     national Conference on Scientific Information, Wash-
     ington, D.C., 1958, *Proceedings* (2 vols.; Washing-
     ton: National Academy of Sciences and National Re-
     search Council, 1959), I, 381.

Chapter IV

STATUS OF THEORY AND RESEARCH: SOME REPRESENTATIVE USE AND USER STUDIES

Hosmer (1890)

Hosmer's previously cited article gives a reasoned and unusually specific account of what "browsing" means to a humanist scholar. Many more recent descriptions by "visiting scholars" in librarianship have added almost nothing. Hosmer defines the process:

> One catches a bite here in a momentary twist: elsewhere, he feeds at length, the pasture proving sweet and nutritious. Browsing is the proper Baconian method of reading. The rapture of having at command an entire alcove! As you pass along the shelves, it is enough, in the case of most books, merely to touch the title page with the antennae; with others, a paragraph may here and there be tasted; as to a few, content does not come until a chapter has been devoured; while, for two or three, the conscience will not be appeased until they have been chewed and digested from cover to cover. Who can tell what books he wants without preliminary tasting? Titles often mislead, and never do more than hint at the contents. Time and again I should have starved had the catalog and librarian's desk stood between me and my problem. ... No librarian performs his task in a proper manner unless, in the midst of his anxiety for the safety of his charge, he at the same time affords abundant liberty to browse--a freedom of access to books far too rarely found, I fear.[1]

In contrast to this ideal browsing state, Hosmer complains, American public libraries have closed-stack collections and inadequate catalogs. He knows of only one American public library, recently opened in a city of 200,000, where browsing is allowed. When he visited the British Mu-

seum in 1886, he could easily obtain special permission to
visit the stacks. Also, a "reference library" whose collection numbered "hundreds of thousands" was conveniently arranged on open shelves for scholars' instant access. [2]

Hardly a belief or suggestion in this 1890 article is
not still a library problem under discussion or experimenta-
tion. Of course, today's scholars and librarians might point
to the vast increase in humanist literature, especially in
journal form, since the time when Hosmer could be delighted
with "an entire alcove!" Noteworthy, though, is Hosmer's
listing of levels of need and therefore of specificity in
browsing, a consideration of perhaps central importance for
any theoretical formulation of the problem. Fussler and
Simon were seventy years later to label such levels "tight
core" and "loose core" browsing. [3]

It is perhaps not surprising to note in available studies that the constituent elements of the browsing concept can
suggest more than one research approach. As indicated in
the preceding chapters, and as will be shown repeatedly in
this chapter, no library use study can avoid consideration of
the browsing function. The studies selected for comment are
meant to provide a representative selection of research reported in the library literature during the last thirty years.
(Kelley's famous study[4] is reserved for the concluding section of this chapter.) Since most of the studies are major
efforts in full cognizance of past research in their own and
related fields, they may in aggregate be assumed to give a
fair and inclusive overview of accomplishment in this area
of theory and research. This review not only documents attitudes towards browsing in open-shelf libraries but also provides a background for the methodology of this study and indicates the source of hypotheses tested by the questionnaire.

Fortunately, as stated earlier, convenient summaries
of the "state-of-the-art" and annotated bibliographies expedite
the investigation. Among the volumes of The State of the Library Art edited by Shaw are those by Frarey on subject
headings, and by Tauber and Wise[5] on classification. Library science dissertations for the period 1925 to 1960 are
recorded in the annotated bibliography prepared by the Library Services Branch of the U.S. Office of Education. [6]
The Davis and Bailey bibliography of use studies often lists
reports which are themselves annotated bibliographies of specialized studies. [7]

In their introduction, Davis and Bailey classify their
selections:

> Actual surveys have been assigned one of four prin-
> cipal categories: (1) citation analysis, which com-
> piles citation counts to determine the use of litera-
> ture in a particular field; (2) questionnaire, sent to
> individuals, requesting specific information as to
> their use of literature; (3) interview, a personal
> query of individuals to determine their use patterns;
> (4) circulation or diary study, which measures the
> use of materials through records kept either by a
> librarian or the individual himself. [8]

Stevens (1953)

Stevens in <u>Characteristics of Subject Literature</u>, published in 1953, describes past research:

> During the past three decades, a number of at-
> tempts have been made to determine quantitatively
> the nature of the library materials used by re-
> search workers.... Quantitative studies of subject
> literatures may be divided into two general groups.
> In one ... is included the study of the number of
> publications in a given field, or productivity of lit-
> erature in the field, for the purpose of comparing
> the amount of research in different subdivisions of
> the field. This kind of study is made by a count
> of the writings which have been abstracted in a
> specialized abstracting journal. The other major
> class of quantitative studies includes the study of
> the literature used by research workers in a given
> field. Such a study is often made by counting the
> references cited by a large number of research
> workers in their papers. Sometimes this kind of
> study is made by tabulating the journals and books
> used in a specialized library. [9]

Stevens is concerned with the second type of study
which has critical practical implications for the organization
of library materials: dispersed or consolidated collections?
remote storage or immediate accessibility? laboratory or
research library collections? Stevens lists as a policy implication for research libraries: "Great sets often cannot be
stored because the scholar does not know what part of the

set he needs; he must work through the whole set or use
many parts of it simultaneously."[10] The study is thus inevitably concerned with direct-shelf approach problems.

Stevens, like Davis and Bailey, acknowledges critiques
of the basic methodological assumptions of the research he
has documented. All, however, feel that more research is
required. Stevens states in his summary of findings:

> It is clear that much remains to be done in this
> field. While some literatures have been studied
> with varying degrees of thoroughness,... other lit-
> eratures of the sciences and technologies have not
> been studied at all. Moreover,... practically no
> investigation has been made of the literatures of
> the social sciences and humanities.[11]

Davis and Bailey contend:

> For a number of years the value of use studies has
> been debated ... [but] a very basic premise of li-
> brarianship and documentation is to meet the needs
> of the user in the most efficient manner. To do
> this it is necessary to talk to him, uncover his
> likes and dislikes, his needs and desires. The
> same method can be followed to determine the needs
> of a whole group with similar interest patterns.[12]

Comments on this last assertion will be deferred to
the end of this chapter. Here one may note again that
Frarey and Dunkin have questioned the need for more catalog
use studies, and that Taube[13] has generally denied the value
of user studies as related to scientific information.

Akers (1934)

The earliest use study to be discussed is Akers' "To
What Extent Do the Students of the Liberal-Arts Colleges Use
the Bibliographic Items Given on the Catalog Card?" In this
1934 study, ten liberal-arts colleges were selected to represent men's, women's, and coeducational colleges in the East,
West, Middle West, and South. Check lists were filled out
by 257 students. The findings indicated that students were
hampered in consulting the catalog because they did not know
how to use it, and because they did not know of other bibliographic aids. Accordingly, "Either the catalog must be made

self-explanatory or there must be a better system of instructing students in its use than now exists. "[14]

     Suggestions were offered by thirty-two of the students
on how to improve the card catalog. These suggestions confirmed how use studies, even presumably only of the card
catalog, are inseparable from wider considerations of stack
use and, hence, of related concepts of browsing or direct access. One student suggested that the card include the color
of the book! Another student, however, might have been
paraphrasing Hosmer:

> Even the best cataloging system cannot give infor-
> mation which is often vital in the selection of a
> book--for instance, its style, the attitude of the
> author to his subject, the print, and paper. If the
> student were admitted to the stacks, it would be
> the work of a minute to find out all this by a glance
> through the book. [15]

Jackson (1956)

     In 1956 Jackson directed the most ambitious catalog
use study to date. The report, edited by Mostecky, appeared in 1958:

> The scope of the present study was much broader
> than that of any previous comparable undertaking.
> Within twelve weeks approximately 5,700 interviews
> with patrons of many different kinds were conducted
> at thirty-nine libraries ranging from academic, pub-
> lic, and special institutions with collections of at
> least 40,000 volumes to smaller high school librar-
> ies....
>
> The facts were solicited by way of a questionnaire.
> With this document in hand, a regular staff mem-
> ber interviewed a patron using the catalog, indi-
> cated how the patron fared by checking appropriate
> boxes on the face of the form, and entered at des-
> ignated places the required background information,
> such as the patron's occupation. [16]

     The libraries represented the larger adult and young-
adult collections. The questionnaire had forty-five items to
be checked.

The general conclusions (of the director, not necessarily of all investigators) were optimistic. All catalogs
tested were on the whole successfully used by the patron, indicating that no change in basic policy was required. Most
difficulties arose from patrons' lack of adequate citation as
well as from their unfamiliarity with the catalog. Failures
increased directly with catalog size.[17] Akers might not have
been surprised by these findings. Dunkin commented in a
review:

> As might be expected, much of it restates in one way
> or another findings of previous similar studies ....
>
> Of these findings, old and new, some appear to be
> relatively insignificant, and others perhaps too ob-
> vious to require statistical proof. A handful might
> offer concrete suggestions about specific problems
> if they could be proved conclusively.[18]

The report frankly admits methodological problems,
not all of which were satisfactorily met. For this discussion,
a detailed analysis is needless. It is of much interest,
though, to see how the study determined to confine itself to
what the patron did or didn't find in the catalog. The study
design was to ignore what the patron could have found on the
shelves. And yet the problems of shelf search and browsing
kept intruding!

Two of the items in the questionnaire related to shelf
search, and the editor comments:

> Furthermore, it is necessary to exclude from this
> discussion the data recorded under Item 29, 'took
> down call numbers for all entries,' and 35, 'prom-
> inence of particular classifications,' which account,
> respectively, for 7 percent of all checks for selec-
> tion factors and 8 percent of those for open-shelf
> libraries. The patron who patiently copies all titles
> under a subject heading (Item 29) is not selecting
> from the catalog; his selection is based on an ex-
> amination of books rather than cards. The same
> thing is true of the reader who uses the subject file
> to determine the classification numbers most fre-
> quently assigned to material on his topic (Item 35)
> and then consults the stacks.[19]

This exclusion may have created an unreal milieu for
catalog use. The conclusions on the effects of access policy

on catalog use were, perhaps not unexpectedly, the following:
"The effects of open or closed-shelf policy are not clear."
Furthermore:

> Owing to the composition of the sample, it is pos-
> sible only to compare the records of all closed-
> stack and all open-stack libraries as groups, ex-
> cluding size brackets where only one type is repre-
> sented....
>
> Less failure might be expected at the catalogs which
> must be used proportionately more often--those at
> closed-stack libraries. The evidence encourages
> such expectations with regard to searches for known
> items. With respect to searches for subject mate-
> rials, however, that factor is obviously not the
> most important one. [20]

The logic is not unassailable. Why should one expect
less failure at catalogs of closed-stack libraries which must
presumably be used more than catalogs in open-shelf collections? Such an expectation rests on the assumption that catalogs for closed-stack collections are more adequate. Hosmer
would not have agreed! In any case, the following table[21]
emphasizes the puzzling lack of evidence on the relationship
of catalog search failure to shelf-access policy:

Table 13. Incidence of Failure by Shelf-Access Policy
(College and University Libraries, Types A, B, Metropolitan-
Central, and Special-Purpose Libraries)

	KNOWN-ITEM SEARCHES	PERCENT UNADJ.	FAILURE ADJ.
OPEN-STACK	993	42	29
CLOSED-STACK	329	32	21

	SUBJECT SEARCHES	PERCENT UNADJ.	FAILURE ADJ.
OPEN-STACK	790	20	15
CLOSED-STACK	421	23	17

("ADJ." = the not in catalog data have been excluded from
failures and total searches.)

The difference between 15 percent and 17 percent appears insignificant. The techniques described in the report would not, in fact, support the significance of any but striking percentage differences. Detailed analysis of the table would be hazardous, but it is not surprising that the director recommends for future study the effectiveness of the use of the card catalog in comparison with the direct shelf approach. [22] Clearly, the browsing role must be assayed. Evidently, there can be no definitive catalog use study which is exclusively concerned with the catalog.

Appended to the main report are six case studies prepared by individual investigators. Some of the comments are at variance with those of the director; but of particular interest are the investigators' remarks on browsing and shelf search. Thus, Mostecky in his case study of five college libraries says of the patrons' use of classification numbers:

> One out of ten patrons [i.e., nine out of ninety] used the subject catalog only to determine the most frequently assigned classification number under a heading and preferred to make his selection directly from the shelves, thus combining the strong points of the alphabetical catalog with those of the classified arrangement to the best advantage. This technique, particularly suitable for students browsing for a topic or collecting material for a term paper, could be further popularized not only by guidance programs, but also by the inclusion of classification numbers on guide and reference cards. [23]

Somewhat differing is a later comment of Mostecky:

> The degree of success is in direct relationship to the clarity of definition of the subject under investigation. The catalog is too complex to be used for browsing for a term-paper topic; a periodical index or a subject bibliography would serve this purpose better. [24]

One may, at very least, infer that the questions thus raised are yet to be answered.

Dunkin, however, wondered whether

any such study even on an adequate basis could re-

ally mean much and whether, even if it did mean a
great deal, it would not have to be repeated again
and again to keep abreast of changes in users' habits and attitudes.... Perhaps readers will adapt to
any method of cataloging if it is logically built on
reasonable principles. 25

Herner (1960)

As noted in Chapter Two, a recurrent defense of allegedly complicated and costly shelf classification has been its
"browsability." The Library of Congress has been much concerned with the cost of maintaining its shelf classification.
In an effort to determine whether its patrons needed such an
organization of library materials, it arranged in 1960 for a
study of how its stacks were used. The report of the pilot
study by Herner26 has not been publicly distributed, though
a review by Dubester will be cited later.

Herner described his study as follows:

The specific areas of concern in the study were the
quantitative use of the various subject areas of the
stacks, the types of users of the stacks, their purposes in consulting the stacks, methods of stack
use, and difficulties or problems encountered in the
consultation of the stacks and in the use of auxiliary guidance devices and techniques. 27

The study, extending over two calendar months, employed face-to-face interviews with a sample of users. The
target number of 200 interviews was reduced to 181 because
of unforeseen time restrictions.

Herner's conclusions were conservative:

The only valid applications that can be made of the results of the study are in assessing them to determine
the potential value of a larger, more exhaustive study,
and in studying them for areas of more detailed analysis that might be undertaken in such a future study. 28

This pilot study, however officially tentative, attempted
a frontal attack on the problem of browsing. Herner in his questionnaire distinguished between "specific and non-specific" book
searches and searchers. He did not, however, disdain the word
"browsing" and employed it in questions exploring the purpose
of "non-specific" searches.

Among his findings was that the majority of interviewees were looking for specific books for which they knew
the call numbers. Only "a minority were browsers, with no
specific books in mind."29

Evidently the major reason why patrons who already
knew the call numbers went to the stacks was dissatisfaction
with the slowness and inefficiency of book deliveries. This
finding was, of course, of much practical value, though a
disappointingly unintellectual motive for direct access. However:

> Another cited reason for going to the stacks for
> specific books was because the interviewees wanted
> 'to see what's on the shelves.' This need 'to see
> what's on the shelves' appeared to be related to a
> rather general feeling that the card catalogs do not
> do a good enough job of giving the searcher a clear
> view of the Library's holdings in a given subject
> field. Thus, specific-book-seekers occasionally
> take on the characteristics of browsers.30

The same reason for "browsing" has been given by
Hosmer and Akers.

The policy implications of the Herner study were not
insignificant. Assuming that the findings, even if of a "pilot
study" nature, had some validity, it seemed clear that certain subject areas within the library's stacks were so seldom
visited by either specific- or non-specific book searchers that
they might without undue inconvenience be stored by a fixed
location system. A central research core of frequently consulted works might be arranged by shelf classification.
(Hosmer's 1890 ideas recur.) Improvements in cataloging and
in delivery service could, on the evidence, drastically reduce
the need for personal visits to the stacks.

As far as the theory of browsing was concerned, the
results of the study were regrettably inconclusive. This, indeed, was the major critical reservation in Dubester's review of the study:

> When the report was reviewed in the Library of
> Congress, principal interest was directed toward
> the non-specific-book seekers. Obviously, more in-
> formation is needed. Although the study provided
> data on reference tools and techniques used prior
> to search in the stacks, it did not permit analysis

of the sequence of specific steps taken by the interviewees before they entered the stacks to seek materials for their purpose, or during the course of
their search in the stacks.   To state this problem
in another manner, the questionnaires were not designed to show whether these individuals could have
obtained the needed information if access to the
stacks had been denied them.   A rigorous answer
to this question can only be obtained from a broader
study. [31]

The findings which prompted this critique by Dubester
were as follows:

Specific-book-seekers and browsers were asked to
describe the information they were seeking in the
stacks.   Actually, there was no clear difference in
the answers of the two classes of interviewees that
would lead one to say that one group would best be
served by browsing in the stacks and one would
best be served by using card catalogs and requesting books in the conventional way.   From the types
of information that the interviewees were seeking,
it would seem that a high proportion of both groups
would have little need for direct access to the
stacks if they had a better familiarity with the facilities and services of the Library, and if these
facilities and services were improved. [32]

Readers wishing to confirm the above conclusion might
try to guess which of the following ten answers were given
by "specific-book-seekers" and which by "non-specific-book-
seekers" when the question was asked: "Could you tell me
the specific information you're looking for right now?"

(1)   'Local History of the Province of Quebec. '
(2)   'I'm looking for a Congressional Quarterly. '
(3)   'Content of the book. '
(4)   'Making a bibliography on technological develop-
      ments in urbanization. '
(5)   'Brain Surgery. '
(6)   'Place a man lived in. '
(7)   'P. G. Wodehouse's works. '
(8)   'Checking the construction of women's wear. '
(9)   'How to dope race horses. '
(10) 'Critical biographies on Walt Whitman. '[33]

The first five responses were from "specific-book-seekers," the second five from "non-specific-book-seekers"! The absence of any distinguishable difference between the two groups of answers might, however, be the result, as suggested by Dubester, of the questionnaire design.

Fussler and Simon (1960)

In 1961 Fussler and Simon published their report on the use of books in the University of Chicago Library. The study, made in 1960, investigated the same general problems faced by the Library of Congress:

> It has long been assumed in American university libraries that all books not actually in use should be momentarily available and should be shelved with all other books related to the same subject. ...
> The presumed necessity for the momentary availability of books may deserve more critical examination. [34]

Chapter Seven was devoted to "Browsing and Non-Recorded Use." Fussler and Simon could not consult the Herner study, but they developed a questionnaire form of their own which was attached to a sampling of books in the stacks. If the questionnaire were returned by the patron, the book had, supposedly, been examined in the stacks. (Of course, this technique does not meet the problem of non-cooperating patrons.) An attempt was made to set various levels of value for browsing. Thus, browsing-use was considered "not valuable" if the patron merely glanced at the title page, or only skimmed through the book while standing up. "Tight core" browsing-use excluded both glancing at the title page and skimming the book while standing up. "Loose core" use excluded merely glancing at the title page. The components of valuable "tight core" browsing-use were: (1) check the book out of the library; (2) carry it to a desk and read it there; (3) note the title for future reference; (4) examine a specific passage in the volume. [35]

Fussler and Simon defined "Browsing-Use" as the use of books not brought to readers by messenger. "Substantially all non-recorded-use is browsing-use. But some browsing-use is recorded, as the reader may well decide, after examining a book in a book stack, to charge it out." [36] Since the major purpose of the study was to determine the feasibil-

ity of placing some of the collection in compact storage--
which would prevent browsing--the most important finding described in Chapter Seven was that books which developed little
recorded use, i.e., which were not often charged out, also
developed little valuable browsing use.   The implication was
that books could be safely removed to compact storage on the
basis of predicted recorded use without jeopardizing browsing-
use habits.

      Although Fussler and Simon went further than earlier
surveyors in distinguishing levels of specificity and of "value" in browsing, they were less interested in the theoretical
basis of the browsing act than in its implications for projected compact storage.   Their questionnaire used such terms
as "casual browsing, " "examine a specific passage, " "skim
through, " "merely glance" without detailed explanation or definition.   Could one skim through a book without examining
some specific passage?   Could not a mere glance at the title
page sometimes confirm or destroy a hypothesis?   Also, the
questionnaire focused on one book at a time and thus ignored
the suggestive relation of that book to nearby ones--a "value"
considered by most classificationists to be perhaps the essential justification of browsing in a shelf-classified collection.

      The conclusions emphasized the non-definitive charac-
ter of the findings on browsing:

            This investigation has only scratched the surface
            of one fascinating aspect of what leads a man to
            read a book. ...

            The amount of influence upon use caused by the
            shelf-level cannot be clearly stated on the basis of
            our data.

            We cannot safely generalize from these data to oth-
            er institutions. [37]

      On the general value of browsing, Fussler and Simon
held opinions which their study evidently did not alter:

            The freedom to browse freely in the book stacks of
            any library--large or small--is greatly cherished
            by American students and faculty members.   There
            is a reader satisfaction and an efficiency in exam-
            ining books directly that cannot be matched through

present library catalogs, reference aids, staff, etc.,
for many kinds of readers' needs.   Furthermore,
open browsing permits a kind of serendipity per-
haps--but not necessarily--less likely to occur if
readers are required to use bibliographies, card
catalogs and other intermediate devices for a portion of their needs.   We were well aware of these
needs and habits before we embarked upon the
study, and our colleagues have seen that we did not
forget them in the course of the investigation. [38]

However, Fussler and Simon pointed out that for
browsing to be fully effective, the library must have acquired
the books and have arranged them on the shelves in an "appropriate" order, and that the books be on the shelves at the
exact time the reader is browsing.   They concluded: "The
complexity of the chain of events does not mean that browsing is unimportant; but it does suggest what every good scholar knows: browsing alone cannot serve as a satisfactory
base for a serious literature search. "[39]

Bowen (1960)

A footnote[40] mentioned that Mrs. Carroll G. Bowen,
a student in the Graduate Library School at Chicago, was engaged in an investigation of stack use that employed a "diary" technique.   The procedure was to present readers in
the stacks with questionnaires which would elicit information
about the next four books touched.   This study resulted in a
1961 Master's dissertation.   Bowen's study was a further exploration of one aspect of Fussler and Simon's:

This study of browsing is an attempt to augment
and recheck the findings of that investigation.   The
method is more direct in that an interviewer approached the browser, asked him a few questions
and handed him a questionnaire to be filled out as
he used the books in the stacks.   It was hoped that
the direct approach ... would provide data giving
a clearer idea of the number of books used by
browsers in a day, by whom they are used, what
kind of materials are involved and their value, and
how they are found.

Bowen defined browsing for her study:

first as the use of materials from the stacks which

are not checked out and not recorded in circulation
records and, second, as the search for materials
through the classified shelving system rather than
the card catalogs whether they are then checked out
or not.

The purpose of this study, as of its predecessor, was
a practical one:

If the results of this study agree with the findings
of the Use Study that browsing and circulation use
of a book are proportional, circulation use could
then be used as a criterion for removing materials
from the classified shelving system with a predict-
able disruption of browsing use. [41]

Bowen used the same questionnaire developed by Fussler and Simon. The survey was conducted in April and May,
1960, and obtained 175 questionnaire returns. Preceding the
survey, a one-day study was made on March 14th to determine a base against which the later interview results could
be checked. The one-day survey, which obtained 183 responses, indicated that on the average 5.4 books were looked
at in 33.8 minutes, i.e., 6.2 minutes per book per patron;
that faculty members looked at more books but spent less
time with each one; that graduate students looked at almost
as many per person but spent a longer time with each one.
The median was 3 books per person, which seemed to Bowen
a more representative measure. [42]

The two-month interview survey indicated that graduate
students were the major users. The one-day survey indicated that quite a few more individual items were involved in
browsing than in circulation. This might be in conflict with
the earlier study's conclusion. [43]

Although the questionnaire was designed by Fussler
and Simon so that the patron could indicate the predicted value of the material, Fussler and Simon did not report in any
detail on this section of the questionnaire. They preferred
to establish levels of value in accordance with their criteria
for "Loose Core" versus "Tight Core" browsing. Bowen,
though she felt that the maximum value of a browsed book
was indicated by the book's being checked out, paid much
more attention to the interviewees' prediction of the material's value, and she tried to correlate such estimates with the
other reported data.

Among the findings of her study were the following:

(1) The type of person who browses is typical of the general population of an academic library.

(2) Only 5.3 percent of all materials used were found by "true browsing" methods, the rest by the card catalog and related means. The value of the groups of materials varied inversely to the proportion found by true browsing, i.e., the card catalog produced the more valued materials whether these materials were checked out or not.

(3) Materials used by browsers generally did not vary much from the total collection's subject distribution; serials, however, seemed to be found more frequently through the catalog and to be more highly valued by the patron. Browsed materials were slightly less likely to come from earlier materials than had been indicated by Fussler and Simon.

(4) Surprisingly, shelf-level showed no significant influence on the proportion of books found by browsing rather than by the card catalog.

(5) Browsers seemed to use a somewhat higher percentage of materials showing a low recorded use.

(6) Confirming a finding of the Herner study, Bowen found that almost half of the people interviewed in the stacks might very well have obtained their materials through non-browsing means, e.g., card catalog. [44]

Bowen concluded with some careful reservations:

> This study of browsing applies only to semi-closed stacks; as regulations for entrance to stacks vary, the type of browsing may well vary too. For most people the card catalogs serve as an adequate guide to the collection, but in a scholarly community a few browsing uses may be important enough to justify an elaborate structure to support such access. Therefore, averages and medians are not particularly satisfactory guides to the value or importance of browsing, but are the only ones possible in this kind of generalized study. [45]

Detailed methodological criticisms of Bowen's study are perhaps obviated by her final statements on the feasibil-

ity of browsing-use studies, statements not dissimilar to
those of Fussler and Simon:

> The results of this attempt to study browsing be-
> havior provide no startling new facts; it does sug-
> gest that more research would be useful....
>
> There is need for a more detailed and personalized
> study of browsing, which would attempt to get a to-
> tal picture of a person's actions in the stacks and
> of all the materials that he consults. Basic to all
> further browsing studies is a better idea of what is
> in the stacks to begin with; with such information
> a much sharper picture of the relative efficiency
> and value of browsing compared with other tech-
> niques for the identification of relevant materials
> might be possible. [46]

Bowen's prescription implies the need to define an experimental framework--a "closed universe"--within which,
as attempted by Cleverdon's Cranfield Project, [47] comparative
measures of "relevance" and "recall" could be constructed.

Hoage (1960)

As part of the research for her 1961 doctoral dissertation on the use of Library of Congress Classification in
American libraries, Hoage[48] conducted a study of patrons:
"Two points of view were expressed: patrons described their
search for material on the shelves, and public service librarians gave their opinions of the extent to which the patrons
that they serve need and receive assistance. "[49] The questionnaires were administered to a sample of 158 librarians
and 476 patrons in university, college, public, and special
libraries.

Hoage's findings were as follows:

> Approximately 41 percent of the public service li-
> brarians in this sample estimated that more than
> half of their patrons need assistance in using the
> classification. Most of the librarians believe that
> the average patron is not aware of the subject ap-
> proach provided by the classification and is igno-
> rant of the full meaning of the call numbers....
> In no instance did the opinions and practices of the

patrons in a specific type of library differ from
those in other types.   Most of the patrons used the
classification as a location device.   They usually
found what they wanted, and only 9. 5 percent sought
help for the search that they described. 50

Hoage acknowledged that her sample of patrons was
not representative of those who would be using special libraries since only one of the latter consented to have its patrons
participate.   More general reservations, however, were
voiced by Hoage on user studies; these reservations and en-
suing suggestions resembled those of Bowen:

> More extensive study of individual patrons is needed.
> Case studies should provide information that it was
> not possible to obtain through use of a written ques-
> tionnaire, such as: (1) the patron's typical behav-
> ior-visits made to the shelves compared with those
> made to the library; (2) the approach to the shelves
> --origin of the search, comparison of the termi-
> nology of the patron with that in the schedules,
> substitutions made by the patron; and (3) factors
> contributing to patron adjustment and maladjustment
> in each situation. 51

Johns Hopkins: Bovey and Mullick (1962)

Ostensibly, the research recommended by Fussler and
Simon, Bowen, and Hoage would be realized by the operations
research and systems engineering approach represented by
the 1961-62 study of the Johns Hopkins University libraries.
As with the studies of Herner at the Library of Congress and
of Fussler and Simon, and of Bowen, at the University of
Chicago, a major question faced at Johns Hopkins was the
value of browsing and how seriously it would be affected by
less accessible storage arrangements or by closed-stack policies.   Accordingly, Section IV of the Johns Hopkins report
describes a survey of library usage.   The survey was conducted on three days in each of three weeks during April and
May, 1962:

> During the time ... a member of the research
> group stationed himself at the entrance of the li-
> brary where he handed a questionnaire to each per-
> son entering the library with the request that it be
> answered.   Respondents returned the form by plac-

ing it in a box at the exit of the library.[52]

The 1,172 returns represented three-days' use of nine branch libraries. Some of the more important findings were:

1. A significant fraction of those using the library conduct both author and subject searches.
2. A significant fraction of those using the library fail to find one or more items they seek.
3. A significant number of wanted items are found by browsing. This in turn points to an "open shelf" policy as desirable and also reinforces the importance of sound decision making with respect to the removal of items to lower-cost, less accessible storage areas.[53]

The library usage study was part of a more general examination of Johns Hopkins library problems. Regrettably, the other parts show most evidence of the rigorous methods of investigation promised by "operations research" and "systems engineering study." The goal of the usage study, however, was no less ambitious:

> The primary purpose of this survey of library usage was to construct a picture of the activities which make up a library day. Such a picture had never been constructed at Johns Hopkins or, to the best of our knowledge, at any other research library.[54]

The questionnaire asked: "Did you browse through the books on the general shelves?" If so, the patron was requested to indicate how many of the books he was charging out had been found in that way. The percentage of patrons who conducted some type of search and who reported browsing was, respectively, 18.1 in Science and Engineering collections, 16.1 in Humanities and Social Sciences collections, and 12.1 in the Main Reading Room collection. The corresponding percentage of charge-outs that arose from browsing was, respectively, 17.7, 7.6, and 8.3. The interpretation of these data was:

> The percentage of charge-outs that arose from browsing cannot be taken as an accurate measure of the absolute importance of browsing since it provides no information on the in-library use of material which arises from browsing. However ... the appropriate conclusion still seems to be that brows-

ing is not inconsequential, particularly in the Science and Engineering branch libraries.

The overall percentage of patrons who reported having browsed in the general shelves is only of limited value since it provides no indication of the difficulty that the patron might have in obtaining needed material if it were absent from the open shelves. [55]

The investigators noted other methodological problems:

A question was included on the questionnaire asking if the respondent had failed to find material and if so why. From a purist's point of view it would have been desirable to identify every failure to find material and to pinpoint the reason for each, but it was apparent that the detailed investigation necessary to truly identify the causes of even a fairly small number of failures would be a monumental task. Therefore the attempt to identify the reasons for failures was restricted to asking whether the failure occurred because the patron could not find the material listed in the card catalog, because the material was already charged out to someone else, or because the patron could not find the material on the shelf. [56]

Many more limitations on this library usage study were described:

In conducting research on human activity one often finds the results to be less clear cut than had been anticipated. . . .

We had anticipated a much more detailed picture of library use than actually resulted.

The primary reason that such detailed statements could not be made is the lack of a sufficient number of observations on each type of search. [57]

Perhaps the climactic difficulty was the following:

The questionnaire was designed on the assumption that searches for specific items and subject searches were more or less mutually exclusive

phenomena; in other words we assumed that if a
patron came to the library in search of some particular books he would not at the same time search
for material on a subject. In fact approximately
one-fourth of the returns were from patrons who
had conducted both types of search, and the design
of the questionnaire did not permit a satisfactory
separation of that portion of their activities attrib-
utable to the subject search. In fact the idea that
such a separation is realistic is questionable in itself.

The situation was made even more difficult by the
lack of homogeneity between the library groups and
patron categories.... Some of the heterogeneity almost certainly represents real differences in library use by the various patron groups. 58

In spite of such elaborate qualification, it may be desirable to cite one of the findings because it contrasts so
sharply with those of Fussler and Simon, though less so with
those of Bowen: "The results ... suggest ... that circulation volume is not suitable as an index of the intensity of use
of material within the library. "59

University of Chicago: Requirements
Study for Future Catalogs (1966)

Has there been more recent progress in research on
the direct shelf approach and browsing? Jackson, director
of the 1955-56 Catalog Use Study, had recommended the study
of the comparative effectiveness of the card catalog versus
the direct shelf approach. In March, 1968 appeared Requirements Study for Future Catalogs 60 which Jackson considered
"probably the most important study of library catalogs in the
United States since the Catalog Use Study of 1955-56. "61
The 1966 study, conducted at the University of Chicago by a
research team from its Graduate Library School, was "an
experiment to test what people tend to remember about books
they have seen. "62 Jackson in his review urged that librarians now pay more attention to the development of subject
headings because in the study:

The reporters note that authors or titles, if accurately known, are quicker means of finding a book
than subject.... However, since such accuracy was

infrequently achieved, the subject approach, for all
its disadvantages, was the most productive under
the circumstances described. [63]

Jackson's emphasis was somewhat different from that
of the study's research team for whom a more pressing concern was to determine "the relative usefulness for purposes
of specific work retrieval of the various types of nonstandard
book information, "[64] that is, of information other than that
of author, title, and subject entries. On this score the findings were not too encouraging. Cooper stated:

> One is led to the tentative conclusion that the non-
> standard information which could be supplied by a
> patron who has had previous contact with a docu-
> ment would by itself usually be adequate in small
> collections, but inadequate in larger collections,
> for the location of the document with a modicum of
> search effort on the patron's part. [65]

However:

> Nonstandard information which is by itself inade-
> quate for retrieval may become adequate when sup-
> plemented by whatever fragments of standard infor-
> mation are available, and this observation tempers
> somewhat the pessimism of the previous conclusion
> stating that nonstandard information would usually
> be useless for retrieval in very large collections. [66]

Nevertheless:

> It does not necessarily follow that it could not be
> exploited with the help of computers.... With an
> automated catalog or retrieval system, it may well
> be within the realm of practicality to perform
> searches for any arbitrary combination of remem-
> bered nonstandard clues. [67]

Disregarding the question whether it is a major duty
of the library catalog to help patrons trying to relocate works
already handled, the implications of this study for research
in browsing, as that term is commonly understood, seem nu-
gatory. Not only did "probably the most important study of
library catalogs in the United States since the Catalog Use
Study of 1955-56" not follow Jackson's suggestion to investigate the relation of direct access to catalog use; it also re-

jected for its purpose any conventional catalog use study because, as Vaughan indicated, "Catalog use studies seem to
be of little value in exploring these questions, since the information library patrons bring to present catalogs is conditioned by their expectation of catalog capabilities."[68]

Morse (1970)

Though not strictly a use or user study, the 1970 article of Morse, "Search Theory and Browsing,"[69] deserves
mention. Morse, an operations research expert, had in his
1968 Library Effectiveness: A Systems Approach[70] used
mathematical probability models in systems analysis of library activities. His article proposes that a mathematical
formula derived from search theory be applied to browsing.
The aim is to "optimize the chance of success" of "the average browser" by separating the collection into directly accessible "high-interest" and less accessible "low-interest"
sections. The separation would be "according to circulation
rate." Morse acknowledges that this method, though "probably optimal failing specific data on browsing habits" yet "demands a greater awareness of book circulation than most libraries have at present."[71]

He defines browsing rather loosely as "a search hope-
fully serendipitous" or as "looking along a section of library
shelves in the hope of finding a book of interest." To justify
his formula, he compares the act of browsing to that of
"spotting a submarine in a given area of the ocean and the
degree of effort spent by a patrol aircraft, for example, in
searching the area."[72] Thus he equates searching for an
object with searching for information.

Also striking is his acceptance of recorded circulation
as a reliable criterion of browsing value, a criterion which
the studies of Fussler and Simon, Bowen, and Bovey and
Mullick could not confidently establish, particularly since non-
recorded library use may be a critical component of "browsing" as understood by most librarians.

Kelley's "Great American Library
Dream"--and After

While the above researchers were engaged in library
use and user studies which nolens-volens acknowledged the

phenomenon of browsing, librarians continued to express their opinions and beliefs on the same topic. Except for a less diffident use of the word itself, the statements of today's librarians are often indistinguishable from those of Hosmer in 1890. Thus, Dix, librarian of Princeton University, spoke in 1963 before the University of Washington Library Convocation as follows:

> The basic test of the quality of any university library is its ability to get into the hands of the reader the book he wants when he wants it. ...
>
> As the number of books increases, the advantage of some system of classification by subject becomes apparent, for the odds are that many of these books will be of the same type and will thus be found in the same part of the building, if not immediately adjacent to each other. ...
>
> Is not the reader more likely to know in general what he wants and to be fully satisfied only after examining briefly the books themselves and then happily taking the right one away to read? ... No catalog card, however complete, no electronic console for scanning a bibliographic store, can quite do the whole job.
>
> I recognize that this may seem an anti-intellectual approach. ... One should of course use all the tools available, but should he not also cultivate by practice the marvelous flair of the true bookman and scholar for skimming quickly through a series of volumes and then almost by instinct finding the one which fits exactly his needs of the moment? The library that facilitates this practice is the open-stack, classified collection.
>
> Only in this sort of collection can one get at one other type of book he wants, that which he did not know he wanted until he found it. ... This kind of browsing is a by-no-means-unimportant by-product of the kind of arrangement of books about which I speak. [73]

In 1964 another librarian-spokesman defended relative shelf classification, a defense based more perhaps on "realism" than on verifiable logic. Angell, chief of the subject

cataloging division at the Library of Congress, presented a
paper, "On the Future of the Library of Congress Classification," at the Second International Study Conference on Classification Research, Elsinore, Denmark. [74] Angell began by
quoting the following anti-browsing paragraphs from the 1964
report, Automation and the Library of Congress, also known
as The King Report:

> Certainly, mechanization will impose a change, be-
> cause a large research library, automatically con-
> trolled to insure the effective location and delivery
> of its holdings, cannot permit open-shelf operation.
> Browsing can now be freed of its dependence on
> classification, from which most of its ills stem,
> and given a functional classification.
>
> Closing the stacks will result in a reduced need for
> subject-related classification as a medium for stack
> arrangement, since the stacks will no longer serve
> as a single large browsing collection. [75]

Angell's reaction was philosophical: "Do we hear in
these words the first faint premonitory stroke of the bell
that will one day toll the death knell of the Library of Congress Classification? It may well be." [76] Angell, though,
gave two reasons why he did not fear the imminent demise
of the LC Classification. First, even if the Library of Congress were mechanized, there would still be need for a core
collection maintained on a subject-classified basis for reference use, and also for browsing in a "best books" group.
(Compare the findings of Herner.) The second reason for
Angell's optimism was that the numerous libraries using the
LC Classification would not be converting to automated systems probably until after the Library of Congress, so that
they would still need LC Classification for their shelf arrangement.

Angell ended with an admittedly unverifiable argument:

> There is also the possibility, which I personally
> find credible, without supporting evidence of scien-
> tific validity, that the impulses to the abandonment
> of relative location of the book stock at the Li-
> brary of Congress will become effective if at all
> at a point so far distant in time as to make a
> worthy enterprise the investment of time, thought
> and funds to the perfecting of the Library of Con-
> gress Classification. [77]

Not all librarians, however, were as sanguine as Angell on the browsability of the LC Classification. On May 15, 1964 the Classification Committee of the American Library Association issued a report on the types of classification available to new academic libraries. The Committee considered browsability as one of the characteristics which would influence the choice of a classification system. Its conclusion, already cited, was: "DC has the advantage of providing browsability. In open-stack libraries, this is important. It is practically impossible to browse with LC although people try it all the time."[78]

The statement was startling for an extreme conclusion given without supporting evidence; equally startling was the apparent assumption that "browsing" was a generally understood term for which definition was unneeded.

Not only librarians have been concerned with browsing. There is considerable discussion by documentalists and information scientists on the nature of this process, though often the terms and emphasis differ from those in library literature. The basic concerns, however, seem very similar.

At the 1958 International Conference on Scientific Information, held in Washington, Menzel presented a paper on "Planned and Unplanned Communication" which posed such questions as: "At what level of efficiency is the scanning of each journal or other medium performed? How many articles or pages must a scientist scan in a journal for each one that he eventually reads? or for each one that he eventually finds to have been worth reading?"[79]

Such questions might be part of a "depth analysis" of the browsing function in a library's stacks. Information scientists have generally shown more theoretical awareness of the browsing concept than traditional librarians. The documentalists have been much concerned with the effectiveness of available information retrieval systems, and much of the research on this effectiveness focuses on criteria for "relevance" of the information retrieved. The Cranfield Project began the systematization of such research on a comparative basis, a point conceded even by the severe criticism of Swanson.[80] But, to use the words of Kyle,[81] the information scientists have been interested not only in "dowsing" but also in "browsing." Thus, the Cranfield Project studied the relation of "recall" and "relevance" ratios. Keenly aware of the possibilities of "heuristic search," information scientists have

given more official status to "browsing" than librarians.   At
the 1965 Symposium on Education for Information Science,
held at Warrenton, Virginia, the technical information specialist, Rigby, presented a paper extolling the virtues of
browsing at all levels of education and research. [82]

Rigby presented the concept of browsing as a highly
desirable, non-conformist, life-time adventure in research
and learning, an activity deserving the utmost encouragement.
He listed the following factors as restricting or abetting
browsing and browsability:

> Browsability is easily restricted by: (a) Closed
> shelf collections or stacks; (b) Randomly or alpha-
> betically arranged stacks or collections; (c) Me-
> chanical or electronic systems not accessible to the
> user; (d) Poorly presented or badly arranged bib-
> liographies, lists, indexes or abstracts.

> Browsing can be abetted by: (a) Open stack librar-
> ies (especially in special libraries); (b) Good sub-
> ject arrangement in stacks, reference or journal
> collections, abstracting and indexing serials, etc.;
> (c) Multi-access card (or printed) indexes; (d) Im-
> proved visual presentation and labeling; (e) Educa-
> tion of students and scientists to encourage, not
> discourage, browsing. [83]

Rigby felt that to facilitate retrievability through
browsing, numerous types of access were desirable, e.g.,
the listing of works by such approaches as place, time,
form, language, affiliation.   Although he did not really "define" browsing, his is one of the few attempts to construct,
even informally, a theoretical framework for its manifold
activities.

It is significant that Rigby's contribution to the theory
of browsing had no recourse to use studies.   Perhaps the
research reviewed above has demonstrated an inherent self-
restriction of use studies in relation to the browsing concept.
A not uncommon opinion among librarians is that research
on the concept of open stacks has been almost nonexistent.
Thus, a librarian wrote in the October 1, 1969 Library
Journal that there was a "glaring dearth of published information" and a "lack of patron opinion studies pertaining to
this subject."[84]   This chapter might modify such an opinion.
Lack of adequate data on open stacks policy and on browsing

is not evidently the result of researchers' indifference, though more research would be desirable.   Rather, there seems to be a lack of <u>successful</u> research.

Perhaps the essential nature of use and user studies prevents the accurate measurement of <u>all</u> necessary factors: those related to the process of library usage and those related to its results.   It may not be too pretentious to suggest that as far as use/user studies of browsing are concerned, there exists an inescapable limitation analogous to that of Heisenberg's "Principle of Indeterminancy" which states that one cannot accurately determine at the same time both a moving particle's velocity <u>and</u> its position.   Insofar as the browsing act is a continuous process, any interruption for record keeping by the patron or the observer may break the continuity and thus distort the nature of the act.   One cannot, to apply the analogy, measure with optimum accuracy both the action and the result of browsing at any point.

Fussler and Simon, describing their investigative procedure, gave suggestive testimony on this issue:

> In studying non-recorded use it is difficult to define the unit of behavior that will be counted as 'use' in such a manner that the unit is unambiguous and practicable to count.   For instance it is possible to count all books that are left on reading tables.   But many books are used in the stacks and then replaced by the readers....

> Or, an observer might follow a reader and observe his behavior.   But the behavior will almost surely be affected by the presence of the observer.   Furthermore, this technique runs into either exorbitant cost or difficult sampling problems....

> Nor does there seem to be a satisfactory mechanical or electronic method of describing browsing. The number of readers is sufficiently small, and stacks are sufficiently large, to make a motion-picture or closed-circuit TV procedure impractical since cameras would have to be placed either in many different areas of the library or on the reader's head.   Furthermore, such techniques are unlikely to tell us <u>which</u> books were used and which were not.

> Perhaps the best unit of behavior for counting pur-
> poses is 'touching the book.'... To determine the
> value of browsing contacts that take place, we must
> also separate the contacts into categories of value.
> And we must determine which contacts would not
> have taken place under a different library organiza-
> tional plan. [85]

Fussler and Simon (and later, Bowen) chose a diary
technique whereby the patron was expected to check off items
in a highly structured questionnaire. The limitations of the
technique have been admitted by the investigators, but they
have urged further and more intensive research.

First, however, one must try to define "browsing."
As suggested in Chapter Two, additional use studies may not
be auspicious, since the problem, as posited, seems to require a less direct and more "theoretical" investigation.
Such an approach was taken thirty years ago by Kelley in
The Classification of Books: An Inquiry into Its Usefulness
to the Reader, a well-known work whose apparent success
with certain specific questions has perhaps obscured the further application of her methods to the general problems of
browsing and browsability, although she recommended more
research. If Kelley's study has been kept for consideration
until now, it is not for lack of significance, but, conversely,
for its importance as a benchmark against which to measure
the quality and effectiveness of the previously considered
studies.

Kelley did not discuss "browsing" or "browsability,"
nor did she undertake use or user studies, though her primary concern was the patron:

> But it is evident that this knowledge, if stored in
> books which are not used, is dead. On the other
> hand, if the subject-matter can be brought into con-
> tact with living or productive minds, it becomes
> alive and in this way new ideas and knowledge tend
> to be created. In helping to make possible this
> vital contact the library assumes an important edu-
> cational function. [86]

Yet Kelley has probably given more convincing data
on the limits of browsing and browsability than have any later
use studies. Her method might be described as inductive,
analytical, and theoretical. Having been both classifier and

readers' consultant, she had learned many practical lessons on what shelf classification could and could not do for the patron. Her doctoral research, which was the basis of her book, consisted of testing her pragmatic knowledge by theoretical analysis. In this sense, her work might be described as a user study, the user being Kelley herself.

Kelley had learned through experience that "the awareness of the great majority of readers of the nature of the detailed, systematic order of books before them does not exist." She tried to determine, by examining library holdings as represented by classification schemes and subject headings, how much the great majority of readers would have missed even if they were fully aware of the detailed systematic order of books before them. She concludes that: "For three definite subjects only about 2.2 percent, 5.9 percent, and 5.7 percent of the total material in the library on those subjects is to be found under the class-number."[87]

As for subject headings:

> Of all the material on a subject which is brought out under that subject in a well-made dictionary catalog, one-third is shelved under the subject's specific class-number, one-third appeard in the form of analytical entries shelved with the main series, and one-third is shelved elsewhere. [88]

From these findings Kelley concluded:

> To know that, on an average, three times as many titles on specific subjects can be traced under the subject in the dictionary catalog as can be found by direct consultation of the shelves; to know, further, that there is no assurance of finding the most important contributions under the number; to keep clearly in mind that the use of classified books is but one of many steps to be taken in searching for subjects--all of these facts tend immediately to diminish the reliance which one can place upon consultation of the shelves for finding desired material. [89]

Kelley described the use of book classification and, to a lesser extent, of subject cataloging as:

> the Great American Library Dream--that dream of librarians which strives to reveal to readers the subject-contents in books. For the well-known and aspiring aim of both is to interpret and record the subject-matter in books in such a way as to make it easily and almost automatically available by the patrons of the library. [90]

Because she believed the "Great American Library Dream" to be more important than any of the means being used to realize it, she was able perhaps to view both classification and subject cataloging in a clearer light than many of her colleagues:

> The present study has made it evident that the important needs of serious library readers can be met but partially through classification. Searching for material on specific subjects through consultation of the books on the shelves is an unreliable procedure. To rely upon classification alone is far less than a half-way measure. Since librarians consider it one of their highest duties to make possible for their readers an adequate subject-approach to books, they are forced to turn to other records to help achieve this end.
>
> One such record is the dictionary and card-catalog. . . .
>
> Yet even the ideal subject-catalog would be limited in the number and kind of entries it would include; it cannot begin to exhaust the possible sources of information on definite subjects. . . . In addition to entries found in the catalog, there still remains the body of general and special indexes and bibliographies which must be utilized in each field. [91]

As the noted cataloger Prevost [92] said in her review of Kelley's work, most of these ideas on the inherent limitations of classification were perhaps part of many catalogers' intimate working knowledge; but it was Kelley's insistence on establishing these facts on an intellectual and theoretical basis that made the study so valuable.

If the status of theory and research on the browsing concept is not satisfactory to librarians, it may be because not enough researchers have continued in the <u>theoretical</u> way demonstrated by Kelley. The numerous use <u>studies have,</u> for all their suggestiveness, often raised more problems than they have solved. In its fullest sense, a theoretical study of basic principles must be use- and user-oriented: the subtitle of Kelley's book was pointedly <u>An Inquiry into Its Usefulness to the Reader.</u>

The plea for theoretical investigation is not a lonely one. Taube[93] felt it was less important to discover what the user wanted, which might not be reliable, than what he needed. Richmond wrote in 1965 that research in the art and science of classification must extend to the areas of how people "learn" as neuro-physiological organisms.[94] On a more modest scale this study of the direct shelf approach and the browsing concept aims at least not to ignore the established methodology of Kelley or the envisioned one of Richmond.

The methodology has been outlined in Chapter Two. It is neither within the intent nor the competence of the investigator to rebut the possible need for future use and user studies. Any study of a library's catalog, its shelf access policy, or its classification scheme, cannot but in some sense be use- or user-oriented research. If this study does not choose to replicate previous use and user studies, it is only out of the belief, prompted by considering past research, that a different approach might lend a different perspective on an established problem--without implying that other approaches are invalid. With abundant time and resources, one could conduct a <u>parallel</u> consumer or usage study which might, indeed, add <u>estimable</u> data to those accumulated by documentary analysis and the opinion questionnaire--the two principal data-gathering tools of this investigation.

It is, however, not a negligible point, and one strengthened by the results of Kelley's method, that the librarian is perforce also a library user. To ask librarians for <u>their</u> opinions on the desirability or effectiveness of various direct access policies as presented by the questionnaire is, in effect, to conduct a user and use study of a certain class of library patron. That class may seem, in statistical sampling terms, professionally "biased" or even suffering from "occupational deformation, " but it would be less than realistic to deny that their opinions may play a decisive role

in determining the conditions under which the other classes
of library patrons, viz., the library public generally, will
have access to the bookstock.

Nor can it be denied that librarians, like members of
almost any profession, do not rely for their policy decisions
exclusively on "objective" data "scientifically" gathered. They
must inevitably engage in introspection which effectually as-
similates the "objective" data to their previous direct experience in the use of library resources.   Much of this experience may be distilled into "opinions."   Again, Kelley's methodology adduces valuable testimony.   If, therefore, it is librarians whose opinions are solicited on library matters, one
cannot categorically claim this to be fundamentally less a
"user" study than soliciting the opinions of laymen consulting
the catalog or browsing among the shelves.   Only the type
of "user" differs.

Another implication deriving from a review of the earlier use and user studies is the permanent status of most of
the questions broached, many of which have been included in
this study's questionnaire.   In this sense, at least, this study
replicates previous efforts.

Hosmer's opinion that "No librarian performs his task
in a proper manner unless ... he at the same time affords
abundant liberty to browse"[95] is reflected in the questionnaire
statements: "Open-shelf access is generally desirable in all
libraries" (IV:1) and "All readers should be encouraged to
browse." (V:1)

Stevens' research on the characteristics of the various subject literatures, and the Johns Hopkins study on
browsing in the sciences and humanities, have been kept in
mind while framing the following set of questionnaire statements:

> Open-shelf access is more needed by readers in the
> humanities than in the sciences. (IV:12)
>
> Open-shelf access is more needed by readers in the
> social sciences than in the biological and physical sci-
> ences. (IV:13)
>
> The validity of the direct shelf approach lessens as
> research in the discipline relies more on topical sub-
> jects and less on personal names and distinctive titles
> for access to information. (IV:15)

Herner's finding in his pilot study at the Library of Congress that the majority of the interviewees were looking for specific books for which they already knew the call number--which confirms a previous study by Hoage--is restated in the questionnaire statement: "Shelf classification has much greater value as a locational device, i.e., getting the book once you know the call number, than as a systematic subject approach." (III:8)

Bowen's conclusions on the effectiveness of catalog use versus browsing--as well as Dubester's critique that Herner's study did not show whether the interviewees could have obtained the needed information if access to the stacks had been denied them--are encompassed in the questionnaire statement: "Nothing can be accomplished by browsing in a general research collection that could not be done more easily and efficiently through the use of the library catalog and other bibliographical tools." (V:13)

Fussler and Simon questioned the influence on use of the shelf-level. They also indicated the potential benefits of serendipity made possible by browsing but concluded by reiterating "what every good scholar knows: browsing alone cannot serve as a satisfactory base for a serious literature search."[96]

These opinions are included, respectively, in the following questionnaire statements:

The possible physical difficulties encountered in browsing (e.g., bad lighting, high or low shelves, lack of working space, effort in lifting or replacing books) make browsing in most large academic collections an undesirable procedure from the standpoint of most users. (V:8)

A major value of browsing is the possibility of "serendipity," i.e., "making desirable but unsought for discoveries." (V:11)

Some of the limitations of shelf classification (e.g., linearity, books not on the shelves at time of search, separate shelving sequences) make relative shelf classification basically undependable as a primary approach to subject materials in the library. (III:5)

Bowen compared open-shelf use by faculty and grad-

uate students.   Such concerns are rephrased and expanded in
these questionnaire statements:

> Direct shelf approach is more useful in a specialized
> or university departmental collection with a homoge-
> neous clientele than in mixed collections with different
> types of readers. (IV:8)

> Open-shelf access is more needed in university or re-
> search libraries than in general undergraduate librar-
> ies. (IV:9)

> The more advanced the student or researcher in aca-
> demic libraries, the less need for open-shelf access.
> (IV:17)

> Browsing is essential for academic research above the
> beginner's level. (V:10)

Bowen also found that the card catalog produced the
more valued materials whether they were checked out or not,
and, also, that serials seemed to be found more frequently
through the catalog than through browsing.   The following
two questionnaire statements refer to these same topics:

> Nothing can be accomplished by browsing in a general
> research collection that could not be done more easily
> and efficiently through the use of library catalogs and
> other bibliographical tools. (V:13)

> Open-shelf access is more needed for use of books
> than for serials. (IV:11)

Hoage reported in her study of the Library of Congress Classification that most librarians did not believe the
average patron was aware of the subject approach provided
by the classification and did not know the full meaning of the
call numbers (points made by Kelley and others), and that
most patrons used the classification as a location device.
The last finding, similar to Herner's, has been discussed in
relation to questionnaire statement III:8.   Hoage's first finding is restated in the questionnaire statement: "Close classification notation is simple enough for the average patron to
follow successfully on the shelves. " (III:10)

Angell's optimism on the future of the Library of Congress Classification was based, among other things, on the

need for browsing in a classified core reference collection or in a "best books" group. The first opinion was enthusiastically anticipated by Hosmer in his description of the British Museum's Reading Room, a model for the great nineteenth-century American research libraries in Washington, Boston, New York, etc. The core collection and "best books" principle (whose implications will be dwelt on in later chapters) are included in the questionnaire statement: "Direct shelf approach is most valuable in collections for beginning students where the books are basic or 'core' titles. " (IV:14)

The opinions of the Classification Committee of the American Library Association on the browsability of the Dewey Decimal and Library of Congress Classifications are rephrased in the two questionnaire statements: "Dewey Classification aids browsing" (V:6) and "L. C. Classification hinders browsing. " (V:7)

Some of Kelley's concerns about the relative usefulness of shelf classification versus subject headings are encompassed by the following statements:

> Close relative shelf classification is necessary for effective direct shelf approach to subject materials. (III:4)

> Some of the limitations of shelf classification (e. g., linearity, books not on the shelves at time of search, separate shelving sequences) make relative shelf classification basically undependable as a primary approach to subject materials in the library. (III:5)

> Subject headings in the public catalog are more useful to the patron than shelf classification. (III:9)

> Adequate catalogs, bibliographies and, when available, reference assistance, would make open-shelf access in large academic libraries largely unnecessary. (IV:16)

Following chapters offer numerous other citations which could as well be sources for the above statements. Even this relatively brief section already evidences overlap and duplication. The purpose is to emphasize that the problems related to direct access are peculiarly obdurate, and that one might, through any representative sampling of past studies, reconfirm their pervasive and still largely unresolved nature. It was this nature of the problems which made it seem mandatory to include them as statements of opinion in a questionnaire which aimed to elicit the reactions of to-day's library profession. The degree to which librarians hold to these opinions may determine to a considerable extent those policies relating to direct access which are subject to professional judgment.

Notes

1. James K. Hosmer, "On Browsing by a Book-Worm, " Library Journal, XV (December, 1890), 34.

2. Ibid., p. 34-35.

3. Herman H. Fussler and Julian L. Simon, Patterns in the Use of Books in Large Research Libraries (Chicago: University of Chicago Library, 1961), p. 196.

4. Grace Osgood Kelley, The Classification of Books: An Inquiry into Its Usefulness to the Reader (New York: Wilson, 1937).

5. Carlyle J. Frarey, Subject Headings, in The State of the Library Art, ed. by Ralph R. Shaw, Vol. I, Pt. 2 (New Brunswick, N.J.: Graduate School of Library Service, Rutgers University, 1960); Maurice F. Tauber and Edith Wise, Classification Systems, ibid., Vol. I, Pt. 3 (1961).

6. U.S., Office of Education, Library Services Branch, Library Science Dissertations: 1925-60: An Annotated Bibliography of Doctoral Studies, comp. by Nathan M. Cohen, Barbara Dennison, and Jessie C. Boehlert (Washington: Govt. Print. Off., 1963).

7. Richard A. Davis and Catherine A. Bailey, Bibliography of Use Studies (Philadelphia: Graduate School of Library Science, Drexel Institute of Technology, 1964). This retrospective benefit has been described, as noted in the preceding chapter, as "the 'entropy' of the system; i.e.,... the amount and skill of the work previously done by some library or bibliographer and available for exploitation by others; or, conversely ... the amount of effort which is expended by the farsighted in putting material in shape for others to

exploit to their advantage or to the advantage of science."--Malcolm Rigby and Marian K. Rigby, "Cost Analysis of Bibliographies or Bibliographic Services," in International Conference on Scientific Information, Washington, D.C., 1958, Proceedings (2 vols.; Washington: National Academy of Sciences and National Research Council, 1959), I, 381.

8. Davis and Bailey, Bibliography of Use Studies, p. iii.

9. Rolland E. Stevens, Characteristics of Subject Literatures (Chicago: Assn. of College and Reference Libraries, 1953), p. 10.

10. Ibid., p. 20.

11. Ibid., p. 18.

12. Davis and Bailey, Bibliography of Use Studies, p. ii.

13. Frarey, Subject Headings, p. 64; Paul S. Dunkin, "Catalog Use Study by Sidney L. Jackson," Library Quarterly, XXIX (April, 1959), 142; Mortimer Taube, "An Evaluation of 'Use Studies' of Scientific Information," in Emerging Solutions for Mechanizing the Storage and Retrieval of Information, Vol. V of his Studies in Coordinate Indexing (Washington: Documentation, Inc., 1959), p. 46-71.

14. Susan Grey Akers, "To What Extent Do the Students of the Liberal-Arts Colleges Use the Bibliographic Items Given on the Catalog Card?" Library Quarterly, I (October, 1934), 408.

15. Ibid., p. 407.

16. American Library Association, Cataloging and Classification Section, Catalog Use Study: Director's Report by Sidney L. Jackson, ed. by Vaclav Mostecky (Chicago: American Library Assn., 1958), p. 1.

17. Ibid., p. 2.

18. Dunkin, "Catalog Use Study by Sidney L. Jackson," p. 140-41.

19. Jackson, Catalog Use Study, p. 34.

68   Access to Library Collections

20. Ibid., p. 18-19.

21. Ibid., p. 20.

22. Ibid., p. 42.

23. Ibid., p. 69.

24. Ibid., p. 70.

25. Dunkin, "Catalog Use Study by Sidney L. Jackson, " p. 142.

26. Saul Herner, "A Pilot Study of the Use of the Stacks of the Library of Congress, " Washington: Herner, 1960. (Typewritten.)

27. Ibid., p. 1.

28. Ibid., p. 5.

29. Ibid., p. 8.

30. Ibid., p. 9-10.

31. Henry J. Dubester, "Stack Use of a Research Library, " American Library Association Bulletin, LV (November, 1961), 893.

32. Herner, "A Pilot Study, " p. 11.

33. Ibid., p. 23-31.

34. Fussler and Simon, Patterns in the Use of Books in Large Research Libraries, p. 2.

35. Ibid., p. 196.

36. Ibid., p. 185-86.

37. Ibid., p. 202, 204.

38. Ibid., p. 204-05.

39. Ibid., p. 205.

40. Ibid., p. 188, footnote 2.

41. Alice Bowen, "Non-recorded Use of Books and Browsing in the Stacks of a Research Library" (unpublished Master's dissertation, University of Chicago, 1961), p. 2-3.

42. Ibid., p. 7.

43. Ibid., p. 10, 14.

44. Ibid., p. 41-43.

45. Ibid., p. 44.

46. Ibid., p. 44-45.

47. Cyril W. Cleverdon, Report on the Testing and Analysis of an Investigation into the Comparative Efficiency of Indexing Systems (Cranfield, Engl., 1962).

48. Annette L. Hoage, "The Library of Congress Classification in the United States" (unpublished D. L. S. dissertation, School of Library Service, Columbia University, 1961).

49. Hoage, "Patron Use of L. C. Classification," Library Resources and Technical Services, VI (Summer, 1962), 247.

50. Ibid., p. 248-49.

51. Ibid., p. 249.

52. Johns Hopkins University, Progress Report on an Operations Research and Systems Engineering Study of a University Library (Baltimore, 1963), p. 58. (The authors of Section IV, p. 53-108, are Robert L. Bovey and Satinder Kumar Mullick.)

53. Ibid., p. 4.

54. Ibid., p. 65.

55. Ibid., p. 75-76.

56. Ibid., p. 80.

57. Ibid., p. 85-86.

58. Ibid., p. 86-87.

59. Ibid., p. 84.

60. Chicago, University, Graduate Library School, Require-
    ments Study for Future Catalogs; Progress Report
    No. 2 (Chicago, 1968).

61. Sidney L. Jackson, Review of Requirements Study for
    Future Catalogs, Library Journal, CXIII (October 1,
    1968), 3525.

62. Don R. Swanson, "Acknowledgment," in Chicago, Univer-
    sity, Graduate Library School, Requirements Study,
    p. v.

63. Jackson, Review of Requirements Study, p. 3525.

64. William S. Cooper, "The Potential Usefulness of Cat-
    alog Access Points Other Than Author, Title and
    Subject," in Chicago, University, Graduate Library
    School, Requirements Study, p. 119.

65. Ibid., p. 118.

66. Ibid.

67. Ibid., p. 83.

68. Delores K. Vaughan, "Memorability of Book Character-
    istics: An Experimental Study," in Chicago, Univer-
    sity, Graduate Library School, Requirements Study,
    p. 2.

69. Philip M. Morse, "Search Theory and Browsing," Li-
    brary Quarterly, XL (October, 1970), 391-408.

70. Morse, Library Effectiveness: A Systems Approach
    (Cambridge, Mass.: M.I.T. Press, 1968).

71. Morse, "Search Theory and Browsing," p. 391, 399-
    401, 405.

72. Ibid., p. 391.

73. William S. Dix, "On the Arrangement of Books," Col-
    lege and Research Libraries, XXV (March, 1964),
    87-89.

74. Richard S. Angell, "On the Future of the Library of Congress Classification," in International Study Conference on Classification Research, 2d, Elsinore, Denmark, Classification Research: Proceedings, ed. by Pauline Atherton (Copenhagen: Munksgaard, 1965), p. 101-12.

75. Gilbert W. King, Automation and the Library of Congress; Report of a Survey Sponsored by the Council on Library Resources, Inc. (Washington: Library of Congress, 1964), p. 23, 43. (Cited by Angell, "On the Future of the Library of Congress Classification," p. 101.)

76. Angell, "On the Future of the Library of Congress Classification," p. 101.

77. Ibid., p. 102.

78. American Library Association, Classification Committee, "Report, May 15, 1964: Statement on Types of Classification Available to New Academic Libraries," Library Resources and Technical Services, IX (Winter, 1965), 106.

79. Herbert Menzel, "Planned and Unplanned Scientific Communication," in International Conference on Scientific Information, Washington, D.C., 1958, Proceedings, I, 221.

80. Swanson, "The Evidence Underlying the Cranfield Results," Library Quarterly, XXXV (January, 1965), 1-20.

81. Cited by D.J. Foskett, Classification and Indexing in the Social Sciences (London: Butterworths, 1963), p. 99-100: "the clear distinction of information retrieval into two types--the search for specific information, and the search for any information about a topic. Bar-Hillel ... describes the two as 'data-providing' and 'reference-providing'; Barbara Kyle calls them 'dowsing' and 'browsing.' "

82. Malcolm Rigby, "Browsability in Modern Information Retrieval Systems: The Quest for Information," in Symposium on Education for Information Science, Airlie House, 1965, Proceedings, ed. by Laurence

B. Heilprin, Barbara E. Markuson, and Frederick L. Goodman (Washington: Spartan Books, 1965), p. 47-52.

83. Ibid., p. 51.

84. Sam Clay, Letter to the Editor on "Open-Stack Study," Library Journal, XCIV (October 1, 1969), 3378.

85. Fussler and Simon, Patterns in the Use of Books in Large Research Libraries, p. 187-88.

86. Kelley, The Classification of Books, p. 5.

87. Ibid., p. 17, 99.

88. Ibid., p. 125.

89. Ibid.

90. Ibid., p. 5-6.

91. Ibid., p. 127.

92. Marie Louise Prevost, Review of Classification of Books, Library Journal, LXIII (January 15, 1938), 69.

93. Taube, "An Evaluation of 'Use Studies' of Scientific Information."

94. Phyllis A. Richmond, Transformation and Organization of Information Content: Aspects of Recent Research in the Art and Science of Classification (Copenhagen: Danish Centre for Documentation, 1965), p. 36. (Pamphlet)

95. Hosmer, "On Browsing by a Book-Worm," p. 34.

96. Fussler and Simon, Patterns in the Use of Books in Large Research Libraries, p. 205.

Chapter V

THE SOCIOLOGY OF DIRECT ACCESS

Although, as Lyster[1] has indicated, the problem of direct access is inextricable from that of classification, this
chapter attempts to segregate factors which may be termed
sociological and which bear on the concept and history of direct access. The purpose is to trace the evolution of the
concept, the better to determine the social expectations of
those advocating open access. One may then try to evaluate
the practical results of open access as documented in the literature: to what extent have they fulfilled the intentions?

The Early Controversy on Direct Access in the United States and Great Britain

Available historical studies make clear that the granting of direct access both in the United States and Great Britain was part of a complicated political, socio-economic development during the last half of the nineteenth and the first
decades of the twentieth century. Some of the numerous factors contributing to the development are, at least in broad
outline, familiar: political democratization, urbanization,
spread of public education, growth of commerce and indus-
try, migration and immigration (especially in the United
States), rapid proliferation of the means of transport and
communication. Precisely how these factors interacted, or
what degree of causality should be assigned to each, is still
uncertain.

There have been only a limited number of studies
which have tried, in a more than elementary way, to apply
sociological analysis to the history of the public library
movement in this country. In his pioneering effort, Shera
acknowledged his debt to Durkheim for the organizing concept
of the public library as a social agency. Shera sought the
origins of the American public library in the milieu of which
it was an effect not a cause: "Historical scholarship and the
urge to preservation, the power of national and local pride,

73

the growing belief in the importance of universal education, the increasing concern with vocational problems, and the contribution of religion--these, aided by economic ability and encouraged by the example of Europe, were the causal factors in the formation of libraries that would be free to all the people."[2]

Shera agreed with Beals on the aims of the founders of the American public library in early New England: "The objectives of its founders were specific and very real.... In short, they were, as Ralph Beals has pointed out, interested in normative ends--in the improvement of men and women and through them of society."[3]

Shera concluded that the public library "followed--it did not create--social change.... The public library is revealed as a social agency dependent upon the objectives of society.... When a people are certain of the goals toward which they strive, the functions of the public library can be precisely defined."[4]

Though Shera strove for a sociological explanation consonant with Durkheim's principle that social laws, not the laws of individual psychology, underly social phenomena, his work seems closer in spirit and results to the descriptive narratives of the "New History" of Schlesinger, Beard, and Adams, the last of whom he quotes to introduce his study. The causal relations of the factors involved in the rise of the American public library seem still undefined. A hint of those topics whose consideration might have been fruitful is to be found in a footnote where Shera mentions the controversy surrounding the motives of the New England textile mill owners in their book-oriented cultural philanthropy.[5] Sociological analysis might be most illuminating when applied to such questions: who set the objectives of the society and to what extent might the furthering of these objectives by influential members of that society through the "normative" free public library be consciously or unconsciously self-serving?

Ditzion, whose dissertation continued Shera's social history into the period 1850 to 1900, reached a conclusion similar to Shera's: "Both the institution and its methods were conceived ... as a contribution towards the self-realization of the broad masses of the people."[6] Rothstein summarized the studies of Shera, Ditzion, and Thompson:

The detailed studies of Ditzion and Thompson indi-

cate that the desire for popular education, a naive
faith in the efficacy of 'good' reading in the preservation of virtue, civic pride, and sheer imitation
all played their part in the creation of the public
library.

But, as Shera makes clear, the interest of scholars, especially the historians, in finding a viable
basis for the preservation and servicing of the materials of research was a compelling and perhaps
decisive motive. 7

Whatever effect the interest of scholars had on the
origins of the American public library, by the time the public library was assuming full growth during the last quarter
of the nineteenth century in Great Britain and the United
States, direct access for all readers was being demanded on
political, educational, and social grounds.   Bostwick provided
an overview of the American development:

But not until very recent years did the library begin to conceive of its duties as extending to the
entire community.... The modern public library
believes that it should find a reader for every book
on its shelves and provide a book for every reader
in its community, and that it should in all cases
bring book and reader together. This emphasis on
the reader as well as on the book ... may be described as a process of socialization. This is the
meaning of ... the lending of books for home use,
free access to shelves....

Some of the greatest steps in advance, like that of
open access to shelves, were at the outset advocated by a small minority. The new ideas were
largely a response to public demand. They had to
win their way, but demonstrated usefulness quickly
broke down opposition and led to general adoption.

Open access, of course, has also been common in
small popular libraries, but was until recently considered by most libraries impracticable for larger
institutions. 8

Opposition to open access during the period 1877 to
1895 was summarized by Bostwick; many of the arguments
against open access were surprisingly non-intellectual: the

risks of pilferage, and of misshelving by the public.   Indeed,
in 1877, Dewey, at an English conference, condemned open
access[9]--interesting confirmation that Dewey's classification
scheme was not originally intended for the shelves or for the
convenience of the public at them.   These "housekeeping" objections to open access, which reflected the traditional pre-
public library custodial character of the librarian, were
voiced well into the twentieth century.

Winsor in 1876 had opposed direct access in public libraries because there was too much danger of books being
misplaced by "prowlers among the shelves." However, such
opponents of direct access in public libraries did not feel
they were depriving the patron of any essential service.
Thus, Winsor, in justifying his position, explained that the
alcove system was excellent for a scholarly or special library where members had unrestricted access to shelves,
but for

> a great collection to which multitudes have access,
> and but a few are personally known to the librar-
> ians ... such a state of affairs ... involves the
> shutting out of the public from the shelves....
> Most prowlers among shelves do not restore books
> they have taken down to the exact place from which
> they took them....

> The service cannot be performed by the readers,
> but must be performed by officials.[10]

Mathews in 1876 and Vinton[11] in 1886 disapproved of
direct access privileges even for college students.   Mathews
conceded that some students might benefit from unrestricted
access to the shelves:

> There are some persons, no doubt, who are op-
> posed to all guidance of the young in their reading.
> They would turn the student loose into a vast li-
> brary and let him browse freely in whatever liter-
> ary pastures may please him.... No doubt there
> is a vein of wisdom in this advice....

> But ... the truth is, the literary appetite of the
> young is often feeble, and often capricious or per-
> verted.   While their stomachs generally reject un-
> wholesome food, their minds often feed on garbage
> and even poison.[12]

Mathews therefore recommended that professorships of books and reading be established to instruct the students in the proper approach.

By 1886 the dispute was being vigorously maintained in the journals, though perhaps the argument had already been resolved in both public and academic library practice. In the March, 1886 issue of Library Journal appeared a letter, from the Librarian of Princeton College, which was accompanied by this editorial footnote:

> Severe attacks have been made on the Princeton College Library for shutting students out from the books, while in most colleges the tendency is decidedly to admit more freely. Mr. Vinton was asked to give his reasons for the change, and replies as above. We expect this note to call out some rejoinders. [13]

Basing his objections, like Winsor, on the housekeeping problems created by direct access and on the need for professional servicing, Vinton stated:

> An ideal administration of a library in an ideal community would allow free access to the books; but in a less perfect condition of things it has never been found safe.
>
> A library is a dictionary; but if the words in a dictionary were movable, how useless would it presently become!... Those who can resort to the shelves certainly lose much time in ineffectual search; and it is surely to be supposed that practiced assistants can find what is wanted sooner than borrowers themselves. [14]

British librarians continued the dispute, in much the same vein, into the first decades of the twentieth century. Thus, a letter to the editor in the 1906-07 Library World from a "Birkdaler" opened indignantly:

> Sir, -- From some of your remarks I have gathered that you do not, personally, care a rap whether libraries adopt open access or any other system. That is where we differ, and I fancy if you saw the working of Birkdale Public Library you would go the whole animal and back up ratepayers who claim

free access to their own property![15]

The editor defended himself: "We have never said we
are indifferent to the question of open access or any other
matter of importance in library administration, but we re-
spectfully decline the role of special pleaders on either side
of this particular question. "[16]

In Britain, as in America, the threat of pilferage was
a frequently employed argument against unrestricted access
for public library patrons. An anonymous letter (possibly
written by J.D. Stewart, the nephew of the British librarian
and classificationist James Duff Brown) in the 1907-08 Library World assailed those opponents of open access who

> interested in concealing the real facts ... drag in
> the American libraries with their large losses.
>
> Not the slightest hint is given in these various doc-
> uments that the difference between safeguarded open
> access and the non-safeguarded varieties are so
> great as to render comparison between them out of
> the question. One might as well compare a motor
> 'bus and donkey-cart. [17]

To prove his point the writer enclosed two photographs, one
of a branch of the Free Library of Philadelphia which lacked
exit-control, the second of a branch of the Islington (England)
Public Library which had such control. He concluded tact-
fully:

> In making this comparison, and illustrating it be-
> yond all question, it is not intended to minimize
> the splendid work of the Philadelphia libraries, but
> merely to point out that variation of minor methods,
> and not the use of a system, is the sole cause of
> those statistical differences as regards losses
> which are being paraded in Britain without proper
> explanation or note. [18]

The principle of direct access for public library patrons in England and America was to overcome these and
other objections. The arguments in favor of direct access
in public libraries were fervent, sometimes redolent of political oratory. Dana in 1891 proclaimed:

> In general, remember always (1) that the public

> owns its public library, and (2) that no useless
> lumber is more useless than unused books....
> Open wide the doors.... Let the shelves be open,
> and the public admitted to them, and let the open
> shelves strike the keynote of the whole administra-
> tion.[19]

The English "Birkdaler" had used a similar political argument in demanding support for "ratepayers who claim free access to their own property!"

Bostwick discounted the two principal arguments
against open access in public libraries--theft and disarray--
because of the overriding purpose of the institution, its usefulness to the public: "The advantage of open access to the
user scarcely needs mention or analysis."[20]

In 1890 Putnam, then of the Minneapolis Public Library, considered direct access a possible function of branch
libraries, but concluded more positively that "freedom of access cannot long be refused."[21] An 1894 survey by Steiner
found only one American library fully accepting the policy,
but after this--particularly with the opening of the Free Library of Philadelphia--the impetus for direct access accel-
erated rapidly.[22] The Committee of Five Report[23] of 1926-
27, which included a special study of shelf access, showed
that almost all American public libraries were granting this
privilege, and that in children's rooms open access was universal.

Savage, summarizing the triumph of the open-shelf
principle for English public libraries, i.e., "popular town libraries," credited James Duff Brown and Louis Stanley Jast
who "nearly forty years ago ... opened their campaign for
classed libraries.... The advocates of classing and open
shelves--the tin-trumpeters in the march of progress in the
late nineties and early nineteen hundreds--out to win adher-
ents at all costs ..." English librarians were evidently at
first uneasy that the public should be admitted to the shelves;
both professional and social reserve are implied in Savage's
description of the English public librarian's reactions: "At
length, realizing that to hand out books by call numbers was
not enough, that they must teach and guide, they admitted,
at first with the cold welcome of a liveried footman to a
tramp, readers to examine books at the shelves."[24]

But what were the specific advantages, claimed by its

early proponents, of direct access for public library patrons?
To say that the library, since it was financially supported by
the public, should grant the public access to its shelves was
not an unimpeachably logical argument that the public would
thus receive the maximum benefits from its property.   This
point was stressed by the advocates of professional service
in libraries.

The educational value of open shelves was emphasized
from the first.   Dana, discussing the architecture of public
libraries, advised that "in arranging the rooms, or building,
plan from the first ... to permit visitors to go to the books
themselves.... The public like to handle and examine their
books, and it is good for them to do it." But why should
this be good?   Because it was "educational."

> It is from this common-folks-education point of
> view that the advocate of the open-shelf system
> looks upon the question of library administration.
> A free public library is not a people's post-gradu-
> ate school, it is the people's common school....
>
> A public library can reach a high degree of effi-
> ciency in its work only when its books are acces-
> sible to all its patrons. [25]

Somewhat later a similar argument was advanced by
Tapley-Soper for the superiority of open access over the traditional indicator system in British public libraries: "There
are two reasons which place open access above all other systems which have been practised.   The first is its educational
value, and the second its simplicity."[26]

Attempts at more precise delineation of the "educational" values of open access are found in discussions concerning open shelves for American college, university, and special libraries.   Although, as indicated, Vinton at Princeton
had defended barring students from the stacks, this was evidently a departure from custom and, thus, a cause for out-
cry.   The principle of direct access to at least some of the
books in great research and scholarly collections was well
established.   Hosmer had been awed by the British Museum
Reading Room's open-shelf reference collection, [27] a plan followed architecturally and bibliothecally by the Library of Congress and the New York Public Library.   Prior to the free
American public library, scholars and members of private
or subscription or student society libraries were accustomed

to open-shelf privileges in their own libraries.

So, Cutter in an 1886 article defending Dewey against
his critics, Perkins and Schwartz, pointed out:

> The writers seek to minimize the merit of Mr.
> Dewey's (and of course of all similar systems) by
> declaring that the convenience afforded in its close
> classification--if there is any convenience--is ob-
> tained only in libraries where readers are permitted
> to go to the shelves. This, of itself, by the way,
> would be considerable, for it applies to most of the
> mercantile, nearly all the proprietary libraries,
> and all the college libraries (in which the profes-
> sors always and often the students are allowed free
> range). A scheme is good that will accommodate
> so many readers, even if the general public of our
> town and city libraries would get nothing from it.[28]

Cutter went on to indicate that even public libraries
were not usually completely closed-stack collections:

> But this is not all. In the first place, the exclu-
> sion from the shelves, where it appears in the
> rules, is seldom absolute.... Some favored per-
> sons ... are allowed ... and these are always not
> desultory readers, but scholars. [29]

The tradition of scholarly access to the shelves characterized the seminar method in German universities. Teaching was in special library areas where books for consultation
by teacher and student were immediately accessible. The
foundation of Johns Hopkins University in 1876 assured the
acceptance by other American universities of the seminar
method for advanced research and scholarship.

Harris, in an 1890 article, saw in the seminar system extraordinary possibilities of expansion:

> I think that our national system of education, or
> the system and methods generally prevalent in the
> United States, is destined to be vastly improved by
> the efforts of librarians. What is called the 'sem-
> inary' method ... can be carried out by aid of the
> library, and it makes the library an essential in-
> strument of school work. At present it is quite
> well developed in some universities (as at Johns

Hopkins and Harvard and some others). But it can
obviously be extended with profit to all colleges and
in some degree to high schools, yes, and even to
lower schools. [30]

A few years afterwards, Little was to warn of the
practical problems rising from such library departmentalization. Although he held firmly that college students should
have free access to the shelves as an integral element of
their education, he noted that the seminar method which had
been made part of college instruction during the previous decade "necessarily leads to the housing in different laboratories
and seminary rooms of a very considerable portion of the
books belonging to the institution. "[31] Such proliferation of
smaller collections threatened the integrity of the general collection and also meant considerable maintenance expense and
difficulty. These administrative problems of academic departmental libraries endure, as may be seen in the Harvard
University reports of Metcalf and Buck. [32]

The 1926-27 Survey of Libraries in the United States
(also called The Committee of Five Report) concluded pessi-
mistically: "The most perplexing problem in the administration of a university library is the scope and function of the
departmental collections, and it is safe to say that a solution
satisfactory to all concerned is scarcely possible. "[33] The
troublesome question was taken up in a 1961 symposium,
"Centralization and Decentralization in Academic Libraries. "[34]
Piternick in 1964 mentioned the need for expensive duplicate
catalogs for such collections. [35] There is no doubt, however,
that the advocacy of such departmentalization was from the
start connected with the belief that instructor and student required direct or convenient access to subject materials. The
following questionnaire statement refers to this issue: "Direct shelf approach is more useful in a specialized or university departmental collection with a homogeneous clientele
than in mixed collections with different types of readers. "
(IV: 8)

The educational benefits of direct access as embodied
in the seminar system were described by Harris as: "studying up a topic, mastering the wealth of knowledge extant on
the subject, sifting and criticizing what is recorded, and ver-
ifying what is true by experiment. "[36] There seems a direct
descent from this concept of seminar teaching to the Library-
College instructional proposals of Knapp, Shores, and others. [37]

Even without the reinforcing influence of the seminar idea, the educational benefits of direct access in college libraries (or public libraries with scholar and student clientele) were proclaimed by the early advocates of open-shelf policy. Cutter in 1886 uttered the apothegm: "To the scholar a book on the shelves is worth two in a catalog." His reasoning was as follows:

> Of course the catalog is an aid in the same direction ... but it is as true for the librarian as for the student that the best catalog is the books themselves. The catalog answers a different class of questions or answers the same questions in a different way. If it is well made, it comes nearer bringing everything together than the shelves can ever do; but it does not show the character of the books as well as does a glance at them or the mere sight of their outsides to one who has seen them before. The difference is like that between text-books and object teaching. 38

Little made similar claims for the educational value of direct access because it aided the student to develop his powers of discrimination and selection:

> Every time a student removes from the shelves four or five books on the same topic, glances at their contents and selects the one that in his opinion will best serve his purpose, he not only takes the most important step toward attainment of the desired information, but also employs his faculties in the manner best adapted to strengthen his power of judgment and to quicken his perception of truth. This tasting before one eats can not be done by proxy. The hand of the attendant and the moments of time intervening between the seeker and his shelf full of books is in practice destructive of this use of the library. 39

Bostwick noted a considerable practical advantage of direct access: "Our catalogs inform the reader what books are owned by the library, but not whether a particular book is in use or not.... The mere statement of this difficulty is in itself sufficient to show the advantages of free access to the shelves. "40

Robinson in 1876 proposed granting college students

access to the shelves: "The time has come to prepare students for the intelligent use of many books and the society
of many readers. With that end in view, for many reasons
the bars should be taken down under proper regulations."
Robinson's list of reasons was imposing:

> First of all, because the study of the library, as
> such, is a very important part of a student's edu-
> cation....
>
> Remove the barriers and make familiarity with
> well-chosen authors as easy as practicable.... He
> wants to know, and has a right to know, a good
> deal more about them than can be learned from
> teachers and catalogs. Deny him this, and he
> turns away disappointed and discouraged; grant him
> this, and his interest is awakened, his love for
> books increased, and the habit of reading will most
> likely be formed. [41]

Another reason adduced by Robinson was that open access trains the student in deciding what he will purchase for
his own library after he graduates. Robinson's probably climactic argument resembled the modern concept of independent study in the Library-College. He felt that if a student
confine himself to a few required books and to what he would
learn from lectures, "servility and narrowness are the result." However:

> There is also a manly and scholarly method of
> making the required study only the nucleus about
> which are to be gathered the results of much in-
> teresting and profitable investigation--the pathway
> of thought through a very wide field of inquiry.
>
> But the condition of all this work is a proper rela-
> tion to the library. No student can do this work
> well, and few will undertake it at all, by calling
> for books from a catalog.... A man must stand
> face to face with the books required. [42]

Robinson ended on a personal note:

> I have written earnestly, almost in the style of an
> advocate, because in ten years' experience I have
> seen the best results from such a use of books as
> I have described. The two hours' work done reg-

> ularly every Saturday in this library by an average
> of forty or fifty students, does them more good
> than any two hours' instruction they receive through
> the week. It is work which develops their powers,
> and begets the habit of independent research and
> the love of books. [43]

The value of direct access in college and university libraries was endorsed in the 1964 Report of the Commission on the Humanities: "The greatest achievement of the American academic library has been its success in making its collections readily accessible to students and faculty, and this has been a contribution to the welfare of the humanist in particular. "[44]

Yet, since the size and complexity of many academic libraries presented obvious difficulties in the provision of direct access, it would not be surprising if such access were not as universal in academic as in public libraries. The Committee of Five Report, the first thorough national library survey since 1876, emphasized access policy. Careful definition was attempted through such terms as "entirely or mainly open-shelf, " "entirely or mainly closed-shelf. " Furthermore --"Under this definition, most of the [academic] libraries which are not entirely open-shelf must be classed as entirely or mainly closed, for in few libraries is the open-shelf collection comprehensive enough to permit classification, with many public libraries, as 'partially open-shelf. ' "[45]

The Report indicated that of 225 college and university libraries of all sizes reporting, 126, or 56 percent, could be classed as "entirely or mainly open-shelf. "[46] The questionnaire for this study attempted to update such statistics by including the following questions: "Is your library principally open-shelf?____ closed stacks?____ Please note any special or unusual situation in your library that might modify your answer. " (II: 9)

Some Claimed Social and Political Benefits of Direct Access

Both government officials and library spokesmen expressed the belief that the benefits of direct access redounded to the progress of the political and social order. Although Shera concluded (or assumed) that the public library did not change the social structure but merely reflected it, obviously

any individual as a result of what he may read in library
books may be so influenced or "inspired" as to try in some
way--through himself or others--to effect social change.
Benjamin Franklin, describing the influence of the first American subscription library, initiated by his efforts, claimed
educational, cultural, and even possibly political effects:

> This was the mother of all the North American sub-
> scription libraries, now so numerous. It is be-
> come a great thing itself, and continually increas-
> ing. These libraries have improved the general
> conversation of the Americans, made the common
> tradesmen and farmers as intelligent as most gen-
> tlemen from other countries, and perhaps have con-
> tributed in some degree to the stand so generally
> made throughout the colonies in defence of their
> privileges. [47]

The example of Karl Marx's research in the British
Museum Library may also come to mind.

The belief that unimpeded access to books produces
beneficial social results can probably be traced to the traditional awe of the "book" as a repository of religious and,
later, of secular wisdom. This belief in the "power" of the
book was implied by the findings of Ditzion and Thompson
that "a naive faith in the efficacy of 'good' reading in the
preservation of virtue" helped create the American public library. [48] Nevertheless, it might not be "naive" to have valued the book, particularly before the development of modern
communication and transportation, as an effective and eco-
nomical medium for transmitting information and influence.

The social benefits of education through the public library were consistently extolled. Bostwick stated:

> The public library has always been regarded by li-
> brarians as an educational institution. It is this
> even in its recreational aspects, if a broad defini-
> tion of education be adopted.... The library ... is,
> or at least can be made, one of the most effective
> agencies in the education of the adult.... There is
> now an attempt to do for the adult reader in the
> public library what has long been done there for
> children and in a similar way. [49]

Bostwick also made plain that direct access character-

ized the modern public library; it was one of the "socializing" features through which the public library could only fully
realize its potential. [50]   Dana in A Library Primer (with
Spofford's A Book for All Readers, one of the two standard
guides for American librarians at the turn of the century)
also, as noted, had connected direct access and the social
benefits of education deriving from the public library: "A
free public library is not a people's post-graduate school, it
is the people's common school" and "A public library can
reach a high degree of efficiency in its work only when its
books are accessible to all its patrons." [51]

    This last opinion is expressed in the questionnaire
statement: "Public libraries cannot serve their readers adequately without offering open-shelf access." (IV:5)

    American officials little doubted that the public library
was a powerful instrument for--and therefore a wise responsibility of--the United States Government.   Warren and Clark,
editors of the officially sponsored 1876 Public Libraries in
the United States of America, wrote in its Introduction:

> For forty years the importance of public libraries
> as auxiliaries to public education has been recog-
> nized and dwelt upon by American educators wher-
> ever common schools have flourished....
>
> The influence of the librarian as an educator is
> rarely estimated by outside observers, and proba-
> bly seldom fully realized even by himself.... The
> librarian has silently, almost unconsciously, gained
> ascendancy over the habits of thought and literary
> tastes of a multitude of readers, who find in the
> public library their only means of intellectual im-
> provement.... Librarians should not only under-
> stand their primary duties as purveyors of library
> supplies to the people, but also realize their high
> privileges and responsibilities as teachers....
>
> Recognizing these conditions the United States Com-
> misioner of Education began in 1870 to gather and
> publish the statistics of public libraries in this
> country....
>
> Free public libraries, established and maintained
> on the same principle that free public schools are,
> ... fulfill for all a function similar to that which

the college libraries perform for those fortunate
enough to pursue a college course; rightly administered, they are indeed what one writer has called
them, 'the people's colleges.'[52]

This official concern for the welfare of the public library system has remained strong; the Library Services
Acts, beginning in 1956, are a continuing manifestation of
the government's willingness to support the American public
library as a vital social-educational agency in a democratic
state.

The connection between "direct access" and the educational function of the public library as defined by Warren and
Clark seems to be found in their phrase, "rightly administered. " As indicated, a considerable body of post-1876 professional opinion advocated direct access as the modern, improved method of rightly administering the public library as
an educational agency for those who must rely on it as their
only means of instruction. The argument was bolstered by
the well known fact that those Americans fortunate enough to
attend college often had unimpeded access to the shelves as
part of their education in a democracy.

Such inferences are supported by later studies. Ditzion's dissertation was significant for its title: Arsenals of
a Democratic Culture: A Social History of the American
Public Library Movement in New England and the Middle
States from 1850 to 1900. Ditzion, as mentioned, had concluded: "Both the institution and its methods were conceived
... as a contribution toward the self-realization of the broad
masses of the people. "[53]

Palmer emphasized similarly the political and social
meaning for America of direct access. He referred to "the
idea of the library providing universal perpetual self-education" and noted:

It is perhaps significant that the compiler of the
first library classification scheme for general libraries should have been an American....

Government by the people implied a need to inform
the people, and to lay open to them the intellectual
treasures of the ages. Access for the many to the
books which enshrined these treasures suddenly produced problems of organization and administration

that did not exist for the occasional scholars browsing in the libraries provided for their exclusive en-
joyment. Among the solutions proposed to some of
these problems was the Decimal Classification. [54]

Although Dewey's scheme was originally designed for
a classed catalog rather than for the shelves and, as shown,
Dewey did not at first advocate direct access in public libraries, his Decimal Classification with its simple-seeming
notation and its use of relative shelf location made direct access possible in the public library. If, as Palmer stated,
democracy had to lay open the treasures of the ages to the
masses, librarians soon decided that only the applying of
Dewey's scheme to open shelves would fully realize this purpose. Indeed, already in 1879 Dewey was concerned with the
most effective method of shelf arrangement. [55] From then on,
he made no protest against his scheme being applied to the
shelves and seemed very aware in later editions that his classification was being used almost universally for that purpose
in open-access public libraries. He stated in the second
(1885) edition: "The system was devised for cataloging and
indexing but it was found on trial equally valuable for numbering and arranging books and pamphlets on shelves. "[56]

In his 1920 autobiographical article, "Decimal Classification Beginnings, " Dewey connected his invention of the
Decimal Classification with his spelling and metric reforms
as showing his determination "to make popular education my
life work, " the free public library being "the true peoples'
university. " Since the Decimal Classification was so widely
adopted by public libraries to facilitate direct access and thus
fulfill their educational function, one would not expect Dewey,
on ideological or pragmatic grounds, to have easily opposed
the practice. He commented in this 1920 article--as he had
often elsewhere--that as long as the system, in spite of major theoretical objections, seemed to be acceptable to so
many libraries, it was far better to keep its uniformity than
to attempt any new, possibly better scheme. [57]

The following questionnaire statement was based on
the above and numerous other sources: "Maintaining open-
shelf access is a significant educational responsibility of libraries. " (IV:2)

The social and political importance of the public library as an educational force had thus been proclaimed since
the beginning of the American public library movement. In

1890, Harris, then United States Commissioner of Education, discoursed on "The Function of the Library and the School in Education":

> The school and the newspaper and the library work-
> ing together may be each helped by the other, and
> all may be united into one very potent instrumen-
> tality of education for the universal democracy that
> is on its procession in all the nations of the world.
> ... On this line we see infinite possibilities of
> growth in perfection, infinite possibilities of that
> education which adds to the individual life vicari-
> ously the life and life's experiences of all his fel-
> low-men. [58]

(Harris, when he had been devising a curriculum as Superintendent of the St. Louis public schools, was con-strained to take library classification into account. His in-version of Johnston's Baconian plan for the St. Louis Mer-cantile Library is generally considered to have influenced Dewey's scheme. Also relevant may be LaMontagne's point that "to Harris classification meant shelf as well as catalog arrangement. ")[59]

The proclaimed role of the public library in achieving national political, social, and educational goals inevitably in-volved the more prosaic matter of direct access which, af-ter initial controversy, was accepted as a natural component of American public library administration. The specific ways in which direct access was presumed to aid the public library in reaching these goals will be considered later.

The Library Surveys as Evidence

Sixty years after Harris' discourse, Ranganathan was to term open access "the greatest human contribution of the library profession by our immediate predecessors to the fullest satisfaction of all the Laws of Library Science. "[60] The role of the public library as an educational agency--im-plemented through direct access--had become almost indis-tinguishable from its function as a socially normative agency. Evidence for this evolving attitude is abundantly available in the major library surveys which documented the increasing concern of the American librarian for his social as well as pedagogical responsibility. These surveys traced an increas-ingly blurred boundary between the librarian as educator and as social worker; between the American public library as an optional educational facility and as a purposeful socializing agency with quasi-missionary responsibilities. This should hardly be surprising since public education, by definition, assumes social goals; the perennial question is: which social goals?

Although there has been no socio-cultural investigation of such surveys, Lyle's 1965 conference paper, "An Exploration into the Origins and Evolution of the Library Survey," presented a suggestive overview. [61]

Lyle noted four national surveys from 1876 to 1952. However, already in 1850 Jewett had conducted his mid-century survey of American libraries and found only five institutions with 50,000 volumes or more: Harvard University, Philadelphia Library Company, Yale College, Boston Athenaeum, and the Library of Congress. [62] Jewett was not interested in statistics per se. His dream of a unified national bibliographic structure was evident in his 1852 On the Construction of Catalogues of Libraries[63] and in his ill-fated attempt to distribute through the Smithsonian Institution catalog plates which could be used by all libraries. Not until thirty years after his death was a printed card service provided by the Library of Congress.

By 1876, when the Bureau of Education released its report on Public Libraries in the United States of America, "all public libraries numbering 300 volumes or more from which returns were received in 1875-76, excepting common or district school libraries," totalled 3,647 and had total holdings of 12,276,964 volumes. [64]

The editors of the 1876 survey, like Jewett earlier, were concerned with more than statistics. Their reasons for their special report have been quoted; but two other of their points should be noted: (1) the need for professional librarian training so that Rullman's goal of a common organization for library science be attained, [65] and (2) the need to consider "public" libraries in the widest possible sense as contributing to a national bibliographic resource.

The first point implied standards to make possible the attainment of national goals. This unification of diverse efforts to achieve a national ideal--political, social, and educational--is still being sought, as witness the 1968 Report of the National Advisory Commission on Libraries: Library

Services for the Nation's Needs; Toward Fulfillment of a National Policy. 66 From the 1850 Jewett survey on, the goal, implicit or explicit, of the national surveyors was to gather information to help plan national programs and nationally standardized methods. Such a goal presupposed an accepted national purpose.

The second point represented an early sophisticated approach to the interdependence of American libraries which has perhaps not been adequately recognized by present-day library program planners. The editors of the 1876 report meant by "public" libraries all libraries to which any public was admitted, whether those libraries were government-supported or not. In their Introduction, already cited in part, they indicated they had considered public libraries

> in their direct relations to education, as adjuncts of common schools and academies, of colleges, of professional schools, theological, law, medical and scientific, and as a necessary factor in the elevation of the unfortunate in asylums, and in the instruction and elevation of the vicious and criminal in reformatories and prisons.
>
> Following this the libraries of historical societies, of young men's mercantile and young men's Christian associations have been sketched, and their influence on the increase and diffusion of intelligence described.
>
> And last, free public libraries, established and maintained on the same principle that free public schools are, receive attention and consideration. These libraries are regarded as fulfilling for all a function similar to that which the college libraries perform for those fortunate enough to pursue a college course; rightly administered, they are indeed what one writer has called them, 'the peoples' colleges. '
>
> The history of the several classes of public libraries ... having been presented, the many details belonging to what may be called the economy and administration of public libraries are considered. 67

Some have been surprised by Rothstein's finding that specialized American reference service had its origin in the

American public library, 68 yet there was in the past little
of the compartmentalization of academic, public, and special
librarianship which since the First World War has been a
distinguishing feature in America.   Only recently, as in the
1968 report cited above, has an effort been made to reinte-
grate all types of American libraries into a coherent system
--which would have seemed only natural to the 1876 editors.

The next major national survey, conducted by Kephart
in 1893, focused on technical problems of shelf classification
and the attendant controversial issues of broad versus close
classification, movable versus fixed location, and mnemonic
versus non-expressive notation.   Like earlier surveyors,
Kephart favored the economy and helpful standardization of
cooperative cataloging, but he felt its day was fairly far off. 69

The American Library Association's 1926-27 Survey
of Libraries in the United States aimed to provide a bench
mark for American libraries on the occasion of the fiftieth
anniversary of the founding of the Association.   Like the
1876 effort, it surveyed university and college as well as
public libraries, and strove to cover all major aspects of
American librarianship: technical services, services to readers, legal problems, statistics, personnel.   Although its
principal goal was the cumulation of statistics, rather than
evaluation, the earlier concern with social and educational
responsibility was apparent.   Thus, Volume Two examined
"Service to Readers in Public Libraries and in College and
University Libraries, " and Volume Three "Public Library
Service to Children; Extension Work and Community Service
of Public Libraries; School Library Organization and Service, " including public library work with special classes such
as foreigners and the blind.

A particular interest of this survey was access to
books in all types of libraries.   The survey questionnaire,
as previously noted, sought information on policy as to closed
or open shelves.   Like earlier surveys, it investigated uniformity in cataloging and classification.   The extent of uniformity in cataloging was measured by collecting data on the
use of Library of Congress subject heading lists and printed
catalog cards.   It solicited information on the resolution of
doubtful classification problems.   The approach and format
were reminiscent of Merrill's Code for Classifiers. 70

Although its Director stated that "the purpose of the
Survey was to present all of the essential facts which could

be ascertained, concerning existing conditions and methods
and service, without critical comment of any kind, " the <u>Sur-
vey</u> could not escape evaluative or critical factors. Thus the
chapter in Volume One on the selection and acquisition of materials for public libraries expressed traditional attitudes towards the library as a formative socio-educational agency:

> Between 'the best books' and the 'best that the peo-
> ple will read, ' a compromise is obviously neces-
> sary in most public libraries. The following re-
> ports illustrate the effort which most libraries ap-
> parently make to keep their standards of selection
> as high as necessary concessions to practical pol-
> icy will permit.
>
> With very few exceptions the reports indicate also
> an effort to do as much as possible to transform
> the potential readers of the community into actual
> readers. . . .
>
> Until there is general agreement as to what consti-
> tutes an 'immoral' book, or a 'sordid' or 'perni-
> cious' or 'unwholesome book, ' it is obviously im-
> possible to present a very exact statement concern-
> ing the books which libraries do and do not buy.
>
> Many libraries endeavor not to buy literature which
> criticizes destructively the institutions of society.
> Many others state that they buy only when there
> are convincing arguments to justify purchase, and
> that much of such literature which is bought is
> kept on closed shelves where some restriction is
> possible of its use by immature readers.
>
> That the librarian should ordinarily select the books
> to be purchased is a principle which apparently is
> accepted in most of the large public libraries and
> in many of the smaller. [71]

The national library surveys revealed recurring major
themes: a search for uniformity in the organization of library materials, the question of access to the shelves, the
librarian's responsibility to select--not only organize--his
collection, and, subsuming all these, the American library
as a formative (or normative) socio-educational institution.

Louis Round Wilson, who became Dean of the Graduate

Library School at the University of Chicago in 1932, both by his philosophy and practice encouraged a sociological or institutional approach in surveying the problems of the American public library. One of his faculty members, Carleton Bruns Joeckel, published in 1935 The Government of the American Public Library which considered the library "primarily as a piece of governmental machinery and its efficiency as such, rather than the practical problem of its internal administration."[72] Joeckel, insisting that the idea of regional library service was sound as a general principle, felt that library units must be large enough to be strong and effective. He prescribed what was to become a reality many years later:

> Regardless, however, of what the national government decides concerning financial aid to public libraries, there is little doubt of its responsibility for leadership in the planning of large-scale coordination and strengthening of library resources.

> It is becoming more and more clear that the library is not necessarily a town, or a city, or even a county affair. To reach its greatest usefulness to all people the library must step out of the strictly local class into a wider field, accompanied, probably, by greatly enlarged units, both of service and of government.[73]

Joeckel thus postulated the public library as an element in the national structure, a structure the government was by its nature obliged to maintain. Joeckel's definition of the public library was one used to justify direct access during the period of early controversy: "The only really essential requirement in the definition of a public library is that its use should be free to all residents of the community on equal terms."[74]

Wilson's 1935 Geography of Reading,[75] which surveyed American libraries within the context of socio-economic factors statistically presented, was the most sophisticated sociological approach yet attempted. Wilson

> collected facts concerning some 200 cultural and economic differences among our 48 states.... But Wilson also determined the extent to which certain of the conditions tend to go together--for instance, large incomes, high schools, and library service.[76]

Out of these descriptions were to grow prescriptions.
Wilson, in his earlier career at the University of North Caro-
lina, worked extensively to expand the benefits of library
service to the Negro. He "firmly believed that the South
could not realize its maximum potential unless all inhabitants
were given equal opportunity to extend their educational back-
grounds. "[77] Realistically, he countenanced at the time the
expensive dual library system of the South.

Faith in the American public library as a social-educational agency serving all the people was considerably shaken
by the findings of The Public Library Inquiry[78] which began
its series of surveys in 1947. Berelson's 1949 The Library's
Public, part of the Inquiry, struck a disheartening note for
those who had assumed the public library was an effective
democratic agency. Berelson concluded that: "Among the
major public media of communication the book attracts the
smallest audience.... As a source of information, the public
library has little reality for most people." He described the
typical public library patron:

> The young use the library more than the old, the
> better educated more than the lesser educated, and
> women a little more than, and differently from,
> men. The public library serves the middle class,
> defined either by occupation or by economic status,
> more than either the upper or the lower classes.
> Single persons patronize it more than married ones,
> and white more than Negroes.
>
> The library clientele is a self-selected minority
> with special characteristics; it includes many of the
> 'culturally alert' people of the community.... A
> plausible argument can be made that under present
> conditions the public library clientele must be small
> and that the library should be organized for those
> relatively few people in the community who can
> make 'serious' use of library materials.
>
> Universality of public library service is practically
> impossible for the public library at the present
> time, regardless of the aggressiveness of the li-
> brary in promoting itself....
>
> The library's problem is a problem of optimum al-
> location of resources.... Since it cannot be all
> things to all men, it must decide what things it will

be to whom.... It is a matter of ranking the library's actual and potential publics in a value hierarchy. [79]

It may be relevant to note that Berelson is a distinguished social scientist.   Most librarians might have drawn
a different conclusion from these data: the need to expand
the library's service to non-users.   The 1963 report on Access to Public Libraries, [80] sponsored by the American Library Association, sought to establish (its critics claimed
"to confirm") whether any citizens were, by law or de facto
arrangements, deprived of their right to use the public library.   The philosophy of most librarians has been apparently that of Ranganathan's "Every reader his book" and "Every
book its reader. "[81]

Thus, Martin, who published his survey of the Chicago
Public Library in 1969, described his philosophy of public librarianship:

> In the past the librarian's question has been: how
> can I get the learner to the library?   The future
> question will take another form: how can resources
> be projected to the learner? ... In a time of new
> communication media, we should more picture how
> resources can be carried to people where they are,
> to be used as an integral part of organizing activ-
> ity, in the classroom, the home, the market place,
> the government office....
>
> I remember the educational thrust among librarians
> in the 1920's.   This is what attracted me to the
> profession.   For a quarter of a century I have
> watched this educational motivation weaken....
> Could it be that one of the drives that kept the pub-
> lic library going has faded just at the stage where
> it is most needed?   Is this an institution for a mi-
> nority at a time when culture finally seeps out
> through the majority?[82]

That this educational thrust was still the official policy
of American librarianship was confirmed at the 1969 American Library Association Conference when the Adult Services
Division presented a preliminary draft version of "Library
Services--A Bill of Rights for Adults" which expressed the
traditional concepts that public ownership of libraries meant
the right to direct access:

Each adult is an important, unique individual, with
individual aspirations, needs, interests, abilities
and responsibilities....

Therefore, every adult has the right to expect:
Full and ready access to all available resources
from the sum of recorded fact, opinion and creative effort, in whatever form is most appropriate
to his need and most acceptable to him.

Free and easy access, in attractive and convenient
facilities, to all the local library's materials ... [83]

Some, however, still accepted Berelson's conclusions.
Gaines of the Minneapolis Public Library felt that Bundy's
1968 survey, Metropolitan Public Library Users, confirmed
Berelson's findings of twenty years earlier, and that the lesson was clear: since the adult users have been lost, the librarian must now turn to study juvenile users in an effort to
influence later favorable attitudes towards public library
use. [84]

Future developments for public librarianship at a time
of unparalleled urban unrest were anticipated by Lacy who in
1963 had already warned there was little incentive for American publishers to produce materials for the poor and half-
educated Negro, Puerto Rican or recent white immigrant in
the cities. He accordingly prescribed:

The library should be the social instrumentality that
can translate the needs of the culturally deprived,
of the non-book-using-urban groups into a demand....

The effective dissemination of print through the efforts of the private sector of the economy is confined and will continue to be confined to the middle
and upper segments of the socio-economic-educa-
tional pyramid, for only there does there exist a
demand adequate to sustain the machinery of distribution. There necessarily therefore rests on the
public sector, on urban schools and on the urban
public library, the responsibility for expressing a
demand for materials needed by the segments of
society not now effectively literate, and for providing a channel of distribution for those materials.
Yet a failure to discharge this responsibility could

be, by omission, to contribute one more element
to an already potentially explosive social situation.[85]

   This function of the librarian as social agent is familiar from previous citations and represents a natural extension
of his role as educator.   The social commitment of the public library and librarian has been vigorously promulgated recently by the younger members of the American Library Association who have challenged the "relevance" of today's public librarianship (as well as of the professional training for
it) in an urban and racial crisis.   The 1968 American Library Association Conference saw the formation of a Social
Responsibilities Round Table.   The 1969 conference witnessed
an even more militant grouping of younger dissidents who
participated in a pre-conference Congress for Change and resolved to discourage membership in the American Library
Association unless demands for "change" were met.[86]

The Implications of the Sociological Background
for the Investigation of Direct Access

   What relationships might exist between such social and
institutional aspirations of the American library movement
and the issues of direct access, browsing, and browsability?
The sociological background of the public library movement
and its direct access policy would suggest similar influences
at work: on the concept of the public library as a means
for the "self-realization of the masses" and on the concept
of open-shelf collections organized by means of shelf classification and relative location.

   A significant clue may be found in "self-realization. "
The belief in self-education and self-improvement through
reading had distinguished the American popular educational
movement from its start.   Faith in the book as a vessel of
wisdom and a medium of instruction implied that the book
through its self-revelation would effect the self-education and
self-improvement of the reader.

   The capacity for self-improvement and self-instruction
was axiomatic in the nineteenth-century campaign for popular
education.   In America, particularly, this trust in auto-didacticism seemed confirmed by the democratic credo.   ("We
hold these truths to be self-evident. ")   If one only be ex-
posed to democratic virtues and truths, clearly he could not
but be convinced.

The almost automatic certainty of progress was an eighteenth-century inheritance from the American Founding Fathers. The enormous influence of Darwin's theory of evolution reinforced during the nineteenth century the belief in continuous, inevitable progress. Thus both the eighteenth and nineteenth centuries provided a sympathetic cultural ambience for the cultivation of autodidactic popular education.

All these factors expressed themselves in librarians' attitudes towards direct access facilitated by shelf classification. This study will test various hypotheses relating to direct access: the design, application, and use of classification schemes--along with the variant assumptions concerning the nature of "browsing" and "browsability." One hypothesis is that the reader seeking instruction who follows the classification in the catalog or on the shelves will be led inevitably to the truths of the subject he is studying and, since all parts of the truth are interrelated, any one part will be correctly (that is, "truly") related to any other by the classification scheme.

The direct shelf approach would thus become a preordained finding of the "truth": the correct scheme of knowledge as exemplified in the shelf classification would reveal to the reader not only the true relationships but also numerous relevant or related facts of which he was unaware. This belief in the self-revealing nature of library classification seemed accepted in a subtle form even by classificationists who denied that Platonic realism was applicable to classification in libraries. Ranganathan insisted that his Colon Classification used the postulational approach to practical "classification without tears" because a postulate was neither "right" nor "wrong, " but only "helpful" or "unhelpful. " Yet this pragmatic scheme was also described by Ranganathan as having the following function:

> The shelf arrangement should display the full field
> of a reader's interest, unexpressed as well as ex-
> pressed. When he looks along the shelves of the
> library, he should find there what he was only
> vaguely conscious of wanting; indeed, it is only then
> that he will be able to realise exactly what it is he
> wants. It is only then that he will feel a sense of
> satisfaction, which will, at bottom, be due to the
> fulfillment of an unexpressed want, and to the get-
> ting of something which he had not known how to
> ask for. This represents a deeper function to be

performed by the arrangement of books in a library. [87]

Ranganathan's belief may be in a concept similar to
Lovejoy's "Great Chain of Being,"[88] a preordained or divine
hierarchy. This idea of a hierarchical order basic to nature
was also an intellectual heritage of Darwinian evolutionary
theory. As will be shown later, much traditional library
classification was based on the Darwinian theory of which
Richardson, Cutter, and Sayers were influential proponents.
Richardson believed that library classification should reflect
the "true order of the sciences"--a belief vehemently denied
by Hulme--and defined "the real order of arrangement of
things in the universe" as "a series of groups and groups of
groups arranged according to degrees of likeness from the
simplest to the most complex." Among the laws of classification he included the Law of History ("The progress of
things in space and time is also in general a genetic progress
in complexity.") and the Law of Evolution ("Things which are
constantly growing in complexity continue to have existence,
while others perish."). Thanks to this Law of Evolution "we
now have a clear view of ... the fact that the whole of things
includes not only things present, but things past."[89]

Richardson, in effect, held a Platonic belief in an evolutionary "Great Chain of Being":

> There is such perfection of order in minor groups
> of things that the more one seeks the more he finds
> growing in him such a sense, strong though elusive,
> that there is, if it could only be grasped, some
> kind of relation for pretty nearly everything that is,
> that he returns to the common habit of mankind of
> taking it for granted that there is such a thing as
> order, and this order one such that it may be found
> out.... There is a curious harmony between the
> most ancient and the most modern views in calling
> it 'living' or 'organic.'
>
> This idea that this whole is a 'living thing,' famil-
> iar to us in Plato's Timaeus, is contained in the
> most primitive myth of the 'world tree' and in the
> most modern philosophies as well. [90]

Documentary analysis thus would suggest how sociological and epistemological factors could reinforce each other,
and how belief in democratic self-education and inevitable

progress might not be unrelated to a faith in the self-teaching nature of the shelf-classified library.

Varying interpretations of the direct shelf approach, browsing, and browsability will be examined in the next chapter. From the evidence in this chapter a number of hypotheses were derived for the questionnaire. Some of these hypotheses have been documented also by earlier evidence.

> An effective library classification scheme will reflect the true order of nature and of science and will reveal this order through the relative location of the books on the shelves. (III:1)

> The chief value of close shelf classification lies in its use by the librarian for teaching and by the patron for learning. (III:3)

> Open-shelf access is generally desirable in all libraries. (IV:1)

> Maintaining open-shelf access is a significant educational responsibility of libraries. (IV:2)

> Public libraries cannot serve their readers adequately without offering open-shelf access. (IV:5)

> School libraries (elementary through high school) cannot fulfill their function adequately without open access. (IV:6)

Notes

1. T.W. Lyster, "Observations on Shelf-Classification," Library Association Record, II (1900), 399. (See also "Prefatory Quotations.")

2. Jesse H. Shera, Foundations of the Public Library: The Origins of the Public Library Movement in New England, 1629-1855 (Chicago: University of Chicago Press, 1949), p. 243.

3. Ibid., p. 247.

4. Ibid., p. 248.

5. Ibid., p. 234.

6. Sidney Herbert Ditzion, Arsenals of a Democratic Culture: A Social History of the American Public Library Movement in New England and the Middle States from 1850 to 1900 (Chicago: American Library Assn., 1947), p. 193.

7. Samuel Rothstein, The Development of Reference Services through Academic Traditions, Public Library Practice and Special Librarianship (Chicago: Assn. of College and Reference Libraries, 1955), p. 16.

8. Arthur E. Bostwick, The American Public Library (4th ed., rev. and enl.; New York, Appleton, 1929), p. 1-2, 9.

9. Ibid., p. 9.

10. Justin Winsor, "Library Buildings," in U.S., Bureau of Education, Public Libraries in the United States of America; Their History, Condition, and Management; Special Report; Part I (Washington: Govt. Print. Off., 1876), p. 466.

11. William Mathews, "Professorships of Books and Reading," ibid., p. 248; F. Vinton, "Shall Borrowers Go to the Shelves?" Library Journal, XI (March, 1886), 74.

12. Mathews, "Professorships of Books and Reading," p. 248-49.

13. Editor's footnote, Library Journal, XI (March, 1886), 74.

14. Vinton, "Shall Borrowers Go to the Shelves?" p. 74.

15. "Birkdaler," Letter to the editor on "Open Access," Library World, IX (1906-07), 76.

16. Editor's note, ibid.

17. Anonymous letter to editor on "American and British Open Access," Library World, X (1907-08), 46-47.

18. Ibid.

19. John Cotton Dana, A Library Primer (5th rev. ed.; Chicago: Library Bureau, 1910), p. 15.

20. Bostwick, The American Public Library, p. 48.

21. Ibid., p. 10.

22. Ibid.

23. American Library Association, A Survey of Libraries in the United States (4 vols.; Chicago, 1926-27), II, 19-21. (Also known as The Committee of Five Report.)

24. Ernest A. Savage, Manual of Book Classification and Display for Public Libraries (London: Allen and Unwin, 1946), p. 13-14, 50.

25. Dana, A Library Primer, p. 25, 130, 132.

26. H. Tapley-Soper, "My Opinion of 'Open Access,' " Library World, X (1907-08), 245.

27. James K. Hosmer, "On Browsing by a Book-Worm," Library Journal, XV (December, 1890), 34-35.

28. Charles Ammi Cutter, "Close Classification, with Special Reference to Messrs. Perkins, Schwartz, and Dewey," Library Journal, XI (July, 1886), 180.

29. Ibid.

30. William Torrey Harris, "The Function of the Library and the School in Education," Library Journal, XV (December, 1890), 31.

31. George T. Little, "School and College Libraries," in U.S., Bureau of Education, Report of the Commissioner for Education for 1892-93 (2 vols.; Washington: Govt. Print. Off., 1895), II, 925.

32. See Keyes D. Metcalf, Report on the Harvard University Library: A Study of Present and Prospective Problems (Cambridge: Harvard University Library, 1955); Paul H. Buck, Libraries and Universities (Cambridge: Belknap Press of Harvard University Press, 1964).

33. American Library Association, Survey of Libraries in
    the United States, I, 168.

34. Maurice F. Tauber, ed., "Centralization and Decentral-
    ization in Academic Libraries: A Symposium," Col-
    lege and Research Libraries, XXII (September, 1961),
    327-40ff.

35. George Piternick, "Duplicate Catalogs in University Li-
    braries," in Chicago, University, Graduate Library
    School, Library Conference, Library Catalogs:
    Changing Dimensions, ed. by Ruth French Strout
    (Chicago: University of Chicago Press, 1964), p.
    75-76.

36. Harris, "The Function of the Library and the School in
    Education," p. 31-32.

37. See Dan Bergen and E.D. Duryea, eds., Libraries and
    the College Climate of Learning (Syracuse, N.Y.:
    Program in Higher Education of the School of Educa-
    tion and the School of Library Science, Syracuse Uni-
    versity, 1966); Louis Shores, Robert Jordan, and
    John Harvey, eds., The Library-College: Contribu-
    tions for American Higher Education at the James-
    town College Workshop, 1965 (Philadelphia: Drexel
    Press, 1966).

38. Cutter, "Close Classification," p. 180.

39. Little, "School and College Libraries," p. 924.

40. Bostwick, The American Public Library, p. 182.

41. Otis H. Robinson, "College Library Administration,"
    in U.S., Bureau of Education, Public Libraries in
    the United States of America, p. 516-17.

42. Ibid., p. 517-18.

43. Ibid., p. 520.

44. Commission on the Humanities, Report of the Commis-
    sion on the Humanities (New York: American Coun-
    cil of Learned Societies, 1964), p. 43.

45. American Library Association, Survey of Libraries in

the United States, II, 168.

46. Ibid., p. 167.

47. Benjamin Franklin, Autobiography, in The Works of
     Benjamin Franklin, ed. by John Bigelow, I (New
     York: Putman, 1904), 172.

48. Rothstein, The Development of Reference Services, p.
     16.

49. Bostwick, The American Public Library, p. 374.

50. Ibid., p. 1-2.

51. Dana, A Library Primer, p. 132.

52. S. R. Warren and S. N. Clark, "Introduction," in U.S.,
     Bureau of Education, Public Libraries in the United
     States of America, p. xi, xiv.

53. Ditzion, Arsenals of a Democratic Culture, p. 193.

54. Bernard Ira Palmer, Itself an Education: Six Lectures
     on Classification (London: Library Assn., 1962),
     p. 9.

55. Melvil Dewey, "Arrangement on the Shelves," Library
     Journal, IV (April 30, June 30; 1879), 117-20, 191-
     94.

56. Dewey, Decimal Classification and Relativ Index for Ar-
     ranging, Cataloging, and Indexing Public and Private
     Libraries and Pamphlets, Clippings, Notes, Scrap-
     books, Index Rerums, etc. (2nd ed., rev. and
     greatly enl.; Boston: Library Bureau, 1885), p. 22.

57. Dewey, "Decimal Classification Beginnings," Library
     Journal, XLV (February 15, 1920), 151, 153.

58. Harris, "The Function of the Library and the School in
     Education," p. 33.

59. Leo E. LaMontagne, American Library Classification,
     with Special Reference to the Library of Congress
     (Hamden, Conn.: Shoe String Press, 1961), p. 175.

Sociology of Direct Access 107

60. S. R. Ranganathan, "Colon Classification and Its Approach to Documentation, " in Chicago, University, Graduate Library School, Library Conference, Bibliographic Organization; Papers Presented before the Fifteenth Annual Conference of the Graduate Library School, July 24-29, 1950, ed. by Jesse H. Shera and Margaret E. Egan (Chicago: University of Chicago Press, 1951), p. 103.

61. Guy R. Lyle, "An Exploration into the Origins and Evolution of the Library Survey, " in Library Surveys, ed. by Maurice F. Tauber and Irlene Roemer Stephens (New York: Columbia University Press, 1967), p. 3-22.

62. Charles Coffin Jewett, Notices of Public Libraries in the United States of America; Printed by Order of Congress, as an Appendix to the Fourth Annual Report of the Board of Regents of the Smithsonian Institution (Washington: Printed for the House of Representatives, 1851), p. 192.

63. Jewett, On the Construction of Catalogues of Libraries and of a General Catalogue, and Their Publication by Means of Separate Stereotype Titles, with Rules and Examples. (Washington: Smithsonian Institution, 1852).

64. U. S. , Bureau of Education, Public Libraries in the United States of America, p. 1010.

65. Ibid., p. xxiii.

66. U. S. , National Advisory Commission on Libraries, Library Services for the Nation's Needs: Toward Fulfillment of a National Policy (Bethesda, Md.: ERIC Document Reproduction Service, 1968).

67. Warren and Clark, "Introduction, " p. xiv.

68. Rothstein, The Development of Reference Services, p. 100.

69. Horace Kephart, "Classification, " in U. S. , Bureau of Education, Report of the Commissioner for Education for 1892-93, II, 861-922.

70. William Stetson Merrill, Code for Classifiers: Principles Governing the Consistent Placing of Books in a System of Classification (2d ed.; Chicago: American Library Assn., 1939). A preliminary mimeographed version had appeared in 1914.

71. American Library Association, Survey of Libraries in the United States, I, 10, 53-55, 57.

72. Louis Round Wilson, "Foreword," in Carleton Bruns Joeckel, The Government of the American Public Library (Chicago: University of Chicago Press, 1935), p. vii.

73. Joeckel, ibid., p. 354-55.

74. Ibid., p. x.

75. Wilson, The Geography of Reading: A Study of the Distribution and Status of Libraries in the United States (Chicago: American Library Assn. and the University of Chicago Press, 1938).

76. Douglas Waples, Investigating Library Problems (Chicago: University of Chicago Press, 1939), p. 50.

77. Tauber, Louis Round Wilson: Librarian and Administrator (New York: Columbia University Press, 1967), p. 78.

78. Robert D. Leigh, The Public Library in the United States: The General Report of the Public Library Inquiry (New York: Columbia University Press, 1950).

79. Bernard Berelson, The Library's Public: A Report of the Public Library Inquiry (New York: Columbia University Press, 1949), p. 18, 49-50, 129-30, 134.

80. International Research Associates, Inc., Access to Public Libraries: A Research Project Prepared for the Library Administration Division, American Library Association (Chicago: American Library Assn., 1963).

81. Ranganathan, Prolegomena to Library Classification (3d ed.; New York: Asia Publishing House, 1967), p. 7.

82. Lowell A. Martin, "The Changes Ahead," Library
    Journal, XCIII (February 15, 1968), 715.

83. American Library Association, Adult Services Division,
    "Library Services--A Bill of Rights for Adults," Li-
    brary Journal, XCIV (August, 1969), 2745-46.

84. Mary Lee Bundy, Metropolitan Public Library Users:
    A Report of a Survey of Adult Use in the Maryland
    Baltimore-Washington Metropolitan Area (College
    Park: University of Maryland School of Library and
    Information Services, 1968); Ervin J. Gaines, "Zenith
    or Nadir?" (Review of Metropolitan Public Library
    Users, by Bundy) Library Journal, XCIV (May 1,
    1969), 1849.

85. Dan Lacy, "The Dissemination of Print," Wilson Library
    Bulletin, XXXVII (September, 1963), 60, 64.

86. John Berry III, "The New Constituency," Library Jour-
    nal, XCIV (August, 1969), 2725-39.

87. Ranganathan, Elements of Library Classification (3d ed;
    New York: Asia Publishing House, 1962), p. 82,
    17.

88. Arthur Oncken Lovejoy, The Great Chain of Being: A
    Study of the History of an Idea. The William James
    Lectures Delivered at Harvard University, 1933
    (Cambridge: Harvard University Press, 1936).

89. E. Wyndham Hulme, "Principles of Book Classification,"
    Library Association Record, XIII (1911), 354-55;
    Ernest Cushing Richardson, Classification, Theoret-
    ical and Practical; Together with an Appendix Con-
    taining an Essay towards a Bibliographical History
    of Systems of Classification (3d ed.; New York:
    Wilson, 1930), p. 1, 7, 12.

90. Richardson, Classification, p. 11-12.

Chapter VI

TOWARDS A DEFINITION OF BROWSING

Chapter Two included a preliminary definition of "browsing":

> Although the study intends to pursue intensively the
> meanings of 'browsing' and its verbal variants, a
> working definition might here be given: a patron's
> random examination of library materials as ar-
> ranged for use.... A goal of this project is to ex-
> amine the possible connotations of 'random examina-
> tion' subsumed under the "browsing" concept. Here
> the phrase can be further defined only through the
> synonymous 'casual inspection.'

Multi-Level Definitions of Browsing

The documentary analysis suggests that any definition
of "browsing"--considered as a related or subsumed activity
of the direct shelf approach--must account for at least two
varying connotations. These connotations constitute a dual interpretation which, though difficult to define precisely, is evident from the literature. It involves varying judgments on
the intellectual purposefulness and, hence, value of browsing.

When the feasibility of this study was being considered,
the opinions of distinguished librarians especially interested
in the proposed topic were solicited. One advised:

> Somehow you should be able to distinguish between
> serendipity browsing and mental-set browsing (pur-
> poseful, more or less). That is the difference be-
> tween 'I was walking through Gimbel's on my way
> to the subway ...' and 'I was looking for a book
> on--when I found....' There is a third kind of
> browsing where the person gets the call numbers of
> areas which he thinks might be interesting and goes
> there. This is often better than the subject catalog
> for finding related material. You may want to de-

110

fine browsing in such a way as to exclude anything
as purposeful as this. 'Just looking' is more your
dish of tea, I think. In that case, don't overlook
the new book shelf. [1]

A second correspondent also assumed a multi-level
definition:

You need a much stronger and precise definition of
'browsing. ' As it stands, 'browsing' seems to
mean inspection of materials on the shelves, and
such aids as catalogs, bibliographies, etc. If you
broaden your meaning to such an extent, it will
merely mean 'securing materials from a library. '
If your problem means basically 'Is a book classification worth the cost of assigning classification
notations on all the records, etc. ?' it should be so
stated. Your problem then becomes simpler.

I believe it is essential to separate 'browsing' in
a college or university library from that in a public library. Most people go to the public library
for the sole purpose of looking over the books on
the shelves and selecting from the collection on the
shelves, rather than what may be available through
the catalog. The client wants a mystery story,
rather than a particular title; an up-to-date book
on how to raise bees, and not all the books on the
subject. Although 'browsing' may give the scholar
'something to start on, ' he will eventually need to
use bibliographic tools. [2]

Definition would, indeed, be simpler if it were possible to accept only one of these connotations as correct. Unfortunately, even though, as shown in Chapter Three, "browsing" is a literary metaphor of fairly recent origin, both the
opposition and the intermingling of its connotations have been
common from the start--with considerable theoretical and
practical consequences for library management.

As noted earlier, Mathews, advocating in 1876 the establishment of professorships of books and reading, interpreted browsing pejoratively, on the whole:

There are some persons, no doubt, who are opposed to all guidance of the young in their reading.
They would turn the student loose into a vast li-

brary and let him browse freely in whatever literary pastures may please him.... No doubt there is
a vein of wisdom in this advice....

There are some minds that have an eclectic quality
which inclines them to the reading they need, and
in a library they not only instinctively pounce upon
the books they need, but draw at once from them
the most valuable ideas.... But these are rare
cases and can furnish no rule for general guidance.
... The truth is, the literary appetite of the young
is often feeble, and oftener capricious or perverted.
While their stomachs generally reject unwholesome
food, their minds often feed on garbage and even
poison. [3]

Cutter, writing at the same time, though not using the
word "browsing," stressed its value:

It is objected to the dictionary catalog, and with
much justice, that it gives no help to the man who
wishes to glance quickly over all the literature on
a comprehensive subject, including the books on its
various branches, and that it treats the desultory
reader as badly.... It is useless to deny that here
is the weak point of the dictionary catalog. Here
is an evil which it tries, not unsuccessfully, to reduce to a minimum, but can never do away with
altogether. Mr. Schwartz gets over the difficulty
by adding a classed catalog to a dictionary--a perfect but a somewhat expensive remedy. That the
cost is not justified by the gain in a library where
the public have access to the shelves, and the
books are their own classed catalog, better than
any that the librarian can make, is undoubted. How
it is in town and city libraries, where the public do
not go beyond the delivery room, the librarians
must say. [4]

Cutter did not despise the "desultory" reader. Explaining in 1893 why he considered alphabetical sub-arrangement preferable in open-shelf libraries, he clearly indicated
that "browsing" was not an unrespectable activity:

The simple numerical order is easier to apply ...
than the alphabetic, but the latter saves time in the
end, and is always more satisfactory to an orderly
mind.

There is, however, a great difference in this matter between the libraries which, like college and
proprietary and some smaller town libraries, admit
either the whole public, or some select part of the
public, to the shelves, and those which exclude all
outsiders, as do the larger town and the city libraries. And there is a difference between those which
are used much for browsing and study and those
which are used mainly for circulation. 5

Cutter's coupling of "browsing" and "study" was not
seconded by Spofford who in 1905 questioned the educational
value of browsing and took a dim view of "desultory reading."
His attitude resembled that of Mathews:

We have to add to the long list of the enemies of
books ... those who demand a right to browse (as
they term it) among the shelves of a public library,
and who displace the books they take down to grat-
ify, it may be, only an idle curiosity....

If library facilities consist in rendering the books
in it unfindable, and therefore unavailable to any
reader, then the argument for free range of the
shelves arrives at a reductio ad absurdum....

The real student is better served by the knowledge
and aid of the librarian, thus saving his time for
study, than he can by ranging about dark shelves
to find, among multitudes of books he does not
want, the ones that he actually does want. The
business of the librarian, and his highest use, is
to bring the resources of the library to the reader.
If this takes a hundred or more volumes a day, he
is to have them; but to give him the right to throw
a library into confusion by 'browsing around' is to
sacrifice the rights of the public to prompt service,
to the whim of one man. Those who think that
'browsing' is an education in itself should reflect
that it is like any other wandering employment, fa-
tal to fixity of purpose. Like desultory reading of
infinite periodicals, it tends rather to dissipate the
time and the attention than to inform and strengthen
the mind. 6

Somewhat later, Richardson expressed opposite views
on the educational benefits of browsing for both scholarly re-

search and general reading:

> What is true of trained scientific research ... is
> still more true of popular work. ... Where there is
> access to shelves especially there is the greatest
> educational advantage in the actual incentive to the
> reader to read or at least, what is of almost
> greater importance, to browse through books in or-
> der to pick out certain things. The 'average read-
> er' will hardly study even a classed catalog and is
> utterly at sea with an alphabetical list or an un-
> classified library. If, however, he can look over
> the shelves in a classified library he is surprised
> to find how much there is that is interesting, he
> learns to get facts that he wants more readily, and
> in the end saves much time for himself and for the
> librarian. [7]

Kelley, in her 1937 landmark work on shelf classification, obviously had in mind a dual concept of browsing:

> One might ask, for instance, what is the relative
> importance of the reasons for seeking material,
> judged in the light of the status and purpose of the
> seeker and of the social importance and value of
> the object for which the material is sought. In oth-
> er words, there may be a great deal of casual and
> ineffective running-over of cards in the catalog or
> of books on the shelves by readers with superficial
> interest which leads to nothing, while other use
> might lead to distinctly worthwhile ends. With an
> answer to this query we are not concerned at the
> present time. [8]

Some principal elements in the varying concepts of
"browsing" as related to the direct shelf approach would now
seem apparent. The resultant definitions might be placed
along a continuum of intellectual purposefulness: from capricious self-indulgence in worthless or even pernicious literature to valuable self-education for the general reader and
highly desirable if not essential research for the scholar.

Browsing As a Research Method

These contrasting, sometimes intermingled, opinions
or assumptions concerning browsing have continued to the

present. Noteworthy, as the following quotations will indicate, is the acceptance by the advanced scholar and researcher of browsing as a necessary sophisticated library approach to intellectual problems, an attitude emphasized by documentalists and information scientists.

Stevens in 1956, investigating the research use of libraries, pointed out the impracticality of sending certain materials to storage, since "the social scientist and the humanist must have freedom to range, with more or less purpose, through books in many fields and cannot be restricted to requesting the items he needs by author and title. The natural scientist usually does the latter." Stevens, however, wondered whether the humanist-social scientist actually needed to browse, or whether, perhaps, better bibliographic aids might make such shelf browsing unnecessary. In any case, Stevens did not consider "browsing" a capricious activity. [9]

Often mentioned as an advantage of the direct shelf approach and browsing is the opportunity to choose a book not only for intellectual content but also format. These two factors were merged by Harry Dewey in his defense of shelf classification:

> However, if the name-approach reader were favored by the shelf arrangement--i.e., if all the books in the library were arranged by author in a single alphabet--what substitute does the subject-approach reader find for the absence of a subject shelf-arrangement, and how satisfactory is it? True, he may find a subject catalog, with all books listed under their subjects, but this is no substitute for the shelves themselves. Who can browse among catalog cards and pick out the most interesting book, or the most attractive illustrations, or the largest print? [10]

Particularly among documentalists and information scientists, "browsing" is accepted as a necessary and venerable research means. Evans, writing on "Documentation" in Landau's Encyclopaedia of Librarianship, stated: "In the nineteenth century it was possible for a scientist to obtain and read personally nearly the whole literature on his special subject and browse in neighboring fields." [11] Foskett, recounting the history of the Classification Research Group to 1962, explained that the Group did not ignore mechanization, but "we believe, however, that there will, in the foreseeable

future, remain a need for classification to provide research
workers with the opportunity for browsing and for imposing
some discipline on a literature that tends always towards
greater disorder. "12   Bourne, in his text on information science, cautioned that a manual file was needed for browsing
with computers; that one could not economically browse with
a computer in searching a coordinate index term file; that
Shaw's "Rapid Selector" did not provide for browsing. 13
Bourne, in other words, maintained a criterion of "browsability" for information retrieval.

Menzel, describing the information needs of scientists,
included browsing:

> One of the important services which the scientific
> communication system renders to the progress of
> science [is] to bring to scientists from time to
> time information about work lying outside of their
> present areas of attention, so as to alter the
> boundaries of that area.   Through what sources and
> channels such redirection of attention is likely to
> come about is a matter under investigation.   But it
> is clear a priori that it depends on one or another
> form of browsing--at any rate, on transactions
> which, from the point of view of the previously dis-
> cussed functions, are wasteful and inefficient. 14

Swanson, in his effort to devise a computer-console
substitute for the conventional card catalog and shelf-classified collection, admitted the need to allow for browsing:
"The ability to request anything 'similar' to some work already in hand could be valuable, particularly as an aid to
browsing.... Browsing is a well-known but little-understood
activity ... rather like shopping in a supermarket. "15

Rigby extolled browsing as a basic activity to be encouraged at all levels of age and education:

> In every human activity involving the quest for ob-
> jects, information, or knowledge, two approaches
> may be used, one the direct or specific approach
> and the other the indirect or exploratory approach.

> Either approach may be equally rewarding, although
> not necessarily so in any given instance, or for any
> given person.   But neither can be ignored in over-
> all planning for education or research, or in de-

signing library or information-retrieval systems,
without drastically inhibiting or even frustrating
progress or achievement. Most activities involve,
however, a combination of the two approaches in
widely varying proportions. [16]

The concern of the information scientist with browsing
continues unabated. Overhage of the M. I. T. INTREX project
was quoted in a 1968 interview as asking: "What are we going to do about browsers?"[17]

The above quotations are not to imply that the documentalist's understanding of browsing is necessarily the same
as that of the traditional librarian. However, this study has
shown that many traditional librarians posit the intellectual
need for "browsing" as facilitated by the direct shelf approach. Such librarians' understanding of the browsing concept seems, at least, related to the respect accorded the
term by the scientific community. Needham described how
English librarians continued Cutter's coupling of browsing and
study:

> An interesting development in shelf arrangement is
> seen at Tottenham [English public library].... All
> books, periodicals, etc., reference or lending, are
> shelved together in the appropriate subject bay
> where provision is also made for study as well as
> browsing.... The librarian hopes to cater for the
> general reader and the student more satisfactori-
> ly. [18]

Humanist scholars also continued to esteem browsability, as indicated by the earlier cited 1964 Report of the Commission on the Humanities:

> The greatest achievement of the American academic
> library has been its success in making its collec-
> tions readily accessible to students and faculty, and
> this has been a contribution to the welfare of the
> humanist in particular. There are several factors
> that now threaten to reduce this accessibility. One
> of them, indeed, is microphotography.... One can-
> not browse through microfilms in the stack; they
> must be read at a machine. [19]

Weber[20] pointed out that developments in computerized
or mechanized indexing did not accommodate browsing needs,

a condition noted also by Bourne.

DeGennaro explained in 1964 one purpose of Harvard's making its shelf list available in computer print-out form: "Copies of the lists of a particular class will be located and prominently displayed in the stack with the class in order to provide a guide to intelligent and systematic browsing."[21] The comment seemed to imply, however, that browsing, not properly guided and pursued, could be unintelligent and unsystematic.

Ranganathan has frequently proclaimed browsing essential for research in libraries. He stated in his Prolegomena to Library Classification:

> The most popular approach is the subject approach. Here, hardly any reader--particularly, a reader engaged in work in the wave-front of knowledge-- can specify the subject in exact terms, with all its 'individualising particularities' as William Blake would put it.... The specific subject of interest is often ineffable. Therefore, browsing through a classified sequence of books or of catalog entries is a necessity.[22]

Gore, introducing the college freshman to research in libraries, advised:

> Any time you want to experience the joys of serendipity, go to the shelves and start browsing in some subject area that has caught your interest. This is called 'reading the shelves,' an activity that is the hallmark of a mature reader. When you have learned to read shelves as well as books, you have made a significant advance along the road to intellectual maturity.[23]

In 1969 Clay suggested that browsing and the concept of open shelves had not been adequately investigated, but he cited one survey of graduate book stack use which found that eighty percent of those interviewed "felt they could not get along without browsing.... Though the catalog does inform the patron of the location of a specific book and/or titles of books in a subject field, it fails to completely satisfy him. He feels he needs more: the physical contact with the book."[24]

Browsing As an Equivocal Activity

Despite these numerous encomia, "browsing" represents for many librarians certain undesirable reading habits,
in particular the aimless handling of materials, with its dangers of misshelving and pilferage.   Such opinion was cited in
the previous chapter on the controversy attending the introduction of direct access.   Also, "browsing" means to these
librarians an activity largely non-study oriented, similar to
the frequenting of "browsing rooms." These definitions and
assumptions may be placed closer to the "unuseful" end of
the continuum described above.   Yet, this less respectful attitude towards "browsing" is often mixed with an acceptance
of its possible research value.   The following statement,
from a brochure given entering college freshmen, illustrates
the mixed attitude:

> OPEN SHELVES: The barriers between you and the
> books have been removed.   You can go directly to
> the shelves for your books.   Once you find where
> materials on a particular subject are shelved, you
> can browse through the entire holdings.   In addition
> to finding materials, browsing is a socially accepted
> form of wasting time. [25]

Ellsworth, in his book on library buildings for colleges
and universities, also expressed this mingled opinion:

> Browsing rooms received much attention in the
> 1930's when college and university libraries seldom
> gave students direct access to the books.   Today,
> however, in an open-shelf library, the entire li-
> brary is thought of as a browsing collection.   What
> does browsing mean?   Why have a browsing room
> in an open-shelf library?   Isn't the idea a little
> corny?
>
> In theory the idea is absurd, but in fact there is a
> real need here.   Readers frequently want to pick
> up a book to read for fun but may not know what
> book to read.   They don't know where to go in the
> jungle of the book stacks.   Their need isn't depart-
> mentalized according to subject.   They want a new
> book--probably a novel or a play.   To meet this
> need, a library should have a place where one can
> go and find a sort of 'week-end' reading group of
> books.   The place may be a large display rack, or

> even a small room. People who are in this mood
> usually want to take the books home, not read them
> in the library. Thus, if the place is a room, it
> needn't have much space for readers. It should,
> however, be in a central place, either in the lobby
> or near the reference desks. The collection
> shouldn't be large--seldom over a thousand books
> --because otherwise the reader has to spend too
> much time choosing, and it should consist of new
> books--not nineteenth-century novels. Some one on
> the staff, and this usually means the reference li-
> brarians, needs to see to it that the shelves are
> kept full. [26]

Thus, Ellsworth, like previously cited authorities, employed a duple interpretation of "browsing." On the one
hand, any open-shelf library is in effect a browsing collection; yet, there can also be a browsing collection for those
who wish to choose quickly new novels or plays for fun-filled
weekends. Ellsworth was not alone in describing an open-
shelf academic library as equivalent in toto to a browsing
collection. Mills, tracing the development of separate undergraduate libraries in American colleges, cited Wagman on
the Undergraduate Library of the University of Michigan:
"Since the entire collection was considered a browsing collection, 'no separate browsing collection was provided.' "[27]

Even when browsing is regarded as a legitimate scholarly pursuit, there is often a suggestion of non-purposeful
self-indulgence. A comment by Palmer may be repeated.
Discussing the need for the nineteenth-century public library
in America to classify its collections, he stated:

> Government by the people implied a need to inform
> the people, and to lay open the intellectual treas-
> ures of the ages. Access for the many to the
> books which enshrined the treasures suddenly pro-
> duced problems of organization and administration
> that did not exist for the occasional scholars brows-
> ing in the libraries provided for their exclusive en-
> joyment. [28]

This implied suspicion of some self-gratifying browsing masquerading as scholarship has been expressed by
Knapp, known for her efforts to convert the undergraduate library into a learning center or "library-college":

>We do not intend to belittle the delights nor, in-
>deed, the educational value of browsing. It is an
>experience which the natural reader will enjoy in
>any case. A student with sufficient imagination can
>use almost any book as a stimulus to creative
>thought. Perhaps we will one day find ways to
>help the average student develop such imagination,
>but, for now, we are concerned with lesser tasks
>of helping all students learn to browse not haphaz-
>ardly but with discrimination and judgment. [29]

A reason given by Knapp for this opinion was that the
freshman had been conditioned "from his pre-college experience with small, selected collections." [30] Recently, similar
opinions, admittedly not based on research, have doubted the
value of browsing in large academic collections. Samore
summarized a conference on the problems of library classification:

>Indeed, browsing among the stacks is probably the
>heart of the matter; what is surprising is that for
>so non-rational a process, librarians should go to
>such 'rational' extremes. Although very little is
>known about what people actually 'do' when they
>browse, very much seems to be known about its
>value.

>With the avalanche of hundreds of thousands of doc-
>uments ... browsing has become physically im-
>practical. The search strategy has shifted from
>direct access to access primarily by surrogate. [31]

Orne delivered a like judgment: "Many are now impressed by the relative unimportance of browsing, long touted
as the best avenue to discovery. The volume of published
material in almost any given field is so great that browsing
is well-nigh impossible and usually unproductive." [32]

The varying attitudes towards browsing documented
above might be summarized, no doubt crudely, as: browsing
is good, or bad, or both good and bad. This range of opinion is covered in Section Five of the questionnaire, whose
fourteen statements extend from "All readers should be encouraged to browse" (V:1) to "Browsing is not a sufficiently
precise term to characterize serious research, so its use
should be limited to describing recreational, non-research activities in 'browsing' collections or their equivalent." (V:14)

Descriptions of the Direct Shelf Approach

The browsing process must be thought of as belonging
to the larger subject of this investigation, i.e., the direct
shelf approach. Therefore, it seemed desirable, before trying on the basis of the documentary analysis to define browsing more strictly, to examine the literary evidence on the
purpose of the direct shelf approach. Thus, perhaps, one
might be helped to define "browsing" in relation to the inclusive heading. Although Samore felt that "very little is known
about what people actually 'do' when they browse,"[33] authorities have given descriptions, based on experience as well as
theory, of what readers "do" or are presumed to "do" when
they utilize the direct shelf approach.

As a metaphorical expression, "browsing" was more
susceptible to pejorative connotations than "open access" or
"direct shelf approach," but much evidence has been cited
that the less "weighted" expressions were not immune--be-
cause of the purported disruptive and dishonest proclivities of
readers accorded the latter privileges. In any case, the following quotations, some previously cited, are intended to
supply detailed descriptions by librarians of the presumed behavior of readers engaged in the direct shelf approach.

Dewey explained in 1876 the value of a shelf-classified
collection:

> Every specialist has his own special library....
> Every subject thus being a library in itself shows
> at once its resources as no catalog can show them.
> A catalog cannot be made that will so quickly and
> thoroughly decide a student's wants as the books
> themselves.[34]

A few years later, Dewey restated this idea:

> No catalog ever did, ever will, or ever can take
> the place of the books themselves. The best work
> is done by seeing the books together. If the li-
> brary is not so arranged, the student must often go
> to great trouble to get his books together, where he
> can see them all at once. If not admitted to the
> shelves, he calls for these books together, and the
> convenience of service demands that they be found
> together.[35]

Cutter also stressed the desirability of seeing books, not surrogates, and of seeing related books physically grouped:

> It is as true for the librarian as for the student that the best catalog is the books themselves. The catalog answers a different class of questions or answers the same questions in a different way. If it is well made, it comes nearer bringing everything together than the shelves can ever do; but it does not show the character of the books as well as does a glance at them or the mere sight of their outsides to one who has seen them before. The difference is like that between textbooks and object teaching. [36]

Sayers quoted Gladstone on the value of visual contact with grouped books:

> It is an immense advantage to bring the eye in aid of the mind; to see within a limited compass all the works that are accessible, in a given library, on a given subject; and to have the power of dealing with them collectively at a given spot, instead of hunting them through an entire collection. [37]

From the evidence, the direct shelf approach involved two activities: comprehensive subject survey and specific title selection. Both were described by Cutter in 1893:

> The reason for [shelf] classifying is that people often wish to see many books on a subject at once; either in order to read the whole literature of the subject, or that they may examine it and select the best works. A classified arrangement is also sometimes an assistance in finding a book whose author's name has been forgotten, tho its subject is remembered. It also frequently enables one to get a book without consulting the catalog to find where it is placed, for when the classes are well defined one knows just where a book of well-defined character must be. No one, for example, would go to the catalog to find the place of a life of Washington, or a novel by Dickens, or a history of France in a library in which there were the classes Biography and Fiction and French History, and an alphabetical subject arrangement. [38]

Lyster emphasized the value of the direct shelf approach for specific title selection:

> Shelf-classification cannot do the work of a subject
> catalog, but, so far as it goes, it is superior to
> a subject-catalog, because it shows the books them-
> selves side by side, and enables a student to decide
> what book will be of service.... The concrete book,
> the book itself, can often be accepted or rejected
> at a glance, while the title in a catalog may leave
> the inquirer doubtful.... In fact, shelf-classifica-
> tion is one of the labour saving devices, and is so
> obviously desirable that it is used in all money-
> making businesses. [39]

Martel seemed to lay equal emphasis on comprehensive survey and specific title selection as benefits of a classified open-shelf library:

> The student or business man in the pursuit of his
> investigation finds the literature which concerns his
> inquiry collected for him ready for examination.
> He is saved the time of bringing it together title
> for title by the roundabout method of referring first
> to bibliographies and then to catalogs, writing out
> separate slips for every item, frequently only to be
> disappointed in the scope or character of the books
> when they reach him. [40]

Still another use of the direct shelf approach was mentioned by Bostwick: "Our catalogs inform the reader what books are owned by the library, but not whether a particular book is in use or not.... The mere statement of this difficulty is in itself sufficient to show the advantage of free access to the shelves. "[41]

Richardson advanced one of the most closely reasoned advocacies of the direct shelf approach as implemented by shelf classification. After explaining the practical object of the library, "a machine got together to instill ... knowledge into men's minds, " he claimed this object realized by shelf classification whose result was the juxtaposition of those books which will be most used together:

> The putting of the most-used books together saves,
> in the first place, actual labor on the part of users
> and librarians in assembling any given mass of ma-

terial for use.   No catalog can take its place....
Any roughed-out group of books is a positive and
great gain to economy in bibliographical search and
promotes economy in the actual use by bringing the
books together in space and thus saving innumerable
steps on the part of the man who goes to the
shelves to consult them.... A prime advantage of
having most used books in classes together, therefore, is the fact that the rough bulk of material so
gathered together saves a vast amount of bibliographical work and a vast amount of work in actual gathering together and use of material. [42]

Richardson then reconstructed the activities of readers
in an open-shelf library:

A second and great advantage of having the most
used books together in the classes in which they are
used together is, that they furnish in this way an
incentive to the user to get a full view of his material.... Men are naturally lazy.... In looking
over much material, too, he is pretty sure also to
be tempted by references to look up other material
... not grouped in the classes.... It often happens
that they find that work in which they have been
wasting much time has already been done by someone else.... They should discover this at the earliest date.... This end is greatly promoted by the
simple fact of having the material grouped together
so that men can glance over it and get their eyes
on what has really been done.... As a guide to see
beforehand what fields are still comparatively un-
worked, this classification of books becomes of still
greater importance....

What is true of trained scientific research ... is
still more true of popular work ....Where there is
access to the shelves especially there is the greatest
educational advantage in the actual incentive to the
reader to read or at least, what is of almost
greater importance, browse through books in order
to pick out certain things.   The 'average reader'
will hardly study even a classed catalog and is ut-
terly at sea with an alphabetical list or an unclassified library.   If, however, he can look over the
shelves in a classified library he is surprised to
find how much there is that is interesting, he learns

to get facts that he wants more readily, and in the
end saves much time for himself and for the librarian....

There is a third advantage in classification ... in
the fact of the psychological or mnemonic training
of those who, through seeing books arranged in certain classes, get in the habit of running over the
categories in their minds and associating their own
ideas in these classes. [43]

A description of the reader's presumed activities in
open-shelf collections was given by Bliss, who posited six
types of approach and use: from the elementary request for
a specific work by a specific author to the process of advanced research and investigation. The earlier stages are
served by the author-catalog, or by the alphabetic subject-
catalog. The advanced stages "involve systematic organization of classes on the shelves and in the catalogs." For the
latter stages "access to the shelves is prerequisite, but this
may need to be supplemented by the complete shelf-list and
by reference to the subject-catalog, extending to a wider
range of classes; and special bibliography may prove extensively serviceable. "[44]

Finally, a non-librarian's description à la Hosmer of
direct access and browsing was offered in the British archae-
ologist Celoria's 1969 article, "The Archaeology of Serendip,"
wherein he pled for "Higher Browsing." Celoria began cau-
tiously:

Librarians are not easily convinced by the reader
who makes vociferous claims about the value of unrestricted browsing. Sometimes the browser in-
sists that this method for hitting on 'pablum for ex-
citing the mind' should automatically command library collaboration. The librarian can be forgiven
if he indulges in a little puritanical disapproval.
To please even a few browsers several trained
members of the staff may be needed to organize
this kind of access. [45]

Celoria then delineates a hierarchy of browsing activities:

It might be better at this point to try and describe
the various kinds of browsing. First we should be-

gin by saying what browsing is not. If a reader
goes to a library to check a reference or get a
straight answer to a question, ... he or she is not
a browser.   If he is distracted by neighboring entries in the encyclopedia and reads away, ... he is
surely a browser.

Less simple to classify is the browsing done by a
reader who sees a run of a particular magazine and
decides to see what these volumes are about.   A
further extension of this kind of browsing is the activity of a person who has heard a talk on Spinoza
and is attracted into the philosophy shelves of a library 'just to have a look at Spinoza.'   A few pages
are leafed over and then no more.   A slightly more
utilitarian browsing is that of a university lecturer
in English who has specialized in the Elizabethan
period but is told by his professor that he might
have to take over ... a subsidiary course on Vic-
torian literature.   He accordingly spends an after-
noon looking through back numbers of PMLA ...
and, doubtless, dozens of other periodicals.   It is
unlikely that notes will be taken; the process is not
one of mastication but rather a preliminary sniff at
the subject.

The next step in the hierarchy of browsing is the
regular 'glance over current literature' which is
(or should be) done by workers in various subjects.
... The aim is to keep up to date.   The work is
not the systematic searching which is the opposite
of browsing, but it still can have some of the casualness of browsing.

There is a further class of contact with books which
is well outside the sphere of the above kinds of
browsing.   This will be solemnly termed 'Higher
Browsing' ... which can refer to something which
is both an art and a science.   A person literate in
Higher Browsing goes at regular intervals, say once
every two weeks, to a library and looks at the literature of other subjects.   Practice enables him to
avoid spending too long on some works, and he
learns very swiftly how to get ideas about the content or range or trends of a new subject. 46

Celoria, who believed that "many theories of classification contain a built-in death-knell for HB, " has modest proposals for implementing HB in libraries:

> It is hoped that librarians will acknowledge the need
> for a few loopholes in any library structure so that
> the HB man can find something.... A librarian
> might unofficially foster HB by making the 'New
> Accessions' section of a library into an attractive
> place.... He might adroitly tempt the browser in
> us by putting up shelves marked 'Newly-bound
> books, ' or 'Reclassified books!' The browsing in-
> duced by this might produce much serendipic suc-
> cess. But one cannot legislate for this sort of
> thing.[47]

Towards a Functional Definition of Browsing

Perhaps a further definition, based on the preceding evidence, could now be attempted for "browsing" as related to the direct shelf approach. One might begin with the assumption, seemingly accepted by all authorities, that the browsing function is related to, or is part of, but is not co-extensive with, the direct shelf approach. The great advantage of the approach is to permit the personal examination of books as arranged on the shelves. Such examination allows one to find a work with a known location symbol or--just as important according to Bostwick[48]--to determine whether the work is available. Though not a prime intended intellectual purpose of the direct shelf approach, this activity has been noted by investigators as constituting perhaps its most common application.[49]

Another use of the direct shelf approach is to ascertain directly what books by a particular author, or in a particular form, or on a particular subject are on the shelves. Such an activity has been frequently described as that used by a reader who wishes to "survey" all the works on a subject or by a certain author or in a particular form that are in the library. (Beginning with Cutter and his "Objects, "[50] most writers on cataloging and classification have emphasized these two contrasting--some say irreconcilable--purposes, and have described them by such terms as location versus collocation.)[51] Barring the need for a comprehensive examination of all the literature in a certain genre or on a topic or by an author, the "survey" usually involves a choice of titles from among those inspected. How that choice is made has not

been definitively explained by library-use and user studies.
Sometimes, non-intellectual criteria may govern, such as
size of print, number and kinds of illustrations, convenience
of format.   Selection of works on this basis would involve a
physical examination or comparison.   Allied to this type of
inspection, but implying intellectual judgment, would be a
sampling of the text for its style, level of sophistication, and
approach.

Undeniably, in the above described search, survey, inspection, and sampling activities, an element of uncertainty
or unpredictability obtains.   One can not know until at the
shelves whether a desired book will be found, or how many
books of any kind.   One can not be certain before opening the
book if the print will be large enough.   One can not be sure
before reading some of the sentences whether the text will
suit one's needs.   Nevertheless, all these activities can be
reasonably encompassed, without recourse to a "browsing"
label, by the general headings of "inspection" and even "sampling" of books made possible by the direct shelf approach.

The "browsing" factor as a distinct element in the direct shelf approach seems to emerge pari passu with intellectual unpredictability.   Such unpredictability may vary greatly in degree and kind.   As in the case of "good" versus
"bad" browsing, a continuum can be traced of librarians' attitudes towards, and definitions of, the browsing process, but
now in terms of its unpredictability.   Kind, rather than degree, seems more significant.   Thus, the most elementary
browsing may, in degree, be the most unpredictable.   For
example, on the simplest level, a reader may enter a library
with no set intention of withdrawing any book, though presumably not averse to deciding on some one.   He is, so to
speak, ready to be "sold" by the display, like a shopper with
no fixed purchase in mind.   This library "customer" may
discover a title by a favorite author, or find a new book on
a subject of interest, or come across a work he "has always
meant to read. "   The motivation is largely that of recreational reading or, on a slightly more intellectual level, of keeping generally well-informed through "worth-while non-fiction. "
For this reader the librarian organizes "browsing collections"
or "new books sections. "   This level of choice is analogous
to "impulse purchasing, " an analogy supported by the comments of authorities that "browsing" in libraries and in shops
are similar. [52]

Related to the above type of unpredictability is that involved when one enters a library with the intention of obtaining a certain book, but ends up withdrawing other books by the same author or by authors whose works are nearby. This, too, may bear comparison with shopping, i.e., "purchase of associated items" stimulated by effectively related displays, e.g., toothbrushes and toothpaste shown together. This kind of choice in libraries is encouraged when literature is shelved by type and author, e.g., novels, or when biographies are arranged by biographee.

As the motivation becomes subject-oriented study and research, the complexity and sophistication of "browsing" needs increase, the element of unpredictability becoming not so much greater in degree as, in an intellectual sense, more serious and critical in kind--and, withal, less definable.

Classificationists like Dewey, Richardson, Cutter, and Bliss[53] have offered numerous descriptions of how the student, researcher, or interested reader will find on the shelves books grouped by subject and physically related to other subject groups. At this point the researcher can "browse" through the works and (1) by the aid of table of contents and index determine whether a specific piece of information is contained therein, or (2) by examining the works' notes and bibliographies obtain other titles which might yield the information.

At the next level of complexity, one may, as part of one's research, survey the available literature and, "reading the shelves" in classified order, search for works treating one's subject or related subjects. This may result in finding relevant expected or unexpected information, and even in redirecting or restructuring one's research.

Because these browsing roles represent such a range of unpredictability, it is difficult to construct an accurate general definition. However, throughout this range appears evidently a common element: the reader's assumption that browsing is possible in an open-shelf collection; that is, the chance is at least worth taking that by examining library materials as arranged for use, one may find, if even unexpectedly, books or data to satisfy, variously, one's needs for recreational reading, specific information, or subject research. A kind of confidence seems to be expressed by the reader in the organization of an open-shelf library. (This confidence or expectation seems to be related to the nature, revealed by the earlier etymological analysis, of "grazing" alias "browsing. ") Thus, a more useful definition of "browsing" might be a functional one, perhaps as follows: "Browsing is that activity, subsumed in the direct shelf approach, whereby materials arranged for use in a library are examined in the reasonable expectation that desired or valuable items or information might be found among those materials as arranged on the shelves. "

"Browsability" accordingly could be defined as "that characteristic of an open-shelf collection resulting from the arrangement of a library's materials for use so that one may examine those materials in the reasonable expectation that desired or valuable items or information might be found among those materials as arranged on the shelves. " For reasons to be discussed later, the degree of "browsability" may vary, that is, one collection may be more "browsable" than another.

These definitions could apply, with appropriate changes in wording, to browsing among surrogates for library materials, e.g., catalogs, bibliographies, and abstracts. One should note, however, the distinction made by Bar-Hillel between "reference-providing" and "data-providing. "[54]

Also, the above definitions could be extended to documentation and to information storage and retrieval by substituting for such terms as "library materials" and "shelves" and "open-shelf collection" and "direct shelf approach" the concept of a store of data arranged so that access is available by mechanical or non-mechanical means.

Two corollaries seem to derive from the above definitions: (1) The library's collection is adequate for browsing. (2) The collection is properly arranged for browsing. Accordingly, a hypothesis of this study is that open-shelf libraries' acquisition policies and classification systems have as their rationale (perhaps not always consciously understood or acknowledged) to implement effective direct shelf access, and, in particular, to maximize browsability--as defined above. The next two chapters will conclude the documentary analysis by dealing, respectively, with acquisition policy and shelf classification as means of "structuring" the situation within which the direct shelf approach and browsing are employed.

"Random Examination" and "Serendipity"

The preliminary definition of browsing in Chapter Two

included the phrases "random examination" and "casual inspection" which do not appear in this chapter's definitions.
It seemed difficult to justify those phrases in a functional definition of the direct shelf approach and browsing. One might
characterize a patron's activity in a recreational "browsing
collection" or "new books section" as "casual inspection, "
but "random examination, " taken literally, seems to belie a
basic purpose of the direct shelf approach and of browsing as
just defined.   "Random" means "being done or chosen at random; having no definite aim or deliberate purpose" and "lacking or seeming to lack a regular plan, purpose, or pattern. "
"At random" means "without definite aim, direction, rule, or
method; at haphazard; aimlessly; irregularly. "   "Random" is
distinguished from "chance" as follows: "RANDOM stresses
lack of definite aim, fixed goal, regular procedure, or pre-
dictable incidence.   CHANCE stresses complete lack of design, intent, plan, or prearrangement.... It suggests lack
of plan, reason, forethought in connection with persons encountered or objects found or discovered in various places."[55]

        The selection and arrangement of materials for use in
an open-shelf collection seem to try to counteract a CHANCE,
let alone RANDOM situation, as defined above.   Even for
"browsing room" activities, one cannot accept the literal
meaning of "random" which would imply that one enters a
"browsing room" with no possible intention of reading or withdrawing a book or of allowing oneself to be persuaded to do
so by the display.

        "Random" may have some relevance within the context
of the direct shelf approach and browsing, as functionally defined, if it be interpreted in one of its scientific senses,
e.g., as in biology, where it may mean: "Made as if at
random but controlled or selected so as to bring together
certain individuals, kinds, or classes, or in biometry, to
make representative of, as a cross section of a class or
group; as, random breeding; a random sample. "[56]   In such
a sense, perhaps, one might describe the purpose of organizing an open-shelf library through acquisition and classification: an effort to produce a "random sample" of the literature.   No collection can be universal; therefore, if the literature sample has been effectively "controlled or selected, "
and made accessible, the patron would, by "random" examination within the limits of the sample, have a reasonably
good chance of finding valuable or desirable items and information.

The "random access" of computer science would seem the opposite of what is sought by the organization of an open-shelf collection. "Random access" is defined as "access to storage under conditions in which the next location from which data are to be obtained is in no way dependent on the location of the previously obtained data."[57] Fixed location on the shelves--the contrary of shelf classification--would represent a system of "random access" as understood by computer scientists.

Another word difficult to justify in a functional definition of browsing is the widely used "serendipity." The word was "coined by Horace Walpole upon the title of the fairy-tale The Three Princes of Serendip, the heroes of which 'were always making discoveries, by accidents and sagacity, of things they were not in quest of.' " Its meaning is "the faculty of making happy and unexpected discoveries by accident," or "the gift of finding valuable or agreeable things not sought for"--changed in a later edition to "an assumed gift for finding valuable or agreeable things not sought for."[58]

Neither on grammatical nor logical grounds would it seem correct to use the word as an apparent synonym for "browsability" as defined above. First, the word signifies a characteristic of the seeker rather than the collection: it is a personal "ability" or "faculty" or "gift." Secondly, the idea of "accidentally finding valuable things one is not looking for" is, strictly speaking, not relatable to any intellectual goal or activity.

Actually, the word as now commonly understood seems to describe the pleasantly surprising discovery of material related to a researcher's intellectual interests; but it is not intellectually plausible that such a discovery would be made, as implied by the strict meaning of the word, by browsing in a subject area completely unrelated to a researcher's interests. Otherwise, there would be little reason for surprise! One would not ordinarily expect to find groceries in a shoe store, nor would a chemist peruse professionally the literature of philology. However, the use of "serendipity," as applied to browsing, is so widespread that to reject it would be as pointless as to demand that "grazing" replace "browsing." One, therefore, should acknowledge the technical connotations, however illogical linguistically, lent the word by scientists.

Celoria announced that "serendipity" was now a re-

spectable scientific term, and cited the United Kingdom MED-
LARS usage: "Serendipity class. Occasionally, a search
produces a reference which is highly interesting to the requestor or his colleagues in an entirely different connection."
(Evidently this "entirely different connection" must still, no
doubt, he related in some not entirely different connection to
the professional interests of the requestor and his colleagues.) Celoria gave more evidence:

> Serendipity is now an O.K. word that labels (though
> it does not explain) a lot that goes on in the world
> of knowledge-making. Robert K. Merton, in one
> of the key works on modern sociological thought,
> discusses it under this rubric: 'The Unanticipated,
> Anomalous and Strategic datum exerts pressure for
> initiating theory.'59

He then related serendipity to browsing:

> In both the arts and the sciences many new discov-
> eries seem to occur either by chance browsing with
> or without meditation of some sort, or by an in-
> cidental observation in an experiment.

> In this article, an attempt is made to see how far
> advances in knowledge can arise through 'brows-
> ing' in libraries.... One could sometimes disre-
> spectfully suggest that a browse through Biological
> Abstracts might produce something interesting for
> chemists. 60

A biochemist might consider Celoria's suggestion less
disrespectful than gratuitous. Serendipity in Walpole's sense
may exist, but since its essence is "pure" unpredictability
and its effectiveness largely dependent on personal ability or
temperament, the organization of library materials to realize
it seems infeasible.

Related Questionnaire Statements

Many statements in the questionnaire relate to definitions of the direct shelf approach, browsing, and serendipity.
The following may be noted:

> Maintaining open-shelf access is a significant educa-
> tional responsibility of libraries. (IV:2)

The direct shelf approach is of value primarily as a means to create for the reader or student a structured learning situation. (IV:3)

The value of open-shelf access is primarily conditioned by the quality and appropriateness of the library's collection. (IV:4)

Browsing provides a valuable learning experience. (V:2)

The greater limits imposed on browsing by acquisition policy and by classification, the more valuable browsing will be. (V:5)

Browsing is essential for academic research above the beginner's level. (V:10)

A major value of browsing is the possibility of "serendipity," i.e., "making desirable but unsought for discoveries." (V:11)

The possibility of "serendipity" is much greater in a library with relative shelf classification. (V:12)

"Browsing" is not a sufficiently precise term to characterize serious research, so its use should be limited to describing recreational, non-research activities in "browsing" collections or their equivalent. (V:14)

Notes

1. Phyllis A. Richmond, personal letter.

2. Marie M. Henshaw, personal letter.

3. William Mathews, "Professorships of Books and Reading," in U.S., Bureau of Education, Public Libraries in the United States of America; Their History, Condition, and Management; Special Report; Part I (Washington: Govt. Print. Off., 1876), p. 248-49.

4. Charles Ammi Cutter, "Library Catalogues," ibid., p. 548.

5. Cutter, Expansive Classification; Part I: The First Six

Classifications (Boston: The Author, 1891-93), p.
14.

6. Ainsworth Rand Spofford, A Book for All Readers; De-
    signed As an Aid to the Collection, Use and Preser-
    vation of Books and the Formation of Public and Pri-
    vate Libraries (3d ed., rev.; New York: Putnam,
    1905), p. 218-19, 222-23.

7. Ernest Cushing Richardson, Classification, Theoretical
    and Practical; Together with an Appendix Containing
    an Essay towards a Bibliographical History of Sys-
    tems of Classification (3d ed.; New York: Wilson,
    1930), p. 27-28.

8. Grace Osgood Kelley, The Classification of Books: An
    Inquiry into Its Usefulness to the Reader (New York:
    Wilson, 1937), p. 108-09.

9. Rolland E. Stevens, "The Study of the Research Use of
    Libraries," Library Quarterly, XXVI (January, 1956),
    41-51.

10. Harry Dewey, An Introduction to Library Cataloging and
    Classification (4th ed., rev. and enl.; Madison, Wis.:
    Capital Press, 1957), p. 54.

11. Arthur Burke Agard Evans, "Documentation," in Ency-
    clopaedia of Librarianship, ed. by Thomas Landau
    (3d rev. ed.; New York: Hafner, 1966), p. 153.

12. D.J. Foskett, "The Classification Research Group,
    1952-1962," Libri, XII, No. 2 (1962), 137.

13. Charles P. Bourne, Methods of Information Handling
    (New York: Wiley, 1963), p. 170, 161, 201.

14. Herbert Menzel, "The Information Needs of Current Sci-
    entific Research," in Chicago, University, Graduate
    Library School, Library Conference, Library Cata-
    logs: Changing Dimensions, ed. by Ruth French
    Strout (Chicago: University of Chicago Press, 1964),
    p. 11.

15. Don R. Swanson, "Dialogues with a Catalogue," ibid.,
    p. 122-23.

16. Malcolm Rigby, "Browsability in Modern Information Retrieval Systems: The Quest for Information," in Symposium on Education for Information Science, Airlie House, 1965, Proceedings, ed. by Laurence B. Heilprin, Barbara E. Markuson, and Frederick L. Goodman (Washington: Spartan Books, 1965), p. 47.

17. Joseph G. Herzberg, "Libraries Going Underground As Colleges Seek Book Space," New York Times, March 25, 1968, p. 36, col. 4.

18. C.D. Needham, Organizing Knowledge in Libraries: An Introduction to Classification and Cataloguing (London: Deutsch, 1964), p. 151-52.

19. Commission on the Humanities, Report of the Commission on the Humanities (New York: American Council of Learned Societies, 1964), p. 42.

20. David C. Weber, "The Changing Character of the Catalog in America," in Chicago, University, Graduate Library School, Library Conference, Library Catalogs: Changing Dimensions, p. 30.

21. Richard DeGennaro, "A Computer Produced Shelf List," College and Research Libraries, XXVI (July, 1965), 312.

22. S.R. Ranganathan, Prolegomena to Library Classification (3d ed.; New York: Asia Publishing House, 1967), p. 544-45.

23. Daniel Gore, Bibliography for Beginners (New York: Appleton-Century-Crofts, 1968), p. 76-77.

24. Sam Clay, Letter to the Editor on "Open-Stack Study," Library Journal, XCIV (October 1, 1969), 3378, 3381.

25. How to Use the M.S.U. Library [n.p., 1959?] (Pamphlet, unpaged)

26. Ralph E. Ellsworth, Planning the College and University Library Building: A Book for Campus Planners and Architects (2d ed.; Boulder, Colo.: Pruett Press, 1968), p. 74.

27. Elizabeth Mills, "The Separate Undergraduate Library,"
     College and Research Libraries, XXIX (March,
     1968), 151-52, citing Frederick H. Wagman, "The
     Undergraduate Library of the University of Michi-
     gan," ibid., XX (May, 1959), 185.

28. Bernard Ira Palmer, Itself an Education: Six Lectures
     on Classification (London: Library Assn., 1962),
     p. 9.

29. Patricia B. Knapp, The Monteith College Library Ex-
     periment (New York: Scarecrow Press, 1966), p.
     113, note 5.

30. Ibid., p. 92.

31. Theodore Samore, "Summary and Analysis," in Prob-
     lems in Library Classification: Dewey 17 and Con-
     version, ed. by Theodore Samore (New York:
     Bowker, 1968), p. 184-85.

32. Jerrold Orne, "The Place of the Library in the Evolu-
     tion of Graduate Work," College and Research Li-
     braries, XXX (January, 1969), 27.

33. Samore, "Summary and Analysis," p. 184-85.

34. Melvil Dewey, "Catalogues and Cataloguing," in U.S.,
     Bureau of Education, Public Libraries in the United
     States of America, p. 629.

35. Dewey, "Arrangement on the Shelves," Library Journal,
     IV (1879), 193.

36. Cutter, "Close Classification, with Special Reference to
     Messrs. Perkins, Schwartz, and Dewey," Library
     Journal, XI (July, 1886), 180.

37. W. C. Berwick Sayers, An Introduction to Library Clas-
     sification, Theoretical, Historical and Practical,
     with Readings, Exercises and Examination Papers
     (7th ed.; London: Grafton, 1946), p. 189.

38. Cutter, Expansive Classification, p. 4.

39. T.W. Lyster, "Observations on Shelf-Classification,"
     Library Association Record, II (1900), 408-09.

40. Charles Martel, "Classification: A Brief Conspectus of Present-Day Library Practice," Library Journal, XXXVI (1911), 411.

41. Arthur E. Bostwick, The American Public Library (4th ed., rev. and enl.; New York: Appleton, 1929), p. 182.

42. Richardson, Classification, p. 26-27.

43. Ibid., p. 27-28.

44. Henry Evelyn Bliss, The Organization of Knowledge in Libraries; and the Subject-Approach to Books (2d ed., rev. and partly rewritten; New York: Wilson, 1939), p. 13-16.

45. Francis Celoria, "The Archaeology of Serendip," Library Journal, XCIV (May 1, 1969), 1846.

46. Ibid., p. 1846-47.

47. Ibid., p. 1848.

48. Bostwick, The American Public Library, p. 182.

49. See discussion in Chapter Four of Herner, "A Pilot Study of the Use of the Stacks of the Library of Congress," and Hoage, "Patron Use of the L. C. Classification."

50. Cutter, Rules for a Dictionary Catalog (4th ed., rewritten; Washington: Govt. Print. Off., 1904), p. 12.

51. Needham, Organizing Knowledge in Libraries, p. 21. See also Paul S. Dunkin, Cataloging U. S. A. (Chicago: American Library Assn., 1969) which considers most major problems of cataloging and classification as manifestations of the conflict among Cutter's "Objects."

52. See Swanson, "Dialogues with a Catalogue," p. 123; Ernest A. Savage, Manual of Book Classification and Display for Public Libraries (London: Allen and Unwin, 1946), p. 9.

53. In addition to the citations in this chapter from these
     authorities, see those from Cutter, Richardson, Dewey,
     Ranganathan, and others, in Chapter Five.

54. Yehoshua Bar-Hillel, Some Theoretical Aspects of the
     Mechanization of Literature Searching, U.S. Office
     of Naval Research Technical Report No. 3 (Washing-
     ton, 1960), p. 8-10.

55. Funk and Wagnalls New Standard Dictionary of the Eng-
     lish Language (1963), p. 2048; Webster's Third New
     International Dictionary of the English Language, Un-
     abridged (1961), p. 1880; Webster's New Internation-
     al Dictionary of the English Language (2d ed., una-
     bridged; 1959), p. 2059.

56. Webster's New International Dictionary, p. 2059.

57. Charles J. Sippl, Computer Dictionary (Indianapolis:
     Sams, 1966), p. 151.

58. Oxford Universal Dictionary on Historical Principles
     (3d ed., rev. with addenda; 1955), p. 1847; Web-
     ster's New International Dictionary, p. 2284; Web-
     ster's Third New International Dictionary, p. 2072.

59. Celoria, The Archaeology of Serendip," p. 1846.

60. Ibid.

Chapter VII

ACQUISITION POLICY AND THE DIRECT SHELF APPROACH

Criteria for Library Collections

Lyster[1] affirmed the interdependence of shelf classification and the direct shelf approach. One might also posit an equally close relationship between the direct shelf approach and library acquisition policy. It is frequently stated that a truly professional characteristic of the librarian is his training and responsibility for collection building. Every collection, ideally, has been selected to meet the needs of its particular clientele.[2]

In the cited studies of browsing and the direct shelf approach, only occasionally did an investigator remark that the prior selection of those works whose use was being studied might be a crucial factor in their usability or "browsability." Fussler and Simon pointed out, in passing, that for browsing to be fully effective, not only must the books have been arranged in an appropriate order, and be available while the reader was browsing, but also that "the library must have acquired the books."[3] Bowen made a related point: "Basic to all further browsing studies is a better idea of what is in the stacks to begin with; with such information a much sharper picture of the relative efficiency and value of browsing compared with other techniques for the identification of relevant materials might be possible."[4]

Studies like the two just mentioned attempted, in effect, to evaluate the success of an acquisition policy in terms of how frequently and intensively the acquisitions were being used. Relating the number of uses to the "value" of a collection is logically defensible in determining which materials might be moved to less expensive if less accessible storage. The selective book retirement study by Ash[5] at Yale also sought to establish such a criterion. (Criteria for book storage should be differentiated from those for "weeding," e.g., the attempted mathematical formulation by Gosnell[6] of an obsolescence curve to be applied in discarding materials.)

141

The pilot study by Herner[7] of the use of the stacks in
the Library of Congress suggested that only a basic or core
collection of the more used materials might be shelf-classified in a conveniently accessible area.   Angell defined such
a "core": "It would have the character of a library-in-min-
iature, a basic reference collection, and a browsing collection in the 'best books' sense."[8]   Fussler,[9] considering the
problem of storing university library materials, suggested
that not all research materials required the same degree of
accessibility; that only works in most frequent demand had to
be made quickly accessible.

Many library surveys have tried to assess collection
quality, either by measuring usage or by soliciting opinions.
Downs[10] evaluated New York City collections through a mail
survey requesting librarians' judgments on the quality of their
collections.   In 1942 Downs[11] published an evaluation of leading American research collections which was based on a survey of scholar-specialists.   In 1940 the faculty of the University of Pennsylvania conducted a self-survey of its collections; and in 1948 Tauber, Cook, and Logsdon[12] in their survey of Columbia University libraries employed a questionnaire
to solicit faculty opinion on the research adequacy of the collections.

Such surveys were necessarily ex post facto, the effectiveness of acquisition policy being judged in terms of "results."   Quantitative criteria are often used, particularly by
accreditation teams, to evaluate collections: minimal or
"liminal" standards are set for the number of volumes of different types deemed necessary to meet basic requirements of
library service.   Such criteria have been included in the various Standards published for different kinds of libraries by
the American Library Association.[13]   Quantitative criteria
have also been employed in the evaluation of academic collections by Wilson-Tauber and Clapp-Jordan.[14]

From the early days of American librarianship, statistics on the number and size of collections provided useful evidence on progress and adequacy.   The 1876 Public Libraries
in the United States of America undertook a statistical survey
to determine the number of libraries established during twen-
ty-five-year periods between 1775 and 1875, and the extent of
these libraries' holdings in 1875.   Warren and Clark stated
in their introduction to the 1876 Report: "It was known that
within the last quarter of a century the number of public libraries had greatly multiplied, and that they had assumed a

position of commanding importance as an educational force, but there were no data for determining the extent of their influence. "15   The official need for such statistics is still recognized; the United States Government issues annual statistics for libraries and holdings. 16

The American librarian, however, has also been concerned with the need for the "right" books, that is, for a "proper" acquisition policy to realize the social and educational goals of his collection.   Cataloging, classification, and personal guidance could then make the collection of maximum usefulness.   This concern was early apparent in both academic and public librarianship.   Beals listed among the marks of a learned profession: moral fervor, wide learning, technical skills and techniques, and research interest and ability.   All the foregoing may fairly be ascribed to the selection and acquisition activities of the librarian.   Moral fervor, however, was most conspicuous in the attitudes of early American librarians towards what the reader should find in the library. Beals described this quality: "The members of any profession characteristically are suffused by a deep sense of moral purpose, by a passion to improve the lot of man and of man in society as the end of this professional endeavor. "17   Such motivation was shown, as discussed in Chapter Five, by the educational zeal of American librarians who advanced the political and social benefits of direct access.

Novel Reading Versus Good Reading

The librarian's "deep sense of moral purpose" and "his passion to improve" were manifested in the early controversy on novel reading in public libraries.   (This motivation has been described as "a naive faith in the efficacy of 'good' reading in the preservation of virtue. ")18   Warren and Clark, introducing the 1876 Report, were constrained to note: "It will be observed that on several subjects, as cataloging and novel reading, different opinions are expressed by different contributors; but as the contrariety in each case respects questions that are still unsettled and matters of discussion, it is thought quite proper that all sides should be heard. "19

A middle-of-the-road stand was taken by Winsor in his "Reading in Popular Libraries, " a contribution to the 1876 Report:

It is not very considerate to establish anything like

a fixed standard of good for all people, whether in
dietetics or literature.

Librarians do not do their whole duty unless they
strive to elevate the taste of their readers, and
this they can do, not by refusing to put within their
reach the books which the masses of readers want,
but by inducing a habit of frequenting the library,
by giving readers such books as they ask for and
then helping them in the choice of books, conducting
them, say from the ordinary society novel to the
historical novel, and then to the proofs and illustrations of the events or periods commemorated in
the more readable of the historians. Multitudes of
readers need only to be put in this path to follow
it.

A reasonable conclusion, then, is that the mass of
readers in popular libraries crave pastime only;
but they can be made to glide into what is commonly called instructive reading quite as early as it is
good for them. [20]

Harris in 1890 took a similar stand: "Fiction is the
bait by which we create a love of reading, and it should lead
out to other reading, especially in the line of science and
history and philosophy. "[21]

The suggested acceptance by Winsor and Harris of
novels as "better" reading was rebuffed by the "contrarieties"
of such opponents as Spofford:

We are told, indeed (and some librarians even have
said it) that for unformed readers to read a bad
book is better than to read none at all. I do not
believe it. You might as well say that it is better
for one to swallow poison than not to swallow any
thing at all. I hold that library providers are as
much bound to furnish wholesome food for the minds
of the young who resort to them for guidance, as
their parents are to provide wholesome food for
their bodies.

As to books of questionable morality, I am aware
that contrary opinions prevail on the question
whether any such books should be allowed in a public library, or not. The question is a different

one for the small town libraries and for the great
reference libraries of the world.   The former are
really educational institutions, supported at the people's expense, like the free schools, and should be
held to a responsibility from which the extensive
reference libraries in the city are free.   The latter may and ought to preserve every form of literature....

Take an object lesson as to the mischiefs of reading the wretched stuff which some people pretend is
'better than no reading at all' from the boy Jesse
Pomeroy, who perpetrated a murder of peculiar
atrocity in Boston.   Pomeroy confessed that he had
always been a great reader of 'blood and thunder'
stories, having read probably sixty dime novels,
all treating of scalping and deeds of violence.   The
boy said that he had no doubt that the reading of
those books had a great deal to do with his course,
and he would advise all boys to leave them alone.

In some libraries, where the pernicious effect of
the lower class of fiction has been observed, the
directors have withdrawn from circulation a large
proportion of the novels which had been sought by
reason of their popularity....   Librarians and library boards cannot be too careful about what con-
stitutes the collection which is to form the pablum
of so many of the rising generation.

Give the common people good models, and there is
no danger but they will appreciate and understand
them.   Never stoop to pander to a depraved taste....

It is no part of your business as a librarian to ca-
ter to the tastes of those who act as if the reading
of endless novels of sensation were the chief end of
man. [22]

Bostwick also likened novels to poison:

The desire of the librarian to increase the circulation of certain classes may also cause a departure
from strict arrangement.   Thus in some open-shelf
libraries a so-called 'ribbon' arrangement of fiction
has been adopted, in which the fiction is placed on
one shelf around the room, with non-fiction classes

above and below it, the expectation being that many
users who read only fiction will in this way be attracted to non-fiction books and begin to withdraw
and read them. Many eccentricities of shelf arrangement are to be credited to laudable aims as
this. In some children's rooms the stories have
been classified and shelved with the non-fiction....
The subclassification of adult fiction and its arrangement in corresponding fashion on the shelves
has been strongly advocated by some librarians.
In at least one library, books in the children's
room are arranged by accession number, without
classified order, so that the users will be more
likely to select non-fiction.

It may be postulated, however, that departure from
classified order should be made on the shelves only
from some compelling reason. Library users may
surely be made to read good books in some other
way than that by which rats are induced to take poison, namely by mixing it with their daily food. [23]

Perkins and Mathews, espousing in 1876 the establishment of professorships of books and reading in college libraries, warned against "the tendency to reading for mere amusement" and that "the literary appetite of the young is often
feeble, and oftener capricious or perverted. While their
stomachs generally reject unwholesome food, their minds often feed on garbage and even poison. " "Scientific guidance
for reading" was prescribed so college students would be
trained to "read by subjects and not by authors. "[24]

The Normative Role of the Early
Printed Library Catalogs

The librarians contributing to the 1876 Report were
much occupied with criteria of quality for book selection.
Robinson, advocating direct access in college libraries, was
yet careful to specify the books to be made so easily available: "Remove the barriers and make familiarity with well
chosen authors as easy as practicable. "[25] Such care for
quality criteria stemmed from the frequently postulated educational responsibilities of the library profession. Cutter in
his Rules for a Dictionary Catalog, originally Part Two of
the 1876 Report, listed as among the objects of notes in library catalogs:

3.   To direct the attention of persons not familiar
with literature to the best books.   The main principles of such annotating are simple.   (a) The notes
should characterize the best books only; to insert
them under every author would only confuse and
weary; if few they will arrest attention much better.   Dull books and bad books should be left in
obscurity.   Under some of the poorer works which
have attained unmerited popularity a brief protest
may be made; it will probably be ineffectual; but it
can do no harm to call Mühlbach unreliable or Trip-
per commonplace.   (b) They should be brief and
pointed.   Perhaps after this direction it is necessary to add that they should be true.

4.   To lay out courses of reading for that numerous class who are desirous of 'improving their
minds, ' and are willing to spend considerable effort and time but know neither where to begin or
how to go on. 26

Cutter's educational prescription has troubled one of
his most loyal modern followers: "Cutter's approach, however, could lead at its best to a subjective judgment of quality, at its worst to a form of censorship. "27

Robinson in the 1876 Report also suggested a didactic
catalog:

Catalogs have grown with the growth of libraries,
but no one has yet given us a science of cataloging.
Hardly can we find two alike, and none can be said
to accomplish all that is desired.   Catalogers have
generally attempted two things: first, to make a
list, alphabetical or otherwise, of all their books;
and, secondly, to furnish a guide to the reader in
selecting what he wishes to read.   Now, has not
the failure to devise any plan of cataloging on which
there should be a general agreement arisen largely
from the impossibility of accomplishing both these
results with the same instrument ?

Let the complete list of books be in any convenient
form-- ... is it not of the utmost importance that
there be also, in addition, a guide to the average
reader ?

> Would it not be practicable to make a reference dic-
> tionary or library manual ... which should contain
> the most important subjects of inquiry in the prin-
> cipal departments of human knowledge, under terms
> general or particular, alphabetically arranged, with-
> out definitions or discussion, but simply with ref-
> erences to the best material to be found upon them,
> by whatever author and under whatever title?[28]

Cutter, writing on "Library Catalogues" in the 1876
Report, praised the Boston Public Library which "in its excellent Class-list of History, Biography, and Travel, has
shown what such a catalog might be and how much can be
done in the way of encouraging, directing, and improving the
popular taste for reading."[29] Spofford considered the Boston
classed catalogs "invaluable."[30]

This type of printed catalog for the public library,
perhaps annotated for the guidance--and sometimes warning--
of the library patron, was described by Spofford in the 1876
Report as "intended solely for the inexpert reader." Spofford
listed the printed catalogs of the major American public libraries, "nearly in the order of the relative importance of
the collections," as those of the Library of Congress and the
Smithsonian Institution, Boston Public Library, Astor Library, Boston Athenaeum, Library Company of Philadelphia,
New York State Library, New York Mercantile Library, Mercantile Library of Philadelphia, Cincinnati Public Library,
and the Mercantile Library Association of San Francisco.[31]
Spofford's comment that such catalogs were "intended solely
for the inexpert reader" is strange--even if "inexpert reader"
be contrasted with advanced scholar--since the wide circulation of these printed catalogs among other libraries indicated
the importance with which the library profession regarded the
acquisition records of major American libraries. At a time
when relatively slow transportation and communication made
access to other libraries' materials difficult, the suggestive
or normative value for other collections of these authoritative
printed catalogs seemed apparent. The earliest European
bibliographies and library catalogs were intended to have normative value. Registrum Librorum Angliae, compiled ca.
1250-1296, was the first example of cooperative cataloging:
it listed the holdings of 183 English monastic establishments.
Gesner's sixteenth-century effort at universal bibliography,
Bibliotheca Universalis, and its supplement, Pandectarium,
was recommended by Gesner to be used by librarians in lieu
of compiling their own catalogs.[32]

The Normative Role of Later Book
Lists and Buying Guides

The American Library Association was early concerned with guidance in collection building, as Spofford indicated:

> The American Library Association has had this sub-
> ject under discussion repeatedly, and while much
> difference of opinion has arisen from the difficulty
> of finding any absolute standard of excellence, near-
> ly all have agreed that as to certain books, read-
> ers should look elsewhere than to the public free
> library for them. 33

Spofford then described how the A. L. A. sent to some seventy public libraries a list of authors "many of whose works were deemed objectionable, either from their highly sensational character, or their bad style, or their highly wrought and morbid pictures of human passions, or their im-moral tendency." The list included Ouida, Mayne Reid, Wilkie Collins, and Bulwer-Lytton ("whose Paul Clifford is a very improper book to go into the hands of young people"). The libraries were to indicate whether they "admitted the authors. "34

More positively, the A. L. A. in 1893 prepared the first in its long series of book lists intended to aid the li-brarian in his acquisition policy. The Catalog of the "A. L. A. " Library: 5000 Volumes for a Popular Library35 was to accompany a model collection organized for display at the Columbian Exposition. Published by the United States Bureau of Education, it included a letter of transmittal by the Commissioner of Education, William Torrey Harris:

> I have the honor to transmit for publication a cata-
> log of a model library of 5000 volumes selected by
> experts of the American Library Association, and
> representing as nearly as possible the 5000 books
> that a new library ought to obtain for its collection.
> Inasmuch as many states have laws permitting the
> establishment of public libraries by cities and
> towns, and the support thereof by taxation, the pub-
> lic library has become one of the most important
> of our educational institutions. This catalog, it is
> hoped, will supply a need that is widely felt for
> expert advice in making the first collection of
> books. 36

It is difficult to see how such a list, prepared under
official auspices by recognized authorities in consultation with
numerous experts, could not fail to exert a measure of pre-
scriptiveness, both as buying guide and criterion for evaluation. However, this catalog, like almost all that followed,
contained a warning against its uncritical use as an obligatory buying list:

> The committee would disclaim the idea that this is
> a model library, in the sense of being an ideal se-
> lection. The wealth of material and the differences
> of opinion are such that no such selection is pos-
> sible. They would claim, however, that it is a
> good working library, representing the best thought
> of competent judges in various departments. No
> board of trustees would make a mistake in ordering
> the collection as it stands. The number of volumes
> in each subject is the result of careful study, and
> editions as well as works have been indicated. [37]

The first A. L. A. Catalog was followed by a 1904 edition listing 8,000 volumes and a 1926 edition listing 10,000. [38]
Supplements were issued periodically. The 1904 and 1926
editions included critical annotations. In his "Editorial Preface" to the 1904 edition, Dewey gave a history and rationale
for the A. L. A. catalogs:

> At its Boston meeting in 1879 the American Li-
> brary association enthusiastically adopted the pro-
> posal of the present editor to prepare and publish
> a list of about 5,000 of the best books with com-
> pact notes indicating scope, character and value,
> to be known as the A. L. A. catalog. It was pointed
> out that such a list would serve:
>
> 1. As a guide to bookbuyers whether for private
> or public libraries,...
>
> 2. As a guide to readers in choosing what books
> they might best take from the library or from their
> own shelves.
>
> 3. As a manual to teach the younger and prompt
> the older librarians or booksellers in answering
> most wisely the constant inquiry for the best books
> on a given subject.

4. To take the place of the printed catalog in
small public libraries....

5. As a most convenient catalog for private libraries, by checking in the margin all books
owned. 39

Dewey then explained how critics were surveyed for
their opinions on the 1893 list which was to serve as foundation for the 1904 edition. Dewey evidently felt evaluative annotations to be greatly needed. The 1893 Catalog lacked
them. He expressed his satisfaction with their appearance
in the new edition: "For twenty-six years the present editor
has persisted in his faith that this Catalog would some time
appear because it was the most important and valuable single
book that could be made to aid in the great public library
movement. "40

The 1904 critical annotations were carefully ascribed
to authorities. Thus, Benvenuto Cellini's Life was described,
via Sturgis and Krebhiel's 1897 Annotated Bibliography of
Fine Art: "Not valuable as a guide to the immediate intelligent knowledge of fine art, but gives a truthful picture of
times of violence and individual independence of law and authority. "41   Sayers, however, called the annotations "generally feeble. "42

To provide current coverage, the A. L. A. began to
publish in 1905 The Booklist, a Guide to Current Books, "an
annotated buying guide for libraries, compiled especially for
small and medium-sized libraries. "43   The editors have
specified the nature of their evaluation as related to collection building:

Reviews in the Reference and Subscription book reviews section are prepared by members of the Reference and Subscription Book Review Committee of
the American Library Association, and represent
the combined opinion of the committee. Both books
recommended for purchase and those not recommended are reviewed.

Books reviewed in the other regular sections are
read, selected, and annotated by the Booklist editorial staff. Selection is made with the help of a
group of librarians in representative types of libraries. Only books and materials recommended

for library purchase are listed in the Booklist sections. Opinions expressed in special lists or articles are those of the contributors. [44]

In 1930 the A.L.A. began publication of Subscription Books Bulletin (now merged with The Booklist) to provide a current buying guide for reference works. Since such works could be very costly, it was important that librarians know which were not recommended for purchase; this was the reason for reviewing, as indicated above, both recommended and non-recommended books of this type.

The A.L.A. also has issued book lists for elementary grades, junior high schools, high schools, junior colleges, and colleges. [45] The last type of list deserves detailed mention.

Shaw's A List of Books for College Libraries, [46] prepared for the Carnegie Corporation, and published by the A.L.A. in 1931, was unannotated, but otherwise provided the kind of selection guidance earlier made available to public libraries by the A.L.A. catalogs. Its 14,000 titles were selected on the recommendation of 200 advisers. A supplement [47] was issued in 1940, but the basic list remained largely out of date until the 1967 publication of Voight and Treyz's Books for College Libraries, [48] a list of about 53,400 titles, based on the undergraduate collections selected for the University of California's New Campuses Program. Current coverage of materials for college libraries was made available in 1964 through the monthly periodical, Choice: Books for College Libraries, sponsored by the A.L.A. division, the Association of College and Research Libraries.

The H.W. Wilson Company, in consultation with the A.L.A. and many librarians, publishes up-to-date buying guides in its Standard Catalog Series [49] which supersedes some of the A.L.A. catalogs. Wilson catalogs, available for public libraries, school libraries, and high school libraries, are kept current by frequent supplements.

Structuring the Collection
through Acquisition Policy

The enumeration of basic lists, buying guides, foundation collection lists, and current review media could be much expanded. It should be evident, however, that in the selec-

tion of materials for libraries of almost any type or size,
many authoritative guides are easily available. It would be
implausible if these guides were not considered by librarians
in forming their collections--even if the only evidence were
the continual publication for more than half a century of new
and updated examples. Although, as noted, disclaimers were
usually made by their compilers that such lists were not prescriptive or obligatory, such editorial warnings seemed to
pale before such self-descriptions as "a suggested guide to
the best books" and "a list of recommended first purchases. "
Nor would it fulfill the purpose or meet the professed standards of these lists and guides if, after consultation with numerous experts in all relevant subject fields, undesirable materials were deliberately included.

     Thus, the hypothesis is suggested that librarians, as
implied by the wide availability of numerous buying guides,
attempt to discharge their selection and acquisition responsibility through the structuring of collections so that the direct
shelf approach may result in finding a maximum number of
desirable and a minimum number of undesirable items. In
terms of "browsing, " structuring the collection in this way
is, in effect, an effort to control the unpredictableness of the
activity. (This hypothesis applies specifically to the direct
shelf approach and browsing in an open-shelf collection. It
is not meant to imply only one possible reason for a librarian to "structure" his collection through acquisition policy.
It neither denies nor contradicts the general effort of librarians to select, on professional grounds, the "best" materials
for any type and size of library. In fact, the hypothesis
might be subsumed under a general one: All competent professional librarians qua librarians attempt to select the "best"
materials for their libraries.)

     College libraries furnish striking examples of how bas-
ic collections could be selected and maintained, with the aid
of buying guides, to provide a highly structured learning environment. After Shaw's 1931 Books for College Libraries,
the most influential of the basic lists for college libraries
was undoubtedly that of the Lamont Library of Harvard College. The Lamont Library was opened in 1949

          in order to serve more directly and sensitively the
          needs of undergraduates. This was then an innova-
          tion in library service. Lamont was conceived and
          assembled with the aim of bringing books most
          needed by undergraduates into closer and freer con-

tact with users. This it does by providing more
than one hundred thousand books on open shelves in
attractive and comfortable quarters and by creating
an atmosphere in which one can read and study with
a minimum of interference. [50]

The Catalogue of the Lamont Library, published in
1953, listed in simplified Dewey Decimal Classification order
some 39,000 titles for a separate open-shelf undergraduate
library--the first of its kind in this country. The titles were
described in the "Introduction" as constituting "a live, working collection of books selected to serve the required and
recommended course reading needs of Harvard undergraduates, in addition to a good general collection of books that it
makes readily available."[51] Since the Lamont list was closely matched to the curriculum requirements of Harvard College, it was not presented by its publishers as a buying guide
for others but as a reference work of possible interest to college librarians. It was, however, widely influential, even
when long out of date--as acknowledged by later guides.

The idea of a separate facility for undergraduates, together with an appropriate catalog, was entertained centuries
before Lamont. Thomas James, first librarian of the Bodleian, wished to establish such a collection:

> James, who is supposed to have been a poor li-
> brarian, retired in 1620, and during his retirement
> he spent much time in making subject catalogs of
> the Bodleian. His great desire was that the stu-
> dents should know exactly what books were in the
> library, and that they should be able to find them.
> He had tried to persuade Bodley to form a special
> library for the Arts students, but the scheme had
> been turned down. [52]

The need to structure and service such college collections was stated by Little in 1893:

> When the books suited to the purpose of the library
> have been thus selected by instructors who may be
> considered experts in their several departments,
> and by a librarian who has access to the best bib-
> liographic aids and has been trained in their use,
> there still remains the problem of bringing the
> books and the students together. This involves at
> least three things, classification of books by sub-

jects, access to shelves by students, and instruction in bibliology by professors or librarian. 53

Mills, in her 1968 article on the history of the separate undergraduate American library, pointed out that many libraries had long set aside separate collections for undergraduates in special quarters within the main university library building: "The idea of separate service for undergraduates, therefore, is not new. The concept of a separate library building ... is a relatively new development which began in 1949. "54

Lamont was to inspire other separate open-shelf undergraduate libraries with collections selected and organized to fit particular curricular needs. In 1958 the University of Michigan opened a separate undergraduate library whose background and purpose were described by Wagman:

> With the coming of the great boom years following the war, however, it became apparent ... what the undergraduate needed: a relatively small collection of books, carefully selected to satisfy the ordinary needs of general reading and instruction, available in open stacks, conveniently located, and informally administered by a friendly and competent staff.
>
> It was decided early in the planning that the entire book collection would be placed on open shelves....
>
> It was agreed that the book collection should represent the best in the human record of the past and in current thought. With the aid of hundreds of faculty members and a process of book selection that went on for more than two years, an initial stock of 60,000 volumes and 150 periodical titles was assembled and catalogued. Important omissions from this collection are being corrected currently and it is the intention to keep the collection current by the addition of new books that contribute to knowledge. Inasmuch as the entire collection is a browsing collection, in effect, no separate browsing collection was provided and no special 'recreational' reading collection, based on the notion that 'recreational' is synonymous with 'second-rate' or even with 'meretricious. '
>
> The faculty members were asked to rethink their

courses and submit new required or recommended
reading lists.... In addition a substantial collection
of reference books was placed on the open shelves
where they are accessible to both staff and students. [55]

Though the University of Michigan Undergraduate Library did not, like Lamont, publish a catalog, its shelf list
was obtainable in microfilm or Xerox copy. Even in this
somewhat cumbersome and/or expensive format, it achieved
a certain circulation among libraries, as will be seen in the
following discussion of the 1967 Books for College Libraries.

As noted above, Choice: Books for College Libraries
was established in 1964 by an A.L.A. division to provide a
current review service for college librarians. During 1965,
it published in installments a book list, later issued as a
special 1967 supplement: "Opening Day Collection ... a list
of 1,776 books the editors of Choice feel should be on the
shelves of every academic library when it opens its doors."[56]
This list attempted for new college libraries what the 1893
A.L.A. Catalog had for new small public libraries. The editors described the purpose of the list as:

> to provide librarians and administrators of new col-
> leges or junior colleges with a book collection es-
> sential to all undergraduate schools. Harried li-
> brarians and administrators working against a dead-
> line would only have to order the listed titles and
> thereby assure themselves of a 'cornerstone' li-
> brary collection when the school first opened its
> doors--hence 'Opening Day. '[57]

The trend to publish catalogs of undergraduate libraries continued in 1966 when Princeton University issued through
Bowker the catalog of the 8,400 titles in its Julian Street Library:[58]

> The catalog of a new undergraduate dormitory li-
> brary at Princeton. Not the catalog of an under-
> graduate instructional library in the sense of Har-
> vard's Lamont collection, but meant to include
> 'those books most frequently in demand by students
> for broad supplementary reading and other books in
> all fields which ... might open new intellectual
> avenues for the student. '[59]

For advanced research, Harvard University began to publish in 1965 its Widener Library Shelflist, "a series of computer-produced shelflists, each volume of which is devoted to a single classification or a segment of a large class of cataloged materials in the Widener Library. "60 The normative role in acquisition policy of such a publication was indicated by the following annotation:

> Although originally intended primarily for use at the Widener Library, the lists are useful elsewhere as good subject bibliographies, especially so in view of the rich resources of the Harvard collections. In addition, they are being maintained on a current basis so that computer printouts for supplements or updated editions can be published in the future. 61

The need for an updated version of Shaw's 1931 list for college libraries had long been apparent, and in 1967 the A. L. A. published, as already noted, Voigt and Treyz's Books for College Libraries, based on the collections of the University of California New Campuses Program. The "Preface" evidenced the cumulative influence of previous lists:

> Books for College Libraries has been published to fill the long-recognized need for a retrospective list of books to serve as a book selection aid for college libraries. It is intended to update Charles B. Shaw's List.... This retrospective list of books has been deliberately and directly related to the reviewing journal Choice, in that it includes only titles prior to 1964. 62

There was a familiar disclaimer:

> The danger in publishing a selection list of this nature is that it may be used as a final authority rather than as a guide. This list does not claim to be a list of the best books or a basic list for any college library, for selection of books for a college library must be made in terms of the needs of that particular institution. 63

Voigt and Treyz explained the scope and genealogy of their list:

> Books for College Libraries is a list of monographs

designed to support a college teaching program that
depends heavily upon the library, and to supply the
necessary materials for term papers and suggested
and independent outside reading.... The collection
is expected to satisfy independent intellectual curiosity (and recreational interests) of students and
faculty.

The size and subject balance of the list are similar to the already successful working collections of
the Lamont Library at Harvard University and the
Undergraduate Library at the University of Michigan. [64]

Title selection was governed at all stages by expert
advisors:

Selections of titles for this work is based on the
selections made for the basic undergraduate libraries of the University of California New Campuses
Program....

The New Campuses Program began operation in
1961 to build three identical, basic, self-contained
libraries for three new California campuses: Irvine,
Santa Cruz, and San Diego. The project was based
on the premise that there is a body of knowledge--
the classics, the important scholarly titles, and the
definitive works on all subjects of interest to an
undergraduate community--which should be in any
college library.

The experience of other institutions indicated that
the size of such a collection could be close to
75,000 volumes, of which approximately 20 percent
should be periodicals....

To select the 50,000-55,000 titles that were to
comprise the monograph collection it was necessary
to set up a special selection department. Librarians with graduate degrees in subject areas formed
the professional staff and were supported by bibli-
ographers.... After the initial selection, the lists
were subjected to review by specialists in undergraduate and college collections throughout the country to perfect the collection and shape it toward the
needs of the average college library.

When the list was accepted for publication, a further refinement of the selection was undertaken.
The selection cards were sent to subject specialists, selected with the assistance of the staff of
Choice, for further review. For the purpose of
the published list, additions and deletions were
made to improve balance and to include some titles
originally omitted. In this process some subject
areas were changed as much as 40 percent. 65

After reading of such meticulous efforts to determine
"the classics, the important scholarly titles, and the definitive works on all subjects of interest to an undergraduate
community--which should be in any college library, " it is
difficult to accept unreservedly that "this list does not claim
to be a list of the best books or a basic list for any college
library" or that it would be dangerous to use it "as a final
authority rather than as a guide. " Other libraries might not
care to have all the list's subjects represented, but for the
chosen subject areas, there would seem little reason to question the quality of the selections.

(Somewhat puzzling is that at the final stage of com-
pilation "some subject areas were changed as much as 40
percent" after further expert-consultation--a startling revi-
sion for a collection representing "the classics, the important scholarly titles, and the definitive works. " This percentage, however, may refer largely to materials other than
the indispensable and which were "to satisfy independent intellectual curiosity (and recreational interests) of students
and faculty. ")66

The Effects of Acquisition Policy on Browsing

The concept of "best books" was implicit in the librarian's professional and educational responsibility for selecting
works most suitable to the needs of their patrons.   Conversely, as Cutter indicated, the librarian should warn
against "bad" books, either on intellectual or moral grounds.
Sonnenschein's long-standard buying guide was entitled Best
Books. 67 The idea of a collection of the world's greatest
books was exemplified in such widely purchased sets as Eliot's The Harvard Classics, Warner Library, and, most recently, Hutchins' Great Books of the Western World. 68 Nor
were manuals and guides lacking to aid the librarian or layman in purchasing the best works in the best editions.   The

nineteenth-century bibliographies of Watt, Lowndes, Grässe, and Brunet[69] served as buying guides for the gentleman's library. More recent vade mecum-titles include Haines's Living with Books, Courtney's The Reader's Adviser (former- ly Bookman's Manual), and the frequently revised Good Read- ing,[70] prepared by the Committee on College Reading.

This study does not aim to investigate statistically the extent to which American libraries have been influenced in acquisition policies by such library catalogs, book lists, and advisory manuals. The quantity of such publications, their new editions, the statements by their compilers of the de- mand for their own and similar works--all seem prima-facie evidence of their interest for those concerned with acquisi- tion policy and book selection. Winchell[71] still lists in her 1967 edition the nineteenth-century printed catalogs of the Astor Library, Boston Athenaeum, and Peabody Institute.

The professional literature testified that librarians worried about the waste and even intellectual harm possible when patrons--laymen, students, or researchers--were al- lowed to browse unsupervised in open-shelf collections. From Perkins and Mathews in 1876 to Knapp in 1966,[72] li- brarians concerned with their educational role have warned against the hazards of unguided direct access for students. Short of personal assistance from the librarian at the shelves, a logical expedient would be to provide a collection of such quality that the browser would not fail to find something of value. This selection principle is seen in the collections of "best books" and "classics" for required or recommended reading in public, school, and college libraries. On a larg- er scale, an entire undergraduate library may be so organ- ized.

The degree of this collection structuring will vary with the type, size, and purpose of the open-shelf library. It seems greatest in academic libraries where the books are selected, usually with faculty advice, with maximum regard to the current curriculum. As Woodruff stated, "The tend- ency is to make the university library to an increasing ex- tent a collection of department libraries round a center con- sisting of those books to the making of which different de- partments have contributed in common, and the method of study requires free access to the books themselves."[73] The seminar arrangement would be suggested by Woodruff's de- scription, as would open-shelf reserve collections for specif- ic courses.

Normative or suggestive book lists, especially for college libraries, can produce prescriptive, prefabricated collections. Thus, in 1969 appeared the following advertisement:

> A lot of colleges are buying library books when they should be buying libraries. When you order your books through the Xerox College Library Program, all you do is unpack it. We can send you the complete 2,000 volume Choice Opening Day Collection, with 4,500 enrichment titles (including Choice's Outstanding Academic Books and 500 out-of-print titles from the ALA booklist, Books for College Libraries).
>
> If you're about to start a new college library--or add to an existing one--write for the free Xerox College Library Program Catalog.
>
> Then you'll be able to stop buying your library book by book and start buying your books by the library. [74]

(Does the above message differ from that in the 1893 A.L.A. Catalog for public libraries: "No board of trustees would make a mistake in ordering the collection as it stands"?)[75]

Related Questionnaire Statements

The following may be noted among the questionnaire statements related to the problems of acquisition policy and the direct shelf approach:

> Maintaining open-shelf access is a significant educational responsibility of libraries. (IV:2)
>
> The direct shelf approach is of value primarily as a means to create for the reader or student a structured learning situation. (IV:3)
>
> The value of open-shelf access is primarily conditioned by the quality and appropriateness of the library's collection. (IV:4)
>
> Reserved book collections and assigned reading lists make largely unnecessary open-shelf access in college

libraries. (IV:10)

Direct shelf approach is most valuable in collections
for beginning students where the books are basic or
"core" titles. (IV:14)

The greater limits imposed on browsing by acquisitions policy and by classification, the more valuable
browsing will be (V:5)

In a large general academic collection, browsing is
likely to be wasteful for most students because they
will spend too much time on inconsequential titles.
(V:9)

Notes

1. T. W. Lyster, "Observations on Shelf-Classification, "
    Library Association Record, II (1900), 399.

2. Ralph Albert Beals, "Education for Librarianship, " Li-
    brary Quarterly, XVII (October, 1947), 302.

3. Herman H. Fussler and Julian L. Simon, Patterns in
    the Use of Books in Large Research Libraries (Chi-
    cago: University of Chicago Library, 1961), p. 205.

4. Alice Bowen, "Non-recorded Use of Books and Browsing
    in the Stacks of a Research Library" (unpublished
    Master's dissertation, University of Chicago, 1961),
    p. 45.

5. Lee Ash, Yale's Selective Book Retirement Program
    (Hamden, Conn.: Shoe String Press, 1963).

6. Charles Francis Gosnell, "The Rate of Obsolescence in
    College Library Book Collections As Determined by
    an Analysis of Three Select Lists of Books for Col-
    lege Libraries" (unpublished Ph.D. dissertation, New
    York University, 1943).

7. Saul Herner, "A Pilot Study of the Use of the Stacks of
    the Library of Congress, " Washington: Herner,
    1960, p. 12. (Typewritten).

8. Richard S. Angell, "On the Future of the Library of

Congress Classification, " in International Study Conference on Classification Research, 2d, Elsinore,
Denmark, Classification Research: Proceedings, ed.
by Pauline Atherton (Copenhagen: Munksgaard,
1965), p. 102.

9. Fussler, "The Problems of Physical Accessibility, " in
Chicago, University, Graduate Library School, Library Conference, Bibliographic Organization; Papers
Presented before the Fifteenth Annual Conference of
the Graduate Library School, July 24-29, 1950, ed.
by Jesse H. Shera and Margaret E. Egan (Chicago:
University of Chicago Press, 1951), p. 163-86.

10. Robert B. Downs, Resources of New York City Libraries, a Survey of Facilities for Advanced Study and
Research (Chicago: American Library Assn., 1942).

11. Downs, "Leading American Library Collections, " Library Quarterly, XII (July, 1942), 457-73.

12. Bibliographical Planning Committee of Philadelphia, A
Faculty Survey of the University of Pennsylvania Libraries (Philadelphia: University of Pennsylvania
Press, 1940); Columbia University, President's Committee on the Educational Future of the University,
Subcommittee on the University Libraries, The Columbia University Libraries; a Report on Present
and Future Needs, Prepared for the President's Committee on the Educational Future of the University
by the Subcommittee on the University Libraries,
Maurice F. Tauber, Chairman, C. Donald Cook and
Richard H. Logsdon (New York: Columbia University Press, 1958), p. 259-75.

13. E.g., Public Library Association, Subcommittee on
Standards for Children's Service, Standards for Children's Services in Public Libraries (Chicago: American Library Assn., 1964).

14. Louis Round Wilson and Maurice F. Tauber, The University Library: The Organization, Administration,
and Functions of Academic Libraries (2d ed.; New
York: Columbia University Press, 1956); Verner W.
Clapp and Robert T. Jordan, "Quantitative Criteria
for Adequacy of Academic Library Collections, " College and Research Libraries, XXVI (September,
1965), 371-80.

15. Warren and Clark, "Introduction," ibid., p. xi.

16. E.g., U.S., Office of Education, Library Services
     Branch, Statistics of Public Libraries Serving Com-
     munities with at Least 25,000 Inhabitants, 1965-
     (Washington: Govt. Print. Off., 1968-).

17. Beals, "Education for Librarianship," p. 296-97.

18. Samuel Rothstein, The Development of Reference Ser-
     vices through Academic Traditions, Public Library
     Practice and Special Librarianship (Chicago: Assn.
     of College and Reference Libraries, 1955), p. 16.

19. Warren and Clark, "Introduction," p. xxxv.

20. Justin Winsor, "Reading in Popular Libraries," in U.S.,
     Bureau of Education, Public Libraries in the United
     States of America, p. 432-33.

21. William Torrey Harris, "The Function of the Library
     and the School in Education," Library Journal, XV
     (December, 1890), 31.

22. Ainsworth Rand Spofford, A Book for All Readers; De-
     signed As an Aid to the Collection, Use, and Pre-
     servation of Books and the Formation of Public and
     Private Libraries (3d ed., rev.; New York: Putnam,
     1905), p. 19-27. For a recent view reminiscent of
     Spofford's on the Pomeroy case, see Pamela Hans-
     ford Johnson, On Iniquity: Some Personal Reflec-
     tions Arising Out of the Moors Murder Trial (New
     York: Scribner, 1967).

23. Arthur E. Bostwick, The American Public Library (4th
     ed., rev. and enl.; New York: Appleton, 1929), p.
     195-96.

24. F.B. Perkins and William Mathews, "Professorships of
     Books and Reading," in U.S., Bureau of Education,
     Public Libraries in the United States of America, p.
     230-51.

25. Otis H. Robinson, "College Library Administration,"
     ibid., p. 517.

26. Charles Ammi Cutter, Rules for a Dictionary Catalog

(4th ed., rewritten; Washington: Govt. Print. Off., 1904), p. 105.

27. Paul S. Dunkin, Cataloging U. S. A. (Chicago: American Library Assn., 1969), p. 61.

28. Robinson, "Titles of Books," in U. S., Bureau of Education, Public Libraries in the United States of America, p. 723-24.

29. Cutter, "Library Catalogues," ibid., p. 549-50.

30. Spofford, "Library Bibliography," ibid., p. 737.

31. Ibid., p. 733-44.

32. Dorothy May Norris, A History of Cataloguing and Cataloguing Methods, 1100-1850; with an Introductory Survey of Ancient Times (London: Grafton, 1939), p. 30-32, 132.

33. Spofford, A Book for All Readers, p. 22.

34. Ibid., p. 22-23.

35. U. S., Bureau of Education, Catalog of "A. L. A." Library: 5000 Volumes for a Popular Library Selected by the American Library Association and Shown at the World's Columbian Exposition (Washington: Govt. Print. Off., 1893).

36. Harris, "Letter of Transmittal," ibid., p. 5.

37. American Library Association, Committee for Purchase and Arrangement of "A. L. A." Library, "Introduction," ibid., p. vii.

38. U. S., Library of Congress, A. L. A. Catalog: 8, 000 Volumes for a Popular Library, with Notes, ed. by Melvil Dewey (Washington: Govt. Print. Off., 1904); A. L. A. Catalog, 1926: An Annotated Basic List of 10, 000 Books, ed. by Isabella M. Cooper (Chicago: American Library Assn., 1926).

39. Dewey, "Editorial Preface," in U. S., Library of Congress, A. L. A. Catalog, p. 5.

40. Ibid., p. 10.

41. U.S., Library of Congress, A.L.A. Catalog, p. 926.

42. W. C. Berwick Sayers, Canons of Classification Applied to "The Subject, " "The Expansive, " "The Decimal" and "The Library of Congress" Classifications (White Plains, N.Y.: Wilson, 1916), p. 125.

43. Constance M. Winchell, Guide to Reference Books (8th ed.; Chicago: American Library Assn., 1967), p. 25.

44. Editorial note, The Booklist, LXVI (November 15, 1969), 353.

45. For an extensive listing, see Winchell, Guide to Reference Books, p. 26-27.

46. Charles B. Shaw, A List of Books for College Libraries (Chicago: American Library Assn., 1931).

47. Shaw, A List of Books for College Libraries, 1931-38 (Chicago: American Library Assn., 1940).

48. Melvin J. Voigt and Joseph H. Treyz, Books for College Libraries (Chicago: American Library Assn., 1967).

49. E.g., Standard Catalog for Public Libraries, 4th Ed. 1958: A Classified and Annotated List of 7610 Non-fiction Books Recommended for Public and College Libraries, with a Full Analytical Index, comp. by Dorothy H. West and Estelle A. Fidell (New York: Wilson, 1959). For a comprehensive listing, see Winchell, Guide to Reference Books, p. 25-27.

50. Harvard University Library, Guide to Lamont Library (Cambridge, 1968), p. 1-2.) (Pamphlet)

51. Philip J. McNiff, "Introduction, " in Harvard University, Lamont Library, Catalogue, prep. by Philip J. McNiff and members of the Library staff (Cambridge: Harvard University Press, 1953), p. vii.

52. Norris, A History of Cataloguing and Cataloguing Methods, p. 149.

53. George T. Little, "School and College Libraries," in U.S., Bureau of Education, Report of the Commissioner for Education for 1892-93 (2 vols.; Washington: Govt. Print. Off., 1895), II, 922-23.

54. Elizabeth Mills, "The Separate Undergraduate Library," College and Research Libraries, XXIX (March, 1968), 145.

55. Frederick H. Wagman, "The Undergraduate Library of the University of Michigan," College and Research Libraries, XX (May, 1959), 179, 184-85.

56. Choice: Books for College Libraries, IV, special supplement (June, 1967).

57. Editorial note, ibid., p. 1.

58. Princeton University, Julian Street Library, The Julian Street Library: A Preliminary List of Titles, comp. by Warren B. Kuhn (New York: Bowker, 1966).

59. Eugene P. Sheehy, Guide to Reference Books, Eighth Edition, First Supplement, 1965-1966 (Chicago: American Library Assn., 1968), p. 4-5.

60. Ibid., p. 2.

61. Ibid. See also Richard DeGennaro, "A Computer Produced Shelf List," College and Research Libraries, XXVI (July, 1965), 311-15, 353.

62. Voigt and Treyz, "Preface," in Books for College Libraries, p. v.

63. Ibid.

64. Ibid.

65. Ibid., p. vi.

66. Ibid., p. v, vi.

67. William Swann Sonnenschein, Best Books: A Reader's Guide and Literary Reference Book, Being a Contribution towards Systematic Bibliography (6 vols., 3d ed., entirely rewritten; London: Routledge, 1910-

35).   First edition 1887.

68.   The Harvard Classics, ed. by Charles W. Eliot (50
        vols.; New York: Collier, 1909); Warner Library
        ..., ed. by John W. Cunliffe and Ashley H. Thorn-
        dike (30 vols.; New York: Warner Library Company,
        1917) (First edition 1896-97 had title Library of the
        World's Best Literature); Great Books of the Western
        World and the Great Ideas, ed. in chief, Robert M.
        Hutchins; assoc. ed., Mortimer J. Adler (54 vols.;
        Chicago: Encyclopaedia Britannica, 1952).

69.   Robert Watt, Bibliotheca Britannica; or, A General In-
        dex to British and Foreign Literature (4 vols.; Edin-
        burgh: Constable, 1824); William Thomas Lowndes,
        Bibliographer's Manual of English Literature (6 vols.,
        new ed. rev., corr., and enl. by H.G. Bohn; Lon-
        don: Bell, 1858-64); Johann Georg Theodor Grässe,
        Trésor de livres rares et précieux (7 vols.; Dresden:
        Kuntze, 1859-69); Jacques Charles Brunet, Manuel
        du libraire et de l'amateur de livres (9 vols., 5.
        éd. originale entièrement refondue et augm. d'un
        tiers; Paris: Didot, 1860-80) (First edition 1810).

70.   Helen E. Haines, Living with Books: The Art of Book
        Selection (2d ed.; New York: Columbia University
        Press, 1950); Winifred F. Courtney, The Reader's
        Adviser (2 vols.; 11th ed.; New York: Bowker,
        1968-69); Committee on College Reading, Good Read-
        ing, ed. by J. Sherwood Weber (35th ed.; New York:
        New American Library, 1969).

71.   Winchell, Guide to Reference Books, p. 9-10.

72.   Perkins and Mathews, "Professorships of Books and
        Reading"; Patricia B. Knapp, The Monteith College
        Library Experiment (New York: Scarecrow Press,
        1966), p. 113, note 5.

73.   Edwin H. Woodruff, "Some Present Tendencies in Uni-
        versity Libraries" (a paper read before the Interna-
        tional Congress of Librarians at Chicago, July 14,
        1893), quoted by Little, "School and College Librar-
        ies," p. 925.

74.   University Microfilms, Ann Arbor Michigan, a Xerox
        Company, Advertisement, Library Journal, XCIV

(June 15, 1969), 2430.

75. American Library Association, Committee for Purchase
     and Arrangement of "A. L. A." Library, "Introduc-
     tion," p. vii.

Chapter VIII

CLASSIFICATION AND THE DIRECT SHELF APPROACH

The literature of classification--philosophical, bibliographical, and bibliothecal--is voluminous and, especially in
regard to libraries, ambivalent. This chapter considers evidence that the ambivalence may both reflect and influence efforts to structure through bibliothecal classification the direct
shelf approach and browsing. Examination of this hypothesis
requires discussion of such related topics as the nature of
the classification of knowledge vis-à-vis books; the value for
patron (and librarian) of shelf classification; the usefulness
of close classification on shelves; the problem of linearity in
library classification; the contribution of subject cataloging to
the organizing of library materials; the purpose and worth of
notation and mnemonics in classification schemes; and claims
for the enhancement of librarians' prestige because of classification. All topics are interrelated and each could be subdivided. To argue a thorough treatment of any would be
gross pretension. This chapter attempts to evaluate them in
accordance with the criterion of usefulness, described in
Chapter One, in the hope that the discussion will, within the
frame of this study, prove pertinent, lucid, and of tolerable
length.

American and European Attitudes
Towards Library Classification

Shelf classification was accepted by American and
British libraries, as described in Chapter Five, along with
the policy of direct access. Dewey's relative shelf location
both insured and facilitated the policy. It is now almost universally believed that an open-shelf library requires shelf
classification of some kind. Tauber, in his 1957 survey of
the shelflisting section of the Library of Congress, stated:
"The consultant is convinced that classification on the shelves
is necessary in open shelf libraries." He reported on the
"Dependence by Readers and Staff Members on the Classification (on Shelves or Shelflist)" as follows:

There is an unmistakable preponderant opinion indicating dependence on the classified arrangement of
books for those persons--staff and users having access to the stacks--who require a subject breakdown of the materials acquired by the libraries....

It is evident in the replies from the librarians that
a classified arrangement of books on the shelves
provides the kind of subject approach that is useful
to the staff and the clientele who have access to
the stacks. Even this testimony, however, has to
be weighed for what it is worth--opinion based on
experience. There is no evidence other than that
discussed in the earlier part of this report: that
libraries which have been organized by fixed number, broad classification, poorly devised local systems, or by some other device have been under
great pressure from the users and staff to reclassify by a modern system.... A common comment
is that 'both faculty and students are in the habit
of going directly to the shelves for their subject
material....' A recent survey of the library services at Columbia University revealed that the faculty members and students overwhelmingly supported access to the shelves, even though it was
pointed out that closed shelves led to a finer control over the materials.[1]

Tauber cited Metcalfe in rebuttal to Shera's criticism
of shelf classification: "It is hard to believe that anyone who
has managed a reference library of any size would agree
with Shera that they can be more economically and efficiently
used with books in accession or author alphabetical order,
than with books classified, or categorized, however broadly."[2]

Opinions similar to Metcalfe's and Tauber's seem to
be held by most librarians on the value of shelf classification
for the direct shelf approach and browsing. Richardson, Cutter, and Ranganathan have, among others, been quoted to
such effect in earlier chapters. Rider, conceding some merits to the older fixed location schemes, concluded:

For all that, we must still insist that classified arrangement is superior to fixed location for two reasons only. First, it enables a 'browser' to go to
one shelf, or to one section, in the stacks to find
there, and to examine there, most of the materials

which the library has on the subject of his immediate interest.

Second: it enables the library's assistants to go to
that one shelf, or one section, to find and later to
return to, all of the books taken out on the subject. [3]

In contrast with American (and British public) librarians' belief in shelf classification, European librarians have
tended to depreciate subject classification, either for catalog
or shelf. Since most European libraries had closed stacks,
the slighting of shelf classification may not be surprising.
Beyond this, however, European librarians seem traditionally
to have suspected subject analysis or classification. Norris'
history of European cataloging to the middle of the nineteenth
century concluded that the classed or subject catalog had by
the middle of the last century been deposed by the dictionary
catalog--at least in public libraries. Like Pettee, [4] Norris
showed how the dictionary catalog evolved over the centuries
from author catalogs with subject indexes, and from subject
listings with supplementary author approaches. Up to 1850
there was ceaseless vacillation between the alphabetical-au-
thor and the subject-classified forms. Though the earliest
catalogs, e.g., the Penakes of Callimachus, were subject-
classified, this principle never monopolized. During the
seventeenth and eighteenth centuries, classed catalogs had become so unsystematic that they lost by forfeit to the competing format. [5]

Subject classification for the library user was derided
by influential librarians. Panizzi, testifying before the British Museum Select Committee of 1836, although agreeing that
an alphabetical subject index should supplement the main
author catalog, excoriated the classed catalog: "The continual
discoveries in science make classification ridiculous, and the
people who talk continually about classed catalogs are the
very people who would not use them if they were provided. "[6]
Panizzi's 1841 Ninety-One Rules for the British Museum were
supposed to have settled once and for all the author-versus-
classed-catalog controversy in favor of the former. Further
--"The Bodleian Library has tried both the classed and au-
thor-alphabetical types, and had finally abolished the classed
one. "[7]

A leading opponent of the Bodleian classed catalog had
been Professor H. W. Chandler who in 1885 delivered a cel-

ebrated diatribe:

> A classed catalogue is a snare and a delusion,...
> an absurdity and something worse because all clas-
> sification is arbitrary; what suits one searcher for
> wisdom will not suit another.... [If ever completed
> it will be] a gigantic sham catalogue which no man
> fit to use the Bodleian library would ever care to
> look at.
>
> Who tied the millstone of a classed catalogue round
> the Librarians neck, I do not know; but the classed
> catalogue and all the work that it entails is so much
> labour thrown away. No real scholar, no man who
> is capable of literary research, wants a classed
> catalogue; he hates the very sight of such a thing;
> it serves no useful purpose; it is a snare and a
> delusion. The sciolist, and he alone, thinks how
> delightful it would be to turn out any given subject
> and there see all the books that have been written
> on it. He does not know how impossible the thing
> is, or what mischiefs result from the attempt to
> compass such a work. Most French catalogues are
> classed, and he who has had the ill luck, as I
> have, to consult them, retains a lively sense of de-
> testation for those who were foolish enough to class
> the books. Could men of real knowledge be con-
> sulted, I am quite certain that a large majority, if
> not all, would infinitely prefer the alphabetical ar-
> rangement under authors' names, to the best classed
> catalogue that could be devised. [8]

As Reichmann indicated, the Bodleian adheres to
Chandler's views, as shown by the 1961 comments of the
Bodleian librarian: "The Bodleian has not succumbed to the
prevailing notion that it is the business of a learned library
to spoon-feed the immature students.... Those who hope to
use the Bodleian as a glorified Children's Encyclopaedia will
soon discover their mistake. "[9]

Reichmann's 1963 survey of European catalogs found
that other British as well as continental libraries were not
as adamantly against the classed catalog as the Bodleian and
the British Museum. He estimated an equal distribution in
European libraries between alphabetical-subject and classified-
subject catalogs, although reports on readers' reactions were
contradictory. However, in regard to shelf classification,

European librarians differed decidedly with American:

> In the majority of American libraries, holdings are shelved according to a logical system. A standardized classification is preferred, such as Dewey's scheme or that of the Library of Congress, and there is general preference for the entire library to be classified by one system rather than by a combination of different ones.
>
> Americans tend to believe that classification schemes are logical arrangements which remain valid and efficient regardless of time and space.... Because of this belief in the semipermanence of American classifications, cataloging and classification have been integrated so that the class notation is at the same time the call number.
>
> European librarians disagree with every one of these positions. Most institutions are of the opinion that the shelving of books according to a classed system is an inefficient and obsolete method, and they discontinued it decades ago. Books are shelved in broadly defined subject groups, and there is a trend to diminish the number of groups and even to abolish them altogether.
>
> Public libraries everywhere prefer open shelves and must have, therefore, a classified arrangement of books. Scholarly libraries have such a system for their subject reading rooms and utilize classification schedules for the systematic catalog only. Fifty years ago Georg Leyh asserted the principle of a 'standort-freien Katalog,' that is, the separation of classification notation from the call number to insure fullest flexibility for the systematic catalog. This doctrine has been generally accepted all over Europe. Librarians overseas reject the conception that any classification system could remain permanently valid and useful. A classification is a historical phenomenon, runs the argument, and is intimately connected with the ideology and conceptual capacity of the period in which it was formed. Basic changes in ideology and scholarly conception will necessarily invalidate the old classification system.[10]

Schneider in his Handbuch der Bibliographie expressed
serious doubts on classification for libraries:

> Classified arrangement of titles is no more an a-
> priori evidence of scientific character than is al-
> phabetical arrangement.... It is the beginner in a
> study, who has mastered very little of its knowl-
> edge, who needs bibliography most.... Philosoph-
> ical schemes ... [are] useless or even disadvanta-
> geous if taken over in toto or copied for biblio-
> graphic purposes.... The higher and weightier their
> trains of thought become, the more untenable do
> philosophical schemes become for the classification
> of publications. Ends and means are too widely
> separated. It is a suspicious recommendation and
> indicates the mediocrity of a philosophical system
> if it be claimed to be applicable to bibliographical
> purposes.... All classification schemes must die.
> Inflexible schemes are successful candidates for
> suicide.[11]

American librarians' use of shelf classification indicated to critics like Dunkin a basic disinterest in the rationale of library classification:

> Classification, beginning with Dewey, has taken lit-
> tle account of theory and principles; instead it has
> sought a practical book-shelving device which would
> best suit the 'convenience of the public.' DDC has
> suffered from the long conflict between the theoret-
> ical notion of 'keeping pace with knowledge' and the
> practical convenience of 'integrity of numbers.'
> Until the present, LCC has been free from these
> slogans because it has remained a 'private' classi-
> fication scheme developed to serve its own need
> only. But if the trend away from DDC to LCC con-
> tinues, LCC may well be dragged into the fray.[12]

Jolley had a similar judgment: "In the United States
librarians tend to regard classification mainly as a method
of shelf arrangement and this, as much as conservatism, has
prevented any real movement for a wider use of the class
catalogue."[13]

Such critiques of American librarians' indifference to
classification theory seem controverted by the extensive literature on problems of library classification, particularly the

sometimes bitter attacks on the Decimal Classification because of reclassifying "required" by its successive editions.
If American librarians were indifferent to theory, and concerned only with the practical need for a convenient shelving
device, would they not long ago have turned to fixed location
schemes employing very broad subject groupings? The pro-
tests against the changes in Dewey editions came from librarians who believed in the need to maintain, even at considerable expense, a consistently logical shelf classification
based on defensible theory. (This will be considered below
in discussing Eaton's "Epitaph to a Dead Classification.") It
was the post-Dewey American librarian Bliss[14] whose two
volumes on the organization of knowledge presented the most
thorough modern scholarly analysis of the underlying theoretical principles of classification--philosophical, scientific, bibliographical, and bibliothecal. Oddly, critics, like Dunkin,
of modern library classification blamed post-Dewey American
classificationists Richardson and Bliss for introducing metaphysical concepts into "practical" library classification. The
next section discusses a hypothesis that one reason why
American librarians continue elaborate shelf classification,
in spite of evident practical contradictions, is that they may
tacitly entertain metaphysical assumptions which absorb paradoxes of bibliothecal classification.

Practical Library Classification and
the True Order of Knowledge

American classificationists stressed their practical,
non-dogmatic aims, even though philosophical--even meta-
physical--theory supplied important elements in their schemes.
Cutter acknowledged: "It is plain that no shelf-classification
can collect in one place all that the library possesses on
each subject.... But within the proper limits of its work,
and in connection with the catalog, classification is of the
greatest value as one of the keys that unlocks the treasure-
house of knowledge."[15] Yet, LaMontagne pointed out that
"although Cutter sought a logical and practical method of arranging books ... he thought a work of permanent value could
be achieved only by a classifier who based his work upon a
classification of knowledge."[16] According to Sayers:

> Cutter explained that 'the expansive classification
> follows the evolutionary idea throughout....' He
> considered each of his classes following internally
> 'logical, or, if you please, natural arrangement.'

Also, 'There are many ... transitions, part of
them, at least, novel in classification. They are
not merely ingenuities, pleasing only to their con-
triver; they have a certain practical value, since
they bring books together, which one may wish to
use at the same time. '17

However, according to Broadfield, 18 the evolutionary
theory is not philosophically tenable as a basis for library
classification; and as for Cutter's avowedly practical yet logical scheme, Bliss commented:

In complexity his schedules are system-mad, more
complicated than those of the Library of Congress,
and more excessive in the notation....

Cutter's Classification has enjoyed the reputation
of being admirably logical in its scheme and adequately scientific in its nature.... This reputation
... was not justified.... Tho the order of the main
classes was indeed logical and philosophic, it was
not correctly scientific even for the science of its
decade, and the less so for the present.

He nowhere ... brought together the general ideas
and principles on which a theory and a system
should be based. 19

In all editions of his scheme Dewey insisted on its
practical purpose, as he had in 1876:

In all the work, philosophical theory and accuracy
have been made to yield to practical usefulness.
The impossibility of making a satisfactory classification of all knowledge as preserved in books, has
been appreciated from the first, and nothing of the
kind attempted. Theoretical harmony and exactness
have been repeatedly sacrificed to the practical requirements of the library or to the convenience of
the department in the college. As in every scheme,
many minor subjects have been put under general
heads to which they do not strictly belong.... The
rule has been to assign these subjects to the most
nearly allied heads, or where it was thought they
would be most sought....

Theoretically, the division of every subject into just

nine heads is absurd.   Practically, it is desirable
that the classification be as minute as possible
without the use of additional figures; and the decimal principle on which our scheme hinges, allows
nine divisions as readily as a less number.   This
principle has proved wholly satisfactory in practice,
though it appears to destroy proper coordination in
some places. [20]

Dewey sometimes so touted his "practicality" as to
elicit reservations even from friendly critics like Sayers:

Dewey claimed that his original contribution in the
scheme was his relative index, 'the most important
feature of the system.' ...

Dewey had no intention of producing a system which
should follow the categories of the scholar; he
aimed at a practical piece of machinery for the
rapid arrangement, filing and finding of books and
library materials, and he describes the system as
a series of pigeon-holes into which this material
may be fitted.   He even went so far as to declare
that it mattered less in what pigeon-hole a book was
put than that all books on the same subject should
be placed in the same one and that that one should
be indexed.... He regarded the system as one for
classifying nine special libraries.... It is, therefore, vainly that we seek to find an evolutionary
order in the main classes. [21]

Bliss, whose critical survey of classification schemes
was to culminate in the creation of his own, scorned Dewey's
"practicality":

The notion that specific subjects, however confused
and dispersed, may by an alphabetical index be located and brought together for reference and research we have termed 'the subject-index illusion.'
The Decimal Classification is still advocated by
those who see classification through the subject-
index illusion.

Two basic principles of systematic classification are
subordination and collocation, but these principles
have been largely ignored in the Decimal Classification.

> The Decimal Classification is disqualified as an organization of knowledge both structurally and functionally. It does not embody the natural, scientific, logical, and educational orders. It fails to apply consistently the fundamental principles of classification. It is disproportionate in its expansions, tho elsewhere lacking in requisite specific details. [22]

Even Metcalfe, an admirer of Dewey's practical approach, rejected Dewey's suggested use of his index:

> And there is much in Dewey's own point that it doesn't matter much where books are classified as long as all those on the same subject are in one place and that indexed. But he went too far in recommending classifying from the index even without check in the tables, an injunction rightly reversed in editions after his death. [23]

Dewey's practical principles were intended to insure his scheme's usefulness for the librarian and reader, a usefulness which most American librarians felt could be fully realized only in an open-shelf library with direct access. Though Dewey had maintained that "in all the work, philosophical theory and accuracy have been made to yield to practical usefulness," his scheme was attacked, particularly in its later editions, as increasingly impractical, because its adherence to theory resulted in more and more relocations and in extreme notational inflexibility. Palmer referred to the Decimal Classification as "an enumerative scheme ... each edition panting after the elusive quarry of a definitive list of subjects. It was a quite unattainable goal, as its author and editors knew." [24]

Eaton, despite Dewey's disclaimer, insisted his scheme was a philosophical one:

> The classification scheme ... is a logical classification. It is based on an outline of knowledge in contrast to practical classification schemes which are based on existing collections of books. A logical scheme, which begins with the universe of knowledge, may provide places for subjects which have not yet been discovered. It allows for unlimited expansion by dividing subjects into their component parts. Anything new is a part of the total universe, therefore a part of all that exists. A

> practical scheme endeavors to provide for books
> which are already in existence, and it tries to
> leave space for the new subjects that will appear in
> the future. When the new subject appears a spe-
> cial place will be provided for it in the scheme.
> Frequently the topic will be added to related ones;
> sometimes new classes will be established.

> The Decimal Classification of Melvil Dewey is an
> outline of knowledge equipped with a numerical nota-
> tion that provides shorthand symbols for the terms
> in the outline. The symbols can be used on the
> back of books to indicate shelf arrangement as well
> as subject content. 25

Eaton limited this description to the fourteen editions
issued in Dewey's lifetime. She asserted that, with the fifteenth, the scheme was no longer true to Dewey's concept:
"We must accept the fact that with the fourteenth edition
Melvil Dewey's classification died.... The resultant scheme
was impossible for classed catalogs and hopelessly inadequate
for large open-access book collections. "26

LaMontagne also emphasized the theoretical basis of
Dewey's scheme:

> Ironically it was not Dewey but his over-zealous fol-
> lowers who exaggerated the importance of physical
> shelving.... Actually, Dewey ... was primarily an
> advocate of the classed catalog and originally de-
> veloped his classification for this purpose, not for
> shelving.

> The physical collocation of books on related subjects
> by classification ... does not provide ... an ade-
> quate approach to their contents.... It is 'informa-
> tion' rather than the containers ... that is impor-
> tant. 27

Custer, in his introduction to the seventeenth edition,
detailed the theoretical-philosophical basis of Dewey's "practical" scheme:

> The system is hierarchical both as to disciplinary
> and subject relationships and, with certain minor ex-
> ceptions, as to notation.

Hierarchy in disciplinary and subject relationships means, for example, that whatever applies to or is true of 600 applies to or is true of all its subdivisions, what applies to 630 applies to all its subdivisions, what applies to the span 631-632 applies to all its subdivisions, what applies to 631 applies to all its subdivisions, on to the finest subdivision. [28]

Dewey's theory of hierarchy seems to express the Platonic realism found in traditional library classification schemes. As indicated in Chapter Five, implementing such a theory might reflect the librarian's tacit assumption that by so structuring his collection, "the reader seeking instruction who follows the classification in the catalog or on the shelves will be led inevitably to the truths of the subject he is studying and, since all parts of the truth are interrelated, any one part will be correctly, that is, 'truly' related to any other one by the classification scheme." Interestingly, Custer, in describing the relationship of any part to the whole, used interchangeably the clauses "applies to" and "is true of." Defenders of the theoretical foundations of Dewey's "practical" scheme, like Eaton and LaMontagne, were probably implying such metaphysics. Dewey indicated it would make no great difference if the universe of knowledge were divided into other than nine main parts. The sine qua non, however, of metaphysical hierarchy was that each of the parts--nine or other --be further divisible and that ultimately all total the original whole.

Hierarchy in library classification derived from Aristotelian logic, particularly as later expressed in the diagram of "Porphyry's Tree." Broadfield[29] carefully demonstrated, from the point of view of Aristotelian logic, the error of transferring the hierarchical genus-species concept of that logic into library classification, an error facilitated by Porphyry's distortion of Aristotle's doctrine.

However, the major library classificationists insisted, despite their acceptance of Aristotelian hierarchy, on the "practical" nature of their schemes.

Metcalfe, an admirer of Broadfield, has criticized at length, often polemically, the metaphysics of most hierarchical library classification schemes:

There are no elemental or nuclear subjects analogical with the elements of chemistry and the nuclei

of physics; no invariable or objective or absolutely
scientific or natural classes or categories or orders of classes or categories of subjects or their
qualities, such as Matter, Life, Mind, Record,
which may be supposed to have some justification
for their order in an analogy with biological evolution, or such as Time, Space, Energy, Matter,
which may be supposed to be justified by discoveries in physics but as applied to indexing are mere
metaphysical speculations of very venerable ances-
try about the ultimate constitution of things....

There is a basic confusion of the theory of information indexing and classifying with metaphysical theory or speculation on a universal classification
based on the constitution and order of the universe,
none of which is proven in itself or in its relevancy to bibliographical indexing and classifying.   Edwards made a comparative study of book classifications, and concluded ... that the conflicting metaphysical classifications were at least no better than
those which aimed at being only practical; Hulme
had essentially the same theory, which led him to
reject Richardson, but Sayers said explicitly of
Edwards, and implicitly of Hulme, that he did not
have 'any theory worthy of record, ' because for
Sayers theory was unproven, irrelevant metaphysical theory, for which he turned to Richardson and
evolution.   Mainly because of Sayers' influence ...
the study of bibliographical classification in Great
Britain is now worse confounded by the addition to
Richardson of Bliss and Ranganathan, and argument
about their divergences with scarcely any questioning of their starting point....

Confusions of purpose and method can arise both
from the way classification may be illustrated in
diagrams and the way classes and subclasses have
to be set out on pages in columns and on cards in
files....

Porphyry's Tree--No other logical diagram has
been more misunderstood by librarians than this
most famous and ancient one.

[As long as] the subdivision at each step of division
is by the same characteristic, which is subject, or

form, and the subclasses are mutually exclusive,...
the requirements of logical divisions are met.

Obviously the heading comes first, but under it and
reading from left to right or any other way there
is no reason in logic why the included class general literature should come first.   The indexing reasons why it should are, first that the study goes
from general to particular, and putting the general
first as a rule establishes a convention which makes
it easier to follow a classification.[30]

Richardson, Sayers, Bliss, and Ranganathan, whom
Metcalfe branded "bibliosophers" because of their "metaphysical" theories, always dwelt on the pragmatism of their
schemes!   Thus, Richardson in his preface to the third edition of Classification defended his scheme against accusations
of theoreticalism:

Dr. Van Hoesen has curiously mistaken the tendency of the work ... as inclining to the 'theoretical'
attitude.   The exact contrary is intended to be the
case and has been the unequivocal teaching and
practice of the author throughout his active career....   The attitude of this book is 'that in case
of conflict the practical always prevails over the
theoretical, ' that 'practical classification is the putting together of books most used together, ' that
'book classification is an art not a science, ' that
'classification is a labor saving device, ' that 'the
object is a practical one just as the object of the
library itself is a practical one' or 'economy and
increased efficiency in the use of books, ' that 'any
variation whatever from the scientific order is per-
missible if so be it promotes this end of the use, '
that the adjustments or modifications ... are so
many and so radical that it may well be asked
whether the theoretical order is anything but a
'hook on which to hang the exceptions. '[31]

Richardson, however, had an important qualification:

The theoretical or scientific order of nature is, in
fact, the backbone and the rule, however many exceptions there may be.   To keep this in mind is to
keep modification from degenerating into disorder.
This is a vastly different matter from a theoretical

attitude or tendency.[32]

When Metcalfe, nevertheless, labelled Richardson a metaphysician, i.e., "bibliosopher," he probably had in mind such Richardsonian dicta as the following on "the theoretical or scientific order of nature":

> Among the chief principles or laws which have to be taken into account in classification are:
>
> (1) The law of likeness. Likeness is the universal principle of the order of things.... In every case the true likeness is the one which determines order.... Likeness is, therefore, characteristic of all things and its law may be expressed as the law that all things in the universe are organized according to their likeness.
>
> (2) The second general principle useful for our task is the historical law that the progress of things in space and time is also in general a genetic progress in complexity.
>
> (3) The law of evolution adds to the law of history the observation that the law of historical progress from the simple to the complex holds good of all things which tend toward continued existence....
>
> In our task of arranging in continuous series according to likeness from the simplest to the most complex, we are arranging not things themselves but our ideas of things.... The first step is, therefore, to make each unit exactly correspond with the reality. Then comes the putting together of the ideas by likeness, or their classification. Thanks to modern science and its laws, every one may now get, if not a perfect idea of the whole, at least a clearer one than was ever possible before, save perhaps to a few seers like Plato and Moses.[33]

Broadfield[34] contradicted on traditional philosophical grounds Richardson's leading ideas on likeness, evolution, complexity, etc. Although Cutter, as noted, also based his scheme on the evolutionary principle, he was not accused by his admirer Metcalfe of "bibliosophy." Cutter, unlike Richardson, did not employ philosophical parlance. Also, he seemed sceptical of revelatory metaphysical effects in library classification:

> Generally an attempt is made [in the classed cata-
> log] to bring all books under a strictly philosophi-
> cal system of classes, with divisions and subdivi-
> sions, arranged according to their scientific rela-
> tions. It is a very attractive plan. The maker
> enjoys forming his system, and the student fancies
> he shall learn the philosophy of the universe while
> engaged in the simple occupation of hunting for a
> book. [35]

Sayers, like Richardson, described his approach to
classification as determinedly practical:

> What does a librarian mean by a library?... To
> the librarian it is a systematic collection of books,
> made as useful as possible by the various guides
> that he provides.

> My classification theory is quite simple. The or-
> der which philosophers, scientists or valid system-
> atic thinkers have discovered in things is the basis
> of book classification.... This statement has made
> me the target of some criticism which may or may
> not be justified.... I am quite aware of the impor-
> tance of order. The question of the right order is
> a later study....

> Classification schemes are simply convenient lists
> of the names of subjects of books or forms of
> books; and as complete statements of intellectual
> activity they must be obsolescent almost with publi-
> cation. It is quite impossible that any scheme can
> set out once and for all the order of knowledge, or
> fix its classes so that their relationships or rela-
> tive importance can never alter.

> Classification ... its simplest meaning is that proc-
> ess of the mind by which qualities in things are ab-
> stracted and the things are grouped by these quali-
> ties into classes....

> When the librarian uses the word 'classification' he
> means the work of sorting and arranging the mate-
> rial--books, manuscripts, documents, maps, prints
> --with which he has to deal. His primary busi-

ness is to select and collect books and other
printed and graphic records for the use of others;
and he is successful if he is able to marshal this
material so effectively that it can be placed before
his readers in the least possible time. In short,
to save the time of readers in their pursuit of
knowledge, information and even amusement, is his
ultimate work as a librarian.[36]

Like Dewey, Sayers sometimes expressed in extreme
form the practical goals of library classification:

Does it matter in what order the groups themselves
are arranged? In the classification of knowledge it
matters supremely ... but ... in book classification we use the order which is most convenient for
the librarian and his readers.

'The order in which readers expect to find books
is that in which they should go' is a sound statement if we have defined 'readers.' ... It is surely
wise to arrange a library for the better type of
reader and to encourage the other to learn how and
why it is done.

The study of the best systems of classification ...
shows that order varies according to the theory of
knowledge held by the classification-maker as well
as by his purpose.[37]

All this did not prevent Sayers in his Canons of Classification from prescribing that a classification "should follow
in its form the order of ideas, history or evolution" nor that,
to express its essential genus-species hierarchical nature, it
"should commence with terms of wide extension and of small
intension and proceed to terms of small extension and great
intension."[38] He fervently espoused Richardson's evolutionary
theory:

In his luminous synthesis of the subject Dr. Richardson arrives with certainty at the conclusion that
the order of knowledge is the order of things, and
the order of classification is the order of things.
Here he reaches a concrete and, it would seem,
complete statement of classification order.... To
object ... to the historical or evolutional order now
that the progress of being from the simplest to the

most complex forms has been traced with some degree of certainty, seems to us to ignore the
achievements of science and the aid they give to
the classifier. 39

Moreover, this evolutionary order was of practical
benefit to the library user:

Generally speaking the natural arrangement enables
us to infer a great many of the properties of the
things arranged; and to attain to evolutionary order
natural characteristics must prevail.

A commonly accepted, and seemingly opposed,
view is that the order shall be the most convenient
to the user of the system.... This is a wider
view, but it is not necessarily antagonistic to our
rule of evolutionary order. An evolutionary order
may be, and as a rule is, most useful to the user
of a general classification; but, for special purposes, men may require special arrangements....
All these are artificial arrangements, but within
each of them history may still prevail.

It is when we come to view knowledge as a whole,
as we must do in a general bibliographical classification, that we postulate the order of ideas, or
history, or evolution as the criterion. 40

The schemes of Bliss and Ranganathan, the most influential classificationists since Dewey, also coupled avowedly practical ends with apparently metaphysical means. Bliss
expressed frequently the utilitarian purpose of library classifications: "for hardly less important than the selection of
books is the classification and grouping of books with regard
to their contents and the interests in which they are most
likely to be used for good purposes. "41 Having in two volumes of the Organization of Knowledge found wanting almost
every classification theory and scheme from ancient times
on, he took pains in introducing his own scheme to assure
potential users that "the entire system has been gradually developed during more than two decades in the libraries of The
College of the City of New York.... It is practical therefore, as well as logical, in its origin and development. It
has been thoroughly tested and has proved to be efficient and
economic. "42 He claimed the right to approach library classification pragmatically. He commented thus on Jevons' fa-

mous dictum that library classification was a logical absurdity:
"But to pronounce so upon this practical problem from the
logical point of view was itself illogical.... Yet this must be
done, the librarian says.   The educator and the scientist
agree that data and subject matters must be classified."[43]

Bliss's "practical" system was based on principles of
gradation by speciality, collocation, alternative location, and
--perhaps most striking--consensus.   His epistemological
principles were as follows:

> The objective realities are correlative to subjective
> concepts, to conceptual subject-matters, to studies,
> sciences, technologies, and arts.   Real and natural
> classes and relations, however diverse and various,
> are more stable and permanent than the conceptual
> classes and relations, which are more variable,
> because subjective.   In so far as all classes and
> relations have conceptual correlates, all classifica-
> tions imply conceptual correlation and they must be
> regarded as conceptual.[44]

Bliss's metaphysical assumptions were denied by critics like Broadfield, Kelley, and Metcalfe.   Kelley's review
of Bliss's second volume summarized many of these objections:

> He quotes Lester F. Ward to the effect that there
> is an 'order of nature [which is the natural ar-
> rangement of the sciences], and if all authors do
> not agree it is because they have not yet discovered
> the true order.'   This order, relatively permanent
> in its structure, may be, for future requirements,
> plastic and developmental.   The conclusion to this,
> then, would be that, for any one period of time,
> there is one order and only one, which is the order
> of nature; and that, at the same time, this would
> conform to what the author calls the 'educational
> and scientific consensus.'   This order, structurally
> adjusted according to certain practical require-
> ments, becomes a tool for the classification of
> books.
>
> But ... is it humanly possible ... to build one or-
> der of nature against which all other orders can
> be measured as correct, 'nearly correct,' or whol-
> ly incorrect?... Partial agreement there undoubted-
> ly might be in the major divisions of subject mat-

ter and also in many subdivisions and relations,
even though the serial order of subject fields,
which the author seems to consider of superimpor-
tance, would not necessarily coincide. But even
though a classification system could be devised
which is so excellent that some of the readers who
consult the shelves would be led by it from one
subject to the next which to them seems most
closely related, still, it is probably true that the
importance of one system of detailed relationships
is fairly small in comparison with the multitudinous
relationships operating in the minds of all readers. [45]

Ranganathan, considered by most critics to be the
most metaphysical of modern classificationists, insisted on
the practical motivation of library classification, particularly
his own scheme:

We shall be able to see the wisdom of translating
the names of subjects into an artificial language of
ordinal numbers if we realize the purpose of library classification. What, then, is the purpose?
It is to arrange books in a helpful sequence, or,
rather to mechanize the arrangement of books in a
helpful sequence. It is also to help mechanize the
correct replacing of books returned after use.
Again, it is to help fix the most helpful place for
a newly added book among those already in a library. [46]

From this "Basic Canon of Helpful Sequence" derived
his well-known "Five Laws of the Library Science":

(1) Books Are for Use.
(2) Every Reader His Book.
(3) Every Book Its Reader.
(4) Save the Time of the Reader.
(5) The Library is a Growing Organism. [47]

Ranganathan is best known for his theory of facet analysis: "that all possible facets of all possible specific subjects can be regarded as manifestations of one or another of
the five Fundamental Categories--Time, Space, Energy or
Action, Matter, and Personality."[48] This basic theory was
rejected by Moss[49] who claimed that the Fundamental Categories could be traced to those of Aristotle which Bertrand
Russell had rejected as neither understandable nor usable.

Metcalfe[50] charged that Ranganathan misapplied the Aristotelian categories.

Thus, library classificationists have claimed the practicality of their schemes, and almost all have conceded there can be no exact congruence between classifications of knowledge and those of bibliographies and libraries. Yet, apparently the schemes rest on certain metaphysical, philosophical, or epistemological assumptions. The resultant ambivalence or duality seems to introduce a "practicality" curiously different from what is claimed. Because of these metaphysical assumptions, librarians may believe that shelf classification will be self-revealing and self-teaching of knowledge for the user of the direct shelf approach and for the browser. As Bliss claimed: "A classification of books consistent with the scientific and pedagogic orders ... has ... educational value as the manifest organization of knowledge."[51]

Such possible beliefs are expressed as a hypothesis by the questionnaire statement: "An effective library classification scheme will reflect the true order of nature and of science and will reveal this order through the relative location of the books on the shelves." (III:1)

The Role of Close Classification

"Close" classification is defined in the questionnaire as follows:

> By 'close' classification, as used in these statements, is meant a library's use generally of the more specific or detailed arrangements or subdivisions available in a classification scheme rather than preferring generally the less minute breakdowns suitable for 'broad' classification. Usually, close classification means longer notations. (III: Prefatory note)

Close classification became a topic of controversy almost as soon as open access was introduced. The basic complaint against close classification remains that its alleged complexity and usually lengthy notation are unuseful to the reader--and frequently to the librarian. Perkins and Schwartz,[52] in reviewing the second edition of Dewey's scheme, had criticized among other features its close classification. Both Dewey and Cutter replied, the latter con-

fining himself to the issue of close classification. Cutter
stated that the complaints against Dewey's close classification applied in effect to all systems "that are worked out in
detail." Perkins and Schwartz had argued that, even if close
classification were of any convenience, it would be so "only
in libraries where readers are permitted to go to the
shelves." Cutter countered that there were now many such
libraries, but even where the public was excluded, "there is
all the more reason for a method which will enable the librarian to supply with the least delay the information that in more
fortunate libraries the inquirer can get for himself. "53

Dewey had been chided by Perkins and Schwartz for
implying that close classification "should bring absolutely everything in the library on each subject into one place." Cutter admitted this was a verbal indiscretion, and explained
that what Dewey really meant was that "not only are all the
books on the subject found together but the most nearly allied
subjects precede and follow. "54 The major objections of
Perkins and Schwartz--which will be returned to in this chap-
ter--were: (1) "Each successive subdivision simply intensi-
fies the difficulty of keeping all the books on a subject together" and (2) "This process of division, if carried out to
its logical result, ends in a reductio ad absurdum. If we
want to keep every distinct subject by itself, we are obliged
to provide a separate place in our scheme for every variety
of animal,... every author that has written a book. "55

To the first objection Cutter replied that the books
"are physically no farther off than they were before subdivision.... You simply look at the same books on the same
shelves in a different order." To the second objection Cutter responded:

> Not exactly. There are not books on 'every variety
> of animal,' etc. Leaving out of view difficulties of
> notation, there is no objection to the fifty million
> heads the Duet calls for, when we have books treat-
> ing of fifty million subjects; till then no one is
> bound to provide so many heads, but only the pos-
> sibility of so many; and that is afforded by the dec-
> imal system.
>
> The practice of division by distinct subjects is ad-
> vocated on the ground that it is convenient, which
> it certainly is up to a certain point.... The real
> question is, what is that point? We say that it dif-

fers for libraries of different size of character.[56]

Cutter conceded that minute classification required
longer notation, but he did not consider this a major problem.   If the class mark was made longer, the author marks
could be shortened; also, by a suitable notation of letters and
numerals, the class marks could be kept to reasonable
length.[57]

Cutter had already opted for close classification in an
1879 article describing his Boston Athenaeum system:

> Minute classification is not needless, it is not con-
> fusing, and, with a movable location, does not
> waste room.   The objections to it arise from mis-
> conception, and possibly, in some cases, from bad
> classification, which is an entirely different thing.
>
> It is not any harder to find books on a given sub-
> ject in a minutely divided library than in one
> slightly divided.   The books in a small subdivision
> are merely brought together within their class;
> they are not taken out of their class.   It is easier,
> to be sure, to find a book by a given author when
> the subdivisions are few, provided the books in
> each class are arranged alphabetically.   It would be
> easier still if there were no classes at all.   But
> the main purpose of classifying a library is not to
> enable one to find a book by a given author.   That
> is the purpose of the catalog.   The object of clas-
> sification is to guide people readily to all the books
> on a given topic.
>
> The general principle that should determine the ex-
> tent of classification in a small library is this:
> when a class may be distinctly and clearly sepa-
> rated into well-known parts, separate them, even
> if the groups of books resulting are very small.
> But when the divisions are vague, indefinite (as in
> Filosofy), let the class remain undivided till the
> number of books in it is large.... The librarian
> who is using a minute scheme of classification is
> not obliged to apply it all.[58]

Cutter's above recommendations applied to the small
library.   The structural principle of his later Expansive Classification was that since libraries of different sizes required

different degrees of classification, the scheme was to supply
seven expansions:

> The classification which I worked out for the Boston
> Athenaeum was the result of much study and
> thought, and it has borne the test and received the
> improvement of five years' use.... But ... the
> Boston Athenaeum contains about 170,000 volumes.
> It is evident that a library, all whose books could
> be put into a single room, all whose work must be
> done by a single person, would not require and
> would never attempt to use this elaborate arrange-
> ment; consequently ... I have been led to prepare
> a scheme applicable to collections of every size,
> from the village library in its earliest stage to the
> national library with a million volumes.
>
> Libraries might be arranged in an ascending series,
> with reference to the need and gain of order....
> The three factors, size, use and degree of shelf
> access enter in varying proportions into each li-
> brary's character, and by the resulting product its
> managers can determine how minute shall be its
> classification, whether there shall be any alphabet-
> ical suborder, and if there is any, whether it shall
> be approximate or exact.[59]

Decimal Classification numbers on printed Library of
Congress cards are now segmented to indicate where the notation may appropriately be cut back--or expanded. The question remains, though, as to how minutely a particular library
should classify. No doubt, as Cutter indicated, size, use,
and degree of shelf access are determinants, but each library
must somehow reach its own decision, and often only for
parts of its collection.

A broader theoretical question, taken up by Schneider,
was whether any general scheme could be valid for any library of any size:

> A priori no general library classification scheme
> may be developed, especially if it should be at-
> tempted to extend it to minor details.... The clas-
> sification schemes must be deduced from the history
> and constitution of the collection, and the best clas-
> sification scheme is the one that expresses the in-
> dividuality of the library using it.[60]

As with the other problems of classification ambivalence discussed above, classificationists conceded the theoretical justness of the argument, but, as before, claimed that the exigencies of practical library classification made compromise inevitable. Most schemes included instructions like the following in the introduction to the seventeenth edition of Dewey: "Every library has its own unique clientele, and, in serving that clientele's special needs, may find it desirable to modify specific printed provisions in ways other than reduction."[61] Also, most classificationists recommended special schemes if needed for significant parts of the collection. Although Ranganathan provided for very minute division in his Colon Classification, he promised, also, an even greater specificity--to be supplied by separate volumes for "Depth Classification of Micro Thought."[62] On the other hand, the Classification Research Group expressed an interest in developing through the theory of "integrative levels" an Ur-classification from which any other particular scheme might be devised. Palmer[63] doubted the possibility. In any case, when to apply a special classification, to what part of the collection, and how minutely, remain matters of judgment. The original problem of close classification thus seems to recur in another form. Furthermore, classificationists conceded that a special classification was per se much more vulnerable to obsolescence than a general one. In fact, classificationists like Bliss[64] drew on this idea to claim the relatively permanent correctness of their own general schemes.

Most libraries offer some temporary grouping of books, e.g., new acquisitions, for the reader's convenience. Savage[65] described many elaborate methods of temporary display for public libraries. The Reader Interest Classification,[66] developed at the Detroit Public Library in the 1940's, temporarily groups books out of regular classification order under such broad interest categories as Current Affairs, People and Places, and Personal Living. Such groupings may be devised for any topic of potential reader interest. Custer disowned the method: "Numerous public libraries have recently organized their collections of current popular interest in somewhat heterogeneous groups according to 'reader-interest' arrangement, rearranging titles and developing new categories as interests of patrons shift. Practical as this has proven to be, it is not classification by subject."[67] Needham denounced it: "Reader interest arrangement in public libraries is the outcome at its most extreme form of the adverse attitude to shelf classification.... Whilst close classification certainly has its limitations, such a solution to the problem is too drastic, alienating, as it does, the serious reader. "68

For the open-shelf library, the problem of close classification could be defined by a question: Of what use is close classification to the reader? Bostwick, discussing the schemes of Cutter, Dewey, and the Library of Congress, echoed Perkins and Schwartz:

> Evidently these systems, and numerous others, provide for classification as 'close' as may be desired. The closer the classification the fewer books in the furthest subclass. Carried to its extreme, this would leave one title in each class, for it may probably be asserted that no two books are so exactly alike that they would defy attempts to place them in separate subclasses. 69

Eaton made the same point:

> The Decimal Classification [up to the fifteenth edition] is an outline of knowledge, provided with exact notation for many minute divisions of our total knowledge. The classifier uses the complete tables to determine the exact location of a book in the scheme but does not necessarily use the full number assigned to this subject as a book shelving symbol. The use of the exact number, covering the most minute division of knowledge, is known as close classification. This kind of classification is valuable for arranging a classed catalog or preparing a subject index to articles in journals.
>
> When the class symbol is used primarily as a book marking device, for the purpose of shelving books in subject order, the classification may be broader. Close classification may be unnecessary, or even undesirable, as a shelf arrangement. Classification that is so close that every book in a section of shelving has a different number may have defeated the purpose of grouping books.... Numbers should be limited in length whenever possible to a minimum number of decimal places. The most satisfactory shelving symbol is as short as it can be and still permit the shelving of books in subject order. 70

Bliss took an opposed stand:

Some classifiers, many librarians, and, perhaps
we should say, most readers do not approve of
such close distinctions.   The difficulties, however,
of classifying books and the uncertainties in locating them, whether on the part of librarians or of
readers, are not much increased by definite and
specific classification, but the special services and
conveniences so often requisite are thereby greatly
enhanced.   The uncertainties may usually be removed by ready reference to the Index of the classification or to the catalog under author or subject.
On the other hand the difficulties of finding special
kinds of books in unclassified collections are much
greater and more vexatious.[71]

Savage disdained the pedantry of "classification" and
preferred the word "grouping," but he nevertheless recommended close classification:

The whole art of display for a general reference library, or a home reading library for that matter,
lies in the intelligent application of three rules:

(1) Break up the heavy mass of books into the
smallest sections that can be indicated without confusion by legible signs....

(2) No matter what the classification requires,
group books which support each other.

(3) Use the classification tables to the fullest extent.

This recommendation is in fact but a continuance of
the process of 'breaking up.'   By differentiating one
book from another we display both.   An ideal class
mark ought to embody signs representing all the
catalog headings (apart from analytics), as well as
signs which cannot be revealed by headings....   If
therefore we employ the tables of a great scheme
to their fullest extent we go far to isolate a book
from its neighbors.   The whole art of classification
consists in so differentiating or displaying the matter in books.[72]

Dunkin seemed diametrically opposed:

With more than one author or with more than one
possible subject heading, we can always rely on
added entries. A book can have only one call number. This, of course, makes the selection of a
call number terribly important--or, looked at from
another point of view, it simply strengthens the argument against close classification. [73]

Custer in his introduction to the seventeenth edition of
Dewey adopted a Cutter-like stance:

We have indicated ... that a valuable feature of the
DC notation is its adaptability to both close and
broad classification. How close or how broad the
classification of a specific library should be is a
matter of administrative determination. It is likely
that only a very large general library or a library
with enormous collections in certain subjects will
follow the present edition to its fully expanded detail, and none of those in every section. In short,
every library using these tables will reduce them
in some or many parts. [74]

The most fervent and influential advocate of close classification today is probably Ranganathan:

Why does a librarian classify at all? He classifies
to uncover to himself, in order to make it readily
available to readers, everything that a library has
on any subject. Comparatively few devote any time
at all to practical classification, yet many would
agree that the resources uncovered by minute classification are extremely important to know.

Library classification is an uncovering of the
thought-content of a book. It is what it should be
only when the thought-content as a whole is uncovered, including the primary and secondary phases,
the facets of each of the phases, and the foci in
each of the facets, by those faculties which appre-
hend in terms of entirety rather than in terms
merely of parts....

Take as your mission the establishment of contact
between the right reader and the right book exhaus-
tively, exactly, and expeditiously and without any
fumbling. You will then see that no scheme of

classification can be too minute or too complicated.[75]

Kelley's The Classification of Books[76] was generally
interpreted as a severe critique of the usefulness of close
shelf classification. Metcalfe[77] thought it may have resulted
in the fifteenth edition of Dewey. That edition, designed for
collections of up to 200,000 volumes, eliminated the close
classification of the earlier editions, and had only one-sev-
enth as many terms as the fourteenth. Although a survey
of catalogers' opinions had shown great dissatisfaction with
the complexity and lengthy notation of the previous edition,
the fifteenth was almost universally condemned. Eaton's
above cited "Epitaph to a Dead Classification" expressed the
opinions of many. It is unclear, though, if the edition might
not have been more successful if its principles had been more
effectively realized. Thus, many of the terms did not seem
well chosen, and the index was judged so inadequate that a
revised version had to be published.

A suggestion emerges from the literature that close
shelf classification in open-shelf libraries may represent an
attempt to structure the learning experience of the patron and
browser by revealing through minute specificity the precise
location of a book in a serial order of knowledge as well as,
to a maximum degree, its subject content--as Ranganathan's
above cited statements proposed. These goals seem self-con-
tradictory, though, as will be noted below, not within the
context of "true" hierarchical order. Such a faith seems to
confuse the idea of library classification with the specification
of documents. Most authorities agree that, however defined,
library classification is not the specification of any one book,
but the placing of any one book in a class with other books,
that is, the assembling of books within appropriate groups for
readers' use. Even an opponent of Aristotelian logic as applied to library classification insisted on this "group-nature"
of class: "A class in logic is any group of things we like to
make a class, however unlike they may be in fact."[78] Perkins, Schwartz, Bostwick, and Eaton all warned that excessive specification could destroy the purpose of classing. Metcalfe[79] extensively criticized the equation of specification with
classification, especially as evidenced in the Colon Classification and the Universal Decimal Classification. Rider, introducing his International Classification, expressed similar
objections:

Why any new classification at all?

The answer is simple. The Classification proposed
in this volume has come into existence for just one
reason, a reason resting on two basic premises.
First, a library classification is a classification intended to place in a practicable retrievable order
the hundreds of thousands of books standing on the
shelves of a general library. Second, a library
classification should have a very short and very
simple symbolization.

Bibliographical classifications are not library classifications: they do not have, as their primary
purpose, the arranging of books on the shelves of
general libraries.... Although a basic classification
scheme may serve as a common starting point for
both a library and a bibliographical classification,
one single scheme can never adequately be both....
Every one of our existing classifications has drifted
into the position of trying to perform just this dual
function; but ... in so drifting, they have all followed a veritable will-o'-the-wisp which, in each of
their succeeding editions, has led them further and
further astray.

The Present Confusion Between Library Classification and Bibliographical Classification--is one that
developed gradually, and indeed unconsciously. The
First Edition of Dewey was ... so amazingly simple and so amazingly practical that his enthusiastic
disciples swallowed whole the entirely natural idea
that, if some classification was good, more of it--
in fact a great deal more of it--would be better.
And, for a while, this idea ... seemed to be a
sound one.... Between its first edition and its six-
teenth Dewey grew from 1,000 heads to nearly
20,000; and the latter figure did not include the
many thousands of additional heads that would result from a consistent and thorough-going use of
its 'divide-likes. '

Nor was this ultra-expansionism something peculiar
to Dewey. All our other important library classifications ran exactly the same course. [80]

A second apparent contradiction in the philosophical
assumptions underlying close classification seems to involve
the confounding of specification with the comprehensive de-

scription of a book's contents.   This will be discussed in the
next section.

Among the questionnaire statements designed to elicit
opinions on close shelf classification, as discussed thus far,
are:

> The chief value of close shelf classification lies in its
> use by the librarian for teaching and by the patron for
> learning. (III:3)

> Close relative shelf classification is necessary for ef-
> fective direct shelf approach to subject materials.
> (III:4)

> Close classification on the shelves, because it places
> too few books under any one subject division, is less
> suitable for the direct shelf approach than for closed
> stacks. (III:6)

> Close shelf classification is as useful and feasible for
> small libraries as it is for large libraries. (III:7)

> Close classification notation is simple enough for the
> average patron to follow successfully on the shelves.
> (III:10)

> Although close shelf classification may not be justified
> by its cost, it is cheaper for libraries now using it to
> continue rather than discard it. (III:11)

The Problem of Linearity

Most classificationists and librarians readily acknowledge the problem of linearity in classification.   However, a
general equanimity before this problem on the part of classificationists in creating their schemes and of librarians in applying them seems to have produced still another ambivalence
of theory and practice.   Needham's comment on linearity in
the classified catalog no doubt applies even more to linearity
in shelf classification:

> However, no matter how perfect the scheme used,
> the only relationships that are immediately apparent
> are those between a subject and the subjects imme-
> diately preceding and succeeding it in the file; this

limitation is inevitable with linear order.   But
there are usually many other relationships apart
from those revealed by juxtaposition. [81]

Just as library classificationists have not been deterred from making their schemes because of the acknowledged discrepancy between the classification of knowledge and
that of books, so their admission of the limitation of linearity
has not discouraged them from elaborate provisions for determining the proper place for the book's subject in the
schemes' linear order.   The problem of linearity clearly increases in direct proportion to the minuteness of the classification.   A reason for the great impact of Kelley's critique
of close shelf classification was, as Prevost[82] pointed out,
not that librarians had been ignorant of linearity, but that
Kelley's measurement of its effects confronted librarians with
the consequences of this "theoretical" limitation.   Sayers and
Bliss[83] dismissed Kelley's methodology and conclusions, but
nevertheless carefully defended the validity of their ideas
against hers.   (Kelley appears about eleven times in the index to Bliss's The Organization of Knowledge in Libraries
and the Subject-Approach to Books, and there is also a
lengthy appended bibliographic note which is in effect a review of her book.)   Bliss had spent a lifetime in an effort to
determine the linear sequence of his main classes, a concern
which oddly did not extend to the divisions within the classes.
For example, his extensive provision of alternative locations
seemed to weaken his concept of a consensus on the correct
order.

Close classification seemed to be expected, at least by
some librarians and classificationists, to perform disparate
feats: indicate the subject of the work--not only at its deepest
level of specificity but also in its most comprehensive aspect,
and also as to its precise relationship within the sequence of
knowledge represented by the classification scheme.   Similar
multifarious expectations in documentation and information indexing were condemned by Metcalfe who accused Otlet, Bradford, Ranganathan, and members of the Classification Research Group of fundamental technical confusions:

> Probably no other words have been so abused in in-
> dexing ... as specific, specificity, and specifica-
> tion.   There is a confusion of specification or de-
> scription of documents, with the specification or
> specificity of subject matter or things, and of both
> with qualifications of subjects and things as limita-

tions of information on them by which information, and documents, may be subdivided or subindexed. [84]

To "specify" connotes ordinarily the exact description of parts of the whole, yet Ranganathan called for the minutest possible classification so as to uncover the book's thought-content as a whole. Of course, one classification symbol could by synthesis detail more than one closely specified top-ic, but a book of any length would obviously contain an un-manageably large number of such possible topics--if complete thought-content were to be embodied in the symbol. There seems to be behind this evident paradox the already noted metaphysical belief in a genus-species hierarchy ultimately derived from--or leading back to--a unitary source of knowl-edge. If the essence of the work could be specified, that specification would represent the true or perfect nature of the work and, by metaphysical or epistemological implication, be equal to its complete thought-content. Accordingly, if the true nature of a work were so defined and named, it would by that very act have been placed in its true position in the ordained hierarchy, or, in Lovejoy's phrase, in the great chain of being. Thus, close classification, in the light of such metaphysical assumptions, would reveal through its es-sential specification not only the complete thought-content of the book but, in so doing, perforce set the book correctly in the serial order. Conversely, Bliss implied that if one de-termined the proper position of a main class in the full se-quence, the essential nature of that class would, by definition, be self-revealed. (The ultimate difficulty, of course, is to define "essence.")

So abstract a concept might help elucidate a physical conundrum of shelf classification. If the meticulously deter-mined position of the subject of a book within the class se-quence is shown on the shelves by that book's juxtaposition with two other books, what can be the continued validity of indicative position when all books are not on the shelves at the same time--because of library or home use, or when lat-er acquisitions have been intercalated? An answer would seem to lie in the assumption that in the "great chain of be-ing" all members are linked. Once in its true place, the book remaining on the shelf can never be in the wrong one. Any level of the hierarchy must, by definition, be in correct relation to any other correctly determined. Indeed, for such an objection to be consistently developed, one would needs de-mand of the classifier that he have already and permanently in his collection at least one specimen of every term in the

scheme before determining the proper position of any book.
Otherwise, that position might be falsified by the appearance
of a work not yet in the library or by the absence of any one
work at any time. In other words, the classifier classes by
the scheme, which is designed for many libraries, and not
by the works constituting his present collection--though he is
usually advised by classificationists to divide more minutely
when a large number of books accumulates in any major division.

Nevertheless, there remains the problem of the patron's not being able to see all the possibly important works
on a topic being researched. He cannot be certain he has
seen all the relevant materials owned by the library, nor
can he recognize the full significance nor richness of the collection's linear sequence if significant items are missing.
Much more perilous is unawareness of this situation! This
problem of availability, as distinct from that of linearity,
seems to present the most intractable difficulty for shelf classification per se as a practical knowledge-revealing device.
As discussed in the next section on subject cataloging, this
problem, along with others of a more theoretical nature, has
elicited the urgent advice of classificationists since Cutter not
to rely solely on shelf classification for adequate, let alone
comprehensive, subject search.

When Cutter was defending Dewey against Perkins and
Schwartz, he significantly commented that minutely classified
books "are physically no farther off than they were before
subdivision.... You simply look at the same books on the
same shelves in a different order."[85] Taken literally, the
statement is false. If the order of two books has been
changed, there is no assurance they will be as close as before. Cutter meant, of course, the books could still be no
farther off than the physical boundaries of the class which had
been further subdivided. More significant, however, was his
point that close classification produced--thus implying it to
be the purpose--a different order on the shelves than did
broad classification. Such a view accorded with the traditional rationale of enumerative library classification based on
genus-species hierarchical relations, a rationale reinforced,
as noted in Chapter Five, by contemporary Darwinism. As
Sayers indicated in his Canons:

> 1. A classification should be comprehensive, em-
> bracing all past and present knowledge, and allow-
> ing places for any possible additions to knowledge.

2. It should follow in its form the order of ideas, history or evolution.

6. It should commence with terms of wide extension and of small intension and proceed to terms of small extension and great intension.

7. In this process the steps should be gradual, each term modulating from the term before it and into the term following, thus exhibiting perfect co-ordination of subjects.

8. The enumeration of parts should be exhaustive. [86]

Justifying such canons was the metaphysical belief that as one classified knowledge more closely, one arrived at a more accurate statement of its genus-species nature, one could show more precisely its complex development, and one was thus enabled to <u>place</u> all of knowledge correctly in the <u>order</u> of nature. These ideas, advocated by Richardson, Sayers, and Bliss, were rebutted by Broadfield:

> Evolution moves forward, whereas the 'logical order,' Richardson thinks, leads back. Evolution is conceived as tending to the production of complex forms, while Richardson is far from sure that the logical order does.... Quotation will show the confusion resulting from these conflicts.

> The notion of evolution as tending to the production of complexity, a characterisation which for Richardson amounts to a definition, is at variance with his mechanistic assumptions ...

> Sayers has suggested that the generic terms, whose extension is the greater, are the simpler, the complex being the specific with greater intension. Bliss offers the same interpretation of simplicity and complexity. But if the complexity of a term consists in the manifold interrelations of the characters entering into it, the genus, as having within itself a wealth of potential modes of expression, is more complex than the species. [87]

Broadfield's detailed analysis of such incongruities suggested that they arose from a misapplication of Aristote-

lian logical categories and predicables, particularly because
of "Porphyry's Tree" which introduced an inconsistency into
Aristotle's theory of predicables by relating them "to an individual subject, not as an individual of a certain sort, but
barely as that individual. "[88]

What Sayers would have replied is conjectural, but he
defended library classification against Jevons' charge of its
"logical absurdity" on the grounds that "to a certain extent
book classification can never be perfect, and this is the justification of Jevons's statement, " but, nevertheless, it was
less imperfect than Jevons thought because:

> At the same time Jevons did not know of the gen-
> eralia and form classes, and form divisions, by
> which composite and other intractable books are
> provided for; ...A book classification must hold the
> minuteness of the knowledge classification as an
> ideal to which it must approximate as nearly as
> possible. [89]

Sayers thus believed in a philosophical or metaphysical basis for library classification, despite practical compromises.   Bliss, as noted, had similarly complained that for
Jevons "to pronounce so upon the practical problem from the
logical point of view was itself illogical. "[90]   Yet Bliss in his
critique of other systems and in creating his own was per-
sistently "logical. "   The inquiry later will consider why such
beliefs may have persisted among the "practical" classifications discussed above.

The Role of Subject Cataloging

In an effort to breach the limitation of linearity in
classification, use has been made of alternative or supplementary means of subject analysis in the library, particularly
subject headings in the catalog.   Pettee upheld the superiority of the alphabetical subject heading over the classification
term because, as Coates put it, "a subject can ... belong to
more than one hierarchy in the dictionary catalog, but to one
alone in the classified catalog. "[91]

Pettee, explaining its superiority, averred as "its su-
preme claim to distinction ... its ability to collect material
from different fields under a topical name. "[92]   In a passage,
termed by Jolley "almost lyrical" and "rather high flown, "[93]

she said:

> The parallel lines of our classification schemes are
> drawn through the flat surface of plane geometry....
> In a dictionary catalog the logical analysis of a
> classed catalog is exalted to a third dimension.
> The logic transcends the limits of a classification
> scheme, for the interrelationships of the special
> topics reach out into the whole field of knowledge.
> Under the particular topical heading all aspects of
> the topic may be collected. [94]

One of Kelley's conclusions had been that "on an average, three times as many titles on specific subjects can be
traced under the subject in the dictionary catalog as can be
found by direct consultation of the shelves, " though Bliss[95]
denied that this conclusion was based on adequate sampling.

Most catalogers and classifiers, e.g., Mann, [96] ac-
cept--in less extreme form than Pettee--a basic distinction
between the classification term and the subject heading. This
distinction may be traced to Cutter's Rules. [97] Ranganathan,[98]
however, rejected the distinction, and advanced a theory of
"symbiosis" of subject headings and classification terms
which was exemplified in his method of chain indexing.
Coates[99] used the method for the British National Bibliography. Metcalfe, a proponent of Cutter's dictionary catalog
principles, opposed chain indexing because between even the
index terms to a classification scheme and subject headings
"there are differences in function which may mean irreconcilable differences in method and form."[100]

Bliss carefully evaluated the subject heading against
the classification term:

> In brief, the subject-catalog may be more complete,
> more inclusive, more analytic, more specific, and
> more plastic; but in becoming these it tends to be-
> come too complicated, cumbersome, and expensive.
> Moreover, to most interests, it is less satisfactory
> than access to the books themselves, even tho the
> groups in the classes are more or less incomplete.
> A mass of cards is so uninviting, to follow through
> their dry details in disconnected succession is so
> irksome, there is so much irrelevant material, so
> much 'dead wood, ' so much bibliographic jargon,
> that the reader thrusts the tray from him and turns

to consult the books, some of which at least are
suffused with vivid interests. It is in consideration
of this desire and need for more intimate and in-
formative contact with the books that classification
is maintained in modern libraries and access to the
shelves is allowed. [101]

Swank[102] suggested that subject bibliographies might
eventually replace both subject catalogs and classification in
libraries. Twenty years later, Reichmann[103] wrote that
Swank's call for research on this problem had gone largely
unheeded.

Most librarians dealing with traditional library classification would probably accept the statement of Bliss on the
usefulness of the subject catalog vis-à-vis classification:

> For the organization of knowledge in libraries a
> systematic subject-catalog is hardly less requisite
> than classification, and hardly less problematic.
> Less direct and satisfactory in some respects, it
> is in other respects more plastic and more com-
> plete. But each complements the other and both
> are essential to complete functional efficiency.
> Cataloging and classifying, tho distinct, are closely
> related steps in bibliothecal service. [104]

Such a comment would reaffirm the need not to rely
solely on classification, particularly as applied to shelves,
for subject research. Kelley,[105] whose investigation had
provided confirmatory evidence, recommended the use of all
available bibliographical tools to insure adequate subject
search. One might note that Cutter created both a classification scheme and rules for subject headings.

The following questionnaire hypotheses refer to the
relationship of subject headings and classification:

> Subject headings in the public catalog are more use-
> ful to the patron than shelf classification. (III:9)

> Adequate catalogs, bibliographies and, when available,
> reference assistance, would make open-shelf access
> in large academic libraries largely unnecessary. (IV:
> 16)

> Nothing can be accomplished by browsing in a general

research collection that could not be done more easily
and efficiently through the use of the library catalog
and other bibliographical tools. (V:13)

The Role of Notation

Palmer gave a post-Broadfield assessment of classification order:

It is assumed ... that the object of library classification is so to group books and other library materials that their subject contents can be related to
each other in the most helpful order. It is not possible to define the most helpful order. Any ten objects can be arranged among themselves in nearly
four million different orders, and the potential number of orders in a collection of books is infinite.
Yet few orders are really helpful, ... It may be possible to base the most helpful order on the alphabet,
and indeed attempts have been made to produce al-
phabetico-classed catalogs; but classification implies
a systematic approach, and all library classifications are, in fact, systems of knowledge. [106]

The literature suggests that librarians in their use of
shelf classification for direct access may assume that it generally provides the helpful order for their patrons browsing
or conducting research. A means of indicating and commu-
nicating this helpful order to the patron has usually been considered notation.

Perhaps in no other area of library classification was
inconsistency so evident as in the classificationist's--and librarian's--use of notation. Every major classificationist
stressed its theoretically subordinate role. The classification
was to be the prime concern, to be devised independently of
the notation which was later to provide a shorthand symbol
for the term. Palmer said: "Sayers declared that while a
good notation did not make a good classification scheme, a
bad one could mar it; and though we were always bidden as
students to regard notation as something added to a scheme
(necessary, but only an auxiliary) it is surprising how important this auxiliary is to classificationists themselves."[107]
Kephart had warned in 1893:

Classification is a method of work; notation is a

mere label to help us in handling the material.   It
is a mischievous error to confound the two.

The scheme of classification should be made without any thought of a notation, and numbers assigned
to it afterwards, taking care to allow for the future
growth of the various classes.[108]

Ranganathan restated Kephart's ideas:

We began with the statement that class numbers
constitute an artificial language of ordinal numbers
designed to mechanise the filiatory arrangement of
subjects.   The determination of helpful sequence
does not necessarily require a scheme of classification.... But to preserve the sequence arrived at ...
for these purposes we do need a scheme of classification.[109]

Yet, Kephart said:

It is a singular fact that many schemes of classification are enslaved to their notation.   The attempt
to make out of the book number a structural formula, showing the dependence of classes by giving
a separate figure or letter to each stage of descent,
invariably results in an irrational classification dis-
figured with long and cabalistic marks.   The object
of a notation is to enable us to find or replace a
book with ease and certainty.   Anything that inter-
feres with this is a mistake.[110]

Ranganathan's Colon Classification has been widely
judged unsuitable for library purposes if only because of its
notation which employs upper and lower case roman letters,
Greek letters, and various symbols.   Foskett commented:

The notational symbols ... are often themselves
difficult to sort out and often prove psychologically
unacceptable....

CC has an extraordinarily complex notation, which
undoubtedly proves repulsive to many who would
otherwise find the scheme attractive.   Ranganathan
is inclined to underestimate the importance of
this.[111]

One of the strongest reasons for the popularity of the Decimal Classification was its easily manipulable decimal notation which, as is well known, tempted many librarians into excessive "number building." Bliss referred to Dewey's notation as a tail wagging the dog: "The rapidity of its success was indeed phenomenal. A happy dog's tail is irresistible."[112] Bliss had given much attention to a simple, short notation for his own scheme: "Short class-marks are a distinguishing feature of the system. Only very special subjects require class-marks of more than three factors."[113] He criticized elaborate notations of other schemes, and gave as example of the superiority of his notation over Dewey's that "for a pamphlet on 'Fire-drills at the Newark Air-port, written in the Slovakian language,'" Dewey's notation would require thirty-three figures against Bliss's only twelve factors: BTR, bdf, P, Qm![114]

A reason given by Rider for his new scheme was that the notation in all other widely used ones had become too cumbersome. Fifty years earlier, Rider[115] had warned not to devise new classification schemes, since none could be perfect or permanent!

Sayers listed the requirements for a notation:

> A notation to be perfect should be a pure notation;....
> Further, that arrangement of the symbols is best
> which shows immediately the sequence;... The use-
> fulness of the notation will be governed by its capa-
> bility of expanding, its elasticity.... The briefer
> the notation is the more likely is it to obtain fa-
> vor.[116]

Palmer thought that the failure of many notational systems could be traced to Sayers' requirements, particularly for an expressive notation: "one whereby at a glance the order of the scheme can be seen, and from an individual number the importance of its subject in relation to its main classes can be inferred."[117] Palmer commented:

> What we can clearly see now is that the conflict
> between some of the headings set out by Sayers can
> never be resolved.... Expressive notation ... tends
> to be wasteful of digits, and to grow less accurate
> in its expression with time....
>
> The wastefulness of this kind of notation is subcon-

sciously offensive even to its greatest advocates.[118]

To illustrate the breakdown of conventional enumerative notation, Palmer cited the history of Dewey's decimal scheme:

> Dewey was aware of the need to provide for growth, and found the capacity for it in the use of a decimal notation.... He would bring out successive editions of the scheme with definitive allocations of digits to new subjects. He, not its users, would ultimately control the reflection of the growth of knowledge in his scheme, for any other way lay chaos.... Today the Decimal Classification has really given up seeking to preserve helpful order: it is sufficient now for it to find reasonably approximate 'places' for subjects (and sometimes not such reasonable ones), and to be a super-pigeon-holing device.
>
> New subjects arise in different ways, but decimal notation can only grow in one way.... Growth ... takes place in two dimensions: hierarchically and collaterally; or, to use the terms brought into fashion by Ranganathan, in chain and array. Decimal Classification can expand indefinitely to take care of subdivision in chain, but it cannot take care of new subjects in array.[119]   cannot take care

Palmer weighed discarding traditional notation à la Sayers:

> The only advantage totally lost in deciding to abandon a notation expressive of structure ... is the mnemonic value.... What are the gains to be set off against this loss?
>
> If we decide ... that we shall simplify our demands upon notation so as to lose expressiveness of structure, what can we gain? A positive retention of order, and some shortening of notation. In the light of the growing complexity of knowledge, and of the consequent tendency of class numbers to lengthen, these are more important considerations than the mnemonic value of structure.
>
> If structure is no longer reflected, we are suddenly

free to insert an infinite number of digits at any
point in the series....

Using a non-structural notation will, therefore, provide us certain economies in the length of notation,
by enabling an appropriate allocation of digits to the
more stable areas of knowledge, which can be set
out in some detail.[120]

But how would a non-expressive notation affect browsing and the direct shelf approach in an open-shelf collection?
Does not the public depend on the mnemonic and expressive
features--however imperfect--of the notation to "read the
shelves"? How would patrons know what they were looking
at--or for? On these questions there was a marked divergence between the theory and practice of classificationists
whose schemes were applied in open-shelf libraries. Even
Sayers stated that mnemonics might be more appreciated by
classifiers than readers, and that its "value need not be ex-
aggerated."[121] Bliss[122] delivered a similar opinion. Although Dewey claimed that his mnemonics aided the user,
Metcalfe[123] said there was no evidence that readers benefited
from Dewey's constant form numbers. Dunkin seconded Metcalfe:

Some people think that mnemonic features are good
in notation. DDC is mnemonic rather frequently....
LCC has rather few mnemonic devices. It has not
been scientifically proved how useful such features
are.[124]

Ranganathan, whose notation attempted maximum expressiveness, belittled its intelligibility to the reader:

No scheme of classification can be too minute or
too complicated.... The reader is not concerned
with your notation, or with the 'how' of your classificatory technique, except in its very superficies.
The service of classification can reach him in difficult situations only through you; in other words,
classification in its deepest embellishments has to
be intelligible only to you, though an intelligent
reader may be prepared to share them with you.[125]

Metcalfe pointed out that "a classification may have
classes not brought out in its notation or in any headings or
summary of the scheme" and that classification "notations are

not primarily or functionally languages of communication."126

Needham also questioned the value of expressiveness and mnemonics:

> No notation can ever be fully hospitable and maintain its expressiveness.... Expressiveness is useful in that it expresses the structure of the scheme to some extent, but it must be sacrificed in the interests of hospitality--and many modern schemes have abandoned the concept.

> Memory may also be assisted by mnemonics, i.e., the use of certain symbols with only one meaning so that in time staff and even possibly users become familiar with this meaning.... Literal mnemonics should be incidental--there is danger that in striving for them order and economy may be affected.

> Class numbers are meaningless to most users of the classified file and therefore an index of subjects is required by which terms in natural language can be converted into class numbers.127

Savage, who advocated extensive regrouping and "guiding" of library materials, also disparaged the usefulness of notation for readers:

> Classification is a mechanical time-saving method which reveals knowledge in books. True, but only to librarians who understand it. To readers, unless the coordination is well guided, it is but a map of unknown country without lettering and without a scale.128

Wiley, librarian of the Naval War College in Newport, ridiculed mnemonics:

> One of the ornaments to notation is mnemonics, the value of which is as difficult for me to understand as its spelling....

> If I were asked, what is the best system of notation, I should frankly admit that I don't know. All of them seem reasonably bad, i.e., none unites the qualities of brevity, clearness and expansibility, and

when adapted to a very minute sub-division, all of
them look very much like the picture of the Cubist
lady descending the stairs.[129]

Bostwick, who, as noted in Chapter Five, considered
an open-shelf policy part of the fortunate socialization of the
American public library, took a negative view of notation for
readers:

> Notation, whatever it may be in theory, is rarely
> of direct practical aid to users of the library, ex-
> cept occasionally, in enabling them to replace books
> on the shelves properly in libraries where the pub-
> lic is allowed to do this.... It is probably too much
> to expect the ordinary user of a library to attach
> significance to the notation of any system of classi-
> fication.... It makes considerable difference to a
> reader whether a given book be replaced in one or
> another class, but very little whether that book be
> marked with one or another combination of letters
> or numerals.
>
> The notation in a public free-access library is for
> the use of the library assistant rather than that of
> the public.[130]

A questionnaire hypothesis, already noted in connection
with close classification, is: "Close classification notation is
simple enough for the average patron to follow successfully
on the shelves." (III:10)

Palmer commented, perhaps ironically: "Notation ...
is the device which makes the handling of works on complex
subjects a matter for trained persons who yet have no insight into the subjects they handle."[131]

The studies discussed in Chapter Four indicated that
a chief use of shelf classification was as a locational device
for patrons and librarians to obtain already known works--as
shown by Herner's study of the stacks of the Library of Congress.[132] Hoage's survey of patron use of the Library of
Congress Classification in various kinds of libraries revealed
that:

> Approximately 41 per cent of the public service li-
> brarians in this sample estimated that more than
> half of the patrons need assistance in using the

> classification.   Most of the librarians believe that
> the average patron is not aware of the subject ap-
> proach provided by the classification and is ignorant
> of the full meaning of the call numbers. ...
>
> In no instance did the opinions and practices of the
> patrons in a specific type of library differ from
> those in other types.   Most of the patrons used the
> classification as a location device.   They usually
> found what they wanted, and only 9. 5 per cent
> sought help for the search that they described. 133

The cumulative evidence would seem to indicate that
for subject search in shelf-classified collections, the position,
not the notation, of the book must be the chief means of revealing its topic in proper relation to those of the other books
in the collection which have also been "placed" according to
the classification scheme.   Such a finding must, at the least,
appear tautological, being in effect a restated definition of
traditional library classification: the arrangement of books
in the order of their subject classes as posited by the scheme
in use.   As noted in this section, notation is in theory logically independent of the classificatory act.   Also, as discussed in the section on linearity, the position--not the shorthand address--of the subject within the scheme is the theoretical essence of traditional hierarchical enumerative library
classification.   From a theoretical viewpoint, therefore, it
should not surprise nor dismay that the patron would seem
largely to ignore the notation as a knowledge-revealing device.   Yet, this seemingly tautological conclusion would have
considerable practical implication for the validity of shelf
classification.   If the correct position of the book on the
shelf must be for the patron his essential epistemological indicator, the adequacy of the scheme which determined that
position is crucial.   The question becomes: How adequate is
the scheme?

(Perhaps a preliminary question should be: Does the
patron understand the position of the book any more than he
would its notation?   Those who advocated direct access and
shelf classification--as cited especially in Chapter Five--ob-
viously believed that shelf order did mean something to the
patron.   A thrust of this inquiry has been to determine to
what extent documentary evidence, joined with the findings of
the opinion questionnaire, would support such a belief.   It
was, indeed, as frontal attacks on this question that many of
the use and user studies cited in Chapter Four were launched.)

There is extensive literature on the supposed defects
of individual library classification schemes, much of it written by those like Bliss and Ranganathan who proposed their
own systems.   If the schemes were thus vulnerable, clearly
none could safely claim definitiveness.   Critics like Palmer[134]
asserted there was no convincing argument for the validity
of the class sequence in any library classification.   Bliss
apotheosized main-class order, and Ranganathan largely ignored it.

Disregarding arguments against the supremacy of any
scheme, it would seem from the cited authorities that librarians and readers in open-shelf libraries are to rely on the
self-revelatory nature of the classification exemplified by the
order of books on shelves.   Nevertheless, there persist all
the previously discussed problems of close classification,
linearity, notation, and the special needs of individual libraries.   Yet, among librarians generally, the faith in shelf classification seems to survive--despite the theoretical limitations
explored by Kelley, the admittedly equivocal usefulness of notation, and the lack of any definitive browsing or direct-ac-
cess research.

What, then, could be that persuasive power of the
classificatory idea to convince the librarian that, as Custer[135]
stated, classification controls the collection for reader-bene-
fit, or, as per a hypothesis of this study, structures the
learning experience of the direct-shelf approach?   Perhaps,
there might be extra-library factors to explain at least partially this loyalty to a system which on many theoretical and
practical grounds was admittedly defective.   Such possible
factors of epistemology, psychology, and sociology will be
considered in Chapter Thirteen.

Classification and Librarians' Prestige

The professional literature exhibits frequent claims of
status-enhancement for librarians because of classification.
Richardson asserted that "classification itself is the highest
function of the librarian's work, calling into play every faculty and every attainment of knowledge--the acme of bibliothecal work" and Sayers[136] considered this an apt description.
Bliss also had no doubts:

> That classification is indispensable to library serv-
> ice is a principle not merely advocated but es-

> poused by the profession of librarians. Their pro-
> fessional happiness, self-respect, reputation, and
> success depend on the virtue, fitness, orderliness,
> and efficiency of their spouse.... If those systems
> were less unsatisfactory, librarians would be more
> respected for this part of their service.
>
> Now the ... need for better classification in librar-
> ies is well recognized. The reputation of profes-
> sional librarianship is involved. [137]

Bliss held great faith in the social and educational po-
tency of classification, as Kelley noted in her review of The
Organization of Knowledge in Libraries:

> The author sees the orderly arrangement of books
> upon the shelves of libraries as contributing to the
> production of a greater harmony and unity in social
> organization. Just as a well-ordered society de-
> pends upon reasonable and well-ordered purposes
> (often the product derived from hard-earned knowl-
> edge), so the transmission of this knowledge through
> the increased availability of the subject matter in
> books becomes of great importance. Thus, the
> nearer the actual arrangement of books conforms to
> the accepted theories and practices of social organ-
> ization, the more effective the distribution of their
> contents. By extending such a service, librarian-
> ship definitely becomes educational in its motives
> and strengthens its position as an educational
> force. [138]

Palmer took a similar view in discussing the rise of
the Decimal Classification:

> The point being made here is the importance of li-
> brary classification in the intellectual life of the
> community, in so far as a change in the social or-
> der was reflected in a need for a new technique in
> organizing libraries. The demonstration of our
> closeness to the center of things is good for our
> professional ego, even if nothing else is to be
> gained from a contemplation of it. [139]

Palmer located in classification the focus of all librarianship:

Classification technique and theory ... pervade the whole work of the librarian....

Classification is a foundation study for librarians.

All the techniques, adopted and developed, of librarianship derive ultimately from the need for economy in the widest sense.... In this sense classification may even be said to be at the heart of library economy. [140]

Metcalfe[141] somewhat ironically commented that librarians might tend to confuse knowledge and book classification because it perhaps fed their educational conceit.

A questionnaire hypothesis refers to this claimed status-enhancement by library classification: "Evidence of a system of library classification enhances the prestige and status of the library profession among the users of the library." (III:2)

* * * * *

The second major part of this study consists of the analysis of the questionnaire. The analysis aims to determine which hypotheses derived from and/or tested against the documentary analysis have been supported--and to what extent--by the opinions of the respondents. It is hoped, too, that volunteered comments may add depth or nuance to topics hitherto discussed.

Notes

1. Maurice F. Tauber, "The Shelflisting Section of the Library of Congress: A Report on Functions, Organization, and Problems Made at the Request of the Librarian of Congress, July, 1957," p. I-7, VI-13, 14, 15. (Typewritten)

2. John Metcalfe, Information Indexing and Subject Cataloging: Alphabetical, Classified, Coordinate, Mechanical (New York: Scarecrow Press, 1957), p. 105, quoted ibid., p. VI-20.

3. Fremont Rider, Rider's International Classification for the Arrangement of Books on the Shelves of General

Libraries (prelim. ed.; Middletown, Conn.: The Author, 1961), p. xvi.

4. Julia C. Pettee, Subject Headings: The History and Theory of the Alphabetical Subject Approach to Books (New York: Wilson, 1946).

5. Dorothy May Norris, A History of Cataloguing and Cataloguing Methods, 1100-1850; with an Introductory Survey of Ancient Times (London: Grafton, 1939), p. 225-26, 228.

6. Ibid., p. 205-06.

7. Ibid., p. 179.

8. Quoted ibid., p. 157-58; and in Felix Reichmann, "The Catalog in European Libraries," in Chicago, University, Graduate Library School, Library Conference, Library Catalogs: Changing Dimensions, ed. by Ruth French Strout (Chicago: University of Chicago Press, 1964), p. 39.

9. J. N. L. Myres, "The Bodleian Library: Organization, Administration, Functions," Library World, LXII (April, 1961), 229, quoted in Reichmann, "The Catalog in European Libraries," p. 39.

10. Reichmann, "The Catalog in European Libraries," p. 42-43.

11. Georg Schneider, Theory and History of Bibliography, tr. by Ralph R. Shaw (New York: Scarecrow Press, 1961), p. 22, 35, 172, 185, 195.

12. Paul S. Dunkin, Cataloging U.S.A. (Chicago: American Library Assn., 1969), p. 139.

13. Leonard M. Jolley, The Principles of Cataloguing (New York: Philosophical Library, 1961), p. 108.

14. Henry Evelyn Bliss, The Organization of Knowledge and the System of the Sciences (New York: Holt, 1929); The Organization of Knowledge in Libraries; and the Subject-Approach to Books (2d ed., rev. and partly rewritten; New York: Wilson, 1939).

15. Charles Ammi Cutter, Expansive Classification: Part
    I: The First Six Classifications (Boston: The Au-
    thor, 1891-93), p. 5.

16. Leo E. LaMontagne, American Library Classification,
    with Special Reference to the Library of Congress
    (Hamden, Conn.: Shoe String Press, 1961), p. 210.

17. W. C. Berwick Sayers, An Introduction to Library Clas-
    sification, Theoretical, Historical and Practical, with
    Readings, Exercises and Examination Papers (7th ed.;
    London: Grafton, 1946), p. 95-96.

18. A. Broadfield, The Philosophy of Classification (London:
    Grafton, 1946), p. 41-68.

19. Bliss, The Organization of Knowledge in Libraries, p.
    233, 236, 321.

20. Melvil Dewey, "Catalogues and Cataloguing," in U. S.,
    Bureau of Education, Public Libraries in the United
    States of America; Their History, Condition, and
    Management; Special Report: Part I (Washington:
    Govt. Print. Off., 1876), p. 625.

21. Sayers, An Introduction to Library Classification, p.
    129-30.

22. Bliss, The Organization of Knowledge in Libraries, p.
    227-28.

23. Metcalfe, Information Indexing and Subject Cataloging,
    p. 150.

24. Bernard Ira Palmer, Itself an Education: Six Lectures
    on Classification (London: Library Assn., 1962),
    p. 47-48.

25. Thelma Eaton, Cataloging and Classification: An Intro-
    ductory Manual (4th ed.; Ann Arbor, Mich.: Ed-
    wards Brothers, 1967), p. 63.

26. Eaton, "Epitaph to a Dead Classification," in her Clas-
    sification in Theory and Practice: A Collection of
    Papers (Champaign, Ill.: Illini Union Bookstore,
    1957), p. 62, 59.

27. LaMontagne, American Library Classification, p. 345, 347.

28. Benjamin A. Custer, "Editor's Introduction," Dewey Decimal Classification and Relative Index (2 vols., 17th ed.; Lake Placid Club, N.Y.: Forest Press, 1965), I, 11-12.

29. Broadfield, The Philosophy of Classification, p. 9-11, 19, 22, etc.

30. Metcalfe, Information Indexing and Subject Cataloging, p. 38-40, 42.

31. Ernest Cushing Richardson, Classification, Theoretical and Practical; Together with an Appendix Containing an Essay towards a Bibliographical History of Systems of Classification (3d ed.; New York: Wilson, 1930), p. v.

32. Ibid., p. vi.

33. Ibid., p. 6-7, 14-15.

34. Broadfield, The Philosophy of Classification, p. 2-3, 6-7, 42-48, etc.

35. Cutter, "Library Catalogues," in U.S., Bureau of Education, Public Libraries in the United States of America, p. 529.

36. Sayers, An Introduction to Library Classification, p. ix, xix-xx, xxii, 2.

37. Ibid., p. 15-17.

38. Sayers, Canons of Classification Applied to "The Subject," "The Expansive," "The Decimal" and "The Library of Congress" Classifications (White Plains, N.Y.: Wilson, 1916), p. 42.

39. Ibid., p. 67-68.

40. Ibid., p. 28-29.

41. Bliss, The Organization of Knowledge and the System of the Sciences, p. 108.

42. Bliss, A System of Bibliographic Classification (2d ed. rev.; New York: Wilson, 1936), p. vii.

43. Bliss, The Organization of Knowledge in Libraries, p. 7-8.

44. Ibid., p. 331.

45. Grace Osgood Kelley, Review of The Organization of Knowledge in Libraries; and the Subject-Approach to Books, by Henry Evelyn Bliss, Library Quarterly, IV (December, 1934), 666.

46. S. R. Ranganathan, Elements of Library Classification (3d ed.; New York: Asia Publishing House, 1962), p. 16.

47. Ibid., p. 8.

48. Ranganathan, "Colon Classification and Its Approach to Documentation," in Chicago, University, Graduate Library School, Library Conference, Bibliographic Organization; Papers Presented before the Fifteenth Annual Conference of the Graduate Library School, July 24-29, 1950, ed. by Jesse H. Shera and Margaret E. Egan (Chicago: University of Chicago Press, 1951), p. 101.

49. R. Moss, "Categories and Relations: Origins of Two Classification Theories," American Documentation, XV (October, 1964), 296-301.

50. Metcalfe, Information Indexing and Subject Cataloging, p. 285-86.

51. Bliss, The Organization of Knowledge and the System of the Sciences, p. 113.

52. F. B. Perkins and Jacob Schwartz, "The Dui-Decimal Classification and the 'Relativ Index,' " Library

Journal, XI (February, 1886), 37-43.

53. Dewey, "The Decimal Classification, a Reply to the
     'Duet,' " Library Journal, XI (April, 1886), 100-06;
     Cutter, "Close Classification, with Special Reference
     to Messrs. Perkins, Schwartz, and Dewey," Library
     Journal, XI (July, 1886), 180.

54. Cutter, "Close Classification," p. 180.

55. Perkins and Schwartz, "The Dui-Decimal Classification
     and the 'Relativ Index,' " p. 38.

56. Cutter, "Close Classification," p. 182-83.

57. Ibid., p. 183.

58. Cutter, "Classification on the Shelves; with Some Ac-
     count of the New Scheme Prepared for the Boston
     Athenaeum," Library Journal, IV (July-August,
     1879), 240-41.

59. Cutter, Expansive Classification, p. 1, 15.

60. Schneider, Theory and History of Bibliography, p. 230.

61. Custer, "Editor's Introduction," p. 38.

62. Ranganathan, "Preface to Edition 6," Colon Classifica-
     tion (6th ed., reprinted with amendments; New York:
     Asia Publishing House, 1963), p. 10.

63. Palmer, Itself an Education, p. 30-34.

64. Bliss, The Organization of Knowledge in Libraries, p.
     78, 155.

65. Ernest A. Savage, A Manual of Book Classification and
     Display for Public Libraries (London: Allen and
     Unwin, 1946).

66. Ruth Rutzen, "Shelving for Readers," Library Journal,
     LXXVII (March 15, 1952), 478-82; Detroit Public Li-
     brary, Home Reading Services, The Reader Interest
     Classification in the Detroit Public Library (Detroit,
     1955) (Pamphlet); Dunkin, Cataloging U.S.A., p. 124-
     26.

67. Custer, "Editor's Introduction," p. 6.

68. C.D. Needham, Organizing Knowledge in Libraries: An Introduction to Classification and Cataloguing (London: Deutsch, 1964), p. 150.

69. Arthur E. Bostwick, The American Public Library (4th ed., rev. and enl.; New York: Appleton, 1929), p. 193.

70. Eaton, Cataloging and Classification, p. 129.

71. Bliss, The Organization of Knowledge in Libraries, p. 132.

72. Savage, Manual of Book Classification and Display for Public Libraries, p. 130-32.

73. Dunkin, Cataloging U.S.A., p. 120.

74. Custer, "Editor's Introduction," p. 31-32.

75. Ranganathan, Elements of Library Classification, p. 150, 152-53.

76. Kelley, The Classification of Books: An Inquiry into Its Usefulness to the Reader (New York: Wilson, 1937).

77. Metcalfe, Information Indexing and Subject Cataloging, p. 98.

78. Ibid., p. 294.

79. Ibid., p. 132-35, etc.

80. Rider, Rider's International Classification, p. xi-xiv.

81. Needham, Organizing Knowledge in Libraries, p. 121.

82. Marie Louise Prevost, Review of The Classification of Books, by Grace Osgood Kelley, Library Journal, LXIII (January 15, 1938), 69.

83. Sayers, An Introduction to Library Classification, p. 17;

Bliss, The Organization of Knowledge in Libraries, p. 91, 94, 157, 323-25.

84.   Metcalfe, Information Indexing and Subject Cataloging, p. 225.

85.   Cutter, "Close Classification," p. 182.

86.   Sayers, Canons of Classification, p. 42.

87.   Broadfield, The Philosophy of Classification, p. 46, 48.

88.   Ibid., p. 22.

89.   Sayers, Canons of Classification, p. 31.

90.   Bliss, The Organization of Knowledge in Libraries, p. 7.

91.   Eric J. Coates, Subject Catalogues: Headings and Structure (London: Library Assn., 1960), p. 82.

92.   Pettee, Subject Headings, p. 59.

93.   Jolley, The Principles of Cataloguing, p. 123.

94.   Pettee, Subject Headings, p. 58-59.

95.   Bliss, The Organization of Knowledge in Libraries, p. 324.

96.   Margaret Mann, Introduction to Cataloging and the Classification of Books (2d ed.; Chicago: American Library Assn., 1943), p. 138.

97.   Cutter, Rules for a Dictionary Catalog (4th ed., rewritten; Washington: Govt. Print. Off., 1904), p. 66-80, especially p. 79.

98.   Ranganathan, Theory of Library Catalogue (Madras: Madras Library Assn., 1938), p. 77-198.

99.   Coates, Subject Catalogues, p. 119-31.

100. Metcalfe, Information Indexing and Subject Cataloging, p. 154.

101. Bliss, The Organization of Knowledge in Libraries, p.
      157.

102. Raynard Swank, "Subject Catalogs, Classifications, or
      Bibliographies? A Review of Critical Discussions,
      1876-1942," Library Quarterly, XIV (October, 1944),
      316-32; "Organization of Library Materials for Re-
      search in English Literature," ibid., XV (January,
      1945), 49-74.

103. Reichmann, "The Catalog in European Libraries," p.
      56.

104. Bliss, The Organization of Knowledge in Libraries, p.
      154.

105. Kelley, "The Classification of Books in Retrospect and
      in Prospect: A Tool and a Discipline," in Chicago,
      University, Graduate Library School, Library Insti-
      tute, The Acquisition and Cataloging of Books; Pa-
      pers Presented before the Library Institute at the
      University of Chicago, July 29 to August 9, 1940,
      ed. by William M. Randall (Chicago: University of
      Chicago Press, 1940), p. 163-86.

106. Palmer, Itself an Education, p. 11.

107. Ibid., p. 36.

108. Horace Kephart, "Classification," in U.S., Bureau of
      Education, Report of the Commissioner for Education
      for 1892-93 (2 vols.; Washington: Govt. Print. Off.,
      1895), II, 862, 892.

109. Ranganathan, Elements of Library Classification, p.
      146.

110. Kephart, "Classification," p. 892.

111. D.J. Foskett, Classification and Indexing in the Social
      Sciences (London: Butterworths, 1963), p. 75, 148-
      49.

112. Bliss, The Organization of Knowledge and the System of
      the Sciences, p. 104.

113. Bliss, A System of Bibliographic Classification, p. 10.

114. Bliss, The Organization of Knowledge in Libraries, p.
      212.

115. Rider, "Old Classifications--and the Excuse for New
      Ones," Library Journal, XXXV (September, 1910),
      387-96.

116. Sayers, Canons of Classification, p. 39-40.

117. Sayers, An Introduction to Library Classification, p.
      55.

118. Palmer, Itself an Education, p. 41-42.

119. Ibid., p. 37.

120. Ibid., p. 43-44.

121. Sayers, An Introduction to Library Classification, p.
      62.

122. Bliss, A System of Bibliographic Classification, p. 16.

123. Metcalfe, Subject Classifying and Indexing of Libraries
      and Literature (New York: Scarecrow Press, 1959),
      p. 115.

124. Dunkin, Cataloging U.S.A., p. 107.

125. Ranganathan, Elements of Library Classification, p.
      153.

126. Metcalfe, Information Indexing and Subject Cataloging,
      p. 114, 243.

127. Needham, Organizing Knowledge in Libraries, p. 84,
      86, 123.

128. Savage, A Manual of Book Classification and Display
      for Public Libraries, p. 114.

129. Edwin Wiley, "Some Sidelights on Classification," Li-
      brary Journal, XLIV (June, 1919), 361-62.

130. Bostwick, The American Public Library, p. 183, 189.

131. Palmer, Itself an Education, p. 13.

132. Herner, "A Pilot Study of the Use of the Stacks of the
      Library of Congress," Washington: Herner, 1960.
      (Typewritten.)

133. Annette L. Hoage, "Patron Use of the L.C. Classifica-
      tion," Library Resources and Technical Services,
      VI (Summer, 1962), 248.

134. Palmer, Itself an Education, p. 16-18, 25.

135. Custer, "Editor's Introduction," p. 5.

136. Richardson, Classification, p. 42; Sayers, An Introduc-
      tion to Library Classification, p. 165.

137. Bliss, The Organization of Knowledge in Libraries, p.
      310; The Organization of Knowledge and the System
      of the Sciences, p. 412.

138. Kelley, Review of The Organization of Knowledge in Li-
      braries, p. 666.

139. Palmer, Itself an Education, p. 10.

140. Ibid., p. 58, 60, 64.

141. Metcalfe, Information Indexing and Subject Cataloging,
      p. 64.

PART II

QUESTIONNAIRE ANALYSIS

Chapter IX

SELECTION AND CHARACTERISTICS
OF RESPONDENTS (I, II)

As described in Chapter Two, the opinion questionnaire was sent to a group of authorities on library classification and reader services representing practitioners in various
types and sizes of libraries throughout the United States and
Canada, as well as teachers of classification and reader
services in the accredited American and Canadian library
schools.

Respondents were selected for knowledgeability and
prominence as manifested by their appearance in the professional literature, reputation among librarians, and inclusion
in standard library directories. The choice was determined
by the investigator in accordance with his own knowledge and
in consultation with his research advisors and other experts. Chief printed sources for names were, for practitioners, the A. L. A. Membership Directory, Who's Who in Library Service, American Library Directory, and, for teachers, "Directory of the Association of American Library
Schools."[1]

The survey aimed for at least one hundred analyzable
responses indicating to what extent a selected group of current practitioners and teachers--the doers and influencers--
accepted the various statements of opinion distilled in the
documentary analysis and suggesting many of this study's hypotheses.

The method of selection was related to--but not statistically identical with--that of stratified random sampling as
employed in parametric statistical estimation. The responses,
as will be shown, may be defined by strata or respondent
characteristics, but any element of "random" selection was
not intended to be equated with "randomness" as applied in
sampling theory for the purpose of statistical inference in its
strict sense, i.e., that random sampling process by which
each member of a population has an equal or known chance

230

of being included in the sample.   As a survey, rather than
a parametric statistical sampling, the analysis of responses
aimed to determine patterns of opinion which seemed to represent fairly the group of respondents qua group.   Such a
survey could, indeed, be considered a "pilot project" whose
findings might suggest further investigation into particular
problems and the possible application to those problems of
parametric statistical sampling procedures.

        In conjunction with the above methods, these further
selection factors were considered:

        (1) Because of a working hypothesis that the problems
of the direct shelf approach were of critical concern in large
academic or research collections, it was decided to emphasize such collections in choosing respondent practitioners.

        (2) Although the larger academic and research librar-
ies were to be emphasized, it was considered important to
have also a representation--not necessarily in strict numerical proportion--of other types of libraries: public, special,
and school and public library systems.

        (3) Although location of respondents was not expected
to be statistically significant, it was thought prudent to obtain
a wide geographical distribution so as to forestall geographical bias, e.g., a majority of responses from the Eastern
Seaboard.   Accordingly, questionnaires were sent to every
state and to the provinces of Quebec and Ontario.

        (4) Because a significant difference might arise from
the respondents' professional function and specialization, i.e.,
practitioner or teacher in the technical or reader services,
questionnaires were sent whenever possible to both technical
services and reader services practitioners and teachers in
the same library or library school.

        (5) Questionnaires were sent to every accredited li-
brary school.   For each school, a questionnaire was sent to
at least one teacher of the reader services and one of the
technical services.

        (6) Since the administrator might represent a distinct
attitude, questionnaires were sent to heads of libraries and
of library schools.

        A total of 244 questionnaires were mailed in the spring

of 1969. Though 152 analyzable responses resulted, there
were 168 total returns of which 16 either declined to answer
the questionnaire or delegated the responsibility.

The 152 analyzable responses represented a slightly
larger number of individual respondents because some of the
returns consolidated the opinions of various individuals--evi-
dently to obtain "specialist" opinion on certain statements.
(No attempt was made to adjust for such "group" responses
in tallying.)

All these selection factors combined to contribute an
element of "stratified randomness" when choosing teachers
or practitioners in the technical and reader services as listed
in the standard directories and as known to the investigator
and his advisors.

In addition to the analysis of responses for each
statement in terms of apparent patterns of opinion as evidenced by the frequency distribution of those responses, it
was decided, in consultation with a statistical expert, to apply non-parametric tests for correlation and consistency--
chiefly the chi-square (X^2) test and that for the determination of the coefficient of contingency (C). As will be indicated below in the analysis of Sections III, IV, and V of the
questionnaire, the purpose of the tests was to determine to
what extent certain characteristics of the respondents, e.g.,
their professional functions, could be shown to be statistically related to their responses to the individual statements,
as well as to all the statements of each section considered
in series. (The questionnaire is reproduced in the Appendix.)

Respondent Characteristics: Location and
Professional Function (I:1, 2)

Geographically, the 152 respondents represented 124
institutions in 85 cities in 43 states, the District of Columbia, and the provinces of Quebec and Ontario. There were
no responses from the following 7 states: Alabama, Alaska,
Arkansas, Mississippi, South Dakota, Virginia, and West
Virginia. (These 7 states represented approximately 8 percent of total United States population per the 1960 census.)

As indicated by the following table, 57 percent of total respondents were practitioners, 28 percent teachers, and

TABLE 1

RESPONDENTS BY PROFESSIONAL FUNCTION (I:1, 2)

Professional Function	Number	Percentage
Practitioner		
Technical services	59	38.5
Reader services	24	16.5
Both	3	2.0
Total practitioners	86	57.0
Teacher		
Technical services	24	16.2
Reader services	19	11.8
Total teachers	43	28.0
Administrator		
Library[a]	16	10.4
Library school	7	4.6
Total administrators	23	15.0
Total respondents	152	100.0

[a]Library administrators are considered "practitioners" in categorizing total responses to questionnaire statements. See Tables 12, 17, 23.

15 percent administrators. Practitioner respondents in the technical services were more than two-and-a-half times as numerous as those in the reader services; teacher respondents in the technical services were about one-and-a-third times as numerous as those in the reader services; and administrator respondents from libraries were about two-and-a-third times as numerous as those from library schools. (In this and all other tables, individual percentage figures have been rounded off to the nearest tenth of one percent, so that the grand total of individual percentages will not necessarily equal 100.0 percent.)

Respondent Characteristics:
Institutional Type (I:2, II:1)

Since questionnaires were sent to personnel in both the

technical and the reader services in the same institution, the
number of respondents was expected to exceed the number of
institutions. Analysis of the responses to Sections III, IV,
and V of the questionnaire is generally in terms of the number of responses, i.e., of individual respondents, not of the
institutions represented. This chapter, however, now considers the characteristics of institution-respondents as reported in Sections I and II of the questionnaire. The following Table 2 summarizes data for individual respondents in
relation to the institutions they represent. Thus, library
schools, making up about 27 percent of respondent institutions, accounted for about 33 percent of all responses; and
libraries and library systems, making up about 73 percent of
respondent institutions, accounted for about 67 percent of all
responses.

TABLE 2

RESPONDENTS BY TYPE OF INSTITUTION (I:2, II:1)

Institution Type	Institutions		Respondents	
	No.	%	No.	%
Library school	33	26.6	50	32.9
College library	8	6.5	9	5.9
University library	43	34.7	48	31.6
Special library	11	8.8	15	9.8
Public library	25	20.1	26	16.5
Library system center	4	3.2	4	2.4
Total non-school	91	73.4	102	67.1
Total	124	100.0	152	100.0

"Library system center" respondents (hereafter usually referred to in tables as "System") represented technical
services processing centers serving a group of libraries. Of
the 4 respondent systems, 2 served public libraries, 1 served
public school libraries, and 1 served both. (Table 3 indicates that these system centers serviced libraries whose total holdings attained a median size of over one and-a-half
million volumes.) Though the number of respondent systems
was small, that of the subsumed libraries was considerable:

one public library system reported 53 autonomous member libraries. The inclusion of such systems in the survey at least gave some representation to the important category of the school library, at any rate from the point of view of the technical services. A further effort to obtain representation for school libraries and children's collections was made by sending five questionnaires to teachers of children's literature and allied subjects in the accredited library schools. Unfortunately, only one was returned. However, it is not unlikely that some teacher respondents, even if not children's literature specialists, either taught such a course or included some aspect of it in their more general courses. A similar conjecture would be that some of the public library practitioners in the reader services had, at least as part of their responsibility, some contact with the children's or young adult collections.

Table 2 shows that public libraries and university libraries contributed about 3.6 and 3.1 percent less, respectively, of all responses than their proportional membership in the total number of institutions. This difference does not seem of major significance, and probably occurs because, per institution, more questionnaires were sent to library schools than to non-school respondents. Thus, of the 244 questionnaires mailed, analyzable responses from library schools were 50 out of 80, or 62.5 percent, and from non-school respondents 102 out of 164, or 62.2 percent.

In other words, libraries showed no less interest, proportionately, than did library schools. This is noteworthy since practitioners would usually seem more pressed for time to respond to non-official inquiries. It may be presumed that the problem of direct access and browsing was of considerable interest to practicing librarians.

There is no intention, as indicated above, to justify the exact "mix" of respondents as between teachers and practitioners, and as among those representing the technical services, the reader services, and administration. The survey was not designed as the equivalent of a random sampling for the purposes of statistical inference to population parameters. The proportions, however, appear not unreasonable in terms of a selection of knowledgeable practitioners, teachers, and administrators from various types of institutions throughout the country. Possible statistical significance of the "mix" will be discussed below in analyzing the responses to Sections III, IV, and V of the questionnaire--i.e., is there evidence of a statistically significant relationship between the type of respondent and the way he reacted to the given statements?

Respondent Library Characteristics:
Type and Size (II:1, 2)

The following Table 3 gives size statistics for the 91 libraries and system centers representing 102 responses. Libraries of library school respondents are excluded as such, but most library school libraries are encompassed in the statistics for the university library system within which the library school library is usually a unit. Although it was anticipated that respondent libraries would be generally of considerable size because of this study's emphasis on large academic and research library situations, the measures of central tendency seemed, nevertheless, surprisingly big. Although the smallest library respondent had only 50, 000 volumes, the median size for its type (university library) was well over a million volumes, and the median size for all libraries was at least one million. These figures suggest a continuing increase in American library size and thus raise at least two basic questions, one of a general import and one more specifically related to this study. The former relates to the desirability of huge collections, of whose problems Rider,[2] for one, had warned thirty years before. Is it possible to control such growth through measures like cooperative acquisition policies? These concerns persist even if, as with most university collections, the reported number of volumes combines a large number of separate facilities.

The second question is more particularly related to this study. After a library has reached the size of a million volumes, can there be any significant change of attitude towards the problems of open-shelf access and browsability as the collection size becomes even larger? Once the one-million mark is reached, do incremental increases bring any significantly new problems? No doubt, the practical problems of storage and spatial organization become more difficult, but might not the limit of theoretical difficulties have already been reached? Such questions relating to collection size will be touched on during the analysis of Sections III, IV, and V of the questionnaire.

Almost no respondent library was able--or chose--to give reliable statistics for number of titles rather than of volumes. Thus, there was not adequate information to jus-

TABLE 3

SUMMARY OF LIBRARIES AND THEIR RESPONDENTS BY TYPE AND SIZE OF LIBRARY (II:1, 2)

(Add 000 Volumes)

Unit	Type of Library					
	College	University	Special	Public	System	Total
No. respondent institutions	8	43	11	25	4	91
No. responses	9	48	15	26	4	102
Total volumes	3,379	72,813	23,748	22,691	7,261	129,892
Mean no. volumes	422	1,693	2,159	908	1,815	1,427
Median no. volumes	285	1,300	750	600	1,512	1,000
Smallest no. volumes	54	50	78	60	1,000	50
Largest no. volumes	1,000	5,300	13,800	3,029	3,236	13,800

tify any tabulation of title data as requested in II:2.   This
raises the question: are statistics for number of titles desirable?   Evidently, most respondent libraries thought not.
To what extent, however, would the lack of such data distort
the qualitative estimate of a collection?   All that could be
deduced from the estimates of the number of titles reported
was the expected fact that public libraries held many more
multiple copies than academic libraries.

Respondent Library Characteristics:
Subject Areas Collected (II:3)

Because many statements in library literature assume
particular problems for particular subject collections, and
because responses to the statements in Sections III, IV, and
V might be analyzable in terms of respondents' collection interests, Question II:3 sought information on the subject areas
to which respondent libraries gave major acquisition attention.
Accepted broad categories of subject interest were listed for
check-off, and space was provided for specifying any other
discipline or subject area.   As shown in the following Tables
4 and 5, which summarize data from 87 respondent libraries, the great majority of the libraries reported collecting
in multiple subject areas.

Thus, 5 out of 7 college libraries, 36 out of 42 university libraries, 5 out of 11 special libraries, 13 out of
24 public libraries, and all 3 respondent systems devoted major collecting attention to at least 3 subject categories.

It was expected that one-half of the public libraries
did not devote major collecting attention to the physical sciences.   More surprising was that almost one-half of the
"special" libraries checked all major subject categories.
This might be because "special libraries" included such
broadly based research collections as those of the Library
of Congress and of the New York Public Library, as well as
of more specifically oriented libraries like the Newberry.
The adjective "special" was, indeed, self-applied.

These data suggest that: (1) most libraries considered themselves as devoting major attention to the majority
of standard collection categories; and (2) most libraries
faced, therefore, along with the problem of increasing size,
that of heterogeneous collections.

TABLE 4

COLLECTION INTERESTS BY TYPE OF LIBRARY (II:3)

Type	No. Respondents	Subject Category			
		Humanities	Social Sciences	Physical Sciences	Special
College	7	5	5	6	4
University	42	39	39	37	23
Special	11	5	6	6	9
Public	24	17	18	12	13
System	3	3	3	3	--
Total	87	69	71	64	49

TABLE 5

NUMBER OF SUBJECT CATEGORIES COLLECTED BY VARIOUS TYPES OF LIBRARIES (II:3)

Type	No. Respondents	No. of Subject Categories			
		One	Two	Three	Four
College	7	1	1	2	3
University	42	3	3	15	21
Special	11	4	2	2	3
Public	24	7	4	7	6
System	3	--	--	3	--
Total	87	15	10	29	33

During the questionnaire analysis, it thus became evident that there was little likelihood of establishing any significant relationship between responses from most libraries and their types of subject collections, except possibly in such a clear-cut case as that of a closed-stacks rare book library.

It appears that most respondent libraries must view the problems of open-shelf access and of browsability within the frame of general collections of heterogeneous subjects--though most libraries could also have particular subject strengths. Most respondent libraries must thus concern themselves with available general systems of bibliographic and bibliothecal organization which have been designed to accommodate a wide range of subjects. They must resolve their problems through the medium of general classification schemes and cataloging codes. As discussed above in the chapter on classification, such general schemes invariably entail bibliothecal compromises and uneven development of subject areas.

Respondent Library Characteristics:
Type of Public Catalog (II:4)

Because the type of public catalog might affect or reflect respondent attitudes towards open-shelf access and browsing, information was sought on the relative frequency of the dictionary, divided, classed, or other type of public catalog in respondent libraries. (No distinction, however, was made between the card catalog and the increasingly common book-form catalog.) The following Table 6 summarizes this information. As generally assumed, the dictionary catalog was the norm for most respondent libraries, but the divided catalog occupied a significant position, apparently increasing, in university and special libraries. About 64.4 percent of respondent libraries employed the dictionary catalog exclusively and about 24.4 percent the divided catalog exclusively. Only three libraries, or about 3.3 percent of the total, employed the classed catalog. There were seven libraries using the divided catalog along with a dictionary catalog. Thus, 29 libraries, or about 32.1 percent of the total, employed the divided catalog at least in part. As anticipated, most divided catalogs were reported by university libraries. One public library reported a divided book-form catalog, a type which may be expected to increase.

Of the seven institutions reporting both dictionary and

TABLE 6

TYPE OF PUBLIC CATALOG USED BY VARIOUS TYPES OF LIBRARIES (II:4)

Library Type	Type of Public Catalog Used									
	Dictionary		Divided		Dictionary & Divided		Classed		Total	
	No.	%	No.	%	No.	%	No.	%	No.	%
College	7	7.8	1	1.1	--	--	--	--	8	8.8
University	24	26.7	16	17.8	2	2.2	1	1.1	43	47.8
Special	4	4.4	3	3.3	2	2.2	2	2.2	11	12.2
Public	22	24.4	2	2.2	1	1.1	--	--	25	27.8
System	1	1.1	--	--	2	2.2	--	--	3	3.3
Total	58	64.4	22	24.4	7	7.7	3	3.3	90	100.0

242 Access to Library Collections

divided catalogs, two special libraries and one university library reported they had changed to the divided catalog for new acquisitions while maintaining a retrospective dictionary catalog. The remaining four reported the use of both types by at least some library unit, e.g., one university library used a dictionary catalog for the undergraduate collection but a divided catalog for the graduate.

An evident trend to the divided catalog, at least among university libraries, might be inferred from the comments of three university libraries which now have dictionary catalogs; two stated they would be changing to the divided catalog, and one that "We are currently discussing the possibility (desirability?) of changing to a divided catalog." One public library, however, commented that it had abandoned an experiment with a divided catalog. The reasons for the university libraries' change to the divided catalog were not detailed, though a general assumption is that the divided catalog makes subject searches easier than in large complicated dictionary card catalogs.

American libraries, as confirmed by Table 6, do not favor classed catalogs--a sometimes prescribed substitute for shelf classification. Perhaps the divided catalog, which usually segregates subject from author and title entries, is an expedient for reducing some of the limitations of subject shelf search: missing books, linearity of shelf classification, possibly inconvenient physical facilities. Such inference is, of course, conjectural.

Respondent Library Characteristics:
Classification System Used (II:5)

As shown by the following Table 7, the Library of Congress Classification (LC) was predominant in academic libraries; five of the eight respondent college libraries and 35 of the 43 respondent university libraries employed it alone or in combination with other schemes. Dewey Decimal Classification (DC) maintained its leading position among public libraries, 22 of 25 respondent public libraries employing it as their only scheme.

TABLE 7

CLASSIFICATION SYSTEMS USED BY VARIOUS
TYPES OF LIBRARIES (II: 5)

Library Type	Classification Type				
	DC	LC	Other	LC & Other	Total
College	3	5	--	--	8
University	7	32	1	3	43
Special	--	4	4	3	11
Public	22	2	--	1	25
System	4	--	--	--	4
Total	36	43	5	7	91

The trend among academic and research libraries to change to LC, usually from DC, was confirmed by respondents. Comments from 10 of the 43 respondent university libraries indicated a change from DC to LC since 1964. A college library reported a recent change to LC from DC, and two special libraries indicated a change to LC--one from DC and one from a local scheme. A public library reported a change from modified to regular LC.

Of the three university libraries reporting use of LC along with other schemes, one was also using the U.S. Superintendent of Documents Classification (SDC) and the other two were retaining older local schemes, presumably for special subject areas. A public library, generally employing DC, used LC only for two special subject areas. LC was used together with the Universal Decimal Classification (UDC) by a special library, and together with the National Library of Medicine Classification (NLM) by two other special libraries. Exclusive use of schemes other than LC or DC was reported by four special libraries, viz., the schemes of Billings, Cutter, UDC, and the Harvard Business School.

These statistics seem to have two major implications for this study. First, as previously indicated, a working hypothesis of this study is that the problems of direct access and browsability are particularly critical for academic and research libraries, especially those with large or complex collections. If the classification scheme used by such librar-

ies, as amply evidenced in the preceding chapter, is inextrica-
bly joined with these problems, then the approach to such
problems must be, because of its increasingly predominant
position, through the medium almost exclusively of LC. To
what extent, however, does LC facilitate direct access and
browsability? Can this one scheme provide the answer to
these often vexing problems? Various opinions on the comparative merits of LC, DC, and other schemes have been detailed in earlier chapters and, as noted, a statement on the
"browsability" of LC is included in the questionnaire. The
responses to that statement will be discussed later.

A second major implication (or problem) suggested by
Table 7 concerns the library which, because of change to LC,
usually has some part of its collection classified by a previous scheme, ordinarily DC. The extent of such dual-classified collections would, of course, be determined by the reclassification policy of the library, a matter to be considered
in the next section of this chapter. Here, however, it may
be noted that respondents' comments on the type of classification used indicated that all of those libraries which had
changed to LC still had some portion of their holdings classified by the previous scheme. (There was even one university library which after more than 20 years had "just about"
completed its reclassification!) Such a situation must affect
the browsability of the collection. The problem will no doubt
intensify as the trend to LC continues.

Respondent Library Characteristics:
Reclassification Policy (II:6)

Even though the trend to LC from DC involves usually
some measure of reclassification, the following Table 8 indicates that reclassification projects, especially frequent among
university libraries, were not thought to handicap the reader
seriously. Approximately one-fourth of respondent college
libraries have undertaken reclassification to some extent; almost one-half of respondent university libraries; about one-
third of respondent special libraries; and about one-fourth of
respondent public libraries. Two university libraries reported they were considering reclassification. About one-
fourth of the reclassifying university libraries reported that
their readers had been handicapped by the reclassification;
one-third of the special libraries; and one-fourth of the public libraries.

TABLE 8

RECLASSIFICATION SUMMARY (II:6)

Library Type	No. Institutions	No. Reclassifying	No. Reporting "Readers Handicapped"
College	8	2	--
University	43	19	5
Special	11	3	1
Public	25	4	1
System	4	--	--
Total	91	28	7

Nevertheless, the comments did not indicate that the handicaps made for a critical problem. Among the five universities reporting that their readers had been handicapped, one commented, "The usual relocation problems," and another, changing from Cutter to LC, explained that "LC and Cutter are very alike in some areas and quite different in others. Great care must be taken in differentiating between the two." Perhaps a reason for this reported lack of inconvenience to the reader was the extent of the reclassification. Most respondent libraries undertaking reclassification implied that it was only partial or selective. A further conjecture might be that readers are less handicapped by the existence of dual-classified collections than by the possible confusion entailed by the process of reclassifying.

Of the four public libraries reporting reclassification, only one was changing from non-LC to LC. The other three were changing, respectively, from modified to regular LC; from 16 DC to 17 DC; and, for its art department, from a local scheme to DC. The only public library which reported its readers handicapped was changing from modified to regular LC, but reclassification was not the sole factor: "Physical reorganization of subject departments, changing to LC and converting from a card to book catalog all took place at the same time."

Some college and university respondents commented that, although reclassification did not handicap the reader, the presence of differently classified parts of the collection resulted in some "normal confusion." (Such confusion, actually, would stem from non-reclassification.) It does not seem, from the reclassification policies reported, that the inconvenience of dual-classified collections was thought to justify extensive or complete reclassification. A public librarian, indeed, cautioned against reclassification because "a thorough study by Denver and Kansas City, Missouri revealed many of the problems of high costs, relative gains limited if such a reclassification instituted." Apparently, this comment referred to reclassification from one edition of Dewey to another. If so, the comment might apply with even more force to reclassification from DC to LC because in that case the different schemes would at least be distinct on the shelves, whereas the various editions of DC would be intermingled.

One might infer that, if conversion from DC to LC is being considered because of possible economic and/or bibliographic benefits, reclassification need not be thought a major possible deterrent unless a thoroughgoing reclassification is planned. Respondents' comments, however, indicated that this course was not ordinarily chosen.

Respondent Library Characteristics: Relative
Shelf Location Policy (II:7)

Fixed location has been sometimes advocated as an answer to the problem of proliferating collections, particularly by critics of shelf classification, but there was no evidence of a trend in this direction on the part of respondents. Of 91 respondent libraries, 87 unequivocally reported a policy of relative shelf location. Only one library respondent--a special technical library with a classed catalog and closed stacks--used exclusively fixed location. There were two other special libraries--both with large non-circulating, closed-stacks collections--which employed fixed location for their main collections but relative location for their much smaller open-shelf reference collections.

The remaining exception, a university library respondent, indicated without comment that it did not use relative location. This library is personally known to the researcher: in his opinion it employs relative shelf location in the generally accepted sense of the phrase. However, its holdings are divided into three major parallel sequences: an open-shelf undergraduate core collection, an open-shelf reference collection, and a main closed-stacks collection of research

and less-used materials. Stack-use permits are granted to
faculty and graduate students. Evidently the respondent interpreted "relative location" strictly as the interfiling of all
books in one sequence. (Another respondent, in fact, had
asked: "Do you mean moved for interfiling or moved as a
block with no interfiling?") As pointed out in the preceding
chapter, most libraries have at least some such separate or
parallel groupings. Some authorities, indeed, recommend
that the works most in demand be shelved closest to the
charge-out desk. That at least two respondents should have
dwelt on this technical distinction emphasizes the "relativity"
of the concept of relative shelf location. As is sometimes
not understood, traditional "fixed" location by alcove or bay
was "relative" by broad subject categories, e.g., philosophy
books being placed in the philosophy alcove.

In conclusion, it appears that the respondent libraries, with either open or closed shelves, generally accepted
a policy of relative shelf location. A basic question considered by this study is the extent to which such a policy can
be justified in terms of its usefulness to the reader as
against the alleged expense and complexity of its implementation. Any suggested answer must be deferred to the concluding chapter.

Respondent Library Characteristics: "Broad" or "Close" Shelf Classification Policy (II:8)

Almost three-fourths of respondent libraries reported
a policy of close rather than broad classification. Table 9
indicates, as expected, that a greater proportion of academic
libraries favored close classification on the shelves than did
public libraries. However, the ratio of public libraries employing close classification was surprisingly high. There
were 45 out of 50 college and university libraries which reported a close classification policy--90 percent--and 13 out
of 25 public libraries--more than 50 percent. Special libraries were about evenly divided between followers of broad
and close classification. This differs somewhat from the
general opinion that "special" collections usually need closer
classification. Perhaps these libraries, lacking an adequately specific classification, preferred the broader categories
of available schemes as being, at least, less misleading.
However, it is also possible that some special disciplines rely more on published bibliographies and on periodical indexes
than on shelf classification for "specific" subject access.

Thus, two medical library respondents reported broad classification.

One respondent each from three types of libraries reported both broad and close classification. The public library respondent, which used DC, gave no explanation; the
system respondent stated that "since we limit the Dewey number to five places to the right of the decimal, we would fall
somewhere between broad and close"; and the special (rare
books) library respondent, using Cutter, explained, "Both--
varying with subject collections."

TABLE 9

SUMMARY OF BROAD OR CLOSE CLASSIFICATION POLICY:
BY TYPE OF LIBRARY (II:8)

Library Type	Classification Policy			
	Broad	Close	Both	Total
College	1	7	--	8
University	4	38	--	42
Special	5	5	1	11
Public	11	13	1	25
System	2	--	1	3
Total	23	63	3	89

The cataloging head of a very large university library
wrote:

> We long ago established a policy of open stacks ...
> for faculty and graduate students, with limited ac-
> cess for others. (The Library for undergraduates
> is completely open.) For a large collection ... a
> fairly close classification must be assumed as the
> norm for an open stack. There have never been
> any studies made to determine 'user satisfaction.'

If almost all respondents evidently accepted the pragmatic definitions of "close" and "broad" classification as
given in the questionnaire, some took pains to comment on
the relative nature of such distinctions. A university library
practitioner in the technical services apparently did not con-

sider the definition adequate:

> You use the terms 'close' and 'broad' classifica-
> tion, but do not define them. I think that I under-
> stand what you mean, but would suggest that you
> should attempt to define the terms. A probable
> problem that one will have in trying to answer
> these questions is that you assume that it is equal-
> ly simple to raise or lower the level of classifying in
> all classification schemes. I think in practice that
> your assumptions are primarily valid for Dewey
> but not LC. LC offers fewer options (in my mind)
> for simplified (or broad) notations.

A public library practitioner in the technical services,
whose library used DC, commented: "Depends on the particular subject classification, i. e., the build-up of certain subjects."

Comments tended to support the belief that LC on the
whole provided closer classification than DC, but that LC
was not as capable of being "cut back." A respondent, whose
public library employed DC for most of its holdings and LC
only for two special subjects, commented: "With Dewey
there is a choice--we use fairly close but not more than six
figures beyond the decimal, occasionally seven. LC--cannot
abridge."

A specialist in DC, however, stated that "the LC
classification is irregular in its development, so that some
areas are quite broadly classified." Respondents from libraries using DC made the point that some areas of their
collections required closer classification than others: "Have
started closer classification for Science books," and "In a
few instances (mostly technology) the numbers have perforce
become relatively lengthy," and "Varies in different parts of
the classification. Usually much less close than standard
DC 16 or 17th ed."

Respondent Library Characteristics:
Open-Shelf Policy (II:9)

Open-shelf policy was the norm for all except special
library respondents. As shown in Table 10, 68 of 91 respondent libraries--approximately three-fourths--were officially open-shelf. (Many open-shelf libraries, though, care-

fully noted that such items as rare books and manuscripts
were exceptions to the rule.) Another eight libraries were
at least partly open-shelf, and almost all officially "closed-
stacks" libraries offered--as noted so long ago by Cutter[3]--
some open-shelf service to their patrons, either for access
to reference works or for special research.

TABLE 10

SUMMARY OF OPEN-SHELF OR CLOSED-STACKS POLICY:
BY TYPE OF LIBRARY (II:9)

Library Type	Shelf Policy			
	Open	Closed	Both	Total
College	7	1	--	8
University	33	4	6	43
Special	4	7	--	11
Public	20	3	2	25
System	4	--	--	4
Total	68	15	8	91

Out of 51 college and university libraries, 46 offered
open-shelf access, completely or in part. The six university
libraries which reported "both" could easily be categorized,
in accordance with their self-descriptions, as "modified open-
shelf." Even the five academic libraries which indicated they
were officially "closed-stacks" might not be judged so by an
outside observer. The only closed-stacks college library respondent still had extensive open-shelf reference collections
but was forced because of increasing student enrollment to
use former open-shelf areas for study carrels. Of the four
"closed-stacks" university libraries, at least three granted
stack privileges to graduate students, faculty, and even upper-
classmen. The fourth "closed" university library had an
open-shelf undergraduate collection.

Only among special libraries, understandably, was the
predominant policy that of closed stacks. Of the seven
closed-stacks special libraries, however, two indicated that
research personnel were given stack privileges, and one commented that "our librarian is very anxious to establish a
small open-shelf, core collection, of the more important

books in each business field. "

Among the three closed-stacks public libraries, one reported "one-fourth to one-third open-shelves" and another explained that "Department reorganization has made it necessary to locate the major part of the collection in closed stacks.... It began as an open-shelf library but with growth of the collections, more than 50 percent of the materials are in closed stacks. "

One may conclude that, except for special libraries, most respondent institutions seemed to wish to follow an open-shelf policy and, if unable to do so completely, tried to mitigate the situation by granting stack privileges to at least some patrons and by making at least part of the collection directly accessible to all patrons.

Notes

1. American Library Association, A. L. A. Membership Directory (Chicago, 1968); Who's Who in Library Service: A Biographical Directory of Professional Librarians in the United States and Canada, ed. by Lee Ash (4th ed.; Hamden, Conn.: Shoe String Press, 1966); American Library Directory: A Classified List of Libraries in the United States and Canada with Personnel and Statistical Data, comp. by Eleanor F. Steiner-Prag (26th ed.; New York: Bowker, 1968); "Directory of the Association of American Library Schools, " Journal of Education for Librarianship, VIII (Winter, 1968), 163-232.

2. Fremont Rider, The Scholar and the Future of the Research Library: A Problem and Its Solution (New York: Hadham Press, 1944).

3. Charles Ammi Cutter, "Close Classification, with Special Reference to Messrs. Perkins, Schwartz, and Dewey, " Library Journal, XI (July, 1886), 180.

CHAPTER X

ANALYSIS OF RESPONSES ON "DIRECT SHELF APPROACH (OPEN-SHELF ACCESS): THE ROLE OF CLASSIFICATION" (III:1-11)

Editing and Tallying Procedures

Respondents were asked to check for each statement in Sections III, IV, and V of the questionnaire either "Agree" or "Undecided" or "Do not agree" (see Appendix). This continuum of possible opinion was chosen after much deliberation. A "Do not know" option was decided against because it might impress as uncomplimentary and create resistance. Although the questionnaire was primarily check-off--to encourage responses--respondents were invited to add comments.

The statements, as demonstrated in the documentary analysis, were almost all based on sources in the literature. Some were phrased categorically, either for brevity or to express an idea unmistakably. Sometimes, more than one factor was included: a method not ideal but deemed necessary to keep the questionnaire to reasonable length rather than risk non-response. Also, it was felt that the unequivocal or multi-variable nature of some statements might stimulate discussion. Such proved to be the case. Although respondents sometimes objected vigorously to the form of some statements, 88 of 152 analyzable responses, approximately 55 percent, contained volunteered comments.

Besides carefully recording these comments--varying from a few words to appended letters and manuscripts--it was decided to tally as "Other" an additional category of responses: those which did not include a check mark against any of the three printed options, but which indicated an opinion verbally. Though it would often have been possible to interpret such responses as representing one of the three options, it was decided for accuracy--as well as for later statistical manipulation--to tally under the first three categories ("Agree," "Undecided," and "Do not agree") only statements unmistakably checked.

252

The resultant summary of responses to the statements in Section III, "Direct Shelf Approach (Open-Shelf Access):   The Role of Classification," is given in the following Table 11.   In Table 12 are summarized the responses to the same statements from practitioners only, that is, responses included in Table 11 which represented the opinions of practicing librarians (and library administrators) rather than of library school personnel. Analysis of the responses in this and later chapters is generally based on the tally of total responses, including those from practitioners.   The tally for practitioner responses will be discussed only if it seems to reveal a "marked" difference from the tally for total responses, including those from practitioners. Unless specifically noted, such a difference was not observed. A "marked" difference was defined as one of at least five percentage points for any response category.   For example, Table 11 indicates that 16. 0 percent of all respondents checked "Do not agree" for Statement III:9, whereas Table 12 indicates that only 10. 9 percent of all practitioners checked this option--a difference of 5. 1 percentage points.   Accordingly, the possible significance of this differential will be examined in the analysis below of the responses to III:9.   (Unless indicated otherwise, "respondents" and "responses" may be considered numerically equivalent in the following discussions of tally data.)

Additionally, all responses were tabulated by: (1) professional function of respondent (cf. Table 1); and (2) type of library represented by practitioner (cf. Table 3).   The purpose was to determine, if possible, any apparent influences of such respondent characteristics.   Such influences were looked for, first, in the researcher's tabular categorization and analysis prerequisite to the discussion in this and the next two chapters.   Further to investigate such possible associations, the tallies by respondent characteristics were subjected, as noted in the previous chapter, to the chi-square test; and, also, coefficients of contingency were calculated to determine consistency of such associations from statement to statement.   Results of this statistical testing--as well as possible size-factor significance among respondent libraries--are considered during the following analysis, in this and the next two chapters, of the responses to each statement.   (The tallies of responses by professional function and by type of practitioner's library are reproduced or summarized only when necessary in discussing affirmative results of the chi-square test.)

TABLE 11

TOTAL RESPONSES TO STATEMENTS III:1-11

Statement No. III:	Agree No.	%	Undecided No.	%	Do Not Agree No.	%	Other No.	%	Total No.	%
1.	50	33.8	15	10.1	78	52.7	5	3.4	148	100.0
2.	48	32.9	22	15.1	66	45.2	10	6.8	146	100.0
3.	17	11.5	16	10.8	108	73.0	7	4.7	148	100.0
4.	83	55.3	12	8.0	50	33.3	5	3.3	150	100.0
5.	83	56.5	13	8.8	45	30.6	6	4.1	147	100.0
6.	23	15.8	15	10.3	106	72.6	2	1.4	146	100.0
7.	35	23.6	11	7.4	96	64.9	6	4.1	148	100.0
8.	87	58.8	19	12.8	30	20.3	12	8.1	148	100.0
8Aa	20	64.5	3	9.7	5	16.1	3	9.7	31	100.0
9.	87	58.0	21	14.0	24	16.0	18	12.0	150	100.0
10.	64	42.7	20	13.3	56	37.3	10	6.7	150	100.0
11.	45	30.1	57	39.0	32	21.9	12	8.2	146	100.0

a For explanation of 8A, see discussion of statement in text

TABLE 12

TOTAL PRACTITIONER RESPONSES TO STATEMENTS III:1-11

Statement No. III:	Agree		Undecided		Do Not Agree		Other		Total	
	No.	%	No.	%	No.	%	No.	%	No.	%
1.	36	36.4	12	12.1	49	49.4	2	2.0	99	100.0
2.	32	32.7	18	18.4	43	43.9	5	5.1	98	100.0
3.	11	11.1	10	10.1	74	74.7	4	4.0	99	100.0
4.	60	59.4	7	6.9	30	29.7	4	4.0	101	100.0
5.	54	55.1	8	8.2	32	32.7	4	4.1	98	100.0
6.	15	15.5	10	10.3	70	72.2	2	2.1	97	100.0
7.	22	22.2	7	7.1	66	66.7	4	4.0	99	100.0
8.	59	59.6	14	14.1	19	19.2	7	7.1	99	100.0
8Aa . . .	18	66.7	3	11.1	4	14.8	2	7.4	27	100.0
9.	62	61.4	16	15.8	11	10.9	12	11.9	101	100.0
10.	43	42.2	11	10.8	42	41.2	6	5.9	102	100.0
11.	36	37.1	34	35.1	21	21.6	6	6.2	97	100.0

aFor explanation of 8A, see discussion of statement in text

Statements III:1-11

III:1. "An effective library classification scheme will reflect the true order of nature and of science and will reveal this order through the relative location of the books on the shelves."

Only a little more than a third of 148 respondents agreed. Almost 53 percent did not agree, about 15 percent were undecided, and about three percent indicated some other opinion. (For the exact figures on this and following statements, refer to Table 11.)

There were 29 comments. Most comments by those who agreed seemed to qualify their agreement, at least in part. Thus, a university reference librarian added: "Unless many books are in use." A college technical services practitioner stated: "Though no present scheme is perfect." Other qualifications were: "But there does not exist such a classification." "If you know what the 'true' order of nature is." A university reference librarian commented at length:

> I hesitate to answer actually, because of the phrase
> 'the order of nature.' There is order in nature, we
> all realize, but there are many interpretations of this
> order depending upon our interests and viewpoints.
> I doubt that any librarian, or anyone for that matter, envisions 'the order of nature' so clearly as
> to be able to classify it faultlessly and permanently. Men's knowledge of 'the order' in nature must
> grow and change. YES, an effective scheme must
> reflect 'the order' of nature as well as we can see
> it! But it will always be variously interpretive,
> e.g., Symbolic logic can be classified in Philosophy
> or in Mathematics, depending upon the user's
> needs. Neither classification is wrong, but can we
> say that one or the other reflects and reveals 'the
> order' of nature more than the other?

On the other hand, a university library administrator also agreed but added: "LC does a pretty good job of this."

Almost all the other comments by those who did not check "Agree" were variations or intensifications of the above qualifications: "Disagree, because I don't think there is a 'true order of nature and of science.' If there is, no clas-

sification scheme known to me reflects it. " "Don't agree.
There are as many orders of nature as there are classifiers. ·
Books themselves do not follow any order of nature. " "The
'true order of nature and of science' may not be reflected in
the material to be classified, and this is what we are reveal-
ing--the content of materials. "

The director of a large special national library declined to fill out the questionnaire and in a letter gave among
his reasons:

> I think that your problem is you are trying to cover
> too many types of libraries.   Your statements are
> necessarily broad.   The qualifications which any
> large specialized library would wish to place on its
> answers are not possible.   For example, your
> statement No. 1 ... is somewhat ingenuous.   I do
> not know of any man, living or dead, who has ever
> determined the 'true order of nature and of science'
> and to agree, disagree or to be undecided about
> this proposition begs the question of the pragmatic
> basis of classification.

Other comments from those who disagreed were:
"Heavens!" and "Nonsense; as Borges says, 'We do not know
what the universe is. ' "

The reactions to this statement indicated that, whatever metaphysical assumptions may underlie the literature on
classification theory and practice for libraries, almost two-
thirds of the respondents would not approve of such assumptions.   The vigor of the printed controversies, however,
might indicate that--despite the avowedly "pragmatic" purpose
of American library classification--there may be a not inconsiderable belief in the "true" order as reflected if even partially in library classification.   It may not be negligible evidence that at least one-third of the respondents were willing
to check "Agree" for a statement unqualifiedly put, and that
ten percent checked "Undecided. "

III:2.   "Evidence of a system of library classification
enhances the prestige and status of the library profession
among the users of the library. "

In view of the testimonials to classification as a hallmark of professional librarianship from such spokesmen as

Bliss, Ranganathan, and Palmer,[1] the lack of agreement with
this statement somewhat surprised. Only about one-third of
146 respondents checked "Agree." "Undecided" made up 15.1
percent, "Do not agree" 45.2 percent, and "Other" 6.8 percent of all responses. Compared with the responses to the
preceding statement, fewer, relatively, did not agree, but
significantly more were undecided or gave some other opinion.

Surprisingly strong feelings were expressed in the 21
comments among all types of responses. There were five
comments from those who agreed: "Yes, but they don't understand it!" "If the system helps find the books." "Probably, but most readers are not concerned with the particular
scheme as long as they can locate their books." "No evidence to support view." "Unknowingly!" "But that is not
the reason for having a classification."

Almost all the remaining 16 comments were negative.
Only two comments, tallied under "Other," were in any way
affirmative: "Undoubtedly, if it serves his purpose," and
"It could, but often works against us in some of the ridiculous positions we place ourselves in through over-emphasis
on its 'perfection.'" All other comments were negative:
"Have no data on which to base a judgment." "Doubtful."
"This statement doesn't seem worth pondering one way or the
other." "Irrelevant and ambiguous." "What a ridiculous
statement!" "Don't know what's meant." "It is the service
readers receive that does this." "This is irrelevant."
"Doubtful and probably unprovable." "Can't imagine what you
mean."

Two lengthier comments emphasized the pragmatic
role of library classification. A teacher of classification
stated:

> Enhances prestige and status??? The fact that a
> library helps them to find what they want makes
> readers pleased, but I don't live in a world where
> prestige and status (whatever they are--do you mean
> the salary a grateful public is willing to pay me?)
> depend on this sort of thing.

A college technical services practitioner commented:

> Don't agree. Users of libraries do not generally
> know what the classifications are, what they mean,

how the classes relate one to the other, and are
generally oblivious to the working of the classification, and I doubt that the best classification will
enhance the prestige of a librarian as much as consistent good service and correct answers to specific
questions.

One might have thought that any visible display of professional technique, comprehensible or not, might be expected
to impress the layman and thus reflect not unfavorably on the
status of that profession's representatives.   The resistance
of respondents to admit such a possible effect of the arrangement of their collections may indicate librarians' disinterest
in (perhaps uneasiness with) classification as an intellectual
process involving advanced professional expertise.   (This
point will be further discussed in the concluding chapter.)

III:3.   "The chief value of close shelf classification
lies in its use by the librarian for teaching and by the patron
for learning. "

This statement was designed to put as broadly as possible the primacy of the pedagogical goals championed by the
advocates of open-shelf libraries, as discussed in the chapters on the sociology of direct access and on its early history.   Reaction was overwhelmingly negative, many questioning the meaning of "teaching" and "learning" or expressing
bewilderment.   Only 11.5 percent of 148 respondents agreed.
The other responses were 10.8 percent "Undecided, " 73.0
percent "Do not agree, " and 4.7 percent "Other. "   (Among
the total 44 questionnaire statements, only seven attracted
more than a 70-percent "Do not agree" response.)

Reluctance to accept the general concept of close shelf
classification as pedagogical in purpose, that is, of teaching
subject relations; or to connect the educational nature of
shelf classification with a rationale of open-shelf libraries--
as expressed in the literature--was apparent in many of the
14 comments.   Even a teacher of technical services who
agreed with the statement was somewhat cautious:

I'm not at all sure I should have checked 'Agree';
what is meant by 'use' and how broadly should we
define 'teaching' and 'learning'?   I'm using a broad
interpretation; if we have works on land distribution
in Southern Rhodesia, Japan, etc., and use area

subdivisions, we are doing so to facilitate 'teaching' and 'learning. '

Another respondent agreed but added: "Probably." Among "Other" responses were two qualified agreements: "Use by the librarian for teaching what? Use by the patron for learning what? If you mean obtaining information, then I agree. I've left this one blank," and "Do you mean trying to assemble like books in the same place? If so, I agree." Other comments were quite negative: "Word shelf is irrelevant." "Function is primarily for organization of resources." "For service. Public library does not instruct." "Archaic." "I don't know what this means." "Not clear. For teaching and learning what?"

A college technical services librarian who disagreed explained:

> Don't agree. Unless one is a teacher in a library science program, I do not think that librarians 'teach' a patron or a patron learns from a classification schedule, except to know that the books he is interested in are in such and such a number.

A university reference librarian gave these reasons for checking "Undecided":

> All of this emphasis on 'teaching' and 'learning' does not clarify what is being taught and learned. The use of the library? What bibliographical materials are available on a subject? I do think that patrons learn much about using a library and much about materials on the subject of interest when they have access to open shelves, but I hesitate to place any one value as primary. One great value to me as a student doing research in open-access libraries was locating supplemental material on my subject by perusing the indexes of related books near the particular books for which I had call numbers. Also, I often found useful material when the books I had located through the card catalog were not on the shelf or proved not as relevant as I had hoped.

The generally negative response seemed to indicate that the respondents did not consider themselves as providing for their patrons an educational experience through the use of close classification on open shelves, nor did the comments indicate that the respondents felt they were "teaching" or should "teach" their patrons by some means other than close shelf classification.

III:4.   "Close relative shelf classification is necessary for effective direct-shelf approach to subject materials."

This statement drew a larger percentage (55.3) of "Agree" and a correspondingly smaller percentage of all other options than the three preceding statements.   Evidently, the majority accepted the opinion that satisfactory subject search in an open-shelf library was not possible without close classification and relative location.   Most of the 22 comments were qualifying rather than negative, even among those who disagreed.   Thus, those who checked "Do not agree" commented: "Depends on type of library."   "How could one check 'Agree' since nothing is said about the time involved, size of collection, etc. ?"   "Helpful, not necessary."   "In a few subject fields, e.g., medicine, geographic divisions in history and economics, other sciences, it is helpful but I would disagree that a very close classification is necessary throughout a collection."   "No, unless collection large and technical."   "May be helpful, but the subject approach in the catalog is better."   "Not in every case."

Comments from those who agreed emphasized that close classification was more desirable in large libraries and for special subjects.

It would thus appear that most respondents admitted the need of close classification on shelves for at least some kind of libraries and subjects.   It should be noted, however, that almost a third of the respondents did not agree, though they gave no reasons.   (Perhaps, individual interpretations of "close" classification had an influence.)   Moreover, the qualifying comments implied the further problem of the feasibility and/or economy of adjusting printed DC and LC notation to meet the varying requirements for specificity in particular libraries and parts of collections.

III:5.   "Some of the limitations of shelf classification (e.g., linearity, books not on the shelves at time of search, separate shelving sequences) make relative shelf classification basically undependable as a primary approach to subject materials in the library."

The distribution of responses was about the same as for the preceding statement, though the grand total was slightly smaller. Almost 57 percent of 147 respondents agreed, 8.8 percent were undecided, 30.6 percent did not agree, and 4.1 percent gave some other opinion. One might be misled, however, by the fact that about the same percentage of respondents agreed that close shelf classification was necessary for effective subject search, and also that such a form of search was not dependable as a primary approach because of certain theoretical and practical handicaps! Indeed, further analysis reveals that only 47 (about 31 percent) of the 150 respondents to Statement 4 indicated agreement with both Statements 4 and 5. (Only 12 of the 150 checked "Do not agree" for both, and only one checked "Undecided" for both.) In other words, only about one-third (rather than 57 percent) of 150 respondents agreed both on the need for close shelf classification and on its severe limitations in subject search. Additional analysis reveals that 38 (23.3 percent) of the 150 respondents both agreed with Statement 4 and disagreed with Statement 5, that is, only about one-fourth of the respondents both accepted the need of close classification for subject search and did not reject it as a primary approach in that search.

There were 21 comments. Of 10 comments from those who agreed, about half qualified their opinion, e.g., by indicating that the agreement referred to a large library or that the public catalog should also be used. Comments from others who agreed emphasized their choice, e.g., "Emphatically," "Not valid in any event," and "I feel quite strongly on this!" Respondents who did not check "Agree" generally objected to a lack of definition. So, a teacher of technical services who disagreed explained:

> What do you mean undependable? Primary approach? As I see it, shelf classification is valuable as a first approach; if the patron finds what he wants, we don't need anything further; if he doesn't, we do. It is valuable because it is immediate--he has what he wants in his hands. The limitation--that we have to go elsewhere if we don't find what he wants--applies to the catalog, to bibliographies, in fact to every indirect source of information, but none of these puts what he wants in the patron's hand immediately. So I suppose I must disagree with your statement, without being too sure that I know what it means.

It might be conjectured from correlating the responses to Statements 4 and 5 that, if only about one-fourth of the respondents felt <u>both</u> that close shelf classification was nec- essary for effective subject search in open-shelf libraries <u>and</u> that it was also a dependable primary approach, the re- maining great majority of respondents did not consider the direct-shelf approach (let alone "browsing") as a serious method of subject search in an open-shelf library with close classification and relative location.   The reasons for close classification did not seem to be necessarily related by most respondents to the activity of subject search in open-shelf li- braries.   Such conjectures will be further examined.

III:6.   "Close classification on the shelves, because it places too few books under any one subject division, is less suitable for the direct-shelf approach than for closed stacks."

This statement meant to test the proposition that, even if close shelf classification were not considered desirable for open-shelf collections, it might still be needed in closed- shelf collections.   Cutter, defending close shelf classification, had claimed that, if the library were closed-stack, such clas- sification was all the more valuable for staff retrieval of ma- terials and for reference librarians' work.   Dewey and Bos- twick expressed similar views. [2]

The response was overwhelmingly negative: 72. 6 per- cent of 146 respondents disagreed, 10.3 percent were unde- cided, 1. 4 percent had "Other" opinions--and only 15. 8 per- cent agreed.   Apparently this would indicate (with the reser- vations to be noted below) that close shelf classification would not be considered worthwhile by the great majority of re- spondents for other than open-shelf collections.

There were only 13 comments, of which five indicated that there seemed no reason for shelf classification in a closed-stacks situation, e. g., "Where stacks are truly closed, see <u>no</u> need for subject classification," and "Actually, in a real closed stack, classification serves no function."

The statement was probably worded defectively in that the reason given for possible dissatisfaction with close clas- sification on open shelves would not necessarily be <u>the</u> reason --if a reason were sought--for close shelf classific<u>ation</u> being more suitable in closed stacks.   (Logically, this would be a violation of the law of the excluded middle.)   Those who dis-

agreed with the statement, therefore, might have disagreed
for a reason other than that specified. A teacher of classification gave a detailed critique:

> This statement is in fact meaningless, because it
> does not say what is meant by 'subject division.'
> Does it mean specific piece of notation? For ex-
> ample, all the books on Heat, Light, Sound, Elec-
> tricity and Magnetism, Nuclear science, Properties
> of Matter, etc., etc., etc., fall within the division
> Physics. Suppose we have four shelves of books,
> say 30 to a shelf; they can be scanned equally easi-
> ly if they are arranged by specific subject or by
> author, title or any other means. BUT suppose
> that we find a book on a specific subject in a col-
> lection arranged by some factor other than subject,
> and suppose that we want another one, having found
> the first. We have to scan the whole group, in-
> stead of finding them both together--and it is cer-
> tainly more work to scan several shelves than to
> pull two books off the shelf from the same place
> instead of one.
>
> I have put 'disagree' because I consider classified
> arrangement to be more suited to open-shelf ar-
> rangement than to stack arrangement. As well as
> the ambiguity in the question, there is a confusion
> of questions here, I think. Q1 is: which is bet-
> ter, close or broad classification on the open
> shelves? Q2 is: what is the best method of ar-
> ranging closed stacks?

It may be confirmatory evidence of the above opinion
on the unsuitability of close classification for closed shelves
that only two respondents from the 23 libraries which had
been described as completely or partly closed-shelf (see II:9)
agreed with III:6. These two represented special libraries
in well-delimited subject fields.

III:7. "Close shelf classification is as useful and feasible for small libraries as it is for large libraries."

This hypothesis intended to test the commonly expressed opinion that close shelf classification is more appropriate for large collections which would tend to have more
works in any one or more subject fields. The implication of

such an opinion would be that a small library--general or
special--did not require close shelf classification.   On the
other hand, Cutter[3] felt that even a small library should use
close classification for those books in its collection whose
classes were adequately definable, regardless of the number
of books represented.   The words "small" and "large" in the
hypothesis were left for individual interpretation or comment.

A great majority (about 65 percent) did not agree.
About seven percent were undecided, and four percent gave
some other opinion.   Only about one-fourth agreed.   It would
thus appear that most respondents would admit the greater
suitability of close shelf classification for larger collections,
though the aggregate percentage of those not checking "Do not
agree" was fairly high: about 35 percent.   This would indicate that a sizeable group of respondents did not unhesitating-
ly accept the opinion that close shelf classification is necessarily dependent on library size.

There were 21 comments.   Those who disagreed emphasized generally the size criterion: "Seems unnecessary
in small collections."   "If library is static and will not
grow, then I disagree."   "Library should be fairly good size
or have growth potential for close classification."   "Generally, the smaller the library, the broader the classification
should be.   If you do not have a book on the Democratic par-
ty, it may be better to put books under the general number
for Political parties in the U.S."

One who "disagreed" evidently meant the opposite: "I
think more feasible."   Some who agreed had reservations:
"Special libraries in particular."   "Useful, not feasible."
"May not be as necessary."   "Unless very small and not
growing."

Cutter's opinion was approximated by two respondents.
An "Undecided" technical services public librarian commented:
"In the case of a highly technical special library there could
be reason for it."

A public reference librarian did not check an option
but stated: "Size of library not always relevant; scope and
kind of classification determine objective."

Many who marked "Do not agree" might have held an
opinion similar to the last two.   In any case, these two were
unwilling to agree on the basis of size alone.

III:8. "Shelf classification has much greater value as a locational device, i.e., getting the book once you know the call number, than as a systematic subject approach."

A common criticism of shelf classification in American libraries is that it is not used primarily for subject search, but usually only as an "address" to retrieve known works. This use of shelf classification seems to have been confirmed by the studies of Herner, Hoage, and Tauber[4]-- among others. Statement III:8 intended to obtain further information. The statement expressed a qualitative judgment: not whether such use of shelf classification was more or less common, but whether it was more or less valuable than its assumed major theoretical justification.

About 59 percent agreed, 13 percent were undecided, 20 percent did not agree, and eight percent expressed some other opinion.

Unfortunately, a typographical omission in most of the questionnaires might have misled some of the respondents, i.e., on 68 of the 87 questionnaires returned, Statement III:8 was printed without the second "as." Comments indicated that this had led to misinterpretation of the statement by at least some. Thus, out of 18 comments, six stated that the statement was not clear or that it denied shelf classification to be a systematic subject approach. Yet, some comments in the uncorrected questionnaires showed a clear understanding of the statement, e.g., a teacher of technical services explained:

> Disagree with the statement as printed. BUT it relates to a book. One of the values of classified arrangement is that if you have to get a lot of books on the same subject for a patron, they will be in the same area on the shelves. On second thoughts, classification is still more valuable as a systematic subject approach than as a locating device, so I disagree anyway.

Because of possible misinterpretation, however, an additional tally for Statement 8A (see Table 11) was prepared, that is, for only those questionnaires whose wording was complete. This tally (8A) indicated a considerably higher percentage of "Agree": 64.5 percent compared with 58.8 percent for the original total. Conversely, the percent-

age of "Undecided" and "Do not agree" fell significantly.
Only for "Other" opinions was there a slight percentage increase for the adjusted as against the original totals.

It would appear that the great majority of respondents
considered shelf classification more valuable as a locational
device.   A public librarian in the technical services who
agreed with the uncorrected statement explained: "There are
so many cross-disciplinary fields of study today that subject
indexes, etc., are required to get at interrelated subject materials."   A teacher of technical services who was undecided
about the statement (in its uncorrected form) commented:

> Basically, I would agree with this statement as far
> as American practice is concerned. But we must
> not forget that shelf classification, and close clas-
> sification, have the great advantage of clustering
> together items on a small subject, even if they do
> tear asunder broader subjects or various aspects
> of a broader subject.

A college acquisitions librarian commented on the corrected statement: "I agree.   I think that for the general user, the classification number tells the user where the book
is or should be, and incidentally that he also finds other
books on the same subject in the same general area."

Differing from this last were the following comments
from those who expressed an "Other" opinion on the corrected
statement: "Agree and do not agree." "This is like asking
whether apples are better than monkey wrenches." "Might."

III:9.   "Subject headings in the public catalog are more
useful to the patron than shelf classification."

This statement expressed unequivocally a controversial
opinion among whose advocates were Metcalfe, Kelley, and
Pettee. [5] Its acceptance could inhibit the development and application of classification for open-shelf collections.

A clear majority (58 percent) agreed.   Only 16 percent disagreed, the remaining 26 percent being about equally
divided between "Undecided" and "Other."   There were 39
comments: 11 from those who agreed, five from those undecided, five from those who disagreed, and 18 from those
expressing some other opinion.

Comments from those agreeing were mostly of a qualifying nature: "Since our stacks are closed." "In a large academic library." "For certain types of patrons--not all." "But not much!" "In practice." "Depends on patron's ability to search by subject." "Probably." Others agreed more affirmatively: "Should be if doing real research." "Because they indicate other classes and shelves to search." The following two lengthier explanations also came from those who agreed:

> (1) Although I have not studied this in detail, I suspect this is true because subject headings provide multiple approaches whereas in our libraries class numbers provide only one approach.

> (2) I agree. The subject headings tell the user what books the library has on the subject and then where it should be found. Unless one has a classed catalog where the subject head (index) directs users to a specific number, I do not think that the user is generally interested in classification.

Comments from those not checking the "Agree" column fell into two classes: those which considered the statement lacking in suitable qualifications, and those which insisted that subject headings and classification were complementary, not opposed.

Examples of the former class were: "More useful for what purpose?" "Too baldly yes-no. How will response be interpreted?" "How do they mean this? By locating a subject or a book? Subject--agree, book--no." "Which patron?" "In all types of libraries?" "What patron?"

Typical of the latter type were the following:

> (1) More useful for what? Under what circumstances? Is drink more useful to man than food? The two things are complementary, not conflicting --but this is because the catalog has to supplement the shelf arrangement, however the catalog is arranged and whatever shelf arrangement you have.

> (2) Both subject headings and shelf classification are useful to the patron under particular circumstances. Why argue which is more important?

(3) Both are useful and indispensable.

The last comment may be compared with that from a university technical services librarian who expressed an "Other" opinion: "Neither is too useful."

As noted earlier in this chapter, Statement III:9 offered the first instance of a possible "marked" difference between the opinion distribution pattern of all respondents and that of practitioner respondents only.   Comparison of Tables 11 and 12 indicates that practitioner reaction to III:9 was about the same as from all respondents except in the category "Do not agree" where practitioners seemed markedly less willing (by a differential of 5.1 percentage points) to reject the idea of the superior usefulness to the patron of subject headings vis-à-vis shelf classification.   Perhaps librarians have learned from experience with patrons that subject headings were not less useful than shelf classification.   Differences in various types of libraries might require qualification, though it is of interest that Table 14 reveals no significant relationship between practitioner reactions to III:9 and the type of library represented.   (However, as suggested in the next paragraph of this section, another factor might have to be considered in analyzing the attitude of librarians towards subject headings.)

Thus, the majority of respondents seemed to feel that their patrons were helped more by subject headings in the catalog than by classification on the shelves.   Responses to previous statements have revealed considerable reservation on the role of shelf classification in American libraries.   It is at least possible, though, that the prevalence of the dictionary or divided catalog in American libraries (see II:4) was a factor in the majority agreement on III:9 as well as in the varying earlier cited opinions on shelf classification.   American librarians may, to a great extent, have had their opinions on subject headings formed by their libraries' policies rather than by personal investigation.   Such a possibility, far from proven, may be worth further study.   Also, opinions held on the comparative merits of LC and DC, or of broad and close classification might be similarly conditioned.

III:10.   "Close classification notation is simple enough for the average patron to follow successfully on the shelves."

The discussion in Chapter Eight of the role of notation

in shelf classification stressed the ambivalence of classificationists and librarians towards this "shorthand" expression of
classification terms. In theory, as reiterated in Chapter
Eight, the value of shelf classification is in its end result,
i.e., the relative position of books on the shelves. Notation
is, thus, only a convenient auxiliary for recording that position. The persistence of Sayers' principle of expressiveness
for notation evidently manifests a feeling of many librarians
that notation should be a mirror--not just a "Zip Code"--for
the classification scheme. Statement III:10 aimed to elicit
professional opinion on whether the average patron in fact
recognized the image in the mirror: whether he was thought
to understand close notation, or at least enough of it to be
helped at the shelves in his subject search or browsing.
Some negative views had been cited in Chapter Eight.

Much less than half (42.7 percent) of the respondents
agreed; 37.3 percent did not agree; 13.3 percent were undecided; and 6.7 percent expressed some other opinion. On
the whole, therefore, most did not believe that the average
patron could follow or "read" the close notation on shelved
books. Whether this "readability" is necessary to be helped
by the scheme is another matter. Again, in theory, the notation should not be of such critical significance; in practice,
however, as shown by many of the comments, notational expressiveness is expected to help. In any case, one may haz-
ard that to be confused or bewildered by symbols on book
spines would not encourage confidence in the shelf arrangement as revelatory of subject relationships.

There were 24 comments, most of which modified the
opinion or questioned "average" and "follow." (The intent
was to use "follow" in the sense of understanding the subject
or form sequence of the books on the shelves as expressed
by the notation.)

Among comments from those who agreed were: "Perhaps depends on the classification used." "I think the 'average' patron and 'average' librarian are fairly bright." "In
LC, yes; probably not in Dewey." "Depending on classification used." "Agree as printed--or 'understand'?" "In university library." "If numbers are not too long and involved."

A college technical services librarian accepted "follow" in its sense of "understand":

I agree. I think that the addition of an additional

digit or two (or year of publication, or volume number) to a classification, or call number should
prove no problem to an average patron. I would
not hold this view for numbers that may be like
860. 073944 which becomes ridiculous.

A classification teacher who agreed expounded the traditional concept of the theoretically subordinate role of notation:

Agree, but why does the patron have to follow the
notation? It is the arrangement which is meant to
be helpful, not the notation, which is merely a convenient way of showing the arrangement. For example, the notation of the LC is much the same,
2 letters, up to 4 figures, no matter how detailed
the arrangement it reflects (or, more likely with
LC, how broad). Patrons should follow the guides
which most librarians omit--guides in the catalog,
on the shelves, everywhere. Are you familiar with
the British National Bibliography? In that work,
the arrangement is shown by a notation which is
often complicated and long--but every heading is also shown in words, and this is what the user will
follow once he gets to the right area. Most librarians are completely incompetent as far as guiding
is concerned.

A university reference librarian who agreed dwelt on
the significance of "follow":

Here again, I think it is necessary to define what
you mean by 'follow. ' I think the average patron
has the intelligence to recognize that certain like
materials seem to be grouped together and to 'follow' the books on the shelves until he comes to
sections which do not relate to his interest. No,
I do not think that the average patron can 'follow'
close classification, if this means understanding
how categories are set up under various subject and
subheading divisions, and then looking for selected
areas. The patron usually begins with a call number which can be obtained from a catalog of some
kind--a dictionary catalog which will give specific
call numbers for books under specific topics, or a
classified list or catalog which will give, perhaps,
a better view of related topics and their classifica-

tion numbers. Then, when he goes to the shelves
to locate the desired book(s), he may or may not
examine other books with the same call number
(except for Cutter numbers, etc.) or nearby books
with related call numbers.

Comments from those who did not check "Agree" were
chiefly concerned with matters of definition, but noteworthy
also was conflicting testimony on LC or DC being easier to
"follow": "Average patron in a public library, often not.
Average good college student, often yes. Librarians can be
asked to assist." "Depends on what system of classification
patron is used to." "Not in Dewey." "College level and
up." "What's an 'average patron'?" "Badly worded. Average? Of what library?" "Ambiguous question." "Who is
he?" "I disagree with the term 'close classification notation.' A broad classification notation might be complicated
also." "Depends on system. Yes for Dewey, no for LC."
"A bit beside the point." "Depends on the patron."

A public technical services librarian expressed an
"Other" opinion which seemed to interpret "follow" literally:

> I hate to bicker over the word 'average,' but our
> average patron in this library, or for that matter
> in this community, is hardly the average patron of
> the school library I used to head or of the Colum-
> bia University Library where you are. To use
> 'average' as a conglomerate term, I would say,
> yes, the classification notation is simple enough.
> Anyone who can read from A to Z and can count
> from 1 to 10 can learn quickly to follow standard
> classification notation, even close notation.

It may not be unreasonable to conclude that most respondents did not think their patrons as a whole understood
the classification notation appearing on the spines of shelved
books and that at least some respondents did not think it necessary to do so.

III:11. "Although close shelf classification may not be
justified by its cost, it is cheaper for libraries now using it
to continue rather than discard it."

Less than a third (30.1 percent) of the respondents
agreed with this statement; 39 percent were undecided; 21.9

percent did not agree; and 8.2 percent expressed some other opinion.

The discrimination of respondents was well demonstrated: the distribution of responses would imply careful weighing of a difficult and complex problem.

About 70 percent were unwilling to check "Agree." "Undecided" and "Other" responses were almost one-half of the total, and were more than double the number of "Do not agree."

Respondents' caution was even clearer in the 22 comments, most of which stressed the complex nature of the problem or questioned "cost."   The following qualifications came from those who checked "Agree": "For broad classification, but not for fixed location." "If done by someone else." "Especially if they use LC." "Can classify new books by close classification and reclassify older volumes after a period of years because by this time, many may have been discarded." "Do not agree that it is not justified by its cost."

A college technical services respondent who agreed explained:

> I agree.   Generally it is cheaper to go along with what you have been doing rather than institute changes which will then divide the collection.   I also question whether close shelf classification is really more expensive than broad classification. What you may be doing is saving some money (?) by shortening the close shelf number and passing on the work to the user who must then do his own close classification, and each user will be doing that, thus making it a greater expenditure of time on the part of the user.

A teacher of technical services who in general agreed made, however, a similar point on assumed cost:

> Discard in favor of what?   I can think of arrangements that would be more expensive than close classification, for example, by color of the cover, which would mean relocating every time we had any binding done.   I suspect that 'cheaper' here relates to the immediate cost to the library staff in terms

of time taken to classify in detail as opposed to broad classification--though of course if LC cards are used it takes longer probably to cut down the Dewey number than to use it as it stands. And do you actually reclassify at a broader heading if LC class numbers are used? Because of course you can't alter LC classification from broad to close or close to broad without reclassifying. If however we have some small degree of concern for the pa-tron, who after all pays whatever it costs, we have to take into account the effect on him of our shelf arrangement--whatever it is.

Comments from those who did not check "Agree" al-most all stressed the complexity of the problem: "No data." "Depends." "Which scheme?" "An unqualified statement that must specify which classification scheme. Cost is rela-tive to schedule and information supplied." "Don't know." "Decision needs to be based on individual case, objectives, etc." "Smaller libraries would find it cheaper in the long run to discard." "Do not agree with premise, and question therefore has no meaning to me." "Poverty mentality!" "I disagree that close classification is more costly." "Close classification does not appear to be the only factor involved--staff, size of collection, and source of catalog copy could be significant." "Depends on more variables than you have in-dicated." "Too many possible variables here for categorical answer."

A specialist in DC gave this "Other" opinion:

Whether or not it is cheaper to continue close clas-sification depends on the system. If one wants to classify broadly with LC, it means relocation. If one uses Dewey, one could change from close to broad by interfiling the longer notation with the shorter ones. In other words, no changes would need to be made on the book spines or the catalog cards.

In the strictest sense, close shelf classification must be more expensive than broad (assuming that closer classifi-cation usually means longer notation) because more time is required to transcribe, type, or shelfread longer strings of symbols. More time is also required to verify close notation even when supplied on printed cards since longer notation of-ten signifies the application of auxiliary tables for various in-

ner and outer form divisions.   Yet, the responses and comments implied that to many respondents the "expense" of
closer classification--even if greater costliness be granted--
was not the significant factor for classification policy.   Usefulness was evidently more important.

The expense factor would become more crucial, of
course, if, as a result of revisions in DC or LC, the library
chose to engage in considerable reclassification to preserve
a consistent close classification rather than rely on broader
classes less likely to change in new editions of the scheme.
However, the general inattention to this matter in the above
comments--along with the evidence of the preceding chapter
on reclassification policy (see II:6)--would indicate that reclassification to maintain a consistently up-to-date close classification was not of great concern, apparently because it was
not much practiced.

Moreover, comparison of Tables 11 and 12 indicates
appreciable difference in the "Agree" category between practitioner respondents and all respondents.   The aggregate response in Table 11 for "Agree" was 30.1 percent, that of
practitioners in Table 12 was 37.1 percent, or a differential
of seven percentage points.   This suggests that library respondents, perhaps out of experience, were markedly more
willing to agree on this statement than were non-practitioners.
Also, this might indicate that, despite objections to the wording from some non-practitioners, the practical implications
of the statement were somewhat clearer to librarians.   This
is all the more likely since comments throughout the questionnaire gave the impression that respondents were unwilling
to check "Agree" for any statement they did not fully understand.

Some General Comments from Respondents

In addition to comments on individual statements, respondents sometimes appended fairly lengthy general discussions of the role of shelf classification in American libraries.   A library school administrator (retired) wrote:

> I comment on Section III, 'Role of Classification.'
> Greatly influenced by the late W. Berwick Sayers,
> with whom I lunched nearly daily at Chaucer House
> during my U.K. Fulbright year, and by the coterie
> of distinguished British librarians whom we under-

estimated for so many years, I came back determined to halt the 'rage' to reclassify, rampant
among my academic colleagues.   I agreed with the
British catalogers who wouldn't be caught dead in
a library classified by LC.   Because I came to appreciate their profound theory of classification.

When I was a Columbia student (1926/27), I was
taught 'the larger the library the closer you classify.'   In Britain I came to understand the opposite
for the physical book.   Close classification means
repudiating our impartiality toward all of the disciplines, which has ever been our strength.

From my Library-College standpoint ... serendipity
is an objective in the learning mode I describe
(your V:11).   Browsing is essential; open shelf;
broad classification; perhaps just the third summary
DC.

The head of technical services in a large university
library wrote:

With regard also to classification in general I have
come to hold some fairly strong views; they were
spelled out in a paper delivered about two years
ago--explaining why this Library decided not to convert to LC classification.   ('One seems impelled to
view with absolute incredulity this fetish that is so
often made of classification.   My own developed
conviction is that classification has just barely
enough value, as one approach to the subject content of a library--totally inadequate as the approach
is--to be worth doing.   It is not worth changing
systems....')   I opine 'just barely enough value'
but I hardly need add that this also emphatically
does mean enough value to be worth doing.

A teacher of technical services interpreted the intent
of Section III as follows:

The whole test is slanted and designed to lead the
respondent to answer the questions in a manner
that will support the compiler's preconceived opinion, namely that classification, and close classification in particular, can be replaced by indexing.
Little or no relationship has been made to the dic-

tionary catalog with a classed arrangement.   (L. C.
filing rules.)   Also, the questionnaire in addition
to confusing direct shelf access with <u>classification</u>
of books confuses the classification and cataloging
of <u>books</u> and <u>information</u>.   Information being bits
and <u>pieces</u> of <u>facts</u> usually located in technical reports and easily identified by one or two specific
terms due to the narrowness of coverage.   Books
contain information and have in themselves indexes.
But they contain many pieces of information and
hence, because of their broader coverage, need to
be handled in a different way than smaller segments
of information.   Each book has many segments
('pamphlets') of information.   Scientific information
is also more readily identifiable than information
in the humanities, which does not lend itself to
clearly defined descriptors as does science.   If this
questionnaire differentiated between <u>types of mate-</u>
<u>rials</u>, books, pamphlets, reports, <u>microfiche, and</u>
<u>types</u> of information, science or humanities, it
might be more valid than it will be.   Clarification
of terms in the questions would also help.

Might suggest that you also query one of the world's
largest closed-stack, but classified systems exist-
ent.   L. C., with its 14 million plus volumes has
somehow not seen fit to give up its classification,
but indeed continuously expands it.   'Browser or
no browser. '

   Another teacher of technical services, a classification
specialist, wrote:

You keep on using the word 'necessary' or 'essential. '   This is seeing things in black and white
when they are nearly all in grey.   Sections III, IV,
and V seem to assume that classified arrangement
is the only possible one for open-shelf access--I
may be reading too much into them, but that is my
deduction.   This is not true; there are other possible arrangements, depending on the material to
be arranged and the use to be made of it.   In general, I do believe that in a library with open access, classified arrangement on the shelves is the
<u>most helpful</u>.   All the questions about provision of
<u>catalogs, bibliographies</u>, etc., are red herrings,
deflecting us from the main question: is open ac-

cess desirable in large collections? general libraries? etc. Of course, you need catalogs and bibliographies as well if you have open access, but that
is not the point. The point is, what do you do with
books? Author? Title? Date? Accession number? None of these looks like a real contender for
shelf arrangement in an open-access library. We
are left with subject; my own belief is that classified subject arrangement is better than alphabetical.

Statistical Measurement of Relationship

A question already mentioned is whether respondent
characteristics, as reported in Sections I and II of the questionnaire, seemed to exhibit any significant relationship with
the kinds of responses given in Sections III, IV, and V.
Some principal characteristics of the respondents, as summarized in the preceding chapter, were their professional
function and the type of institution they represented. For
purposes of statistical testing, all responses (as summarized
in Table 11) were also categorized and tallied by respondent
professional function, i.e., practitioner, teacher, or administrator. Practitioner responses were further categorized
and tallied by type of library represented, i.e., college, university, special, or system center. (Library school libraries were excluded as separate units for reasons previously
noted.)

In consultation with a statistical expert, two standard
non-parametric statistical measures of significant relationship were calculated for type of response vis-à-vis type of
respondent: chi-square (X^2) and coefficient of contingency
(C). The chi-square test asks: Assuming there might be
such a relationship, is there reliable evidence of a statistical association between the type of respondent and the manner in which that type expressed his opinions on the questionnaire statements? The chi-square technique aimed to test
the following null hypothesis: "There is no evidence of a
statistically significant relationship between the type of respondent and the way he reacted to the questionnaire statements." The alternative hypothesis would be: "There is
evidence of a statistically significant relationship between the
type of respondent and the way he reacted to the questionnaire statements." The latter hypothesis could be entertained
only if there were adequate statistical evidence to reject the
null hypothesis.

The coefficient of contingency (C), based on chi-square values, measures how strongly related is the type of respondent to his possible responses on a relative and comparative basis from question to question.   This measure would give statistical evidence of the degree of correlation.

It must be emphasized that, although these measurements were chosen and calculated with statistical advice, no claims to "scientific" precision are made.   Even within the frame of non-parametric measures for social science data, the limited quantity of such data here involved, as well as the aggregating of subtotals to obtain class frequencies large enough for testing, would make the results at best only suggestive.   There also exists the problem of "randomness," as discussed in the preceding chapter.   The statements, furthermore, could include so many possible variables, many perhaps unsuspected, that it would be unrealistic to present the test results as "valid" or "reliable" in the strict statistical sense.   However, the results can be useful for comparison with those of earlier studies, and be suggestive for further research, possibly pointing to more precise measurements in future work.   It is within the framework of these qualifications that the following statistical procedures and results are described.

The next Tables 13 and 14 summarize the outcomes of the two chi-square tests and present the coefficients of contingency for Statements III:1-11 discussed in this chapter. An explanation and interpretation of the tables ensue.

To obtain the data whose test results are shown in Table 13, the four types of responses ("Agree," "Undecided," "Do not agree," and "Other") were tallied by three types of respondents: practitioners, teachers, and administrators. Because of the need to accumulate adequate subtotals for the first chi-square test, "administrators" included both library and library school administrators, probably not an ideal grouping.   (The same definition of "administrators" is reflected in the analogous Tables 18 and 24 for the first chi-square tests in Chapters Eleven and Twelve, respectively.) However, for the second chi-square test and for the general analysis of response tallies, library administrators were considered practitioners (see Tables 12, 14, 17, 19, 23, 25). Such a variation added to the already admittedly tentative nature of the statistical measurements.   Certain mitigating factors, however, may be noted: (1) The possibility is tested that responses of library and library school administrators

TABLE 13

STATISTICAL MEASURES OF RELATIONSHIP BETWEEN
PROFESSIONAL FUNCTION OF RESPONDENT AND TYPE
OF RESPONSE FOR STATEMENTS III:1-11

Statement No. III:	Chi-Square Value	Level of Confidence	Coefficient of Contingency
1	7.201	50%	.212
2	6.547	50%	.204
3	0.840	01%	.063
4	7.783	70%	.219
5	4.042	30%	.161
6	3.244	20%	.144
7	1.803	05%	.104
8	2.095	05%	.114
8A	5.145	30%	.375
9	12.522	90%	.275
10	4.637	30%	.170
11	18.301[a]	99%[a]	.333

Notes:

Critical value of chi-square for 95% level of confidence is 12.592. Critical value for level of confidence is 95%. Maximum value for coefficient of contingency is 1.000.

[a] Equals or exceeds critical value.

might be statistically related; (2) The second chi-square test on the relationship between practitioner respondents' types of library and their type of response could serve as a counterbalance or corrective, since this second test considers library administrators as practitioners; (3) In analyzing possible statistical relationships suggested by the first chi-square tests (Tables 13, 18, 24), care was taken to indicate if library and library school administrators appeared to differ drastically in their patterns of opinion--evidence of the relative validity and reliability of this first test.

The critical chi-square value necessary to reject the null hypothesis at a 95-percent level of confidence (a level commonly chosen in social science research) was equal to 12.592. The first column gives the actual value for each

TABLE 14

STATISTICAL MEASURES OF RELATIONSHIP BETWEEN
PRACTITIONER RESPONDENTS' TYPE OF LIBRARY AND
THEIR TYPE OF RESPONSE FOR STATEMENTS III:1-11

Statement No. III:	Chi-Square Value	Level of Confidence	Coefficient of Contingency
1	.919	50%	.095
2	.215	25%	.031
3	.038	10%	.000
4	.020	10%	.014
5	.030	10%	.014
6	1.808	75%	.135
7	.190	25%	.042
8	.677	50%	.082
8A	.187	25%	.082
9	.001	05%	.003
10	.004	05%	.006
11	.014	05%	.012

Notes:

Critical value of chi-square for 95% level of confidence is 3.841.   Critical value for level of confidence is 95%.   Optimum value for coefficient of contingency is .707.

statement as derived from the chi-square test.   The next column gives the test results in an alternative form: at what level of confidence the null hypothesis could be rejected for each statement.   Thus, for Statement III:1, the first column indicates a value of only 7.201 as against the critical value of 12.592 required for rejecting at the confidence level of 95 percent the null hypothesis being tested.   The second column indicates that the null hypothesis could be rejected for the statement only at a 50-percent level of confidence, as against a required level of 95 percent.   The last column indicates a coefficient of contingency for the statement of only .212 as measured on a scale from .000 to 1.000, the latter figure being the greatest possible degree of association.   Thus, the null hypothesis cannot be convincingly rejected for Statement III:1, since there is inadequate evidence of a statistically significant relationship between the professional function of the respondent and the manner in which he reacted to this and, comparatively, the other statements.

Table 14 presents analogous data for the responses of practitioners (including library administrators) categorized by the type of library represented. For this testing--because of the technical need to obtain large enough class frequencies-- two classes of libraries were related to two types of responses. The first class of respondents combined those from college, university, and special libraries; the second class combined those from public libraries and library system centers. The two classes of opinions were "Agree" and "All other." The critical value of chi-square for a 95-percent level of confidence was 3.841. The optimum value for the coefficient of contingency was .707.

There was almost no indication of a statistically significant relationship between the type of response and the type of respondent as characterized either by his professional function or by the type of library he represented. In Table 13, only Statement III:11 had a chi-square value which met or exceeded the critical number for the 95-percent level of confidence. Though the coefficient of contingency was quite low, the level of confidence at which the null hypothesis could be rejected for the one statement was 99 percent. This was the sole instance in either Table 13 or 14 of a possible significant relationship, though Statement III:9 in Table 13 came closer than the others. The relevant tally for Statement III:11 is given in the following Table 15.

Table 15 indicates that only one out of 20 administrators (5 percent) agreed with the statement, compared with nine out of 43 teachers (20.9 percent) and 35 out of 83 practitioners (42.1 percent). (However, library administrators were less undecided and disagreed more than library school administrators.) For this statement, at least, the statistical measures suggested a relationship perhaps deserving further study. The generally very low measures for all other statements in Section III implied a decided lack of significant relationship between the type of respondent (or his library) and how he answered the questionnaire. This might indicate-- though, of course, it is not statistically demonstrated--that the type of library and professional function represented by the respondents did not significantly affect opinions on the various problems relating to the direct shelf approach and the role of classification.

Might the same be conjectured about the size factor of the library represented? This characteristic was considered for testing. Preliminary test results, however, gave insuf-

TABLE 15

RESPONSES TO STATEMENT III:11 CATEGORIZED BY
PROFESSIONAL FUNCTION OF RESPONDENT

Professional Function	Agree		Undecided		Do Not Agree		Other		Total	
	No.	%	No.	%	No.	%	No.	%	No.	%
Practitioner	35	24.0	29	19.9	14	9.6	5	3.4	83	56.9
Teacher	9	6.2	19	13.0	9	6.2	6	4.1	43	29.5
Administrator[a]	1	0.7	9	6.2	9	6.2	1	0.7	20	13.7
Total	45	30.1	57	39.0	32	21.9	12	8.2	146	100.0

[a]Includes library and library school administrator.

ficient reason to assume that such a relationship--if it ex-
isted--could be tested in this study, especially because of the
limited data. (With class intervals of 500, 000 volumes, 91
libraries would be distributed over 12 classes of which the
first three classes--up to a million volumes--would include
47. 2 percent of all respondent libraries.) Previous studies
have not shown significant association between library size
and respondents' attitudes towards basic problems of library
classification, e. g. , the 1966 survey by Tauber. 6

Of course, as already shown, respondents' opinions
were sometimes couched in terms of the size of their own libraries, e. g. , the comment of the head cataloger in a large
university library who wrote that close shelf classification
would be the norm for a large open stack such as that of her
library. 7 However, the cataloger in a small library might
well hold the same opinion in relation to large open stacks
in large libraries generally. Indeed, it would be very difficult to guess the size of library represented by the respondents if one had only unidentified comments as evidence.

Notes

1. Henry Evelyn Bliss, The Organization of Knowledge in
    Libraries; and the Subject-Approach to Books (2d ed. ,
    rev. and partly rewritten; New York: Wilson, 1939),
    p. 310; The Organization of Knowledge and the System
    of the Sciences (New York: Holt, 1929), p. 412;
    S. R. Ranganathan, Elements of Library Classification
    (3d ed. ; New York: Asia Publishing House, 1962),
    p. 150, 152-53; Bernard Ira Palmer, Itself an Educa-
    tion: Six Lectures on Classification (London: Library
    Assn. , 1962), p. 58, 60, 64.

2. Charles Ammi Cutter, "Close Classification, with Special
    Reference to Messrs. Perkins, Schwartz, and Dewey,"
    Library Journal, XI (July, 1886), 180. Melvil Dewey,
    "Catalogues and Cataloguing," in U. S. , Bureau of Ed-
    ucation, Public Libraries in the United States of Amer-
    ica; Their History, Condition, and Management; Spe-
    cial Report: Part I (Washington: Govt. Print. Off. ,
    1876), p. 629-30; Arthur E. Bostwick, The American
    Public Library (4th ed. , rev. and enl. ; New York:
    Appleton, 1929), p. 182.

3. Cutter, "Classification on the Shelves; with Some Account

of the New Scheme Prepared for the Boston Athenae-um," Library Journal, IV (July-August, 1879), p. 241.

4.   Saul Herner, "A Pilot Study of the Use of the Stacks of the Library of Congress," Washington: Herner, 1960 (Typewritten), p. 8; Annette L. Hoage, "Patron Use of the L. C. Classification," Library Resources and Technical Services, VI (Summer, 1962), 248; Maurice F. Tauber, "Review of the Use of the Library of Con-gress Classification," in Institute on the Use of the Library of Congress Classification, New York, 1966, Proceedings, ed. by Richard H. Schimmelpfeng and C. Donald Cook (Chicago: American Library Assn., 1968), p. 9.

5.   John Metcalfe, Information Indexing and Subject Catalog-ing: Alphabetical, Classified, Coordinate, Mechanical (New York: Scarecrow Press, 1957), p. 27-28, 64; Grace Osgood Kelley, The Classification of Books: An Inquiry into Its Usefulness to the Reader (New York: Wilson, 1937), p. 126; Julia C. Pettee, Sub-ject Headings: The History and Theory of the Alpha-betical Subject Approach to Books (New York: Wilson, 1946), p. 58-59.

6.   Tauber, "Review of the Use of the Library of Congress Classification," p. 3-4.

7.   See discussion of II:8 in Chapter Nine.

CHAPTER XI

ANALYSIS OF RESPONSES ON "DIRECT SHELF APPROACH
(OPEN-SHELF ACCESS): ITS SUITABILITY
IN VARIOUS LIBRARIES" (IV:1-19)

IV:1. "Open-shelf access is generally desirable in all libraries."

This statement epitomized a philosophy documented in the earlier chapters on the sociology and history of the direct shelf approach. The response was heavily in favor, though a considerable proportion did not agree. (For the tally of responses to statements discussed in this chapter, see the following Table 16.) Slightly under two-thirds agreed; almost three percent were undecided; a little less than one-third did not agree; and less than one percent expressed some other opinion. The small totals for "Undecided" and "Other" indicated that almost all respondents were willing to take a "yes or no" stand on a broadly stated principle. Nonetheless, the 19 comments--17 from those agreeing--carefully pointed out unavoidable exceptions. Thus, six comments from respondents who agreed excluded rare books and similar materials. One respondent remarked: "Security-classified library regulations actually prohibit open-shelf access."

Other qualifying comments from those agreeing were: "I've put 'Agree' here, but I can, of course, think of situations where it is clearly undesirable to have open access, e.g., in a library for the blind. A pity you had to include the word all." "In all public and academic libraries." "Public libraries." "This is my personal opinion. I dislike restrictions--but this may be a public library response." A college reference librarian, though agreeing, explained:

> 'All libraries' could include even rare book libraries and special collections, such as the Folger Shakespeare Library. It would be foolish to say that every library must have open-shelf access, although I think that this is a distinct advantage in public and school libraries.

TABLE 16

TOTAL RESPONSES TO STATEMENTS IV:1-19

Statement No. IV:	Agree No.	%	Undecided No.	%	Do Not Agree No.	%	Other No.	%	Total No.	%
1.	98	65.3	4	2.7	47	31.3	1	0.7	150	100.0
2.	88	59.1	21	14.1	38	25.5	2	1.3	149	100.0
3.	41	28.7	23	16.1	75	52.4	4	2.8	143	100.0
4.	79	54.9	10	6.9	52	36.1	3	2.1	144	100.0
5.	108	73.0	15	10.1	21	14.2	4	2.7	148	100.0
6.	113	79.6	15	10.6	8	5.6	6	4.2	142	100.0
7.	88	59.9	14	9.5	40	27.2	5	3.4	147	100.0
8.	39	26.4	19	12.8	85	57.4	5	3.4	148	100.0
9.	21	14.3	12	8.2	110	74.8	4	2.7	147	100.0
10.	15	10.3	6	4.1	124	84.9	1	0.7	146	100.0
11.	80	54.1	10	6.8	55	37.2	3	2.0	148	100.0
12.	37	25.0	22	14.9	86	58.1	3	2.0	148	100.0
13.	33	22.3	25	16.9	86	58.1	4	2.7	148	100.0
14.	48	33.3	25	17.4	68	47.2	3	2.1	144	100.0
15.	38	26.6	19	13.3	83	58.0	3	2.1	143	100.0
16.	32	21.8	12	8.2	100	68.0	3	2.0	147	100.0
17.	36	24.5	10	6.8	99	67.3	2	1.4	147	100.0
18.	6	4.0	10	6.7	132	88.0	2	1.3	150	100.0
19.	89	61.4	17	11.7	37	25.5	2	1.4	145	100.0

Other comments from those agreeing were less specific: "Most libraries." "Ideally." "At least to some extent." "Add 'except in isolated cases.' " "But perhaps not to total collection." A respondent raised the problem of expense: "Despite the cost of housekeeping of open shelves, I agree that the open-shelf concept is a good one."

Only two comments came from those who disagreed, one from a teacher of reference services who asked: "Rare book library?"--an exception which evidently did not influence others not to check "Agree." A second lengthier comment came from a teacher of technical services:

> I know I am in the minority, but this is where I usually am. As I mentioned in III:5, to get really the full range of subject approaches you need the combined subject word and subject number approach in our libraries. And the latter can often be given only by direct access to the shelves. To this extent, I agree with the statement. Nevertheless, there are many types of material in all libraries which are not suitable for open access, and if a library had a really good classed catalog, open shelves would not be needed. So I accept the questionnaire statement with reservations.

It may be noted that this last respondent's negative opinion was based not only on the unsuitability of certain types of materials for direct access but also on a special issue: the claimed superiority of the classed catalog for subject approach.

Table 17 summarizes practitioner (including library administrator) responses to the statements in Section IV discussed in this chapter. Unless specifically noted in the discussion of a particular statement, it may be understood that the pattern of practitioners' opinions on that statement did not differ markedly from that of all responses as shown by Table 16. As defined in the previous chapter, a "marked" difference in the opinion distribution would be one of at least five percentage points for any category of response to any statement.

Although there was no marked difference between the opinion distribution of practitioner respondents and all respondents on this statement, a point of interest was the type of library whose respondents did not check "Agree." Categorization of the responses to IV:1 by the type of library represented (this tally is not shown in Table 17) indicated that within each type of library the percentage of all responses other than "Agree" was, respectively, university library--43.5, college library--44-4, special library--53.3, public library--23.1, public and school system center--0.0. These data would indicate that more opposition to "blanket" approval of open shelves came, as might be expected, from academic and special libraries. Yet, except in the case of special libraries, a majority of the responses from each library type was "Agree."

Thus, almost two-thirds of all respondents were willing to check "Agree" on a statement expressing, in a deliberately broad form, the desirability of open shelves. This would imply, if it were not already evident from its widespread use in American libraries, the continuing loyalty of American librarians to the basic principle of direct access whenever possible. Further analysis of practitioners' responses indicated that opposition to open-shelf policy was stronger, proportionately, among academic and special libraries; though only in the case of special libraries was a majority unwilling to check "Agree."

IV:2. "Maintaining open-shelf access is a significant educational responsibility of libraries."

This statement, related to III:3, attempted to assay opinion on a pedagogical concept of direct access and open shelves, as exampled in the description of the public library as the "people's university." Table 16 shows that somewhat fewer, proportionately, checked "Agree" for IV:2 than for IV:1; somewhat fewer checked "Do not agree"; and about the same percentage expressed an "Other" opinion. Significantly greater in number and proportion, however, were those who checked "Undecided" for IV:2 as compared with IV:1--more than five times as many. Evidently, a pedagogical rationale for open shelves, while still eliciting majority agreement, fostered more indecision or unwillingness to express a definite opinion than did the general principle of open shelves.

The 12 comments were mostly from those agreeing and mostly of a brief and generally qualifying nature. Among the comments from those agreeing were: "I think there are many exceptions, of course." "Not sure I know what this means, but I'll agree." "It is a helpful service responsibil-

TABLE 17

TOTAL PRACTITIONER RESPONSES TO STATEMENTS IV:1-19

Statement No. IV:	Agree		Undecided		Do Not Agree		Other		Total	
	No.	%	No.	%	No.	%	No.	%	No.	%
1.	62	62.0	4	4.0	34	34.0	--	--	100	100.0
2.	59	59.0	15	15.0	25	25.0	1	1.0	100	100.0
3.	30	31.6	15	15.8	49	51.6	1	1.1	95	100.0
4.	52	54.2	8	8.3	36	37.5	--	--	96	100.0
5.	73	73.7	10	10.1	13	13.1	3	3.0	99	100.0
6.	74	78.7	12	12.8	4	4.3	4	4.3	94	100.0
7.	58	59.2	12	12.2	25	25.5	3	3.1	98	100.0
8.	24	24.2	14	14.1	59	59.6	2	2.0	99	100.0
9.	15	15.2	8	8.1	73	73.7	3	3.0	99	100.0
10.	13	13.3	4	4.1	81	82.7	--	--	98	100.0
11.	55	55.0	7	7.0	36	36.0	2	2.0	100	100.0
12.	26	26.0	12	12.0	60	60.0	2	2.0	100	100.0
13.	24	24.0	13	13.0	61	61.0	2	2.0	100	100.0
14.	32	33.3	15	15.6	47	49.0	2	2.1	96	100.0
15.	28	29.2	12	12.5	54	56.3	2	2.1	96	100.0
16.	20	20.2	6	6.1	71	71.7	2	2.0	99	100.0
17.	26	26.3	7	7.1	65	65.7	1	1.0	99	100.0
18.	5	5.0	8	7.9	88	87.1	--	--	101	100.0
19.	60	61.9	11	11.4	24	24.7	2	2.1	97	100.0

ity. " "Basically. Educational locational responsibility. "
"Certain libraries. " "Yes, but a responsibility only for those
libraries which determine that open-shelf access is feasible,
e.g., not rare book libraries. " "In most instances. " A library school administrator added: "This may be by dial access, also, in the future. "

The two comments from those who checked "Do not
agree" were not very specific: "Depends on type of library, "
and "Do not agree for all. " These might have been categorized as "Qualified Agree. " The remaining comment, from
a college technical services librarian, who was undecided,
expressed his philosophy of teaching: "Undecided. I think
that the 'educational responsibility' of the library is limited,
and therefore open-shelf access is educational in a haphazard
or unplanned way. "

When responses to this statement were tallied for practitioners only, the pattern of opinion among librarians was
found to be almost the same as among all respondents. Within each type of library, however, the following percentage
distribution of "Agree" responses was observed: university
library--63. 0; college library--55. 6; special library--40. 0;
public library--61. 5; public and school library system center
--75. 0. Thus the percentage of agreement from public library respondents was slightly less than that from university
library respondents--even though the educational motivation
of the modern American public library had been so strongly
advanced in the early struggle for direct access. Also of
note was the considerably lower percentage of agreement
among college compared with university librarians. One
might have thought the former would have been at least as
concerned with an educational potential of direct access. The
comments on this statement were neither especially numerous
nor definite. This might point to absence of firm convictions,
or even to disinterest.

IV:3. "The direct shelf approach is of value primarily
as a means to create for the reader or student a structured
learning situation. "

This statement, which drew only weak agreement, presented a further hypothesis on a pedagogical rationale of the
direct shelf approach, i.e., that the selection and arrangement of materials for open shelves were meant to create a
structured ("programmed, " so to speak) learning environment

wherein the patron would be led to learn, from purposefully
acquired materials organized by shelf classification, what
those materials were capable of teaching. "Structured learning situation," borrowed from current educational psychology
literature, was intended to suggest a teaching function of direct access as fulfilled through the structuring of the collection by acquisition policy and, though not primarily, to imply
the revealing of the "structure" of knowledge through bibliothecal classification.

The majority (52. 4 percent) did not agree; less than
one-third (28. 7 percent) agreed; 16. 1 and 2. 8 percent were,
respectively, undecided or of some other opinion. Of the 11
comments, six questioned the meaning: "Quite certain I
haven't the least idea of what this means." "Don't know what
such language means." "Question too vague." "Ambiguous
to me." "Undecided. I don't know what a 'structured learning situation' is." "Meaning?"

Some protested the phrasing: "Choice of terms?
'Structured learning situation'--gobbledegook!" "Less jargon,
please."

A college reader-services librarian who was undecided stated: "Only for libraries which determine that open-
shelf access is feasible"--a comment he made also on the
preceding statement. Comments from two respondents who
checked "Do not agree" seemed to show comprehension of the
statement's intent. Thus, a teacher of technical services remarked: "Other resources available for such learning," and
a teacher of reference: "I hope not."

The responses to IV:3 reinforced the inference that
respondents were by no means unanimously agreed on a pedagogical purpose of direct access, i. e., to be self-teaching or
to provide a kind of "programmed" instruction. Although
IV:3 may have been too abstract to be acceptable to many respondents, that in itself might suggest that librarians and
teachers were not inclined to conceptualize shelf classification
and direct access, or to relate them pedagogically to current
educational ideas.

IV:4. "The value of open-shelf access is primarily
conditioned by the quality and appropriateness of the library's
collection."

This hypothesis aimed to measure opinion on the significance of acquisition and selection policies in "structuring" the collection and, thus, in "controlling" the benefits to be derived from direct access.   The statement reflected the discussion in Chapter Seven on the relation of acquisition policy to the direct shelf approach.   One might suppose that IV:4 was a truism--indeed, as shown below, this was sometimes a reason for disagreeing with it!   Strictly as worded, IV:4 would imply that the materials rather than their arrangement would constitute the principal value of a collection on open shelves.   Such a view might be more congenial to those preferring subject approach through catalogs and bibliographies, since they would probably consider preliminary bibliographic approach more effective for any type of shelf arrangement. Collection quality would accordingly assume paramount significance.

More than one-half (54.9 percent) checked "Agree"; 6.9 percent "Undecided"; 36.1 percent "Do not agree"; and 2.1 percent expressed some other opinion.   Almost twice as many were willing to agree with IV:4 as with IV:3, though the statements were not logically unconnected.   Of course, the abstraction of IV:3 may have caused many to disagree. It is also possible, however, as just discussed, that most respondents did not connect theoretically their acquisition and classification policies with the "structuring" of their collections in any pedagogical sense, particularly in terms of direct access.

Only nine comments resulted, many emphasizing the obviousness of the statement--though, as indicated above, this did not necessarily mean agreement.   Among the four comments from those agreeing was: "But true of any situation."   The other comments from those agreeing made significant qualifications: "Plus the nature of its catalog."   "And its size."   "Not 'primarily conditioned by'--'related to.' "

Those who disagreed commented: "All 'access' is so conditioned."   "I don't agree.   If you have an open-shelf library, the quality of the collection or the appropriateness has nothing to do with the idea of open-shelf access."

Those who held "Other" opinions remarked: "The value of a library is primarily conditioned, etc.   If the collections are lousy, open access, closed access, catalog, it's all the same--lousy."   "Question is irrelevant--a poor, inappropriate collection is worthless, open or closed!"   (One

may note that, as shown earlier, respondents will cite the
same reasons for differing with others on the same state-
ment--another complication for accurate statistical measurement.)

     IV:5.   "Public libraries cannot serve their readers
adequately without offering open-shelf access."

     This statement reflected the generally held opinion
that open-shelf access was a hallmark of modern American
public library development.   Bostwick[1] had called it part of
the socialization process of the American public library.   The
hypothesis implied that the "philosophy" of the American public library could not be satisfactorily implemented without direct access.

     Response was generally affirmative.   Almost three-
fourths (73.0 percent) checked "Agree"; 10.1 percent "Undecided"; 14.2 percent "Do not agree"; and 2.7 percent expressed an "Other" opinion.

     There were 14 comments, usually qualifying the basic
choice.   (Some comments referred to the Reference Department of the New York Public Library as a "public" library.
More accurately, the Reference Department is primarily a
privately supported, closed-stack, non-circulating research
collection which is open to the public.   Like the Library of
Congress, it was described by its staff responding to this
questionnaire as a "special" research library.)

     Comments from those agreeing were: "But not central
stack of 2 million volumes!"   "In non-rare or highly specialized materials, and in other exceptions, e.g., it would be a
national disaster if the New York Public Library opened up
the stacks of the Reference Department to all comers!"   "Depends on type of 'public' and type of material."   "But does
not have to be totally open-shelf."   "At least for part of the
collection."   "With qualifications as to some collections."
"Notable exception: New York Public Library."

     A respondent who disagreed explained: "I don't agree.
I can foresee where a public library can serve its clientele
well without open-shelf access.   New York Public Library at
42nd Street and Fifth Avenue does very well with its closed-
stack policy."

Some "Other" opinions were qualifying or cautious.
A university library administrator stated: "I do not feel qualified to make a judgment."   A university reference librarian
commented: "Don't know your criterion for 'adequate service.' "   Another university library administrator remarked:
"Wouldn't know."   A teacher of reference qualified: "In general.   Again, can't there be a qualification here?"

In summary, almost three-fourths of all respondents
were willing to accept open-shelf access as necessary for
public libraries to fulfill their service function.   The comments of those agreeing suggested that not all the collection
was necessarily equally suitable for direct access; and a respondent who disagreed evidently felt that the catalog and other bibliographical devices could substitute adequately for direct access.

IV:6.   "School libraries (elementary through high
school) cannot fulfill their function adequately without open access."

As explained in Chapter Nine, practitioner or teacher
respondents specializing in children's librarianship were few,
so this statement probably evoked general professional opinion
on whether direct access was as important in school libraries
as in other types, e.g., public libraries of IV:5.

There were 142 responses out of a possible 152, the
second largest "abstention" from any statement.   Comments
confirmed that the specialized nature of the libraries involved
made respondents reluctant to express an opinion in so "foreign" a field.   However, the 142 who did respond were generally affirmative: 79. 6 percent agreed; 10. 6 percent were
undecided; 5. 6 percent did not agree; and 4. 2 percent expressed some other opinion.

It may be surmised that most of those who agreed believed generally in the desirability of open shelves in a "public" situation--as evidenced in reactions to the previous statement.   An "Undecided" respondent qualified this general belief: "I do not know.   Open access is good basic principle,
but I do not think that a closed-shelf library cannot function
adequately.   Again, I suppose one would have to know what
the 'function' of the library is supposed to be."

A teacher of technical services who agreed added:
"Based on my view of their function."

Remaining comments from those with "Other" opinions questioned either the wording or their own competence: "No experience." "I do not feel qualified to make a judgment." "Don't know your criterion for 'adequate function.' " "Wouldn't know." "What is their function?" "In general. Again, can't there be a qualification here?"

Contributory to the generally high percentage of agreement might be an inferred analogy with children's collections in public libraries which are traditionally open-shelf. Also, the usual publicized examples of school libraries are relatively small one-room collections arranged to encourage the young reader to make direct use of the materials. To conclude, at least for the lower educational levels most respondents seemed to accept the idea of open access as part of the learning process, an opinion less widely held, apparently, as the educational level rose.

IV:7. "The smaller the library, the more valuable is open-shelf access."

This hypothesis expressed a judgment on the benefits to be gained from direct access; it did not raise the issue of whether direct access was more feasible for smaller than for larger collections, though feasibility might be implicit. One possible reason for agreement could be that a patron would have more opportunity to benefit from direct access to the entire collection, if it were small, than to only part of a large collection to which direct access was limited because of considerations of time and effort. The hypothesis might imply that open-shelf access was more useful for general surveys of broad fields of knowledge by non-specialist patrons than for very specific subject research by advanced scholars. Of course, a small collection could be specialized and, to follow the above reasoning, thus enhance direct access for subject investigation. However, this last possibility evidently did not particularly influence--if the responses for IV:7 be compared with those for III:7. (Also, the median size of special libraries represented by respondents was, as shown in Table 3, 750,000 volumes, hardly a "small" collection.) This point will be further discussed in connection with IV:8.

Responses for IV:7 were: "Agree"--59.9 percent; "Undecided"--9.5 percent; "Do not agree"--27.2 percent; and "Other"--3.4 percent. The 17 comments mostly raised the problem of feasibility, denied the validity of size as a criterion, or questioned the possibility of any opinion.

Those agreeing commented: "I'm not sure about valuable, but more feasible." "You must except the rare book
collection in this statement." "And less reason for closed
stacks." "I agree. Generally, the smaller the collection,
the greater the need for open shelves." "I guess so."

Those disagreeing gave the following reasons: "I
found the open access valuable for graduate research." "Valuable in all libraries." "Not size of library but nature and
content of material and patrons determine value of open-shelf
access." "Not necessarily." "Size is no determination of
value." "Depends on staff and service. Some small special
libraries O. K. with closed shelf." "To whom? The librarian?"

"Other" respondents stressed inability to judge: "No
opinion." "Wouldn't know." "Depends on type of library."
"Have not measured their comparative value."

Of interest, as suggested above, is a comparison of
the responses to IV:7 with those to III:7, "Close shelf classification is as useful and feasible for small libraries as it
is for large libraries." The earlier statement covered both
the feasibility and value of close shelf classification, whereas
IV:7 focused on the value of open-shelf access. Yet, the decidedly contrary patterns of "Agree" and "Do not agree" for
these statements raised the possibility that the elements of
open-shelf access and close shelf classification were not as
logically connected in respondents' minds as those of direct
access and small collection size. A common opinion in the
literature was that the larger the collection the closer usually
should be the shelf classification. This idea was not contradicted by the responses to III:7. Reactions to IV:7 would indicate that open-shelf access was thought more valuable in the
smaller library. Hence, the opinions on III:7 and IV:7, if
taken together, seemed to imply a general belief in broad
classification for small open-shelf libraries. The next statement is relevant to this issue.

IV:8. "Direct shelf approach is more useful in a specialized or university departmental collection with a homogeneous clientele than in mixed collections with different types
of readers."

The statement expressed a value judgment and left
"useful" open for interpretation. The hypothesis represented

an opinion often met in the literature that direct access was
most productive for subject search by specialists in special
collections which were usually provided with close shelf classification.   (The opposite opinion has also been advanced,
i. e. , that subject specialists prefer bibliographic to shelf access.   This latter view is included in later statements, particularly in IV:17.)

     A clear majority (57. 4 percent) did not agree; only
26. 4 percent agreed; 12. 8 percent were undecided; and 3. 4
percent held some other opinion.   Thus, about three-fourths
were not willing to check "Agree. "

     There were eight comments.   The only one from a
respondent who agreed, a teacher of technical services, expressed belief in the virtues of the classified catalog along
with close shelf classification:

          To summarize my reaction to the last few ques-
          tions, for a school, public, or specialized library
          serving a homogeneous clientele, I agree with open
          access to most materials because (1) my ideal, the
          classed catalog, would not be feasible in a school
          or public library and (2) a specialized library tends
          to serve a bibliographically sophisticated clientele
          which can make serious (rather than browsing) use
          of close shelf classification.

     A college acquisitions librarian was undecided:

          I really don't know.   Direct shelf access is as use-
          ful to the Donnell branch of the New York Public
          Library where its users are varied as it is useful
          in the Frick Art Reference Library where its users
          are practically all 'art' students or researchers.

     A library school administrator who disagreed added:
"Not necessarily. "   A teacher of technical services who disagreed emphasized format: "Here again, departmental libraries are more likely to be composed of documents, pamphlets,
etc. , which affects access and classification needs. "

     Those not checking an option expressed inability to
judge: "No opinion. "   "Wouldn't know. "   "Have not measured
their comparative value. "

     A possible motive for the preponderantly negative atti-

tude might be found in the first quoted comment from the
teacher of technical services who agreed but distinguished
"serious" direct access from "browsing," and also implied
that close classification was primarily for serious research.
For much the same reasons, the majority of respondents
might have favored the benefits of direct access for the non-
specialist, "non-serious" browser in general libraries, public
or academic.   Presumably, the majority, as indicated by response to III:7 and IV:7, would also favor broad shelf classification.

Since specialized or university departmental libraries
tend to be smaller than general collections, the responses to
IV:8 might be thought inconsistent with those to IV:7.   Opinion on IV:7 was strongly for open shelves in smaller libraries, whereas that on IV:8 did not accept the greater need for
open shelves in specialized collections.   The statements, however, may not be logically comparable, and there is confirmatory evidence in the comments on IV:8 that collection size
and collection specialization were not considered equally relevant in determining shelf policy.   In other words, the majority did not seem to give great weight to collection specialization in decisions on direct access.   This may be another
instance of a general reluctance to limit the benefits of direct
access to any particular type of library.

IV:9.   "Open-shelf access is more needed in university or research libraries than in general undergraduate libraries."

This statement tested acceptance of a hypothesis that
direct access would be of greater usefulness in the larger,
more advanced academic research collections than in college
libraries, since the latter would tend to be less specialized
or scholarly, and their users less in need of materials for
advanced, independent research.   ("General undergraduate libraries" was not intended to designate only physically separate undergraduate libraries, like Harvard's Lamont Library,
which have been established as units within university library
systems.   It was meant to refer to undergraduate libraries
generally, as distinguished from university or research libraries.)   The statement implied that direct access was more
valuable for higher than lower levels of study.   (Statements
IV:10 and 14 are related to IV:9 and stress the possibility of
"structuring" undergraduate learning experience through the
provision of "pre-selected" titles.   Statement IV:17 presents

an hypothesis on the general need for direct access in advanced research.)

Response was largely negative: 74.8 percent disagreed; only 14.3 percent agreed; 8.2 percent were undecided;
and 2.7 percent had some other opinion.   Most of the 12
comments confirmed the general negative opinion.   A university library administrator who checked "Agree" gave a pragmatic reason: "Because faculty would rebel if it were otherwise."   Comments from those disagreeing were: "If you
mean the general collection." "It's valuable for any library,
may not be feasible for some!" "Equally needed." "More?
More helpful?" "It is equally useful in the public library
branch because people may not know exactly what they are
looking for and in the research library where the researcher
can see other books he may not have found primarily through
the card catalog, and also because of the loss of time making
out request slips, and delivery from closed-shelf libraries."
"Other" comments were: "No experience." "It is useful in
both." "No opinion." "Have not measured their comparative
value."

Most respondents thus did not agree that direct access
was more important for advanced academic and research than
for undergraduate collections.   This would tend to confirm
the response to IV:8 that direct access was no less valuable
for general than for specialized subject research.

IV:10.   "Reserved book collections and assigned reading lists make largely unnecessary open-shelf access in college libraries."

This hypothesis raised a pedagogical issue: to what
extent does the traditional instructional use of "pre-selected"
reading make open shelves inessential for the major study
activities of college students?   (Not unrelated is the wide
availability of inexpensive, paperbound critical anthologies for
numerous major works in the humanities.)   Though IV:10 did
not express a value judgment on such an instructional policy,
some respondents did so in their comments.

Response was even more negative than to the preceding: 84.9 percent did not agree; 10.3 percent agreed; 4.1
percent were undecided; and 0.7 percent expressed some other opinion.   Only five comments resulted.   The administrator
of a school library system center who agreed added: "Yes!

but that doesn't make them desirable." A library school administrator with an "Other" opinion explained: "Not related unless <u>total</u> curriculum is based on reserve reading and reading list." Remaining comments were from those disagreeing: "If you are thinking only of the junior students." "But still desirable!" A college acquisitions librarian remarked:

> I would hope that college students do more than just assigned or required readings, and that the college is giving them a choice of recreational reading, and doing more than insisting on the reading lists. Honors courses, of course, require students to go on their own and explore the collection.

Despite frequent complaints by librarians on the expense and inconvenience of maintaining large reserve collections in college libraries, and despite the prevalence of assigned reading lists, most respondents evidently felt it a responsibility of the college library to maintain direct access for students. This principle was expounded in a letter appended by a teacher of classification:

> For those readers who are working within the confines of a set reading list, you don't need a library. Just a locked room with enough copies of each text, and a strong man to turn the key. If catalogs and bibliographies will give us all the answers, all we need is a central lending service, not a whole lot of libraries. Take for example the National Library for Science and Technology in Britain. If you know what you want, you send them a request by 3:00 P.M., and you will get the item next morning through the mails. This is not a substitute for going into a local library, to see what is available, to get ideas, to handle the contents. It serves a very different function, equivalent to a closed-access stack. Open access has a very different purpose.

IV:11. "Open-shelf access is more needed for use of books than for serials."

This hypothesis implied an opinion frequent in the literature that serials are more effectively approached through indexes and bibliographies, the usual reasons being that journal articles are too numerous, varied, and specific to be ef-

fectively searched through shelf inspection. The statement
intended to refer to bound volumes of serials, since current
issues in most libraries are usually made available immediately on open racks for review or browsing. The responses
and comments indicated that this was generally understood.

The majority (54.1 percent) agreed; 6.8 percent were
undecided; 37.2 percent did not agree; and 2.0 percent had
some other opinion.

There were seven comments. A teacher of reference
who agreed qualified: "Back files but not for current issues."
A technical services public librarian who agreed explained:
"Shortage of staff which might require more self-service
would affect this decision. Closed stacks for serials also
gives more security to back files of important resources."
A college acquisitions librarian who agreed gave these reasons:

> I agree. One needs to explore the shelves. Seri-
> als generally are not explorable, unless one ex-
> plores the indexes to periodicals. I would think
> that when one asks for a periodical other than one
> for light or recreational reading, that he is looking
> for something very specific.

"Other" comments were: "Here again, I feel no useful point is served by arguing whether open-shelf access is
more needed for use of books than for serials," and "Perhaps." The head of a university library's technical services
department who disagreed explained his reasoning at some
length:

> You will readily identify me, after a glance at my
> answers on the enclosed questionnaire, as a firm
> advocate of open-shelf access whenever possible.
> My stance on the question does not derive primari-
> ly from its browsing values, although I recognize
> that these can at times be quite real. Far more
> important, to my mind, is the gain to the reader
> in the efficiency with which he can go directly to
> the specific items which he has already identified
> as probably the ones he needs. May I take the lib-
> erty of enclosing a reprint of an article I co-au-
> thored in 1962; please note the marked passage:
> 'Open stacks are of tremendous benefit to students
> and library staff alike. Brooklyn College com-

ments: "Since our collection is on open shelves,
the urgent desire of the student to get his books is
simply reflected in the rapidity of the student's
own progress from the card catalog to the book
shelves." '   The same statement surely applies to
a faculty member doing research.

I would register this view with particular vehemence
relative to your IV:11.   I have never appreciated
open access more than when engaged in a fast literature search, emerging with a list of citations to
periodical articles which I could check rapidly right
at the shelves.   I strongly disagree with Orne, 2
feeling that he misses the main point.

A teacher of reader services who disagreed gave as
his reason: "Bibliographic access only is generally poor policy."

Though the majority evidently believed that direct access was more needed for books than serials, differing opinion was not inconsiderable, 46.0 percent being unwilling to
check "Agree."

IV:12.   "Open-shelf access is more needed by readers
in the humanities than in the sciences."

Statements IV:12 and 13 attempted to test opinion on
the relative need of open-shelf access in broad subject areas:
humanities vis-à-vis sciences, social sciences vis-à-vis
"hard" sciences.   The hypotheses implied that open shelves
became less valuable as the disciplines became "harder" and
presumably more susceptible to precise specification.   Statement IV:12 presented the humanities-sciences dichotomy.

Only 25.0 percent agreed; 14.9 percent were undecided; 58.1 percent did not agree; and 2.0 percent expressed
some other opinion.   There were eight comments.   The dominant reason for agreement was that as the subject became
more "scientific," the information sought would become more
specific, and thus indexes and bibliographies would be more
helpful than shelf inspection.   "Other" comments were: "No
opinion."   "Wouldn't know."   "How can you generalize?"
Remaining comments were from those who agreed: "Because
sciences use indexes and periodicals more."   "Probably."
"Agree only because indexing is poorer."   "Add 'in most sit-

uations.' " A college acquisitions librarian offered the following remarks, which he extended also to IV:13 and 14:

> Generally, I agree that the users in the humanities
> need to browse more than those in the sciences.
> I would think that those doing work in the sciences
> are looking for specific materials and do not expect
> to stumble on what they are looking for by fumbling
> among the books that a specific library happens to
> have on the shelves at a time that he is looking.

Thus, only a fourth of all respondents would agree on
the greater need of open access for materials in the humanities vis-à-vis the sciences.

IV:13. "Open-shelf access is more needed by readers
in the social sciences than in the biological and physical sciences."

This hypothesis extended the above mentioned "soft-
hard" dichotomy to the sciences. General opinion is that the
social and/or behavioral sciences are less "hard" than the
life and physical sciences. (An analogy for such a continuum
of hardness might be that of an intellectual Mohs scale.) Response was consistent with that for IV:12. Opinion distribution was similar: 22.3 percent agreed; 16.9 percent were
undecided; 58.1 percent disagreed; and 2.7 percent expressed
some other opinion. There were seven comments, none adding substantially to those on IV:12. Those not checking an
option remarked: "No opinion." "Wouldn't know." "How
can you generalize?" "Oh, for God's sake?" The last comment, from a library school administrator, apparently expressed impatience with the cumulative intent of IV:12 and 13.
Those who agreed added: "Probably." "In most situations."
The comment by the college acquisitions librarian on IV:12
applied also to IV:13.

Responses to IV:12 and 13 indicated that the great majority were not willing to accept the idea that direct access
became less necessary as the subject materials became more
scientific and, thus, presumably more specific and quantifi-
able as to the information contained. One implication might
be that the majority did not accept the adequacy of bibliographic access to the sciences. A complicating factor could
be the relative quantity and importance of science literature
in journals as compared with the literature of the humanities

and the "softer" disciplines. Responses to IV:11, however, would suggest that this factor was taken into account.

IV:14. "Direct shelf approach is most valuable in col-lections for beginning students where the books are basic or 'core' titles. "

This statement, connected with the concept of the di-rect shelf approach as providing a "structured learning situa-tion," tested reaction to the hypothesis that open shelves in academic libraries were of greatest benefit when students were on a beginning level and were presented with a "core" or "foundation" or "opening day" assemblage--a principle dis-cussed in Chapter Seven on acquisition policy. (This state-ment is related in varying degree to most of the previous hypotheses concerned with the pedagogical nature of direct ac-cess, especially to IV:3 and 4.) More abstractly, IV:14 might read: "The direct shelf approach in academic libraries is most valuable when performing a propadeutic function. "

Reaction was mostly negative or undecided. Only one-third agreed; 17. 4 percent were undecided; 47. 2 percent did not agree; and 2. 1 percent held some other opinion.

Most of the nine comments were either qualifying, or disclaiming competence to judge. Comments from those agreeing were: "Well, at least it is ALSO valuable--but sure-ly too for the chemistry department library serving graduate students and researchers. " "No supporting data. " "I inter-pret this to mean an 'undergraduate reading room' or some-thing similar. These two terms, 'basic' and 'core' are very vague. " The previously cited remarks by the college acquisi-tions librarian on IV:12 and 13 were also applied to this statement.

A teacher of reference who was undecided explained: "The word 'most' fills me with doubt. " Comments from those not checking an option were: "Probably. " "No experi-ence. " "No opinion. " A college technical services librarian who did not agree remarked: "Not necessarily. Believe all libraries should have open stacks, but do not know really in which situations it is 'more needed' than in others. "

Though there could be many reasons for rejecting this statement--depending on the context within which it was taken --the responses and comments for previous hypotheses in-

volving the "structuring" aspect of acquisition and classification policies lead one to surmise that one reason might be
dislike of the idea that students would be "constrained" within
pre-selected collections and thus not free to exercise their
privilege of direct access in a more diversified, less conditioned learning environment.   Related to this surmised reason might be the faith--to be examined when analyzing the
next section of the questionnaire--in the benefits of serendipity assumed to be provided by the browsing process.

        IV:15.   "The validity of the direct shelf approach les-
sens as research in the discipline relies more on topical subjects and less on personal names and distinctive titles for
access to information."

        This statement offered a hypothesis, related to IV:12,
that the direct shelf approach had greatest value or effectiveness for works, as in the humanities, adequately identifiable
and arrangeable by author and title, e.g., Hamlet by Shakespeare or a biography of Proust by Maurois.   Such works,
though highly accessible through bibliographic agency, would
tend to be more easily recognized, assayed, and retrieved
on open shelves than works in the sciences whose specific
topical subject matter might not be clear from the classified
arrangement (or title) and whose author's name might not be
significant to the patron.   Such a hypothesis accords with the
opinions in the literature that study and research in the sciences depend more on bibliographies and periodical indexes
than on shelf arrangement.

        The majority (58.0 percent) disagreed; 13.3 percent
were undecided; only 26.6 percent agreed; and 2.1 percent
expressed some other opinion.   Almost three-fourths, thus,
were unwilling to check "Agree," though the somewhat abstract wording may have confused some.

        None of the 10 comments came from those who agreed.
A significant number questioned the theoretical assumptions
of the hypothesis.   A teacher of reference who was undecided
reworded the hypothesis: "As form of publication varies with
discipline."   A teacher of technical services who was also
undecided explained:

            I disagree violently with this statement because I
            believe its reasoning is wrong.   Surely as the re-
            search knowledge in the discipline increases, the

> researcher uses the direct approach less (though he
> will still use it) and relies more heavily on biblio-
> graphic identification, for the location of specific
> information, through specialized subject bibliogra-
> phies. His approach here may be specialized top-
> ical subject, but he will rely heavily on personal
> names of other researchers known to him in his
> subject field.

The last comment seems more to agree than disagree
with the statement. "Other" comments questioned wording or
assumptions: "Don't know what a 'topical subject' is." "What
do you mean 'validity'???" "I question the basic premise
underlined: as research in the discipline relies ... less on
personal names and distinctive titles."

Comments from those disagreeing also, in general,
doubted the assumptions: "I am not sure your premise is
valid." "No evidence that such a transition takes place."
"I don't agree. Direct shelf approach does not necessarily
become less valid as research continues along various lines."
A college reference librarian detailed his opposite view:

> On the contrary, I think that when research relies
> on personal names and distinctive titles, open-shelf
> access can be a bother when all a researcher need
> do is present a list of call numbers so that a deck
> boy will retrieve the needed material. As in IV:4
> above, I think that topical research is aided by
> open-shelf access, since library catalogs and bibli-
> ographies inadequately present specific, and ab-
> stract topics especially.

Most respondents--assuming the statement's intended
meaning was clear--thus seemed opposed to downgrading the
direct shelf approach in topical subject research as compared
with its use in research involving works with distinctive auth-
or and title names, such works being presumably more common in the humanities than the sciences. This overall opinion would be consistent with earlier responses evidencing a
general belief in shelf classification as a means to display
topical subject relationships.

IV:16: "Adequate catalogs, bibliographies and, when
available, reference assistance, would make open-shelf access in large academic libraries largely unnecessary."

This statement advanced the hypothesis, not infrequent in the literature, that direct access in large academic (or research) libraries could be replaced on the whole by bibliographic and personal assistance. Any such library with closed stacks would be assuming this service policy, one more common in European institutions. The hypothesis would probably be favored particularly by advocates of the classed catalog who stress bibliographic over bibliothecal organization.

Less than one-fourth (21.8 percent) agreed; 8.2 percent were undecided; 68.0 percent did not agree; and 2.0 percent had some other opinion. Thus, almost 80 percent were unwilling to accept the idea that direct access could be unnecessary, under certain circumstances, in large academic libraries.

There were 13 comments. Most either questioned the probability of the assumed circumstances or, even granting such aids available, still defended the need for direct access. Comments from those agreeing were: "But would have to be generously adequate." "But still desirable." "Perhaps." A teacher of technical services who agreed gave criteria for adequacy:

> I agree. But, to me, an adequate catalog in a research library must (1) be classified; (2) be closely coordinated with the bibliography collection; (3) make far more use of analytics, especially subject analytics, than is customary--I am thinking of documentation approach here; (4) be staffed by a sufficient number (I don't mean 1 at a time, I mean 6 at a time) of the best staff members available to help coordinate all bibliographical approaches.

A public library technical services practitioner who was undecided differentiated "browsing" from research:

> Browsing and research seem to me two different things, but both require access to shelves; research requires shelves with reasonably close classification. Not all information can be put into catalogs and bibliographies, and access to books and their indexes is needed.

A college reference librarian, also undecided, challenged the assumptions:

This statement really seems too hypothetical for a
definite answer. 'Adequate' tools and staffing seem
so far distant that they seem impossible. Tools
must be much more elaborate in detail, or I'm
afraid that browsing will still be necessary, only
the browsing will take place after materials have
been retrieved from closed stacks. Locating materials through the broad, and often inconsistent
and unclear, subject headings now used in catalogs,
for instance, will result in a patron's request for
great numbers of books to examine for relevancy
and a great number of books for the library staff
to shelve. This does not overlook the fact that
many more rejected volumes may be off the shelves
than in cases where browsers work directly at the
shelves.

Comments from those disagreeing were as follows.
A public reference librarian asked: "Adequate? What is
that?" A reference teacher questioned the phrasing: "Adequate when available???" A college acquisitions librarian
remarked:

I don't agree. Adequate catalogs, bibliographies,
etc., certainly are a great help (for those who are
looking for specific information) but for the more
general user, the browser, the person unsure of
what he really wants, he would find the open-
shelves approach still useful.

A teacher of classification analyzed the hypothesis in
detail:

I think this question is a very interesting one, for
what is implicit in it rather than what is actually
asked. Open-shelf access is not necessary in any
library. Closed access implies that readers will
select what they want through catalogs, bibliographies, and reference assistance; open access implies that some readers will find what they want
directly; so open access makes catalogs, bibliographies, and reference assistance largely unnecessary for those readers. No matter how good the
bibliographical tools provided, it is helpful to some
readers if they can look at a helpful shelf order.
As with III:9, it doesn't seem to me to be a question of necessity, but of what is--overall, and in-

cluding the patron--the most helpful way of doing things.

Some not checking an option made the same point: "None of these approaches is 'necessary'; they all help." "Would possibly make it less important--'unnecessary,' I doubt." A final "Other" comment was from a technical services practitioner in a public library: "No experience."

To conclude, a majority would not approve of access to large academic (or research) collections exclusively through bibliographic and personal assistance. Comments were that one still needed to examine the shelves either for selection of works or retrieval of specific information. Another belief was that, although IV:16 posited adequate bibliographical and personal assistance, the likelihood of such assistance was not acceptable, at least to some.

IV:17. "The more advanced the student or researcher in academic libraries, the less need for open-shelf access."

This statement, related to IV:9, 14, and 16, advanced a hypothesis based on the literature that direct access was most necessary for beginning students; those at more advanced levels of scholarship were presumed either to know their special literature thoroughly or to rely on bibliographies and indexes for subject search and information retrieval.

The predominant negative response was consistent with that for IV:9, 14, and 16. About one-fourth (24.5 percent) agreed; 6.8 percent were undecided; 67.3 percent did not agree; and 1.4 percent expressed some other opinion. Thus, about three-fourths would not agree with an opinion not uncommon in the literature and one widely held by European librarians. The eight comments took various stands. Those agreeing remarked: "I interpreted this to mean open-shelf access for the majority of the collection. I still do believe in access to the books, for an advanced researcher, although they may be shelved in closed stacks." "Less need or less important?" "I agree. The more advanced the user, the more he would rely on bibliographies, catalogs, indexes, etc. The more general user would still prefer an open-shelf arrangement."

Those who disagreed commented: "Ideally, yes. But with our traditional catalogs and lack of service, No." "Just

the opposite!"   "For him. "   An "Other" comment was:
"Partly true, but misleading in its generalization. "

Though most respondents felt that direct access was
no less needed by advanced researchers, the comments did
not much elucidate the reasons.   Probably a general belief
in the need for direct access--regardless of bibliographic or
personal assistance--as expressed in previous responses and
comments, especially IV:16, also extended to IV:17.

IV:18.   "A reader whose early experience has been
with the Dewey classification will not be able to use effectively a collection classified by L. C. "

This statement tested acceptance of a hypothesis that,
since most readers in their earlier use of public libraries
became accustomed to the Dewey classification scheme, they
would not, when faced with LC--presumably later in academic and research collections--be able to utilize the new
scheme effectively.   Surveys of the use of LC[3] have indicated a general lack of understanding of the scheme by patrons, a situation attributed to absence of experience and instruction.   The hypothesis, however, was phrased categorically to elicit clear-cut reaction.

No other statement was so overwhelmingly rejected:
4. 0 percent agreed; 6. 7 percent were undecided; 88. 0 percent disagreed; and 1. 3 percent expressed an other opinion.
Almost all the 10 comments confirmed the consensus.   A
specialist in DC who agreed added: "At least not for some
time. "   A library school administrator who did not check an
option explained: "For a considerable period--perhaps the
entire Freshman college year. "   The remaining comments
were from those who disagreed: "Needs some indoctrination
certainly. "   "Do we now have any measures of effectiveness ?"   "General public or student?   Who ?"   "Not necessarily so. "   "Exclamation point!"   "Assuming an IQ above 80. "
"Personal adaptability is the factor, not the scheme. "   A
college acquisitions librarian stated:

> I do not agree.   It does not necessarily follow that
> because one has become used to DC, he can not
> come to know and use the LC classification.   We've
> had this situation. ... We still have both DC and
> LC and to my knowledge, there is not any difficul-
> ty.

(The college library referred to in the last comment
was forced by space limitations to make most of its collection closed-shelf, at least to undergraduates.)

In summary, almost all respondents believed that it
was possible for readers whose previous experience had been
with DC to adjust to LC for effective utilization of the new
collection.   Comments, however, indicated that some instruction might be needed, and that it might take a certain amount
of time--perhaps up to a year--to become adept.   (Related
statements on whether DC and LC promote browsing are discussed in the next chapter.)

IV:19.   "Provision of direct shelf approach for readers is not in itself a valid reason for close classification on
shelves in general academic and research libraries."

This hypothesis returned to the issue of close classification as related to direct access and proposed that direct
access per se did not logically justify close shelf classification.   Implied was that broad classification could be "successfully" used for direct access even in academic and research libraries for which close classification is often recommended.

Substantial agreement was recorded: 61.4 percent
agreed; 11.7 percent were undecided; 25.5 percent disagreed;
and 1.4 percent expressed some other opinion.   Evidently,
a decisive majority agreed that broad classification and open
shelves were not incompatible in general academic and research libraries.

There were nine comments.   Those agreeing remarked:
"Depends."   "Fairly broad classification is sufficient."   A
college acquisitions librarian stated:

> I agree.   You can have closed shelf arrangement
> with broad classification.   New York Public Library
> has very broad classification in its Reference De-
> partment.   You can have a very close classifica-
> tion as we have at our library, and still have a
> closed setup.

Comments from those disagreeing included: "Are you
using the term 'direct shelf approach' interchangeably with
classified or relative location by subject heading?"   "It is

the only reason." "Assuming a typical American situation where the public has no access to the shelflist, and thus approaches books subjectwise by subject words, is ANY classification needed in a closed stacks library?" (This last comment was also given for III:6.) The two "Other" comments stated that the meaning was not understood.

Statistical Measurement of Relationship

The following Tables 18 and 19 summarize the results of the chi-square tests and indicate the coefficients of contingency for the responses to IV:1-19 as discussed in this chapter. Table 18 shows total responses in relation to the professional function of the respondent, and Table 19 shows practitioners' responses in relation to the type of library represented. (As explained previously, Table 18 for the first chi-square test treats the library administrator as "administrator," but Table 19 for the second test treats him as "practitioner.")

Only for IV:18 did the chi-square test summarized in Table 18 indicate a possibly significant relationship with the professional functions of the respondents. The corresponding tally for IV:18 is given in Table 20. Inspection of Table 20 confirms the consistently negative reaction from all professional groups, i.e., 72 of 85 practitioners (84.7 percent), 39 of 42 teachers (92.8 percent), and 21 of 23 administrators (91.3 percent) checked "Do not agree." (The percentages just given--84.7, 92.8, 91.3--do not appear in Table 20 but result from inspecting the totals in Table 20. They are, of course, proportionately equivalent to the percentages actually appearing in Table 20 which presents the data as grouped for the chi-square test. This inspection method will be employed for analogous data in this and the next chapter.) However, the 84.7-percentage for practitioners' "Do not agree" responses was lower than the aggregate 88.0-percentage for that type of response, whereas the percentages for teachers and administrators, respectively 92.8 and 91.3, were correspondingly higher. This could indicate a less determined opposition to the statement by practitioners than other professional types.

The coefficients of contingency were all very low, indicating extremely weak probability of correlation among the responses to the statements in series.

TABLE 18

STATISTICAL MEASURES OF RELATIONSHIP BETWEEN
PROFESSIONAL FUNCTION OF RESPONDENT AND
TYPE OF RESPONSE FOR STATEMENTS IV:1-19

Statement No. IV:	Chi-Square Value	Level of Confidence	Coefficient of Contingency
1	6.745	50%	.204
2	3.431	20%	.148
3	7.380	70%	.219
4	6.712	50%	.211
5	4.768	30%	.176
6	2.827	10%	.140
7	3.547	20%	.153
8	5.771	50%	.193
9	3.348	20%	.149
10	9.050	80%	.241
11	5.712	50%	.192
12	5.270	50%	.185
13	10.096	80%	.253
14	2.553	10%	.132
15	3.539	20%	.155
16	6.440	50%	.205
17	3.881	30%	.160
18	15.813[a]	98%[a]	.309
19	4.050	30%	.165

Notes: Critical value of chi-square for 95% level of confidence is 12.592. Critical value for level of confidence is 95%. Maximum value for coefficient of contingency is 1.000.

[a]Equals or exceeds critical value.

TABLE 19

STATISTICAL MEASURES OF RELATIONSHIP BETWEEN
PRACTITIONER RESPONDENTS' TYPE OF LIBRARY
AND THEIR TYPE OF RESPONSE FOR STATEMENTS IV:1-19

Statement No. IV:	Chi-Square Value	Level of Confidence	Coefficient of Contingency
1	4.785[a]	95%[a]	.214
2	.125	25%	.035
3	.644	50%	.082
4	.020	10%	.014
5	4.736[a]	95%[a]	.216
6	.334	25%	.059
7	1.491	75%	.122
8	5.447[a]	98%[a]	.228
9	.024	10%	.016
10	3.383	90%	.183
11	4.060[a]	95%[a]	.198
12	.000	01%	.002
13	.048	05%	.022
14	.055	10%	.024
15	.033	10%	.018
16	1.682	75%	.129
17	.878	50%	.094
18	.002	02%	.004
19	.007	05%	.008

Notes: Critical value of chi-square for 95% level of confidence is 3.841. Critical value for level of confidence is 95%. Optimum value for coefficient of contingency is .707.

[a]Equals or exceeds critical value.

Table 19 included four statements for which the chi-square test indicated a possible significant relationship between practitioners' responses (including those of library administrators) and the type of library represented. The corresponding tallies for these statements--IV:1, 5, 8, and 11 are given in Table 21. (The subtotals in Table 21 are those required by the test, i.e., two types of libraries and two types of responses.)

Inspection of IV:1 in Table 21 indicates that a significantly higher percentage of respondents from public libraries and public and/or school library system centers agreed on the general desirability of open-shelf access in all libraries than did respondents from academic and special libraries. Of 70 responses from academic and special libraries, 38 (54.3 percent) agreed, compared with 24 out of 30 (71.0 percent) public and system responses.

Similar inspection of the other statements in Table 21 indicates the following. For IV:5, 66.7 percent of academic and special library responses agreed on the necessity of open-shelf access in public libraries, compared with 90.0 percent of public and system responses. For IV:8, 31.4 percent of responses from academic and special libraries agreed on the greater usefulness of the direct shelf approach for specialized collections, compared with 6.9 percent of responses from public libraries and library systems. For IV:11, only 47.9 percent of academic and special library responses agreed that open shelves were more needed for books than serials, compared with 72.4 percent of responses from public libraries and library system centers. One might deduce, in conclusion, that academic and special libraries were less in favor of direct access for general library situations than were public libraries and library systems, but more disposed to approve of it for special collections, and less disposed to limit it to monographs rather than serials.

The coefficients of contingency were all extremely low.

Notes

1. Arthur E. Bostwick, The American Public Library (4th ed., rev. and enl.; New York: Appleton, 1929), p. 1-2.

2. Jerrold Orne, "The Place of the Library in the Evolution of Graduate Work," College and Research Librar-

TABLE 20

RESPONSES TO STATEMENT IV:18 CATEGORIZED BY
PROFESSIONAL FUNCTION OF RESPONDENT

Professional Function	Agree		Undecided		Do Not Agree		Other		Total	
	No.	%	No.	%	No.	%	No.	%	No.	%
Practitioner	5	3.3	8	5.3	72	48.0	--	--	85	56.7
Teacher	1	0.7	2	1.3	39	26.0	--	--	42	28.0
Administrator[a]	--	--	--	--	21	14.0	2	1.3	23	15.3
Total	6	4.0	10	6.7	132	88.0	2	1.3	150	100.0

[a]Includes library administrator.

TABLE 21

PRACTITIONERS' RESPONSES TO STATEMENTS IV:1, 5, 8, 11 CATEGORIZED BY TYPE OF LIBRARY REPRESENTED

Type of Library	Agree		Non-Agree		Total	
	No.	%	No.	%	No.	%
Statement IV:1						
Academic & Special	38	38. 0	32	32. 0	70	70. 0
Public & System	24	24. 0	6	6. 0	30	30. 0
Total	62	62. 0	38	38. 0	100	100. 0
Statement IV:5						
Academic & Special	46	46. 4	23	23. 2	69	69. 8
Public & System	27	27. 2	3	3. 0	30	30. 3
Total	73	73. 7	26	26. 2	99	100. 0
Statement IV:8						
Academic & Special	22	22. 2	48	48. 5	70	70. 8
Public & System	2	2. 0	27	27. 2	29	29. 3
Total	24	24. 2	75	75. 7	99	100. 0
Statement IV:11						
Academic & Special	34	34. 0	37	37. 0	71	71. 0
Public & System	21	21. 0	8	8. 0	29	29. 0
Total	55	55. 0	45	45. 0	100	100. 0

ies, XXX (January, 1969), 27. (The respondent may
particularly have had the following sentences in mind:
"Present standards put a premium on direct access
to the book collections, and for decades this has been
considered one of the essential perquisites of the
graduate students and faculty. Yet many are now impressed by the relative unimportance of browsing,
long touted as the best avenue to discovery. The volume of published material in almost any given field
is so great that browsing is well-nigh impossible and
usually unproductive.")

3.   Annette L. Hoage, "Patron Use of the L. C. Classifica-
     tion," Library Resources and Technical Services, VI
     (Summer, 1962), 248-49; Maurice F. Tauber, "Re-
     view of the Use of the Library of Congress Classifica-
     tion," in Institute on the Use of the Library of Con-
     gress Classification," New York, 1966, Proceedings,
     ed. by Richard H. Schimmelpfeng and C. Donald Cook
     (Chicago: American Library Assn., 1968), p. 4, 10.

CHAPTER XII

ANALYSIS OF RESPONSES ON "DIRECT SHELF APPROACH
(OPEN-SHELF ACCESS): THE ROLE OF 'BROWSING'
AND RELATED ACTIVITIES" (V:1-14)

V:1.   "All readers should be encouraged to browse."

As noted in Chapter Six, "In a sense the overarching
purpose of this study has been to arrive, via documentary
analysis and opinion survey, at clarifying definitions of the
direct shelf approach and of browsing." Section V focused
on those browsing and related activities referred to implicitly in the earlier hypotheses. In none of the earlier statements was "browsing" used. "Direct shelf approach," "open-
shelf access," or "open access" appeared instead. Though
in a broad sense these terms may be said to encompass
"browsing" and related activities, they do not effectively define or explain. "Browsing" and related activities are made
possible when a library provides open-shelf access. The latter is an instrumentality. "Browsing" and related activities
are the ends.

This distinction between "open-shelf access" and
"browsing and related activities" was reflected in V:1 which
was the counterpart of IV:1, "Open-shelf access is generally
desirable in all libraries." Thus, V:1 presented a similarly
general hypothesis vis-à-vis "browsing." ("Browsing" was
defined in the introductory paragraph of Section V: "By
'browsing' is meant the inspection of books on shelves to select appropriate or desirable material for research or recreational use. It usually involves at least a cursory inspection of the contents.")

The response was heavily affirmative. (For the tally
of total responses to statements discussed in this chapter,
see Table 22.) More than three-fourths (77.7 percent) of all
respondents agreed; 5.4 percent were undecided; 16.2 percent
did not agree; and 0.7 percent expressed an other opinion.
Comparison of these responses with those to IV:1 indicated a

noticeably higher percentage of agreement (12. 4 percentage
points more) than on IV:1.   Almost twice as many disagreed
with IV:1 as with V:1, but only about one-half as many were
undecided on the earlier statement--though the absolute numbers of "Undecided" responses were comparatively unimportant.   It would appear that though most respondents would approve in general terms both the desirability of open-shelf access in all libraries and also the encouragement of browsing
in (presumably) all libraries, there seemed to be measurably
greater approval of the latter--even though "browsing" was
defined in the questionnaire as encompassing research as well
as recreational use.

Table 23, which summarizes practitioner responses to
V:1-14, shows for V:1 an almost identical pattern of response
from practitioners (including library administrators) as from
all respondents, including practitioners.   (Nor was there a
signal difference between practitioner responses to V:1 and
to IV:1 as shown in Table 17.)

In view of the evident, though not major, difference
in the percentage of agreement on V:1 as against IV:1, a
comparative tally was made of the responses to these statements.   Of the 150 responses to IV:1, 81 (54. 0 percent)
agreed both on IV:1 and V:1; 10 (6. 7 percent) agreed on IV:1
but disagreed on V:1; 32 (21. 5 percent) did not agree on
IV:1 but did agree on V:1; and 13 (8. 7 percent) disagreed on
both.

Thus, only slightly more than half of the respondents
who had agreed on the general desirability of open shelves
(IV:1) also agreed on the need to encourage browsing (V:1),
and slightly more than 20 percent did not agree on the need
for open shelves (IV:1) but did agree on the need to encourage browsing (V:1).   Such an analysis of "voting behavior"
indicated considerably more divergence of opinion on the relation between open shelves and browsing than would be suspected from the separate responses to individual statements.
(No doubt, discussion of every statement would benefit from
such analysis.   Regrettably, the limits of this study preclude
so elaborate a methodology, though its application may be
promising for future studies.)

Additional comparison of the responses to IV:1 and
V:1 as categorized by professional function of respondent
showed that teachers and library school administrators followed about the same pattern of agreement and disagreement

TABLE 22

TOTAL RESPONSES TO STATEMENTS V:1-14

Statement No. V:	Agree No.	Agree %	Undecided No.	Undecided %	Do Not Agree No.	Do Not Agree %	Other No.	Other %	Total No.	Total %
1.	115	77.7	8	5.4	24	16.2	1	0.7	148	100.0
2.	121	81.2	17	11.4	10	6.7	1	0.7	149	100.0
3.	116	78.4	6	4.1	24	16.2	2	1.4	148	100.0
4.	42	28.2	21	14.1	82	55.0	4	2.7	149	100.0
5.	19	13.9	42	30.7	54	39.4	22	16.1	137	100.0
6.	90	60.8	15	10.1	36	24.3	7	4.7	148	100.0
7.	18	12.2	18	12.2	108	73.0	4	2.7	148	100.0
8.	42	28.8	14	9.6	88	60.3	2	1.4	146	100.0
9.	17	11.7	27	18.6	99	68.3	2	1.4	145	100.0
10.	67	45.6	20	13.6	56	38.1	4	2.7	147	100.0
11.	134	89.9	5	3.4	9	6.0	1	0.7	149	100.0
12.	103	71.0	20	13.8	17	11.7	5	3.4	145	100.0
13.	16	10.8	12	8.1	112	75.7	8	5.4	148	100.0
14.	41	28.3	15	10.3	81	55.9	8	5.5	145	100.0

TABLE 23

TOTAL PRACTITIONER RESPONSES TO STATEMENTS V:1-14

Statement No. V:	Agree		Undecided		Do Not Agree		Other		Total	
	No.	%	No.	%	No.	%	No.	%	No.	%
1.	77	77.8	5	5.1	16	16.2	1	1.0	99	100.0
2.	80	80.0	13	13.0	6	6.0	1	1.0	100	100.0
3.	78	78.8	6	6.1	14	14.1	1	1.0	99	100.0
4.	27	27.0	14	14.0	56	56.0	3	3.0	100	100.0
5.	11	12.0	28	30.4	39	42.4	14	15.2	92	100.0
6.	62	62.6	11	11.1	22	22.2	4	4.0	99	100.0
7.	10	10.1	16	16.2	71	71.7	2	2.0	99	100.0
8.	27	27.8	11	11.3	58	59.8	1	1.0	97	100.0
9.	11	11.5	20	20.8	64	66.7	1	1.0	96	100.0
10.	40	40.8	16	16.3	39	39.8	3	3.1	98	100.0
11.	91	91.0	2	2.0	6	6.0	1	1.0	100	100.0
12.	70	72.2	15	15.5	10	10.3	2	2.1	97	100.0
13.	11	11.1	7	7.1	77	77.8	4	4.0	99	100.0
14.	32	33.3	10	10.4	49	51.0	5	5.2	96	100.0

on the statements. However, practitioners were decidedly more willing to approve of browsing than to endorse the general principle of open-shelf access. This is seen by comparing Tables 17 and 23 which indicate that while 62.0 percent of practitioners agreed on the general need for open-shelf access (IV:1), 77.8 percent agreed on the need to encourage browsing (V:1).

Analysis of practitioner responses by type of library represented showed that 38 of 70 (54.3 percent) university, college, and special librarians agreed on the need for open-shelf access (IV:1) as compared with 24 of 30 (80 percent) public and system librarians. Similar analysis of V:1 indicated that 51 of 69 (73.9 percent) university, college, and special librarians agreed on the need to encourage browsing, compared with 26 of 30 (86.7 percent) public and system librarians. Thus, it appears that practitioner approval of open-shelf access was greater among public and system librarians than among academic and research librarians; and that encouragement of browsing was even more heavily supported by public and system librarians than was open-shelf access, though on this issue the difference with academic and research librarians was narrower.

The 10 comments on V:1 were almost all from those agreeing and tended to qualify their opinion: "I cannot bring myself not to check 'Agree' although 'all readers' obviously have no need to browse on all occasions." "At times." "I believe it is natural for readers to browse. No special encouragement is needed." "I have always worked in technical services of a university library. Open shelves were introduced January, 1969 so there is no experience in my answers here." (The respondent applied this disclaimer to all of Section V.) "But not for all purposes." "I agree. It is not the most efficient way of selecting materials, but it does have the advantage of enabling the user to see and handle a large number of books." A teacher of classification modified his agreement: "If by 'encouraged,' you mean 'given the opportunity,' I agree; but to my mind it has a far more positive connotation, implying a degree of moral coercion, and I'm not sure I agree with that."

Those disagreeing were generally not completely negative: "It depends upon his need at a particular time." "I prefer: 'Most readers should be given the opportunity of browsing. Selectively, they should be encouraged to browse.' " "All? Top-flight scientists?"

To summarize, almost 78 percent of all respondents agreed on the need to encourage patrons to browse, a greater proportion than had agreed on the general desirability of open-shelf access in all libraries (IV:1).   Further analysis, however, indicated that only a little more than one-half accepted both the general desirability of open-shelf access in all libraries and the need to encourage all readers to browse. Split response was more apparent among practitioners, particularly among academic and special librarians who were less willing to agree to open shelves than to the encouragement of browsing by all readers.   Nevertheless, almost two-thirds (62 percent) of all practitioners accepted the principle of open shelves and more than three-fourths (77.8 percent) agreed that browsing should be encouraged.   Public and system librarians were even stronger in approving both open shelves and browsing, though academic and special librarians were not so far behind other practitioners in approving or browsing.

Perhaps, respondents felt that IV:1 and V:1 were not necessarily logically related.   However, the above analysis hints that many respondents, particularly academic and special librarians, did not in any way connect open-shelf access with "browsing."   This possibility will be watched in the following.

V:2.   "Browsing provides a valuable learning experience."

This hypothesis, related to III:3, IV:2 and 3, tested acceptance of an educational concept of browsing, i.e., an activity in which the reader or student gains knowledge from the works whose inspection is facilitated by the direct shelf approach.   (Implicit is that the works have been arranged--perhaps even selected--so that browsing is possible.)

This statement elicited the second highest percentage of agreement for any in the questionnaire: 81.2 percent agreed; 11.4 percent were undecided; 6.7 percent did not agree; and 0.7 percent had some other opinion.   Less than 19 percent of all respondents would not agree to the general educational value of browsing.   Agreement on V:2 may be compared with that on III:3, IV:2 and 3--respectively, 11.5 percent, 59.1 percent, and 28.7 percent.   Reaction to V:2 confirmed the general attitudes expressed on those earlier statements.

When the hypothesis was stated in broad terms, as in
IV:2, fairly high agreement ensued.   There seemed to
emerge a belief in the general educational value of open
shelves, evidently in terms of some informal learning process.   When, however, as in III:3 and IV:3, elements of conscious pedagogical influence were introduced, much opposition resulted.   The intrusion of the idea of a librarian
"structuring" the learning situation or consciously "teaching"
the patron was evidently disapproved.   Although IV:2 obtained
majority agreement, it drew 22.1 percentage points less in
the "Agree" category than did V:2, probably because--as suggested in comments--the pedagogical role of open-shelf access was expressed as a formal responsibility of libraries,
perhaps even implying what a respondent to V:1 described as
"a degree of moral coercion."

The 14 comments, eight from those agreeing, generally either gave qualifications or questioned the wording.   Those
in agreement commented: "Qualified.   It can, if there is
sufficient knowledge on the part of the user."   "Can provide."
"I don't know what is meant by a 'valuable learning experience.' I'm agreeing to the question: does browsing help
readers to find what they want?"   "Learning or discovery?"
"I agree.   As above, it is not the best use of one's time,
but the browser is not necessarily looking for something specific."   "May provide."   "Potential, not guaranteed."   "Generally."

Those undecided remarked: "Random access."   "Always?"   The remaining comments, from those disagreeing,
were: "It's just fun."   "Is this value measurable?"

In summary, the reaction to V:2 seemed consistent
with that to related statements on the general educational
value of open shelves, particularly as discussed at the end
of the previous chapter.   Even after being defined in the
questionnaire as not necessarily confined to recreational use,
"browsing" was described by some respondents as "not the
best use of one's time" and "just fun."

V:3.   "Shelf classification is necessary for non-recreational browsing."

This hypothesis, related to most of those in Section
III, attempted to assay reaction to what might seem an obvious point.   Acceptance of V:3 was quite high: 78.4 percent

agreed; 4.1 percent were undecided; 16.2 percent did not
agree; and 1.4 percent expressed some other opinion. Agreement was slightly less than for the preceding, disagreement
almost 10 percentage points more.

When opinions were categorized by professional function of respondent, it was found that 78.8 percent of practitioners agreed, 73.8 percent of teachers, and all library
school administrators. Teachers seemed noticeably less willing to accept the need for shelf classification for non-recreational browsing. When practitioner responses were categorized by type of library represented, it was found that 80.2
percent of academic and special librarians agreed, in comparison with 75.0 percent of public and system librarians.
Thus, though academic and special librarians seemed to accept V:3 more than public librarians, the major divergence
of opinion was not among types of library represented but
between teachers and non-teachers.

The seven comments did not particularly illuminate
the reasons of those disagreeing. Only one comment was
added by a respondent who disagreed: "Not necessary but
often helpful." "Other" comments were: "Meaning?" "Do
you mean 'necessary' or do you mean 'desirable' or 'helpful'?" (This last comment was from a university library administrator.) The remaining comments were from those
agreeing: "Or recreational." "Useful." "I agree. For
browsing, one should have together books in a certain area,
rather than have books thrown together as one might find an
attic or second-hand store." "Writing a term paper after
consulting card catalog is this?"

To summarize, though general agreement was expressed on the need for shelf classification for "non-recreational browsing," the reasons for the greater disagreement
on V:3 than on V:2 were not clear. Perhaps the categorical
"necessary" may have kept respondents from agreeing. Another reason might have been reluctance to accept "browsing"
in a non-recreational sense. This reluctance would be consistent with opinions on earlier statements involving any formal specification of the educational roles of open-shelf access and shelf classification.

V:4. "Close classification on shelves is necessary
for non-recreational browsing."

This hypothesis developed the preceding, and was related to those on close classification in Section III, particularly III:4, and also to IV:19. It attempted to test reaction on a categorical assertion that "serious," presumably subject-oriented, browsing was not possible without close shelf classification.

Majority response was negative: only 28.2 percent agreed; 14.1 percent were undecided; 55.0 percent disagreed; and 2.7 percent had some other opinion. This pattern was not inconsistent with IV:19, but its ratio of agreement to disagreement was almost the reverse of that for III:4, which hypothesized that close shelf classification was necessary for effective direct shelf approach to subject materials. Thus, respondents seem to have distinguished between "direct shelf approach to subject materials" and the perhaps more general "non-recreational browsing." One might surmise, again, that respondents were unwilling to accept "browsing" as being sometimes, at least, non-recreational in purpose--at any rate not to the extent of approving of close shelf classification to make such browsing possible. Of course, another reason for disagreeing could be a general belief in the efficacy of broad shelf classification for any "browsing" purpose.

There were 11 comments, mostly questioning "necessary." Those who agreed commented: "Necessary? Close classification is more helpful than broad for non-recreational browsing." "Helpful." "Size? In most situations." A reference teacher who was undecided explained: "Helpful."

Those who disagreed remarked: "Helpful, but not 'necessary.' " "Not entirely, but may sometimes be helpful." "I do not agree. You can have non-recreational browsing with either close or broad classification." (The author of the preceding comment, a college acquisitions librarian, had agreed with III:4 and had remarked: "I think that it is better for the user to know that books on apples are under a certain number rather than know that he has to look under a number for fruit; or that a book on bowling is in such a number rather than looking under a general number for sports.")

"Other" comments were: "Not always 'necessary,' perhaps, but usually helpful." "Do you mean 'necessary' or do you mean 'desirable' or 'helpful'?" (This preceding comment was also applied to V:3.) "Desirable." "How close?"

It will be noted that some who agreed made the same
qualifications as some who disagreed or were undecided or
who expressed an "Other" opinion--another instance of the
difficulty of precise categorization for statistical testing.

In summary, although a majority did not accept the
need of close shelf classification for "non-recreational browsing," this majority negative opinion seemed inconsistent with
the majority agreement on an earlier hypothesis stating the
need of close shelf classification for effective shelf approach
to subject materials (III:4). Evidently, many respondents
felt that "non-recreational browsing" was distinct from "direct shelf approach to subject materials." However, a general belief in broad classification might have affected the pattern of opinion. (Further analysis of V:4 will be found below in the section of this chapter on "Statistical Measurement
of Relationship.")

V:5. "The greater limits imposed on browsing by
acquisition policy and by classification, the more valuable
browsing will be."

This hypothesis, related to IV:3 and 4, and V:3 and
4, attempted a rephrasing of the "structured learning situation" by directly associating the potential benefits of browsing
with the degree of conscious assembling and organizing of the
collection for open-shelf access. "Limits" intended a non-
pejorative concept of purposefully chosen boundaries, analogous to use in mathematics, or to "constraints" in information science. Less technically, the statement might have
read: "The more strictly and consistently the works have
been chosen and classified, the greater benefits the browser
will derive from their inspection and use." It aimed also to
consolidate hypotheses discussed in Chapters Seven and Eight
on the roles of acquisition and classification in the direct
shelf approach. The resultant statement sought to test acceptance of a pedagogical principle worded at a level of theoretical abstraction. Also involved, at least partially, was
the use of V:5 as a "control statement," since V:5 subsumed
elements from other statements on the relationships of acquisition and classification to open-shelf access. Responses
to V:5 could be compared with those to the related statements and, thus, seeming inconsistencies might be uncovered.

To judge from the total number of responses, the pattern of opinion, and the nature of the comments, this state-

ment must be considered the least satisfactory in the questionnaire, though, as will be explained below, such reaction was not valueless for the study. Only 137 of a potential 152 responses were recorded, the greatest abstention from any statement. Only 13.9 percent agreed; 30.7 percent were undecided--by far the highest percentage in this category for any statement; 39.4 percent disagreed; and 16.1 percent did not check an option but expressed an "Other" opinion--again, the highest percentage in this category for any statement.

There were 29 comments (only III:1 received as many) and almost all remarked that the statement was not understood. Only two comments could be said to offer additonal substantive opinions. A college reference librarian who agreed remarked:

> Again, I do not see why browsing need be singled out for justification and value. Of course, a good selection policy (if this is the meaning intended by 'acquisition' policy) will make browsing more valuable. But certainly any kind of library use is made more valuable by a good acquisition policy, not just open-shelf use. And I think that close classification is a necessary location aid in large libraries, especially, which contain many various editions of the same works and foreign language materials. Of course, close classification aids in browsing, but it is difficult to say that this is its main value or purpose.

A college acquisitions librarian who was undecided commented:

> I do not know. I do not know how acquisition policy affects browsing. To browse, you must have books and a location. If your acquisition policy is narrow, you have a narrow range in which to browse, and if you have a broad range, you have a broader range of materials in which to browse. But it does not affect browsing. It may affect what you find as a result of your browsing.

Although clearly the statement's intended meaning was not grasped by numerous respondents, neither the opinion pattern nor the comments lacked research value. First, the conscientiousness of the many respondents in recording their incomprehension showed that the statements were not being checked mechanically. Secondly, even though the statement was apparently not understood by many, the recorded reactions were not inconsistent with those on previous hypotheses which presented a concept of the structuring effects of acquisition and classification on open-shelf access, particularly effects pedagogically interpreted.

At the level of abstract educational theory represented by V:5, most respondents were unwilling to accept or assimilate "limits" in a scientific or mathematical sense. Of course, this might be almost completely due to inadequate wording. Still, it may be significant that respondents did not relate this statement to any others, e.g., IV:3 and 4, and V:3 and 4, which implied a concept of "limits" placed on collections by acquisition and classification policy. Most respondents may very well have considered "limits" a pejorative term. This would reflect earlier attitudes suggested by the comments on those statements in Section IV which implied to the respondents some restriction of patrons' freedom of choice.

A university technical services practitioner who did not check an option added the question: "How can acquisition policy and classification limit browsing?" Yet, it would seem a truism that collections to be useful must be acquired and organized within defined limits, or that the pedagogical process is in a basic sense the "structuring" of students' experience. At controversy is to what extent these limits and "structuring" should be applied for maximum benefit. Reaction to V:5, however, suggested that many respondents were concerned with opposition to "limits" in general. This would be consistent with earlier responses.

The last quoted comment expressed this opposition to "limits." Also, the two immediately preceding comments suggested that V:5 was indeed a truism, an opinion which led one respondent to qualify his choice and the second to indicate an "Other" opinion. Implied, too, by the first quoted comment was a reluctance to accept "browsing" as a serious activity: "Of course, close classification aids in browsing, but it is difficult to say that this is its main value or purpose."

In summary, the quite small percentage of agreement on V:5--despite the admitted possible inadequacy of the statement--was not inconsistent with earlier reaction to hypotheses relating to goals of direct access as implemented by con-

scious use of acquisition and classification policy, and also
with earlier reaction to hypotheses presenting such ideas on
levels of abstract pedagogical theory.

V: 6.   "Dewey classification aids browsing."

As discussed above in Chapter Two, a 1964 American
Library Association Classification Committee[1] report had indicated that DC provided "browsability" but LC did not.
Statement V: 6, phrased categorically, intended to elicit opinion on whether DC facilitated browsing.   The next statement
dealt with LC.   The hypotheses V: 6 and 7 were worded in
accordance with the Committee report--positively for DC and
negatively for LC.   Also, as in the Committee report,
"browsing" was not qualified or explicitly defined, though the
introductory definition in the questionnaire would be implied.

Majority response to V: 6 was affirmative: 60. 8 percent agreed; 10. 1 percent were undecided; 24. 3 percent did
not agree; and 4. 7 percent had some other opinion.

There were 21 comments, many of which pointed out
that not only DC aided browsing.   Those who agreed commented: "So may other systems." "Any subject classification aids non-recreational browsing." "As a blanket statement as opposed to no classification, agree; as compared to
other classification schedules, 'aids' yes, but more or less
than what other schedule?" "But are exceptions, i. e., 500
and 600's separated.   Also depends on policy concerning
Dewey's relocations displayed in every new edition." "Dewey
(Third Summary) is now taught in sixth grade and junior high
schools." (This last comment came from a DC specialist.)
"So does LC." "Mnemonics a factor."

Those undecided added: "Meaning?" "Have not worked
with Dewey since 1951." Those disagreeing commented: "Not
if browsing section is arranged by reader interest." "Not in
business literature." (This last comment was from a cataloger in a special business library with its own scheme.) A
college acquisitions librarian added the following which he
applied also to V: 7:

> I do not agree.   I don't really see how classifica-
> tion affects browsing.   If the LC classification puts
> Anthropology in Class D, and the DC in Class 572,
> it does not make much difference.   If you are in-

terested in Anthropology, you can look in either
section, depending on what your own library uses.

Those with "Other" opinions stated: "Not necessarily."
"What does this mean?" "Any classification aids browsing."
"Aids? Cannot answer with choices given." "Depends on
the browser." "Any classification scheme aids browsing."

Further analysis by professional function of respondent
indicated that 62 of 99 practitioners (62.6 percent) agreed,
compared with 23 of 42 teachers (54.5 percent) and five of
seven library school administrators (71.4 percent). The corresponding percentages of "Do not agree" for these professional groups were, respectively, 22.2, 30.9, and 14.3.

When practitioner responses were categorized by type
of library represented, the pattern of agreement on V:6 was
found to be as follows: 38 of 46 university librarians (60.9
percent), five of nine college librarians (55.5 percent), nine
of 15 special librarians (60.0 percent), 19 of 25 public librarians (76.0 percent), and one of four system center librarians (25.0 percent) accepted the statement that DC aided
browsing.

It was not unexpected that more public librarians, proportionately, would accept V:6 than academic and research
librarians, since DC was most heavily used in public libraries. Surprising, however, was that only one of four library
system center respondents agreed, while the other three
checked "Do not agree" without comment. The reasons were
not clear. All system centers serviced public and/or school
libraries, employed DC, and described a policy of fairly
broad classification. Perhaps the system respondents did not
consider their use of broad classification as necessarily aid-
ing "browsing" as they interpreted it. Perhaps they interpreted "aids" as a very active function. In any case, this
disagreement seems inconsistent with the broad approval from
public librarians.

It was somewhat unexpected that almost one-fourth did
not agree, that at least 10 percent were undecided, and that
almost five percent were unwilling to check any option. One
may say "somewhat unexpected" because an oft-claimed virtue of DC is its easily understandable notation which is said
to facilitate inspection of works on open shelves. Academic
and special librarians, of course, contributed more to the
disagreement but almost one-fourth of public librarians would
not check "Agree."

334 Access to Library Collections

To recapitulate, over 60 percent agreed that DC aided browsing, but almost one-fourth did not agree, and over 10 percent were undecided. Practitioners agreed proportionately more than teachers, but noticeably less than library school administrators, while public librarians gave considerably more support to the statement than practitioners from other types of libraries. An apparent anomaly was that only one of four system librarians agreed. Comments indicated that some disagreement may have been occasioned when V:6 was interpreted as implying a comparative evaluation of DC against LC or other schemes, but there was also evidence that respondents from libraries which used LC more than DC, i.e., academic and special libraries, agreed less on the "browsability" of DC than other respondents.

V:7. "L.C. classification hinders browsing."

The intention and wording of this hypothesis were explained above in relation to V:6. In contrast to the previous response, that to V:7 was decisively negative: 73.0 percent disagreed; 12.2 percent were undecided; 2.7 percent had an "Other" opinion; and only 12.2 percent agreed.

There were 15 comments. Those agreeing stated: "Qualified. It can, if patron does not understand the scheme." "Not designed for browsing." "Mnemonics a factor." (This last comment was applied also to V:6 on which the respondent agreed.) A technical services practitioner in a public library who was undecided explained: "I have not used LC. It may be somewhat more difficult to learn."

Comments from those disagreeing were: "Any classification helps." "Any subject classification aids non-recreational browsing." (This comment was applied also to V:6.) "Potential--should add." "Aids browsing." "Hinders to some extent as LC was originally planned for Library of Congress use, not general use in libraries." "Not necessarily." A college acquisitions librarian repeated his comment on V:6: "I don't really see how classification affects browsing...." The "Other" comments were: "Meaning?" "What does this mean?" "Don't know." "Not necessarily."

Further analysis revealed no great difference in opinion distribution among the various professional groups. Noteworthy, perhaps, was that only one of 19 teachers of technical services, and none of 16 library administrators, agreed--

the lowest agreement percentages for V:7 among the professional groups.   Similarity of opinion pattern was also found
among the types of libraries represented by practitioners,
except that the percentage of public librarians in agreement
was almost twice that of university librarians--16. 0 and 8. 5,
respectively.

One might conclude that most respondents did not confirm the view of the Classification Committee that LC hin-
dered browsing, and that any support for this view was more
likely to come from public librarians, in whose institutions
LC was not common.

V:8.   "The possible physical difficulties encountered
in browsing (e. g., bad lighting, high or low shelves, lack
of working space, effort in lifting and replacing books) make
browsing in most large academic collections an undesirable
procedure from the standpoint of most users. "

This statement focused on possible non-intellectual obstacles to browsing in large academic libraries and tested
acceptance of the hypothesis that they were sufficiently common and serious to contraindicate browsing for most patrons.
This view is not rare among advocates of exclusive bibliographic access.   The hypothesis would probably imply, since
"large academic collections" and "working space" were specified, that a significant part of such "browsing" would be
non-recreational.

Reaction was largely negative: only 28. 8 percent
agreed; 9. 6 percent were undecided; 60. 3 percent disagreed;
and 1. 4 percent held an "Other" opinion.   Many of the 14
comments questioned the assumptions of the hypothesis.
Those who agreed remarked: "Except in a special browsing
collection. "   "Not 'undesirable, ' less desirable. "   "If these
conditions are present, browsing is discouraging. "   "Probably. "

Those undecided stated: "No experience in an academic library. "   "Silly question. "   (This comment was from
a library school administrator.)   Those disagreeing commented: "Some users are confirmed browsers and will put
up with bad lights, etc. "   "They'll go to any extent if they
are used to it and endure any hardship. "   "The implication
here is that all we have to do is to make our libraries thoroughly uncomfortable and we can get rid of all these damn

readers altogether. I have a letter on this appearing in ...
in the near future." "Eliminate the difficulties!" "Many
academic collections have good lighting, access to shelves,
working space, etc." "I do not agree. If browsing is a
good thing, and I think that it is, I don't think that bad lighting or anything else will make browsing an undesirable activity for the user."

"Other" comments were: "Meaning?" "Assuming that
most libraries described have all or most of the deficiencies,
one would have to agree, but the basic assumption is probably faulty."

Further analysis of responses by professional function
of respondent showed that 27 of 97 practitioners (27.8 percent) agreed, compared with 15 of 42 teachers (35.7 percent),
and none of seven library school administrators. Analysis of
practitioner responses by type of library represented showed
that 11 of 47 university librarians (23.4 percent) agreed,
compared with two of nine college librarians (22.2 percent),
four of 15 special librarians (26.6 percent), 10 of 22 public
librarians (45.4 percent), and none of four system librarians.
Thus, the extent of agreement by public librarians was at
least twice that of academic librarians and somewhat less
than twice that of special librarians. (Of interest is whether
the reaction of public librarians is based on firsthand experience or reflects a general attitude of that group.)

Thus, at least 60 percent did not agree that physical
obstacles in the stacks of large academic libraries were serious or common enough to render browsing undesirable for
most users. Teachers tended to agree more than practitioners, and public librarians more than academic and special
librarians. Comments suggested that some respondents recognized a basic allegiance to "browsing"--claiming that even
with conditions as assumed by the hypothesis, browsers
would "endure any hardship." The hypothesis was framed in
terms of specific physical conditions in a particular type of
library, but the pattern of response and some of the remarks
implied, as in earlier instances, that a general loyalty to the
idea of open shelves and of browsing held sway.

V:9. "In a large general academic collection, browsing is likely to be wasteful for most students because they
will spend too much time on inconsequential titles."

This hypothesis, related to IV:4 and 14, and V:5, presented a variation of a "structured learning situation" concept, suggesting that because usually the situation was not ideally attained in large academic collections, students (presumably undergraduate and graduate) would be inspecting or browsing through too many works of negligible importance to their purpose. As defined in the questionnaire, such activity would include non-recreational browsing. This statement might be considered as presenting an intellectual counterpart to the physical disadvantages described in V:8. "Inconsequential" was intended primarily as relative to the student's purpose in browsing, though some respondents might have interpreted it as an absolute judgment, that is, a book inconsequential in itself, with the corollary implication that a large general academic collection would be apt to include an appreciable proportion of such inconsequential works.

The response was one of the most negative for any statement. Only 11.7 percent agreed; 18.6 percent were undecided; 68.3 percent did not agree; and 1.4 percent expressed some other opinion. However, a not insignificant combined total of at least 30 percent agreed or were undecided, thus not definitively rejecting the hypothesis.

Of the 10 comments, only two questioned the validity of "inconsequential." This might signify that there was not strong opposition to the implication that a large general academic library would include "inconsequential" titles. (Of course, it is not known whether the respondents not challenging "inconsequential" were interpreting it in the relative or absolute sense.) Those who agreed commented: "If collecting material for a research paper." "That is, can be and sometimes is." A teacher of technical services remarked:

> This is an extremely bad statement as browsing can be excellent for recreational reading and at times very bad if the student is doing research and the catalog could save time. Your definition on page 5 for 'browsing' covers both research and recreation. Which is meant in this question?

A university technical services practitioner who was undecided stated: "This is part of the learning process." Those who disagreed explained: "Inconsequential? Says who?" "What are 'inconsequential titles'? Who decides? This raises an interesting sideline: what do we mean by university education?" "A moot point. Is the time wasted in brows-

ing any greater than the time wasted waiting for a book to be
brought from the stacks? Or the need to review subject
headings to request another title when the first was unattainable?" "Depends on student and subject." "I do not agree.
I suppose that this can be true. But you can go through a
large number of inconsequential books in the browsing area
of a general public library collection. It is not limited to
academic collections."

Thus, reaction to V:9 expressed strong reluctance to
agree that browsing in a large general academic collection
would be wasteful because students would likely be using too
much time inspecting or sampling inconsequential works. The
general tenor of comments seemed to acknowledge existence
of inconsequential titles and of wasted effort, but not of so
serious a nature as to justify condemnation of browsing by
students in large academic collections. The overall response
was consistent with that to other hypotheses which advanced
the general desirability or undesirability of open shelves and
browsing. Evidently, here, too, loyalty to the idea of open-
shelf access governed. The comment of the university technical services librarian who was undecided, "This is part of
the learning process," would denote a philosophy of education
which, though not necessarily opposed to "programmed learning," would consider as also necessary a trial-and-error
learning experience. Such a philosophy was not inconsistent
with the earlier cited views of Little and Robinson[2] who felt
that a benefit of open shelves for college students was the
opportunity to develop powers of discrimination and selection
through the examination of many books.

V:10. "Browsing is essential for academic research
above the beginner's level."

This hypothesis stated categorically the need for
browsing on higher levels of academic research. It did not
imply, if strictly interpreted, that browsing was unneeded for
"academic research" at beginning levels, though this might
have been suggested to some. The statement aimed to assay
support for "browsing" as a necessary component of serious,
advanced academic research.

Reaction was varied. Although more agreed than disagreed, there was no majority view, the spread between affirmative and negative not being wide: 45.6 percent agreed;
13.6 percent were undecided; 38.1 percent did not agree; and

2.7 percent expressed some other opinion. Practitioner responses were as follows: 40.8 percent agreed; 16.3 percent
were undecided; 39.8 percent did not agree; and 3.1 percent
had some other opinion. The closest to a "marked" difference between the responses of practitioners and those of all
respondents--i.e., a difference of at least five percentage
points in any opinion category--was in the "Agree" class
where the percentage of practitioner responses was 4.8 points
less than for all respondents. (See Tables 22 and 23.) Since
the typical practitioner respondent represented a large open-
shelf academic library, one might guess that this difference
was based on experience in such a library.

Further analysis of practitioner responses by type of
library seemed to confirm stronger support from university
librarians than from college, special, and public librarians.
Thus, 23 of 47 university librarians (48.9 percent) agreed,
compared with one of nine college librarians (11.1 percent),
five of 15 special librarians (33.3 percent), nine of 23 public
librarians (34.7 percent), and two of four system librarians
(50.0 percent).

Most of the 16 comments questioned or qualified "essential." Those agreeing stated: "Most professors think so."
"Desirable." "Essential? Useful." "The way our catalogs
and libraries are set up--yes." An undecided public reference librarian remarked: "It's nice, though." Comments
from those disagreeing were: " 'Essential' is a rather strong
word." "The fact that browsing may not be 'essential' for
academic research does not mean it is not often valuable."
"Desirable, not essential." "Desirable." "I do not agree.
I would think that browsing becomes less important as one
goes further on into his studies and deeper in his research."
"Depends on subject."

"Other" comments were: "It is helpful." "Essential?
That depends." "Useful at any level." "Practically."

In summary, there was no clear majority stand on the
necessity of "browsing" for advanced academic research, although more checked "Agree" than any other choice. Practitioners agreed more than all other respondents; university
librarians supported the hypothesis more than college and
special librarians, and considerably more than public librarians. Comments suggested that, though the general desirability of browsing was accepted, the majority were not convinced that it was "essential" for advanced academic research.

Presumably, "browsing" was here interpreted by most respondents as non-recreational. Although less clear-cut than
the response to IV:9 on the greater need for open-shelf access in university and research than in undergraduate libraries, the response to V:10 was not inconsistent with that to
IV:9.

V:11. "A major value of browsing is the possibility
of 'serendipity,' i.e., 'making desirable but unsought-for discoveries.' "

This hypothesis restated a common belief in one of the
claimed chief intellectual benefits of browsing, i.e., the unexpected discovery of valuable information or materials, a
concept discussed in Chapter Six which attempted to define
functionally "browsing" and "serendipity." Very strong ap-
proval--the highest for any statement in the questionnaire--
was elicited: 89.9 percent agreed; 3.4 percent were undecided; only 6.0 percent did not agree; and 0.7 percent had
some other opinion.

The seven comments mostly qualified or questioned
"major." Comments from those agreeing were: "If you had
a classed catalog, it would provide serendipity." "Qualified:
a value not a 'major' value." "One of the major values."
"I agree. Serendipity is probably the most useful result of
browsing." A library school administrator who disagreed explained: "A value, but not a major value." (Note that this
qualification did not prevent others from agreeing.) A technical services practitioner in a special library (with closed
stacks) who did not check an option remarked: "Supposedly;
is there any concrete evidence?"

The favorable reaction to V:11 was in accord with that
to such hypotheses as IV:2 and V:1 which generalized the desirability of open shelves and browsing without specifying the
purpose of the library or the activity. However, the much
greater agreement on V:11 compared with that to earlier related hypotheses might indicate that almost all could accept
V:11 because it did not specify either serious or recreational
browsing, and also because "serendipity" is frequently used
in the professional and lay literature to describe one of the
pleasures of recreational browsing: the unforseen discovery
of enjoyable reading. The next hypothesis is not unrelated
to this point.

V:12. "The possibility of 'serendipity' is much greater
in a library with relative shelf classification."

This statement attempted to test acceptance of a hypothesis positing a direct relationship between shelf classification (with relative location) and serendipity, that "major
value of browsing" overwhelmingly acknowledged in the responses to the previous statement. Although V:12 was not
categorical, "much greater" would imply a significant causal
connection between serendipity and shelf classification (with
relative location).

Response was decidedly affirmative: 71.0 percent
agreed; 13.8 percent were undecided; 11.7 percent did not
agree; and 3.4 percent held some other opinion. Though unmistakably affirmative, reaction to V:12 was obviously not
as close to unanimity as that to V:11. Total responses to
V:12 were four fewer than to V:11; agreement was 18.9 percentage points less than for V:11; disagreement 5.7 points more;
and "Undecided" 10.4 points more. The increased abstention
as compared with V:11, together with the evidence of the below cited comments, suggested that some might have been unsure of the meaning of "relative shelf classification," which
was intended as a contraction for "shelf classification with
relative location." However, the decline in agreement was
suggestive more of a general attitude previously evidenced:
that hypotheses relating to specific implementation of an open-
shelf policy elicited less agreement than those advancing the
general desirability of such a policy.

There were seven comments, of which four questioned
the meaning: "Meaning of 'relative'?" "Than in one with
what else?" "Meaning?" "What do you mean 'relative'?"
A college technical services librarian confirmed his agreement but gave no specific reason. A library school administrator who did not check an option explained: "Size is a factor." Finally, a dual response--classified as "Other"--was
noted on one questionnaire: the college reference librarian,
to whom the questionnaire had been sent, checked "Agree,"
but a technical services colleague who had been consulted
checked "Do not agree."

A concluding observation is prompted by the "Other"
comment of the university reference librarian: "Than in one
with what else?" This implied that the statement could be
interpreted as a truism. As a college acquisitions librarian

commented on V:3: "For browsing, one should have together books in a certain area, rather than have books thrown together as one might find an attic or second-hand store." Assuming that most respondents understood the wording, one might surmise that the lessened agreement with a self-evident statement like V:12, as compared with that to V:11, was occasioned by the specification in V:12 of "conditioning" elements--even those so obvious and ubiquitous as shelf classification and relative location.

V:13. "Nothing can be accomplished by browsing in a general research collection that could not be done more easily and efficiently through the use of the library catalog and other bibliographical tools."

This hypothesis, related to IV:16, expressed categorically a position taken perhaps less unequivocally by most of its advocates in the literature: bibliographic access can satisfactorily replace browsing. As explained in connection with IV:16, this view, though at first glance apparently extreme, is in fact attested by the many large European academic and research libraries which are commonly closed-stack. (Any book, of course, might be rejected as unsuitable after inspection, but the book need not be first retrieved by the patron from the shelves. Advocates of bibliographic access would claim that the number of rejections would be much reduced by preliminary screening with catalogs and other bibliographic aids.)

More than three-fourths of all respondents disagreed: only 10.8 percent agreed; 8.1 percent were undecided; 75.7 percent did not agree; and 5.4 percent had some other opinion. Negative reaction to so unequivocal a statement was not unexpected. However, of considerable interest was a comparison of the pattern of opinion with that for IV:16 whose wording seemed to differ significantly chiefly in the use of "open-shelf access" instead of "browsing."

Table 16 indicates that negative response to IV:16 was 7.7 percentage points less and affirmative response 11 percentage points more than the corresponding responses to V:13 as shown in Table 22. Apparently, respondents, though clearly unwilling to approve of exclusively bibliographical access in general academic or research libraries, were less unwilling to do so for "open-shelf access" than for "browsing." It is possible, though, that this was not because

"browsing" was taken more "seriously" by the respondents
than "open-shelf access" but, on the contrary, was thought
a less critical activity producing a direct personal satisfaction not necessarily connected with serious subject research
and, thus, less replaceable by bibliographic access.   (As a
public reference librarian commented on V:10: "It's nice,
though.")   This possibility was encompassed in the final statement of the questionnaire.

Most of the 19 comments confirmed the general negative view.   There were only two comments from those who
agreed.   A technical services librarian in a very large,
closed-stack research library stated: "Tend to agree."   A
teacher of classification who had previously advocated classified catalogs agreed with V:13 and added: "Through the use
of the classed library catalog."

Comments from those who disagreed were: "If they
are truly adequate."   (Evidently this respondent felt the tools
were not truly adequate.)   "Making available the shelflist in
published form as Harvard has done can facilitate browsing
and increase the value of classification to readers."   "I have
yet to meet a catalog or bibliography that put a book in my
hand. ...   V:13 and 14 both imply that browsing cannot be performed in catalogs and bibliographies."   "Book is of no value
if it is not available.   Browsing indicates its availability or
non-availability."   "General book may have specific material
never mentioned nor never analyzed."   "Browsing is useful
supplement even in research collections."   A college acquisitions librarian remarked:

> I do not agree.   The library catalog and biblio-
> graphical tools become more important as one
> delves more deeply into his field of interest.   How-
> ever, the card catalog is an imperfect tool, the
> bibliographic tools may be outdated or too selective,
> and browsing will tell you what the library has
> rather than what books are available in certain
> areas.   When one starts a question with 'Nothing'
> or 'Always' and like terms, the answer is invari-
> ably 'No.'

A cataloging department head in a large university library who disagreed added a note:

> I foresee a point sometime in the future when large
> research libraries may have to turn to fixed loca-

tion arrangements, similar to that used by the New
York Public Library. The reason is simply one of
sheer quantity of material, and most institutions of
some size may no longer feel they can afford the
luxury of 'wasted' space. Some type of compact
shelving by size will evolve, simply so that the
greatest possible number of volumes can be housed
in a given building. More sophisticated, automated
means of subject approach might have to replace
browsing in these instances. In the case of universities, a 'browsing' or 'instructional' or 'undergraduate' library probably would remain with a relative shelf classification.

Is a question (or statement) on the browsing value
of a shelflist or classified catalog relevant to your
study?

    "Other" opinions were: "Need both." "Perhaps."
" 'Nothing' a broad sweeping term. Depends on library's
catalog." "More efficient to use available tools, but at times
may not be as easy as browsing." "Meaning?" "This would
be true if books were carefully analyzed in depth through subject cataloging and bibliographic listings. No library can afford to catalog in depth." "They complement each other and
both are necessary or certainly desirable." "Accomplished
towards what goal?" "If you know what and how."

    The preceding comment was from a public reference
librarian who appended a letter of which the following part
seemed to refer to this statement:

        A good card catalog for someone who is doing pre-
        cise research might be most useful. However, the
        skill would need to be directed towards researching
        the catalog and the catalogers, not the books. In
        a sense, this is second-hand research and should
        be rejected by the dedicated researcher.

        'Me want to do it myself.' And who would trust a
        cataloger--even (especially) the Library of Con-
        gress!

    In summary, more than three-fourths would not accept
exclusively bibliographic access in lieu of browsing in a general research collection. This was consistent with earlier
approval for general principles of open-shelf access and

browsing.   Nevertheless, comparison of responses to V:13
and to IV:16--together with the evidence of comments--sug-
gested that "browsing" might not be as seriously regarded as
"open-shelf access" which was presumably less likely to be
interpreted as recreational or not "serious." Indeed, some
comments emphasized "browsing" as chiefly valuable for as-
certaining availability of works on the shelves.   The most
specific intellectual benefit of browsing to be mentioned was
that of determining through inspection what specific information was contained in the book, information not usually noted
in catalogs or bibliographies.   With a notable exception, little
attention was paid to browsing as possibly related to subject
study by means of shelf classification.   The next hypothesis
attempted to test the acceptability of "browsing" to describe
serious research.

     V:14.   " 'Browsing' is not a sufficiently precise term
to characterize serious research, so its use should be limited to describing recreational, non-research activities in
'browsing' collections or their equivalent."

     The purpose of this statement was just described.
Strictly speaking, the statement required respondents to react
only to the suitability of a word to describe a certain type of
activity.   However, reaction would necessarily involve intellectual assessment of the activity "browsing."   (The word is
frequently used by documentalists to denote a component element in subject-oriented examination of materials or bibliographic records.)   The comments cited below indicate how
respondents in fact grappled with this problem of identifying
the process before deciding on its appropriate name.

     A small majority was negative: 28.3 percent agreed;
10.3 percent were undecided; 55.9 percent did not agree; and
5.5 percent expressed some other opinion.   Comparison of
Tables 22 and 23 indicated a "marked" difference between the
extent of agreement by practitioners and that by all respondents, and possibly also a "marked" difference in the "Do not
agree" category.   That is, practitioners' "Agree" response
was 5.0 percentage points more, and their "Do not agree"
response was 4.9 percentage points less than the corresponding percentages of all respondents including practitioners.

     Inspection of "Agree" responses by professional func-
tion of respondent showed that 32 of 96 practitioners (33.3
percent) agreed on V:14, compared with eight of 42 teachers

(19. 0 percent), and one of seven library school administrators
(14. 3 percent). Within the practitioner group, technical services and library administrative personnel agreed more than
five times as often as reader services personnel, that is, 23
of 55 technical services personnel (41. 8 percent) and seven
of 16 library administrators (43. 8 percent) agreed, as compared with two of 25 reader services personnel (. 08 percent).
Accordingly, it appears that practitioners rejected "browsing" as a serious research activity markedly more often than
teachers and library school administrators, and that technical services and library administrative practitioners rejected
"serious" browsing over five times more frequently than reader services practitioners.

Inspection of "Do not agree" responses--though there
was not quite a "marked" difference of five percentage points
--by professional function of respondent showed a distribution
similar to but not as extreme as that in the "Agree" category. That is, practitioners were clearly less disposed to disagree with V:14 than were teachers and library school administrators: 49 of 96 practitioners (51. 0 percent) disagreed,
compared with 27 of 42 teachers (64. 3 percent), and five of
seven library school administrators (71. 4 percent). Technical services and reader services practitioners in this "Do
not agree" category did not differ as greatly as in the "Agree"
category, though technical services practitioners were still
much less disposed to disagree with this hypothesis than were
reader services practitioners: 24 of 55 technical services
librarians (43. 6 percent) disagreed on V:14 as compared with
16 of 25 reader services librarians (64. 0 percent). Library
administrators were heavier in the "Do not agree" than they
had been in the "Agree" category: nine of 16 (56. 3 percent)
disagreed, compared with the 7 (43. 8 percent) who had
agreed.

Further analysis of practitioner responses by the type
of library represented showed that academic and special librarians tended much less to agree and correspondingly more
to disagree with V:14 than did public and system librarians.
Thus, 19 of 69 academic and special librarians (27. 5 percent)
agreed as compared with 13 of 27 public and system librarians (48. 5 percent); while 40 of 69 academic and special librarians (58. 0 percent) did not agree on V:14 as compared
with nine of 27 public and system librarians (33. 3 percent).

The reasons for the various opinions were suggested
by some of the 16 comments. Those who agreed remarked:

"The term 'browsing' does not refer to serious research."
"Browsing with a purpose, or searching more accurately describes what was meant." A college acquisitions librarian who checked "Undecided" added a comment that seemingly indicated agreement:

> I agree. [sic] I would agree that in research
> 'browsing' is not too good a term. It seems to
> me to go in hand with recreational, or non-technical pursuits, and other time-wasting activities,
> rather than more direct and goal-oriented activities.

Those disagreeing remarked: "Research is not a sufficiently precise term to characterize serious research."
"V:13 and 14 both imply that browsing cannot be performed in catalogs and bibliographies." "If browsing is limited to title reading, then would agree." "The deficiencies of catalogs, indexes, abstracts, and other bibliographical approaches led me to check 'Do not agree.' " "General book may have specific material never mentioned nor never analyzed." (This point was also applied to V:13.)

"Other" comments were: "While 'browsing' does not characterize serious research, neither must its use be limited only to browsing collections." "Depends on subject matter on which researcher is working." "Meaning?" "Nonsense! The term is not precise, true, but the practice is."
"I don't understand its relevance here!" "Only if you have a substitute for the research-oriented 'look-see.' " "Baffles me, as seeming to be in the have-you-quit-beating-your-wife category, and I must let it pass." A technical services practitioner in a public library remarked:

> The question seems to be too black-or-white to
> answer with the choices you have offered. I will
> agree that 'browsing' is not serious research in
> the way that most people understand the term 'research.' But that does not lead me to the conclusion that its use is then generally recreational,
> non-research oriented. Browsing can and does furnish a product that will greatly enhance most serious research. I do not feel that the term must be
> made to characterize serious research; but it is
> sufficiently important a function of research to be
> a definite complement of it.

In summary, a majority would not agree that "brows-

ing" should be confined only to recreational, non-research
activities. The minority view was more likely to be held by
practitioners than other professional groups and, within the
practitioner group, more likely to be held by technical services and administrative personnel in academic and special libraries. The reaction to this statement was not clear-cut,
as shown by the small majorities of 55. 9 percent of all respondents and of 51. 0 percent of practitioner respondents who
checked "Do not agree. " Some comments suggested considerable difficulty in deciding on a term for that activity which,
though not exclusively recreational or non-serious in purpose,
still bore no designation other than one which to many de-
noted only recreational and non-serious activity. This problem of nomenclature will be considered in the subsequent
chapter.

     During the analysis of the responses to V:13, a com-
parison was made with those to IV:16 and the suggestion was
broached that a possible factor in the differing opinion patterns was that respondents considered "browsing" (as in V:13)
a less serious, thus intellectually less critical, activity than
"open-shelf access" (as in IV:16). To test this conjecture,
a further comparative tally was made of the responses to
IV:16 and to V:13 and 14. Results were as follows:

     Of the 81 respondents who disagreed with V:14, 10
(12. 3 percent) agreed with IV:16, and only one (1. 2 percent)
agreed with V:13; while 64 (79. 0 percent) disagreed with
IV:16, and 75 (92. 6 percent) disagreed with V:13. Of the 41
respondents who agreed with V:14, 19 (46. 3 percent) agreed
with IV:16, and 15 (36. 6 percent) agreed with V:13; while 17
(41. 5 percent) disagreed with IV:16, and 21 (51. 2 percent)
disagreed with V:13.

     The above data did not convincingly confirm the con-
jecture. The modal opinion pattern was definitely substanti-
ated, that is, those who disagreed with V:14 also disagreed
overwhelmingly with IV:16 and V:13; and, conversely, gave
very light support to IV:16 and V:13. However, the pattern
of opinion of those who agreed with V:14 was much less
clear. There emerged no majority of opinion on IV:16,
though there was a bare majority (51. 2 percent) of disagreement on V:13. Although one could not draw "statistical" inferences from these patterns, one might conclude that those
who did not accept "browsing" as a serious research activity
(V:14) were (compared with those who did accept) much less
certain about substituting exclusively bibliographic access for

"open-shelf access" in large academic libraries (IV:16). At the same time, though they expressed majority disapproval of replacing "browsing" by exclusively bibliographic access (V:13), they were much more willing to entertain such a proposition than those who did agree that browsing could be a serious research activity (V:14). A possible explanation of such complex patterns--assuming, of course, the adequacy of the statements--might be that many respondents did not think of "open-shelf access" and of "browsing" as logically related, so that their reactions to statements involving these terms should be considered discrete rather than possibly inconsistent.

Statistical Measurement of Relationship

The preceding analyses in this chapter of responses categorized by professional function of respondent or type of library represented by respondent practitioner were not intended to imply statistical significance such as would be sought by the chi-square tests. The nature of the hypotheses in Section V made it desirable in this chapter to pay more than usual attention to possible patterns of opinion relating to certain respondent characteristics. Although such patterns could be meaningful in the context of the discussion, they were not presented as statistically "valid" or "reliable." The statistical tests, however, aimed to ascertain whether the total pattern of opinion represented by certain characteristics of all possible responses seemed to reveal statistically significant relationships. The following Tables 24 and 25 give the chi-square test results and the coefficients of contingency for, respectively, all responses categorized by professional function of respondent and all practitioner responses categorized by type of library represented.

Table 24 indicates that only Statement V:4 ("Close classification on shelves is necessary for non-recreational browsing.") met or exceeded the critical value of X^2 for the 95-percent confidence level. Table 26 gives the tally for V:4 as prepared for the chi-square test reported in Table 24. (As previously explained, this first chi-square test treats library administrators not as practitioners but as administrators.)

Inspection of Table 26 which summarizes the responses to V:4 as categorized for the first chi-square test indicates that 23 of 84 practitioners (27.4 percent) agreed, as com-

TABLE 24

STATISTICAL MEASURES OF RELATIONSHIP BETWEEN
PROFESSIONAL FUNCTION OF RESPONDENT AND
TYPE OF RESPONSE FOR STATEMENTS V:1-14

Statement No. V:	Chi-Square Value	Level of Confidence	Coefficient of Contingency
1	6.372	50%	.202
2	3.171	20%	.141
3	9.927	80%	.248
4	13.854[a]	95%[a]	.289
5	1.629	02%	.100
6	8.132	70%	.225
7	7.716	70%	.221
8	8.638	80%	.234
9	2.812	10%	.134
10	7.570	70%	.219
11	5.834	50%	.192
12	3.580	20%	.151
13	2.204	10%	.114
14	6.004	50%	.197

Notes: Critical value of chi-square for 95% level of confidence
is 12.592.   Critical value for level of confidence is
95%.   Maximum value for coefficient of contingency is
1.000.

[a]Equals or exceeds critical value.

TABLE 25

STATISTICAL MEASURES OF RELATIONSHIP BETWEEN
PRACTITIONER RESPONDENTS' TYPE OF LIBRARY AND
THEIR TYPE OF RESPONSE FOR STATEMENTS V:1-14

Statement No. V:	Chi-Square Value	Level of Confidence	Coefficient of Contingency
1	1.303	50%	.114
2	.074	10%	.024
3	.095	10%	.028
4	.042	10%	.017
5	1.158	50%	.111
6	.374	25%	.060
7	.174	25%	.040
8	1.336	75%	.116
9	.116	25%	.033
10	.049	10%	.017
11	.007	05%	.008
12	.018	10%	.014
13	.077	10%	.024
14	2.840	90%	.169

Notes: Critical value of chi-square for 95% level of confidence is 3.841. Critical value for level of confidence is 95%. Optimum value for coefficient of contingency is .707.

TABLE 26

RESPONSES TO STATEMENT V:4 CATEGORIZED BY
PROFESSIONAL FUNCTION OF RESPONDENT

Professional Function	Agree		Undecided		Do Not Agree		Other		Total	
	No.	%	No.	%	No.	%	No.	%	No.	%
Practitioner	23	15.4	14	9.4	46	30.9	1	0.7	84	56.4
Teacher	14	9.4	6	4.0	22	14.8	--	--	42	28.2
Administrator[a]	5	3.4	1	0.7	14	9.4	3	2.0	23	15.4
Total	42	28.2	21	14.1	82	55.0	4	2.7	149	100.0

[a]Includes library administrator.

pared with 14 of 42 teachers (33. 3 percent) and five of 23 library and library school administrators (21. 7 percent). Thus, teachers seemed to favor close classification for nonrecreational browsing more than the other groups, especially administrators. In the "Undecided" category, the distribution by professional group was: 14 of 84 practitioners (16. 7 percent), six of 42 teachers (14. 3 percent), and one of 23 administrators (4. 4 percent). Practitioners thus seemed slightly more undecided than teachers and both groups decidedly more so than administrators.

In the "Do not agree" category, the distribution was: 46 of 84 practitioners (54. 8 percent), 22 of 42 teachers (52. 4 percent), and 14 of 23 administrators (60. 9 percent). Here again, administrators seemed more extreme in their attitude, tending more to disagreement than the other groups, especially teachers. The pattern in the "Other" category was: one of 84 practitioners (1. 2 percent), none of 42 teachers (0. 0 percent), and three of 23 administrators (13. 0 percent). One might summarize that administrators responding to V:4 were shown by the first chi-square test to express less agreement, and more "Other" opinion than either practitioners or teachers, especially the latter.

Considering the nature of the questionnaire data and the need to aggregate them in certain combinations for testing purposes, these test results could not be regarded as more than preliminary or suggestive. Accordingly, a more detailed inspection was made of the two "administrator" subcategories: library administrator and library school administrator. Library administrators were found to agree with V:4 almost twice as often as library school administrators, that is, four of 16 library administrators (25. 0 percent) agreed, but only one of seven library school administrators (14. 2 percent). No library administrator checked "Undecided"--as compared with one of seven library school administrators (14. 2 percent). Library administrators disagreed somewhat more than library school administrators: 10 of 16 of the former (62. 5 percent) checked "Do not agree," compared with four of seven library school administrators (57. 1 percent). Both types expressed about the same proportion of "Other" opinion: two of 16 library administrators (12. 5 percent) as compared with one of seven library school administrators (14. 3 percent).

Perhaps the salient conclusion is that library administrators tended to agree more with V:4 and be less unde-

cided than library school administrators.   Thus, to compare
the responses only of library administrators with those of
practitioners (as defined for the first chi-square test) and
teachers, library administrators seemed close to practitioners in proportionate agreement on V:4; but considerably higher
in disagreement, not at all "Undecided," and more inclined to
an "Other" opinion than practitioners and teachers.   One
might repeat here the comments of the two library administrators who expressed an "Other" opinion: "Do you mean
necessary or do you mean 'desirable' or 'helpful'?" and "Desirable."

There was no statement in Table 25 for which the chi-
square value and level of confidence indicated a statistically
significant relationship between practitioner respondents' type
of library and their type of response.   Also, Tables 24 and
25 indicated that, as for the other sections of the questionnaire, no coefficient of contingency was high enough to suggest a significant correlation.

Notes

1.   American Library Association, Classification Committee,
     "Report, May 15, 1964:   Statement on Types of Clas-
     sification Available to New Academic Libraries," Li-
     brary Resources and Technical Services, IX (Winter,
     1965), 106.

2.   George T. Little, "School and College Libraries," in
     U.S., Bureau of Education, Report of the Commis-
     sioner for Education for 1892-93 (2 vols.; Washing-
     ton: Govt. Print. Off., 1895), II, 924; Otis H. Rob-
     inson, "College Library Administration," in U.S.,
     Bureau of Education, Public Libraries in the United
     States of America; Their History, Condition, and
     Management; Special Report; Part I (Washington:
     Govt. Print. Off., 1876), p. 516-17.

CHAPTER XIII

GENERAL ANALYSIS AND INTERPRETATION

Some General Respondent Comments

The difficulty of answering precisely the complicated questions raised by this study was made evident in general comments from respondents and from those who declined to complete the questionnaire. The director of a large special library wrote:

> When I received your questionnaire on the Direct Shelf Approach, I assigned it to technically responsible staff to be filled out. They did so but in so doing called my attention to the difficulties your questions presented to them. I reviewed their comments and agree with them that the way in which you ask your questions cannot elicit meaningful answers from this library.
>
> I think that your problem is you are trying to cover too many types of libraries. Your statements are necessarily broad. The qualifications which any large specialized library would wish to place on its answers are not possible.

A teacher of technical services answered: "I am returning your questionnaire because I am unable to answer your questions using the three possible answers. Answers to some of your questions depend on many factors and are not always clear-cut."

A technical services practitioner in a large university library wrote:

> I've spent an hour filling out your questionnaire and must say that it interested me, but also frustrated me. The subject matter is important and in general the questionnaire I think is good. The frustration comes in trying to fit rather complex and

355

often subtle replies into one of your three categories.   I realize that this is purposeful probably on
your part, wanting people to give you precise answers.   But people are reluctant to be pinned down
to an answer, preferring to qualify and comment
only.   Perhaps this is a malaise of our times and
possibly I suffer more acutely than most.

A teacher of technical services chose not to complete
the questionnaire beyond Section III because: "It is too tedi-
ous to say of nearly every statement: 'I don't know because
nuances are lacking or data are not available.' "

Evidently, many librarians believed that the problems
of their own libraries made it difficult to accept without extensive qualifications a generalization on the direct shelf approach.   Numerous comments expressed this need to qualify.
Teachers also wished to delimit their opinions.   Even admitting the categorical nature of many questionnaire statements, one may wonder if the concept of the direct shelf ap-
proach--along with the various means to realize that approach
--could be so amorphous as not to allow of opinions valid for
more than one respondent's library.   Proposals are now being made for national standardization of bibliographical controls and for national information transfer networks.   Such
developments would place a premium on general answers to
problems of organizing library materials.

Many librarians also have denied the existence of the
"average" patron.   Prevost asked the unanswered question:
"What is the 'public' which we, in general libraries, serve
through the catalog?"[1]   Yet, a library can ordinarily employ
only one scheme of bibliographic control to serve all its patrons.   Purported inadequacies in general schemes of classification are claimed to render the schemes unuseful to most
libraries without extensive adaptation.   Evidence collected by
this study suggested that the difficulties of application might
stem from misunderstanding and ambivalence directed towards the direct shelf approach (with its subsumed browsing
activities) and towards current schemes for organizing library materials to implement that approach.

Modal Respondent Characteristics

Geographically, the 152 individual respondents represented almost all States plus the Provinces of Quebec and

Ontario. Library institutions accounted for about two-thirds of all responses, and library schools for about one-third. University libraries contributed almost one-third of total responses. The median size for all libraries was one million volumes. Thus, the modal library would reflect the problems of organizing huge collections for effective direct use. The size factor would point up the need for procedures generally applicable to such libraries, e.g., cooperative or shared bibliographical organization. Libraries of such size find it increasingly hard to deal, unaided by other institutions, with their acquisition and bibliographical problems. Furthermore, most respondent institutions--not excluding "special" libraries--maintained comprehensive and/or heterogeneous collections. This in turn would involve the acceptance of a classification scheme which, though perhaps not ideal for any one library, would have to be general enough in scope and treatment to cover the great variety of subjects encompassed in the modal collection. The degree of specificity in such a scheme would not be the same for all subject areas.

About a third of all library respondents reported reclassification, chiefly as a result of academic and special libraries changing to LC from DC--but reclassification was almost always partial or selective. At least three-fourths of reclassifying libraries reported their readers were not handicapped by such reclassification. Those reporting their readers handicapped did not, evidently, deem the handicap serious. It would thus appear that about a third of all library respondents, i.e., those reclassifying, maintained without due inconvenienve to the patron collections classified by more than one scheme.

There seemed to be almost no completely "closed" respondent library. Almost all libraries followed a policy of open-shelf access, at least for some patrons, and for part of the collection. Cutter[2] in 1886 had described the prevalence of such a policy.

The modal opinions reported in the questionnaire derived from a large academic library with a heterogeneous general collection on open shelves classified by LC. The library employed a dictionary catalog, close shelf classification, and relative location. There was almost a fifty-percent chance that this library was in the process of partial reclassification occasioned by conversion from DC to LC. The modal individual respondent was a technical services practitioner in a large academic library.

If these modal respondent characteristics were a "representative" sample, the policy makers in today's libraries—at least as regards the problems considered by this study—would tend to be technical services practitioners. Such inference is conjectural. One library administrator, for example, could outweigh in his influence many practitioners in the same library. There is evidence, however, that administrators may leave classification policy to the technical services department. This was suggested by the reluctance or refusal of library administrators to answer questions concerned with classification.

Respondents' opinions on such issues as subject headings and shelf classification, broad and close shelf classification, LC and DC, may have been conditioned by modal institutional characteristics: public dictionary catalog, large heterogeneous collection closely classified on open shelves by LC for academic study and research. Thus, predominant opinion may have been formed more by actual practices and policies rather than by "objective" judgment. Informed opinion, however, usually relies heavily on experience. Respondents frequently disclaimed the value of their opinion on a particular issue because they lacked experience.

Although the opinion patterns for various statements often revealed noticeable differences in relation to professional functions of respondents or in relation to characteristics of the libraries represented by practitioner respondents, statistical tests yielded almost no reliable correlations for the responses as a whole. These results might be attributed to the complexity of many statements, the imprecise nature of many responses, and inadequacy of response frequencies for required test categories.

However, the visual inspection and analysis of response tallies also suggested that most types of respondents—e. g., practitioner or teacher, public or academic librarian—did not respond consistently to the statements, either as presented in series or considered as logically connected. This would imply that most respondents had not formed opinions distinctive to their professional specialization. This might mean that respondents had not clearly defined the questions related to direct access, nor related them constructively to any particular area of library practice or theory.

Nor did size of library represented by the practitioner respondent seem to affect the opinion patterns. It might well be that, after attaining the modal size of one million volumes, libraries tended to discount the further effect of collection size on open-shelf policy. Smaller libraries with rapidly growing collections would probably have a different attitude.

Generally, the modal respondent characteristics were appropriate to a working hypothesis of this study that the problem of the direct shelf approach would be most severe in large academic and research libraries.

The Direct Shelf Approach (Open-Shelf Access): The Role of Classification

As anticipated by the documentary analysis, the opinions and comments on Section III of the questionnaire suggested ambivalent attitudes on the role of classification in the direct shelf approach. Numerous practitioners and teachers seemed unwilling to commit themselves without many qualifications and reservations even to an opinion on problems of classification as related to the direct shelf approach. Most comments stressed local library situations or the need for exacting precision in defining the problem. The reluctance to accept words like "average" and "basically" might also derive from this ambivalence. An implication emerged that American librarianship has not attained consensus on classification in the direct shelf approach nor conviction in the values, theoretical or practical, of library classification generally.

Unease or ambivalence in regard to classification was hinted by the general comments at the start of this chapter. Other comments expressed unease more specifically. A teacher of reader services apologized for not answering the questionnaire because: "Of all the areas--and there are many--in which I have little or no competency, classification heads the list. I would like to help out, but believe me, my contribution would be less than useful to you." A special library administrator declined to respond and explained: "This is in reply to your letter concerning relative shelf classification. You have also written to our Cataloger, which was the logical thing to do. She is a good Cataloger and very knowledgeable, and she will be able to answer your questionnaire very competently." As discussed in Chapter Nine, questionnaires were sent to various types of librarians in the same library (or teachers in the same school) so that complementary opinions might be obtained.

A dichotomy between technical and reader services
was stressed by the head of a technical services department
in a very large university library who declined to fill in the
questionnaire because, among other reasons: "Many of the
questions seem to require information of the sort that is most
likely to come to the public service departments--especially
feedback on the effectiveness of the classification system."

Reactions to Section III on open access and the role
of classification did not--as stated earlier--seem to have
been influenced to a major extent by either professional function of respondent or, in the case of practitioners, by type
and probably size of library represented.

Almost 60 percent thought shelf classification more
important as a locational device than as a means of systematic subject approach.   This confirmed opinions in the literature, but seemed inconsistent with the concern expressed by
many librarians over the "inadequacies" of available classification schemes, particularly the numerous relocations and
revisions in new editions--or sometimes the lack of them!
On the questionnaire evidence, the practical effects of such
concern were not great--unless the conversions from DC to
LC by academic and research libraries may be thought one
effect.

About 60 percent agreed that subject headings in the
catalog were more useful to the patron than shelf classification, an opinion advanced by Pettee and Kelley. [3]   Only 43
percent thought the "average" patron could "follow" close
classification notation on the shelves.   This opinion was consonant with the published views of most classificationists who
relegated notation to a theoretically minor position.   Such a
view, however, seemed contrary to the demands of theoreti-
cians like Sayers[4] for an expressive notation.

Only 30 percent felt it desirable on economic grounds
alone to continue close classification rather than change to
a (presumably) broader and less expensive kind.   Many denied that close shelf classification was more expensive than
broad, though it would seem that just the copying of longer
notations would entail more man-hours.   Comments suggested
that the "expense" of close classification was largely obviated by the acceptance of LC and DC assignments on the
printed cards.   The point was made that trying to "cut back"
LC notation as printed on the cards would make broad classification more expensive.   Similar reasoning would apply to

cutting back DC notation, particularly if the DC notation printed was not segmented. Such opinions emphasized the growing reliance of American libraries on centralized classification services despite purported inadequacies for local needs.

Significantly, almost two-thirds of the respondents did not believe that evidence of classification per se enhanced their professional status among patrons. Such an attitude, as noted, contradicted the literature, and furthermore was not completely consistent with general endorsement of classification for libraries. It might indicate disinterest, perhaps uneasiness, towards classification as an intellectual process involving professional expertise. Classificationists like Bliss, Ranganathan, and Palmer--all of whom claimed professional status enhancement from classification--also stressed its rigorous intellectual demands. Most respondents might therefore have preferred to consider its chief value that of a locational device.

In this matter of status enhancement librarians perhaps projected feelings onto patrons. As a student and later teacher of classification, this investigator found classification courses rather intimidating to pupils. It would not be surprising if some librarians declined to answer the questionnaire because they were not "specialists," though classification is said to affect almost every aspect of librarianship. Because of this pervasive influence, classification was termed the hallmark of professional librarianship by Bliss, Ranganathan, and Palmer.[5]

Despite respondents' denial of its status-enhancement, shelf classification was almost universal among reporting libraries. Except for an occasional advocacy of the classed catalog and indirect, i.e., bibliographic access to collections, as expressed in the literature by Shera and Egan,[6] almost all respondents approved the continuance of shelf classification.

The general approval, however, was not necessarily precise as to its reasons. Thus, a university reference librarian added in a letter:

> After fifteen years of research and study in various fields, I have found browsing in collections classed by any subject scheme to be vitally productive, and would hate to see myself or anyone else

deprived of that wonderful opportunity. If you would
like a specific example, I have recently begun a
most fruitful study of Karl Popper's philosophy, in
consequence of a (failed) search for a copy of Plato's
Republic beside which a most engaging book about
Popper had been shelved. Except for that failed
search in a classified collection, I might never
have discovered Popper. You might want to study
Popper yourself. His writing is a model of clear
thought and clear expression.

Such an experience would suggest a successful accident of "serendipity" more than the intended benefits of a
classified open-shelf collection. It is difficult to understand
how a work about a modern European philosopher of science
would stand classified next to a work by Plato. This type
of serendipity would tend to minimize an assumed value of
subject shelf classification for browsing. Chapter Six proposed functional definitions of browsing and serendipity based
on the probability of fortuitous discoveries in organized collections. Those definitions attempted to clarify the apparent
confusion in the kind of example just cited.

Elements of Epistemology, Psychology, and Sociology in the Role of Classification

Chapter One suggested that helpful hypotheses concerning the direct shelf approach might be derived from sociology,
psychology, and philosophy. The theories of Durkheim, Lovejoy, or Piaget might contribute to understanding the nature
and limits of practical library classification. Some reference
to those theories has already been made. Chapter Eight
promised a later more detailed discussion of such extra-library factors. The first to be considered is epistemology,
specifically that of Platonic realism.

There seems to survive a faith in the knowledge-revealing role of library classification despite the many ambivalences, compromises, and even contradictions involved in
"the presentation of multi-dimensional thought in unilinear
form."[7] This faith apparently descends from the epistemological principle, traceable to Plato via Aristotle, that our
world reflects an ideal order; and if we could ascertain this
order, we would perceive the true nature and relationships
of all phenomena. This order is unitary and hierarchical,
as described by Lovejoy in The Great Chain of Being. [8]

Therefore, any level in the hierarchy (in classic logic a
genus-species order) should reveal its true nature and relationships vis-à-vis all superior and subordinate levels. (See
"The Problem of Linearity" in Chapter Eight.) As Bliss
claimed: "A classification of books consistent with the scientific and pedagogic orders ... has ... educational value as
the manifest organization of knowledge."[9] All traditional
classificationists have defined classification as the process of
distinguishing those characteristics of likeness and unlikeness
stemming from genus-species differentiae. Although Jevons
and Broadfield denied, on traditional logical grounds, that
such a classificatory process was applicable to library materials, all widely used library classifications are examples of
it.

The Platonic doctrine of forms may help explain not
only the epistemology of traditional classification, but also
the relative unimportance to classificationists and librarians
of its apparent contradictions and inadequacies. Plato[10]
taught in his allegory of the cave that men were prisoners in
a world of shadows, i.e., sense perception, and must be
taught the true reality whose light he likened, in another allegory, to the sun. Men must strive, regardless of difficulties and disappointments, to approach the ideal knowledge
distorted by our senses. The perfect union of the terrestri-
al and the supernal remained an ideal.

If such history is relevant to the development of classification, it suggests a philosophical explanation as to why
the classificationists in search of their correct order will-
ingly conceded the inadequacies of their human schemes but
were not deterred thereby. Richardson and Bliss[11] insisted
that classification, regardless of compromises and exceptions,
be based on an order of knowledge. The striving for a basic
order, no matter how approximate because of our human
limitations, had to proceed. Defects and inconsistencies only
confirmed the importance and difficulty of the challenge. In
this sense, the classificationist, admitting the "absurdity" of
his schemes, reaverred: "Credo quia absurdum." This
would be his response to Jevons.[12]

There may also be strong psychological motivation for
the librarian's faith in classification, despite its inconsistencies and contradictions. The "faith" may express an inerad-
icable mental need. Even opponents of traditional classification based on hierarchical classes admitted the importance
of a classification system, even if it be only based on the

immediate or ephemeral purpose of the inquirer. Since this
purpose will vary with the individual, critics like Shera advocated a "referential classification" described by Whitehead.

Shera claimed that the sociology of knowledge, as developed since Durkheim, denied Bliss's faith in a "fundamental order of nature ... the belief that there is a universal,
logically divided classification of knowledge," and that we must
"free classification from the strait jacket of hierarchical systems of knowledge." Accordingly, relational "properties
rather than the essential objects themselves should ... become the axes of their respective special classification
schemes." This would result in "multiple approaches to the
relata rather than multiple or alternative locations for the
individual units."13

Shera's views on practical library classification appeared ambivalent. Metcalfe commented that although Shera
seemed to reject hierarchical classification for both shelves
and catalog, "it turns out later Shera doesn't mean what he
says ... at least for the shelf, on which classification does
help" because it lets the researcher "do some indexing of
his own" so that "he may satisfy needs that not the most an-
ticipatory cataloging ... will anticipate."14

The Baconian tradition of classification, usually contrasted with that of Brunet, is to base the divisions of the
scheme on subjective or psychological activities, i.e., on
"the individuals doing the considering, and indeed each according to his individual intellectual powers."15 Contemporary philosophical and scientific opinion is that classification
represents a basic mental process. Sayers gave the "simplest meaning" of classification as "that process of the mind
by which qualities in things are abstracted and the things are
grouped by those qualities into classes."16 Ranganathan
averred: "Classification is a way of thinking. It is a way
of thinking systematically and purposefully."17 Palmer echoed this thought:

> Classification is at the basis of all intelligent work,
> and is resorted to unconsciously by intelligent peo-
> ple. It is a thousand times more effective if con-
> sciously used as a tool, as every librarian knows.18

Bliss cited William James: "Any classification of
things into kinds ... is a more rational way of conceiving
the things than is that mere juxtaposition or separation of

them in time and space which is the order of their crude
perception."[19] Ansteinsson, considering the dilemmas of
classification, quoted Jespersen on the classifying instinct:
"Man is a classifying animal."[20]

Ranganathan described the possible neuro-psychological
basis of the classification process:

> In common usage, as distinct from the technical
> definition ... classification means what has been
> denoted by the term 'assortment,' ... viz., divi-
> sion into groups and arranging them in a definite
> sequence. In its essence, then, classification as
> used in popular language means only arrangement.
> To arrange things in a more or less helpful se-
> quence is an inherent habit of man.... Perhaps,
> this inherent tendency to arrange is a concomitant
> of the finiteness of the speed of nervous impulse
> within human body. When speed is finite, struc-
> ture is inevitable. When structure is sensed, se-
> quence is but natural. This gets expressed extra-
> neurally also. Thus arrangement is a neural ne-
> cessity. It is instinctive, almost bio-chemical in
> nature, and involuntary. The result is involuntary
> classification.[21]

The best-known non-traditional scheme created by psychological analysis of classification is the Relational Classification of Farradane "who bases his nine categories of relations on the mode of operation of the human mind (as shown
by experimental psychology), [and] has advanced the theory
that there are only nine distinct stages in the progress of
the mind towards complete understanding of concepts ... and
that these stages can be identified in their correct sequence."[22] Farradane defined classification as a "representation of the true structure of knowledge."[23] A related concept of the development of the powers of human thought was
advanced by Piaget in his "genetic epistemology."[24]

The psychological testimony just cited suggests another reason for the faith of classificationists and librarians:
classification is a mental faculty whose expression will not
be balked. This equation of classification with cognition
leads to approval and advocacy: both in theory and practice,
classification becomes a priori a necessary means of organizing library resources for apprehension.

Besides the possibility of classification as a recognized psychological need--of classificationist, librarian, and
reader--it may also represent a sociological drive. In this
respect, a statement of Palmer was suggestive:

> In all exercises of the intellect it behoves man to
> be humble; but in this one of devising systems for
> the organization of knowledge humility is essential.
> Nothing gives us librarians such a sense of power
> as our systems of bibliographical control. [25]

This "sense of power," as well as Platonic-Aristoteli-
an ideas of classification, might be elucidated by some of
Durkheim's sociological research--to which Shera[26] has had
recourse in part. In Primitive Classification, written with
Mauss, he claimed to prove that man's logical faculties,
hitherto considered innately given to the individual, were social in origin:

> Society was not simply a model which classificatory
> thought followed; it was its own divisions which
> served as divisions for the system of classification.
> The first logical categories were social categories;
> the first classes of things were classes of men,
> into which these things were integrated. It was
> because men were grouped, and thought of them-
> selves in the form of groups, that in their ideas
> they grouped other things, and in the beginning the
> two modes of grouping were merged to the point
> of being indistinct. ... Things were thought to be
> integral parts of society, and it was their place in
> society which determined their place in nature....
>
> Not only the external form of classes, but also the
> relations uniting them to each other, are of social
> origin. It is because human groups fit one into
> another--the sub-class into the clan, the clan into
> the moiety, the moiety into the tribe--that groups
> of things are ordered in the same way.... And if
> the totality of things is conceived as a single sys-
> tem, this is because society itself is seen in the
> same way. It is a whole, or rather it is the
> unique whole to which everything is related. Thus
> logical hierarchy is only another aspect of social
> hierarchy, and the unity of knowledge is nothing
> else than the very unity of the collectivity extended
> to the universe. [27]

Although Rodney Needham[28] judged that Durkheim and Mauss did not prove their thesis, he considered their essay of seminal importance. The ideas of Durkheim and Mauss suggest for this study that classification, besides being a neuropsychological need, may be also a sociological one: to structure one's experiences so that they correspond to the individual's social organization in which he is "at home." In this way the individual finds a means of dealing with the "world": he domesticates the alien experience. The "sense of power" classification bestows on librarians may be the motive, psychological and sociological, for men to classify: to feel they control, that is, gain power over, their environments, their worlds of outer and inner experience.

Classification exercises power over phenomena through its imposition of order, arrangement, and system. Whether the power sensed is "real" involves problems beyond the pretensions of this study. Evidently, classificationists like Richardson and Bliss, who accepted certain metaphysical assumptions, did not doubt that reality. This study offers as a possible conclusion that the use of library classification to structure the collection, despite numerous theoretical and practical objections, reflects this need to feel in control, to experience, in that meaning at least, a "sense of power." (On a more obvious level, this resembles the satisfaction of a teacher in "molding" his students, that is, structuring their learning experience.) Before this potent motive, the inconsistencies and ambivalences evident in library classification could fade into insignificance. The need--almost compulsion --of classificationists to create schemes, despite cautionary historical failures, seems more understandable. The faith of librarians in classification schemes--though many librarians admit they do not understand them fully--also becomes more plausible. There is implied a belief, perhaps largely unconscious, that classification can exert power over that world of which the library has often been termed the microcosm. This belief would not be weakened by the metaphysical reassurances of Platonism.

If classification can be defined as a method of division by which classes and groups are determined and ordered, a motto for the strong faith in the validity of library classification might be "Divide and conquer!"

Although, as explained in Chapter Two, this study did not aim at direct investigation of library use and user, it may be appropriate to ask whether, and in what degree, these

factors of epistemology, psychology, and sociology could affect the patron in an open-shelf collection. To the extent
that such factors would apply to all members of a society,
it may be surmised that the reader's behavior and reactions
could be explained accordingly. Thus, the reader would respond to shelf classification analogously to the librarian. If
the librarian aims through shelf classification to create a
structured learning situation, the patron in his direct shelf
approach should feel a confidence in the apparent structure:
the materials are so ordered that the direct shelf approach
will uncover appropriate materials and produce answers to
his questions. As noted in Chapter Six, "browsing" defined
functionally would include the "reasonable expectation that desired or valuable items or information will be found among
those materials as arranged on the shelves."[29] The degree
to which the reader must "understand" this structure is, as
discussed above, uncertain. Most classificationists agreed
that he need not comprehend how the collection has been classified, but only be enlightened by the results--though, to be
sure, professional guidance would be ideal.[30]

     If, as believed by Bliss, Ranganathan, and Palmer,
classification procures for the librarian the respect of the
reader, then the reader must in some way be favorably impressed by the order on the shelves. It might be conserva-
tively assumed, especially in light of contemporary psychology and sociology, that the patron, particularly student or
researcher, must share the need to believe in an order for
that knowledge he pursues. Study and scholarship in themselves constitute socially sanctioned activities conducted in
accordance with conventional standards and means. Palmer
described some social conventions of classification structure:

          Whilst I stressed that main classes of knowledge
          were not inherent in the nature of things, but mere-
          ly a convenient device for helping us to control the
          bibliographic output (or, in the case of scientists,
          to retain in the mind the varieties of things to be
          remembered), I nevertheless assumed that the con-
          cept of the main class should not therefore be dis-
          carded. My reason for adopting this viewpoint is
          that the main class concept springs from a mode
          of thought which is deeply ingrained in human be-
          ings. Main classes are related to the logical con-
          struction of the earliest western philosophers, and
          the formal logic of the Greeks has been the main-
          stay of our rational thought for nearly 3,000 years.

This is not lightly to be cast aside. [31]

The patron, no less a social being than the classificationist or librarian, must also be concerned with the control
of experience. Thus, the classificationist and librarian may
feel that in controlling their experience through the imposition of order, they acknowledge and derive confidence from
a higher order ultimately controlling all experience. On his
part, the reader may feel that by relying on revealed order,
he can put his own experience "in order" and, thus, strength-
en his sense of security. Insofar as he depends on the
shelf-sequence to expose the structure of the collection, he
expresses his faith in the self-revelatory power of classification. The reader may not be too conscious of the man-made
nature of the structure. It may be enough for him, as for
the librarian, that the "order" teaches. What Metcalfe[32]
referred to as the educational conceit of the librarian may
be a belief that the patron learns what the librarian has arranged for him to learn. The librarian may thus identify
with the classification. The patron may be reassured by discovering an order which his extra-library conditioning has
led him to expect. So, he, too, may identify with the
scheme.

Classificationist, librarian, and reader may all feel
they deduce their order from a grand overarching one. Such
a feeling of being part of a greater system need not impair
individual initiative and purposeful activity, in short, the
sense of being in control of oneself. This is copiously documented in cultural and intellectual history.

These suggested psychological and sociological factors
affecting the patron, like the classificationist and librarian,
would be reflected in his sense of power in discovering and
organizing relevant materials. Knapp said that "a student
with sufficient imagination can use almost any book as a
stimulus to creative thought."[33] For this discussion,
"thought" might be interpreted as "structuring," an activity
which for the reader, no less than for the classificationist
and librarian, appears to satisfy a human need to exercise
power over experience by assimilating it into a socially
sanctioned order.

The practical danger is that the patron may waste
his time looking for information that may not exist in the
collection nor be accessible through shelf classification. Certainly, some direct shelf consultation must involve fairly def-

inite research problems or subject searches.   Contrariwise,
the librarian may be so influenced by his beliefs as to assume, albeit unconsciously, that shelf classification can somehow compensate for absent or even unacquired materials.
Cutter, Bliss, and Kelley[34] advised that all bibliographical
tools be used.   Chapter Seven emphasized the need for an
adequate acquisition policy.

The Direct Shelf Approach (Open-Shelf Access): Its Suitability in Various Libraries

Reactions to Section IV of the questionnaire affirmed
allegiance to the general principle of direct access, though
a rationale was not made especially clear or specific.   Thus,
a teacher of technical services wrote: "I found your questions a little hard to answer, but I firmly believe in an open-
stack library for everyone."   There was a strong suggestion
that direct access reflected patron preference.

At least 65 percent of all respondents agreed on the
desirability of open shelves for libraries generally, an opinion stronger among public than academic and special librarians.   Slightly fewer were willing to accept open-shelf policy
as "a significant educational responsibility of libraries."
This view was not stronger among public than academic and
special librarians.   Although about 62 percent of public librarians agreed, a more nearly unanimous vote might have
been expected.   This seemed a surprising decline in support
for the educational and social goals proclaimed by the early
advocates of the American public library as the people's
common school and university.   Martin, as already noted,
recently confirmed this inference: "I remember the educational thrust among librarians in the 1920's.   This is what
attracted me to the profession.   For a quarter of a century
I have watched this educational motivation weaken."[35]

Academic librarians did not conspicuously disapprove
of the educational goals of their libraries, but they seemed
particularly unwilling to acknowledge the possible influence
of acquisition policy on such goals.   This might have been
a factor in the wide disagreement (only one-third agreed)
with a hypothesis that direct shelf approach was most valuable in basic or "core" collections for beginning students.
Of course, disagreement could have been chiefly motivated
by reluctance to limit the approach as most valuable in any
one type of collection.

One might, however, speculate on how many of those disagreeing would approve of separate open-shelf undergraduate libraries. The educational philosophy for the establishment, beginning with Harvard's Lamont Library, of such libraries was basically that of the "core" collection. The reaction to the preceding and related hypotheses suggested that many respondents were averse to acknowledging or endorsing the possible "conditioning" effects of collection building and organizing, particularly in an educational context, though in practice the examples of libraries like Lamont have been very influential.

An apparent ambivalence might thus be seen in the responses to this section of the questionnaire. There was acceptance of the general desirability of open shelves and its general educational value, but opposition to the concept that direct access, viewed as an educational means, involved the conscious structuring of a collection through acquisition and shelf classification so as to prepare for the patron a learning experience. An extreme instance was the only 29-percent agreement with the proposition that the educational responsibility of the open-shelf library was to create for the reader a "structured learning situation." So, also, a surprisingly small 55 percent agreed with what might be considered a truism: that the benefits of direct access were primarily conditioned by the contents of the collection. This attitude might be interpreted as expressing the assumption that "free choice" in libraries produced maximum benefits for the patron, and that any apparent "constraint" reduced or imperiled those benefits. A "structured learning situation" might be regarded as exemplifying such constraints.

Over 60 percent thought open shelves did not require close classification in general academic and research libraries. Though this seemingly implied acceptability of broad classification in such collections, the modal respondent institution had reported close rather than broad shelf classification.

Eaton described the origin of the broad classification policy of the unsuccessful 15th edition of DC:

> One of the chief aims to be achieved by a new edition was some reduction in the size of the schedule. The 14th edition was a massive volume of 2,000 closely printed pages, elaborately expanded in certain areas.... Catalogers had been polled to

determine the kind of schedule they wanted and a
very large portion of the total number complained
about the excessive length of the numbers assigned
to certain topics. The librarians completely ignored the fact that it is not necessary to use close
classification for shelf marks. Dorcas Fellows
gave sound advice on this point many years ago
when she recommended that in the small library
the abridged edition could serve as a useful guide
to the length of numbers and the complete edition
could serve as a reference work for locating topics. [36]

Perhaps the questionnaire responses just summarized
indicated a change of opinion on the feasibility of broader
shelf classification. The availability of segmented DC notation on Library of Congress cards would facilitate such a
change.

Statistical evidence was minimal that opinion patterns
were correlated with professional function of respondent or
type of library represented by practitioner respondent.

Probably the salient point to emerge from this analysis of responses to Section IV was that respondents made almost no reference to the subject-revelatory role theoretically
played by shelf classification nor--perhaps consistent with
the wary attitude to specific educational goals of direct ac-
cess--to the use of shelf classification for subject research.
There seemed little association by respondents of what would
appear logically related issues, e.g., broad and close classification, homogeneous and heterogeneous collections or clienteles. The common advantages, given in comments, of direct access in various types of libraries were such immediately practical ones as being able to choose quickly among
certain titles, to determine what was available, and to examine indexes. None of these would be primarily dependent
on shelf classification order. Also, as previously noted, almost 60 percent agreed that shelf classification was more
important as a locational device than as a means of systematic subject approach; about the same proportion agreed that
subject headings were more useful to the patron than shelf
classification; and only 43 percent thought the average patron
could "follow" close shelf classification notation. Such opinions contrasted with the intellectual benefits claimed for classification by Richardson, Bliss, and Ranganathan. [37] A pedagogical rationale for shelf classification--at least for subject
research--seemed largely ignored or rebuffed.

Similar negative attitudes were expressed on structuring the collection through acquisition policy. Respondents seemed unwilling to agree that their choice of works should be considered a conscious attempt to structure the reader's experience at the shelves. The documentary analysis presented much evidence of the normative role of acquisition policy as expressed in catalogs, "best books" lists, etc. [38] Such lists were officially sponsored by professional groups like A. L. A., or reflected the prestige of the academic institution whose collection was cataloged, or represented the consensus of library experts enrolled by the publisher. The continuous existence of these normative aids perpetuated the original educational and social goals of the open-shelf library. Yet, the editors of these lists usually took pains to disclaim what must be a principal reason for their uninterrupted popularity: providing an authoritative prescription for purposive collection building. The disclaimers did not seem unrelated to the reluctance of respondents to endorse what might be interpreted as a constraint on "complete" freedom of choice at the shelves.

It might be concluded that librarians, in implementing their open-shelf policy through shelf classification, have tended to underestimate or be unaware of the importance for direct access and browsing of their selection activity--despite their consciousness of the need for professional judgment in acquisition, as evidenced by recourse to printed catalogs, basic lists, and review media.

A conscious acknowledgment of his desire to "structure" the collection might confirm a self-image of the librarian as educator or even social worker, as described in the chapter on the sociology of direct access. Conversely, the lack of acknowledgment might indicate librarians' abdication, noted by Martin, of an educational and social role.

(It was not within the purpose of this study to investigate possible restrictive effects of review media which may ignore many worthwhile works. The acquisitions concern of some practitioners, particularly in public libraries, has recently shifted from the problems of choosing the "best" books to those of censorship, intellectual freedom, and the provision of materials for the "functionally illiterate" and the "culturally deprived." Like Martin, these librarians have been occupied with how to bring the educational influence of books into the <u>community</u> rather than readers into the educational ambience of an <u>existing</u> library building.)[39]

Though selection and acquisition have been described as the "apex of library practice,"[40] it has not been systematically taught in library schools. Indeed, as Downs[41] pointed out, the acquisitions department is probably the least planned in goals in libraries of any kind, and well-thought out acquisitions statements are a rarity. Beals, almost twenty-five years ago, diagnosed the problem during his discussion of education for librarianship:

> The traditional approach to book selection and reference tended to obscure the forest by detailed consideration of many trees. It is essential that the attention of the student be focused on the library as a library, i.e., a collection of books chosen and organized for the use of a particular body of readers. Such an approach demands, on the one hand, a consideration of the criteria that determine which of the fifteen-million-odd books theoretically available are best suited to a particular library; and, on the other, the needs and abilities of the particular group of readers for whom the library exists.... Of the innumerable combinations theoretically possible, one particular combination will best meet the requirements of the persons to whose use the library is intended. [42]

The ideal of the "one particular combination" has become in today's libraries increasingly difficult to attain. Often, indeed, it seems forgotten or ignored.

Because of this common taken-for-granted attitude to acquisition policy, the librarian in organizing materials for direct access may tend to consider cataloging and classification in isolation from the particular collection. The effectiveness of shelf classification could thus be seriously impaired by a misconception of its relative value vis-à-vis the materials comprising the collection. Such misconception may also contribute to misunderstanding the role of shelf classification in organizing materials for use. The self-evident importance of the preexisting collection in relation to the intellectual results which may be derived from its organization has, because of its obviousness, perhaps helped render acquisition and selection almost invisible factors in most considerations of the problems of direct access.

Shelf classification seems sometimes to be expected by librarians to substitute for unacquired or absent materials. Only a misconception of how acquisition and classification principles are related could generate such an expectation. Acquisition policy seems to be exercised often with little consciousness of its normative or educational implications. The acquisitions or order department usually operates fairly or completely independently of the cataloging, classification, and reader services departments, particularly in large libraries. This may be another reason why the organization of the open-shelf library is often not properly related to acquisition policy. The knowledge and skill required to select a collection should, ideally, also be available to help organize that collection and guide patrons in its use.

As noted, an implication of the various patterns of opinion--made even clearer by comments--was that librarians held as an article of faith the patron's right to uninhibited freedom of choice at the shelves. Such freedom would evidently be considered threatened by efforts to influence the reader through acquisition and classification policy--at least if the effects of such efforts could be characterized as "conditioning" or "structuring" or "limiting." Complete freedom of choice at the shelves would be, of course, a literal impossibility. Choice can be exercised only on what has been acquired and arranged for the patron's inspection. Respondents may have confused the intellectual and political connotations of "freedom of choice" with the bibliothecal. Such confusion would be fed by misunderstanding of the technical aspects of acquisition and classification. However, this allegiance to uninhibited "freedom of choice" might also be another instance of librarians' reluctance to accept an official role as educator or teacher, that is, of "conditioner" or "influencer." In this sense, the patron should be "self-taught" and have complete "freedom of choice."

Another factor influencing this faith in patrons' uninhibited freedom of choice might be the Platonic influence on librarians' assumptions. The librarian might be expressing the idea that the book as an instrument or depository of knowledge was self-revealing. The shelved work, a link in the "Great Chain of Being," must in itself be allowed to reveal all its treasures to the patron. The nature of the book might thus be confused with its subject-revelatory powers made possible by its assigned position within a classified order on the shelves. Traditional reverence for the "Book" as a repository of wisdom would reinforce this feeling. Such a technical confusion would not be unrelated to that--much dwelt on by Metcalfe[43] in his critique of traditional library

classification policies--of classification, specification, and
qualification.

The Direct Shelf Approach (Open-Shelf Access):
The Role of "Browsing" and Related Activities

Response to the questionnaire section on the role of
"browsing" and related activities followed the trend revealed
in the preceding section. Respondents confirmed their loyalty
to the general ideas of open-shelf access and of browsing:
that all readers should be encouraged to browse; that browsing provided a valuable learning experience; that shelf classification and even close shelf classification were necessary
for non-recreational browsing; and that, most especially,
the possibility of "serendipity" was a major value of brows-
ing--a value made more likely by shelf classification. However, when hypotheses undertook to specify how the benefits
of browsing were to be effected, particularly through acquisition and classification policy, noticeably divided opinion and
conflicting comments ensued. Many respondents seemed to
deny connection among open-shelf access, browsing, and research. "Open-shelf access" and "browsing" seemed separated by many respondents so that apparent inconsistencies
of opinion might represent discrete rather than contradictory
attitudes.

Although the questionnaire defined "browsing" as encompassing both recreational and research functions, responses and comments often indicated unwillingness to accept
"browsing" as a "respectable" or significant component in
subject search or research-oriented activity. (In contrast,
as shown in the documentary analysis, "browsing" was accepted in a serious sense by documentalists.)[44] This attitude was expressed earlier by the public library technical
services practitioner who commented on Section IV: "Browsing and research seem to me two different things, but both
require access to shelves; research requires shelves with
reasonably close classification. Not all information can be
put into catalogs and bibliographies, and access to books and
their indexes is needed." Analysis suggested that many respondents, particularly academic and special librarians, did
not think of "open-shelf access" and "browsing" as constructively related.

Although over 81 percent agreed that "browsing provides a valuable learning experience"--the second highest

percentage of agreement in the questionnaire--there was considerably less support for open-shelf access as "a significant
educational responsibility of libraries." As in the previous
section, disagreement increased when hypotheses introduced
elements of conscious pedagogical "conditioning" by librarians. One respondent feared that for a librarian to "encourage" browsing might mean "a degree of moral coercion."
(This possible confusion of political, intellectual, or social
censorship and restriction with educational "molding" of the
individual has already been noted.) Others were still of the
opinion--despite a definition in the questionnaire--that "browsing" was "just fun" or "not the best use of one's time."

Only about 14 percent agreed that "the greater limits
imposed on browsing by acquisition policy and by classification, the more valuable browsing will be." This statement,
intended to rephrase the "structured learning" concept presented in Section IV, was evidently unclear to many. The
wording was plainly unsatisfactory to numerous respondents
and evoked expressions of bewilderment. (Respondents also
seemed to show unease generally with abstract formulations
of psychological-educational theory.) However, the predom-
inantly negative opinion was not inconsistent with that on earlier hypotheses concerning the structuring effects--particular-
ly in a pedagogical sense--of acquisition and classification on
open-shelf access. Comments again expressed opposition towards implied restrictions on readers' freedom of choice.

The heaviest agreement (almost 90 percent) for any
statement was accorded the hypothesis that "a major value
of browsing is the possibility of 'serendipity,' i. e., 'making
desirable but unsought-for discoveries.'" This reaction corresponded with that for earlier statements on the general desirability of open shelves and of browsing but which did not
specify the kind of library or browsing. It also accorded
with earlier implications of belief in uninhibited freedom of
choice by patrons. Many respondents might have considered
the browsing connected with "serendipity" as largely recreational. This inference was strengthened by response to the
next statement that "the possibility of 'serendipity' is much
greater in a library with relative shelf classification." Although 71 percent agreed, this was obviously much less than
for the preceding.

More than three-fourths disagreed with a categorical
statement that nothing could be accomplished by browsing in
a general research collection that could not be done better

by indirect bibliographic means. The rejection of exclusively
bibliographic access corresponded with earlier general support for open-shelf access and browsing. As in the preceding section, the defense for browsing was little couched
in terms of intellectual benefits for subject study in classified stacks. The commonly mentioned advantages were,
again, the determination of works' availability and the inspection of their indexes to identify information not revealed by
the card catalog.

Only about 28 percent agreed with a hypothesis that
rejected "browsing" as a term precise enough to characterize serious research. The overall disagreement, however,
was not clear-cut. A somewhat small majority of about 56
percent disagreed and, among practitioners, a bare majority
of 51 percent. Comments attested the problem of deciding
what term suited an activity analogous to "browsing" but not
implying non-serious research. Thus, a respondent remarked, "Nonsense! The term is not precise, true, but the
practice is." Another noted, "While 'browsing' does not
characterize serious research, neither must its use be limited only to browsing collections." Such opinions reflected
difficulty and uncertainty in defining the various open-shelf
activities carried on by patrons and in determining how
"browsing" was to be related to these activities.

The problem thus was not strictly or exclusively one
of nomenclature but rather of identification: what constituted
the process of browsing and related activities? Earlier documentary frequency analysis[45] revealed the great resistance
to employ "browsing" as an indexing term or an "official"
designation in the professional literature, although the activity was frequently referred to in print, often by name. An
academician like Hosmer[46] employed the word in 1890 with
a self-consciousness approaching embarrassment. He seemed
uneasy with the relatively new agricultural metaphor which
equated humans with cattle. This unease seemed to survive
in the ambivalence of many respondents who would not accept
the word as a "respectable" element in the direct shelf approach but who yet would not disown it. This was implied
by the responses and comments for the last hypothesis. Opinion patterns for earlier hypotheses repeatedly suggested a
radical separation of the "browsing" activity from that of the
direct shelf approach. However, most respondents--like
Hosmer--were generally convinced that direct access to
books, regardless of the appropriateness of the word "browsing, " was of such beneift as to merit wide encouragement.

Etymological analysis[47] showed the inaccurate general use of "browse" for "graze," the latter implying the existence of pasture--and thus a more purposive and "reliable" activity. From whatever viewpoint the direct shelf approach be considered, the roles and effects of acquisition policy and shelf classification cannot be ignored. Theoretical and practical difficulties seem to arise in libraries when these two complementary means and their interrelationship vis-à-vis the direct shelf approach are not fully recognized. The manifold types of "browsing" cannot be confined to pleasurable exploration in a recreational "browsing" collection, though for many librarians this seemed the only type to which the name should apply. The literature showed that so narrow a definition was not in the minds of authorities like Cutter and Richardson,[48] nor was so unintellectual a one as that of aimless or "random" riffling of pages.

As noted in Chapter Six,[49] the "browsing" factor as an element in the direct-shelf approach seems to manifest itself in ratio to intellectual unpredictability of varying degree and kind. The patron in a "browsing room" or a "new books section" is faced with considerable unpredictability as to the books he will find and select, but such unpredictability, though perhaps great in degree, is not of an intellectually serious or critical kind: any choice may prove suitable or enjoyable. At advanced levels of subject-oriented study and research, the unpredictability confronting the "browser" can be intellectually critical. Only those items or information relevant to the topic under investigation can fill his needs; the intellectual requirements are more demanding, the allowable tolerances narrower. For this kind of browsing the intellectual organization provided by acquisition policy and shelf classification aims to minimize, or at least reduce, unpredictability, that is, to structure the browsing situation more strictly. Whether a "browsing room" patron finds novels of equal interest juxtaposed may be intellectually unimportant; but for a researcher in the stacks, the juxtaposition of works on the same and related subjects can be crucial.

It is not essential--perhaps not even desirable in the light of convention--to establish the word "browsing" as a possibly serious activity to be accepted by librarians as a bibliographic or pedagogic responsibility. Evidence is abundant in the literature and in the response to the questionnaire that many librarians were very reluctant to accept the word in that sense. Respondents, however, by being asked to react to hypotheses employing "browsing" were forced to redefine the term. It became clear that some librarians were using "browsing" as a convenient means to encompass subject-oriented aspects of the direct-shelf approach without having to define those aspects or relate them to the building, organizing, and servicing of their collections. (Witness the almost unanimous endorsement of "serendipity.") It became necessary, in other words, when denying that certain activities did not constitute "browsing" as generally accepted by the librarian or teacher, to focus more sharply on what constituted those activities not belonging to the browsing process but which were related to it as another element of the direct shelf approach.

The questionnaire thus tested not what patrons did at the shelves but what librarians thought patrons did or expected them to do. As Taube[50] indicated, it is more important for librarians to see that patrons get what they need rather than what patrons think they need. This approach is not necessarily arrogant nor usurping nor epistemologically arbitrary. The professionalism of librarianship has been described as the ability to lead patrons--whose subject expertise may be far greater than the librarian's--to information in the patron's subject field. This is accomplished through means of bibliographical organization in whose theory and application the librarian has been trained. A common analogy is that of the librarian plotting the contours of the landscape from a hovering airplane while the scholar afoot painstakingly measures the road.

The Validity of the Open-Shelf Concept

To what extent did this inquiry confirm "the validity of the direct shelf approach as a concept for the organization of library materials"? If the definition of a library as "a collection organized for use" be adopted, undoubtedly the general belief was confirmed that some kind of shelf arrangement or classification is needed to facilitate that use in an open-shelf library. But how valid is the concept of the open-shelf library or direct shelf approach? Defense of the open-shelf library rested chiefly on a philosophy of democratic self-education and academic self-teaching. Kelley, among others already cited, questioned the validity of the philosophy --at least for public library practice:

From the origin of the free public library in the

middle of the last century ... one is constantly
impressed with the vague and high-sounding assumptions as to its aim and function....

The function of the free public library has been to
serve the people as a whole, collectively; the
masses, the general public, the ordinary folk,
were to be supplied with books in preparation for
the duties which democracy was thrusting upon
them.... It was to fill a broad and indefinite need
and to be all things to all men....

It is evident from the beginning that librarians had
no trustworthy way of judging the specific needs
and interests of the individuals who composed their
heterogeneous groups of patrons.

Ideals and convictions to the contrary, the notion
that the thirst of knowledge for the sake of knowledge can be counted upon appears to be almost
mostly romance.

Thus the duty of keeping the reader interested and
satisfied has been shifted to the shoulders of the
librarian, as in education it has fallen upon the
teacher. [51]

The validity of the open-shelf library or the direct
shelf approach must, on the evidence, be accounted a postulate, rather than an objectively demonstrable truth. American preference is unquestionable--whether that of the browser in a public library, the reader services librarian in a
reference collection, or the faculty member or student in an
academic institution. Nevertheless, how the direct shelf approach is implemented remains a matter replete with unresolved issues of theory and practice, both bibliographical and
bibliothecal.

The previously cited comments of Tauber[52] from his
study of the Shelflisting Section of the Library of Congress
probably summarized adequately this aspect of the validity
of the direct shelf approach. To support his conviction that
shelf classification was necessary in open-shelf libraries, he
adduced librarians' testimony which was admittedly only opinion based on experience.

Recent predictions are that use of the public and academic library may not require patrons to visit the collection, let alone use the direct shelf approach. "Direct access," described by Jordan[53] as including home delivery of public library materials, could eliminate patrons' physical contact with the library. Public library mail-order catalogs are already in use. Interrogation by console of computerized stores of bibliographic information could produce desired text displays at the inquiry terminal and eliminate travel to public, academic, or research libraries. The development of audio-visual materials along with increasing interest in library "social service field work" may also restrict the direct shelf approach. However, none of these developments has yet assumed major significance. (Indeed, if the direct shelf approach were eliminated, the same problems of organizing and indexing library materials for use would probably reappear in intensified form.)

For the foreseeable future, libraries will remain largely collections of books which must be organized for use, commonly by shelf classification. Even librarians who on theoretical grounds reject shelf classification would probably agree that, in most American libraries as presently organized, it would be far preferable--for staff or patron benefit-- to continue using DC or LC numbers from printed catalog cards if only as a locational device rather than attempt fixed location.

Notes

1. Marie Louise Prevost, "An Approach to Theory and Method in General Subject Heading," Library Quarterly, XVI (April, 1946), 140.

2. Charles Ammi Cutter, "Close Classification, with Special Reference to Messrs. Perkins, Schwartz, and Dewey," Library Journal, XI (July, 1886), 180.

3. See "The Role of Subject Cataloging" in Chapter Eight.

4. W. C. Berwyck Sayers, An Introduction to Library Classification, Theoretical, Historical and Practical, with Readings, Exercises and Examination Papers (7th ed.; London: Grafton, 1946), p. 55.

5. See "Classification and Librarians' Prestige" in Chapter Eight.

6. Jesse H. Shera and Margaret E. Egan, The Classified Catalog: Basic Principles and Practices (Chicago: American Library Assn., 1956).

7. Bernard Ira Palmer, Itself an Education: Six Lectures on Classification (London: Library Assn., 1962), p. 12. Palmer is paraphrasing S. R. Ranganathan, "Colon Classification and Its Approach to Documentation," in Chicago, University, Graduate Library School, Library Conference, Bibliographic Organization; Papers Presented before the Fifteenth Annual Conference of the Graduate Library School, July 24-29, 1950, ed. by Jesse H. Shera and Margaret E. Egan (Chicago: University of Chicago Press, 1951), p. 96.

8. Arthur Oncken Lovejoy, The Great Chain of Being: A Study of the History of an Idea. The William James Lectures Delivered at Harvard University, 1933 (Cambridge: Harvard University Press, 1936).

9. Henry Evelyn Bliss, The Organization of Knowledge and the System of the Sciences (New York: Holt, 1929), p. 113.

10. Plato, The Republic, 6.7.

11. See "Practical Library Classification and the True Order of Knowledge" in Chapter Eight.

12. W. Stanley Jevons, The Principles of Science; a Treatise on Logic and Scientific Method (2d ed.; London: Macmillan, 1877), p. 715. ("Classification by subjects would be an exceedingly useful method if it were practicable, but experience shows it to be a logical absurdity.")

13. Shera, "Classification as the Basis of Bibliographic Organization," in Chicago, University, Graduate Library School, Library Conference, Bibliographic Organization, p. 82-83, 88. Shera restated these ideas in "Classification: Current Functions and Applications to the Subject Analysis of Library Materials," in Institute on the Subject Analysis of Library Materials, Columbia University, The Subject Analysis of Library Materials; Papers Presented at an Institute, June 24-28, 1952, ed. by Maurice F.

Tauber (New York: School of Library Service, Columbia University, 1953), p. 29-42.

14. John Metcalfe, Information Indexing and Subject Catalog-
     ing: Alphabetical, Classified, Coordinate, Mechanic-
     al (New York: Scarecrow Press, 1957), p. 99.

15. Georg Schneider, Theory and History of Bibliography,
     tr. by Ralph R. Shaw (New York: Scarecrow Press,
     1961), p. 173.

16. Sayers, An Introduction to Library Classification, p.
     xxii.

17. Ranganathan, Elements of Library Classification (3d ed.;
     New York: Asia Publishing House, 1962), p. 149.

18. Palmer, Itself an Education, p. 64-65.

19. Bliss, The Organization of Knowledge and the System
     of the Sciences, p. 116.

20. John Ansteinsson, "Dilemmas of Classification," Li-
     brary Quarterly, IV (April, 1934), 137.

21. Ranganathan, Prolegomena to Library Classification
     (3d ed.; New York: Asia Publishing House, 1967),
     p. 547.

22. D.J. Foskett, "The Classification Research Group,
     1952-1962," Libri, XII, No. 2 (1962), 132.

23. J.E.L. Farradane, "Psychology of Classification,"
     Journal of Documentation, XI (December, 1955), 188.
     This was updated by his "Relational Indexing and
     Classification in the Light of Recent Experimental
     Work in Psychology," Information Storage and Re-
     trieval, I, No. 1 (1963), 3-11.

24. See the convenient recent summary: Jean Piaget,
     "Genetic Epistemology," Columbia Forum, XII (Fall,
     1969), 4-11.

25. Palmer, Itself an Education, p. 34.

26. Shera, "Classification as the Basis of Bibliographic Or-
     ganization," p. 73.

27. Emile Durkheim and Marcel Mauss, Primitive Classification, tr. and ed. by Rodney Needham (Chicago: University of Chicago Press, 1963), p. 82-84.

28. Rodney Needham, "Introduction," ibid., p. xii-xliv.

29. See "Towards a Functional Definition of Browsing" in Chapter Six.

30. See "The Role of Notation" in Chapter Eight.

31. Palmer, Itself an Education, p. 25.

32. Metcalfe, Information Indexing and Subject Cataloging, p. 64. ("Librarians tend to confuse the organization and systematization of knowledge with the organization of its material, perhaps because this confusion feeds their conceit that they are not only administrators but Educators as well. They confuse the role of the dispenser with that of the doctor.")

33. Patricia B. Knapp, The Monteith College Library Experiment (New York: Scarecrow Press, 1966), p. 113, note 5.

34. See "The Role of Subject Cataloging" in Chapter Eight.

35. Lowell A. Martin, "The Changes Ahead," Library Journal, XCIII (February 15, 1968), 715.

36. Thelma Eaton, Cataloging and Classification: An Introductory Manual (4th ed.; Ann Arbor, Mich.: Edwards Brothers, 1967), p. 71.

37. See "Classification and Librarians' Prestige" in Chapter Eight.

38. See "The Normative Role of the Early Printed Library Catalogs" and "The Normative Role of Later Book Lists and Buying Guides" in Chapter Seven.

39. See Dan Lacy, "The Dissemination of Print," Wilson Library Bulletin, XXXVII (September, 1963), 60, 64; Martin, "The Changes Ahead," p. 715; John Berry III, "The New Constituency," Library Journal, XCIV (August, 1969), 2725-39.

40. Roger C. Greer and Douglas L. Zweizig, "An Overview of Present Selection Courses in American Library Schools," in Conference on Library School Teaching Methods: Courses in the Selection of Adult Materials, University of Illinois, 1968, Proceedings, ed. by Larry Earl Bone (Urbana: University of Illinois, Graduate School of Library Service, 1969), p. 12, 19; citing Ralph Ulveling, "Foreword," in Mary Carter and Wallace Bonk, Building Library Collections (New York: Scarecrow Press, 1959), p. iii-iv.

41. Robert B. Downs, "Research in Problems of Resources," Library Trends, VI (October, 1957), 157.

42. Ralph Albert Beals, "Education for Librarianship," Library Quarterly, XVII (October, 1947), 302.

43. Metcalfe, Information Indexing and Subject Cataloging, p. 132-35, etc.

44. E.g., Malcolm Rigby, "Browsability in Modern Information Retrieval Systems: The Quest for Information," in Symposium on Education for Information Science, Airlie House, 1965, Proceedings, ed. by Laurence B. Heilprin, Barbara E. Markuson, and Frederick L. Goodman (Washington: Spartan Books, 1965), p. 47-52.

45. See "Documentary Frequency Analysis: Indexes and Bibliographies" in Chapter Three.

46. James K. Hosmer, "On Browsing by a Book-Worm," Library Journal, XV (December, 1890), 33-37.

47. See "Etymology" in Chapter Three.

48. See "Multi-Level Definitions of Browsing" in Chapter Six.

49. See "Towards a Functional Definition of Browsing."

50. Mortimer Taube, "An Evaluation of 'Use Studies' of Scientific Information," in Emerging Solutions for Mechanizing the Storage and Retrieval of Information, Vol. V of his Studies in Coordinate Indexing (Washington: Documentation, Inc., 1959), p. 46-71.

51. Grace Osgood Kelley, "The Democratic Function of Pub-
     lic Libraries," Library Quarterly, IV (January,
     1934), 2, 6-8.

52. Tauber, "The Shelflisting Section of the Library of Con-
     gress: A Report on Functions, Organization, and
     Problems Made at the Request of the Librarian of
     Congress, July, 1958," p. I-7, VI-13, 14, 15.
     (Typewritten)

53. Robert T. Jordan, Tomorrow's Library: Direct Access
     and Delivery (New York: Bowker, 1970).

CHAPTER XIV

IMPLICATIONS FOR PRACTICE AND RESEARCH

The questionnaire evidence would imply that most libraries should accept their present classification scheme with an absolute minimum of adaptation, prompted either by assumed local needs or by relocations in new editions of the scheme. Respondents reported that thorough reclassification, attendant on conversion from DC to LC, was almost never attempted or contemplated. Reasons for minimizing changes in assigned classification numbers are numerous--and have been adumbrated in the documentary and questionnaire analysis:

(1) The precise use of subject shelf classification by the patron was not clear to the librarian. Its most reported use was as a locational device. The reader then examined the work--not necessarily in relation to others in the same subject class--for evaluation or detailed information. Accordingly, there was no reliable evidence that adherence to assigned classification numbers on printed cards would impair subject-oriented research at the shelves. It has not been definitively shown by use studies how this research is carried out.

(2) Classificationists, in criticizing others' schemes and emphasizing the general pragmatic nature of classification, demonstrated that exact and permanent "accuracy" in shelf classification was unattainable.

(3) The majority of librarians and teachers recommended recourse to all means of bibliographic access: catalogs, subject headings, bibliographies--as well as personal assistance. Shelf classification, no matter how valuable, was not accepted as the sole guide to use of the collection. Striving for utmost precision in shelf classification would thus seem even less necessary.

Some respondents complained that the questionnaire sought generalizations without regard to necessary qualifications. Clearly, however, most libraries must to some extent generalize, that is, compromise, before the numerous competing claims of a heterogeneous clientele on a heterogeneous collection. The almost universal acceptance of the available general classifications, LC and DC, attested this necessary compromise. (Even a very large special library might safely, in the cause of national cooperation and standardization, sacrifice "custom-tailored classification"--unless the resultant scheme was the standard for numerous other special libraries.) Academic library respondents evidenced that LC was more suited to their needs than DC, apparently because of its more complete and specific coverage for a large heterogeneous collection.

The prevalence of DC in public libraries was confirmed and defended. It is suggested that DC thus consider itself not a rival of LC for all libraries, but as a complementary scheme for popular or smaller libraries requiring a less comprehensive and specific classification for less complex or scholarly works. Its relation with LC would be roughly analogous to that of the Sears List of Subject Headings with the LC list. [1] (The need for an abridged DC might be reconsidered.) The philosophy underlying the 15th edition of DC might be revived--and adequately implemented--to provide a broader shelf classification. This could result in less frequent and less extensively revised editions. A chief aim would be to reduce relocation drastically. This broader DC for bibliothecal organization would not forestall intensive development of UDC, the offshoot of DC, for documentation.

Librarians need to acknowledge unequivocally a responsibility to instruct the patron in use of the classification scheme. Surveys[2] continued to reveal that patrons generally did not "understand" the scheme and that they, nevertheless, received little or no instruction. Such instruction could be given through carefully planned and well-publicized lectures, informal teaching while answering individual inquiry, and through greatly expanded "guiding" as advocated by Savage. [3] "Guiding" would be applied in academic and research as well as public libraries. An example would be the book-form shelf list of Harvard's Widener Library;[4] copies of various parts of the list are placed in the stacks with the relevant subject groups

Encouraging the use by staff and readers of classified and alphabetical subject guides to library materials would be most desirable. There seems much justice to charges that

American librarians in practice are generally content to regard classification symbols as locational devices only--an
obvious waste of rich potential. Although the fully developed
classed catalog is not likely to be widely adopted, the shelf
list should be more fully exploited, as at Harvard, for patron use. The American Book Publishing Record (BPR), [5]
especially its bound cumulations, seems to be under-used as
a public classified guide. The Library of Congress Catalog;
Books: Subjects[6] should also be more actively applied to patrons' subject search problems. (One respondent library
keeps the work in the technical services department as a cataloger's tool.) In the fostering of such aids, librarians
should instruct not only in their use but also in the basic distinction between catalog and bibliography.

        Instructional functions involve the larger issue of the
librarian's general educational responsibility. Documentary
and questionnaire analysis suggested strongly that earlier educational and social ideals of the library as a public institution have been much weakened or even denied. A recently
intensified concern has expressed the need to revive these
ideals. Martin, [7] in his survey of the Chicago Public Library, concluded that the educational and social responsibility
of the urban public librarian was to project library resources
into the community instead of expecting the patron to come
to a central resource for voluntary self-education. In academic libraries, the pedagogical role of the librarian has
been elaborately detailed by advocates of the Library-College
concept of education. [8] Not irrelevant is the current demand
for full faculty status for academic librarians. The Association of College and Research Libraries, in its 1970 "Proposed Standards for Faculty Status for College and University
Librarians," stated that the academic librarian "bears central responsibility for developing college and university library collections, for extending bibliographic control over
these collections, and for instructing students (both formally
in the classroom and informally in the library), and advising
faculty and scholars in the use of those collections." Accordingly, "college and university librarians must be recognized as equal partners in the academic enterprise, and they
must be extended the rights and privileges which are not only
commensurate with their contributions, but are necessary if
they are to carry out their responsibilities."[9]

        Ambiguity and ambivalence of respondents in regard
to bibliographic and bibliothecal organization would indicate
a need for greatly revised training in library schools--and

for continuing education of practitioners. Such training ideally would integrate bibliographical and bibliothecal aspects into
almost every curriculum offering. (Similar efforts have been
undertaken to integrate "automation and information science.")
This would follow logically from defining the library as a collection organized for use. The general failure of librarians
to instruct patrons in the use of classification may reflect an
uneasiness with classificatory procedures as well as tacit acceptance of a Platonic belief that the scheme is self-revealing, that is, self-teaching. Similar assumptions--or unease
--may underlie respondents' insistence on patrons' uninhibited
freedom of choice at the shelves.

Another implication for library school curricula is
much increased emphasis on acquisition policy as a vital element in the educational responsibility of the library.   Respondents seemed averse to acknowledge the effects of acquisition policy on patron library experience.   This might not
be unrelated to the librarian's retreat from pedagogical responsibilities. A more sophisticated teaching of acquisition
policy would seem in order, particularly since--as indicated
by recent testimony--it is the least systematized subject in
library schools. 10   Teaching of acquisition must also clarify
methods of collection evaluation and the surprisingly unques-
tioned role of standardized or "best books" lists.

Such restructured curriculum would imply a much
closer relationship between the reader services and technical
services functions.   Compartmentalization of the two in library school curricula must have some influence on their
well-known separation in practice.   Lundy11 at the University
of Nebraska encouraged a merger of the functions by assigning librarians to serve in each area.   Expansion of such a
program would seem highly desirable so that every practitioner, even the binding supervisor, would be considered to
have a "major" responsibility in one and a "minor" in the
other.   This neither would nor could obviate the need for expertise in specialized areas of the technical services, e.g.,
subject classification for foreign-language or technological
works; or for subject specialization in the reader services,
e.g., social science reference work or humanities bibliography.

The need of theoretical comprehension by all practitioners of bibliographical-bibliothecal controls is heightened
by current trends to centralized processing.   Presumably,
fewer hours would be spent in individual libraries on actual

cataloging and classification. More time should be available, and is needed, for interpreting to the patron the products of such centralized services. A probable factor in the inconsistent patterns of opinion on many questionnaire statements was that any inquiry into the problems of the direct shelf approach and "browsing" unavoidably involved both the technical and reader services. A major interest of this investigator is the coordination of the technical and reader services, towards which it was hoped this inquiry might make a theoretical contribution with possibly significant practical implications.

Kelley, after serving in the technical services department of a large special library, performed reader services functions in a large public library. Reviewing her investigation of shelf classification, she concluded that all means of bibliographic access were useful, and that the reference librarian would have to deepen his subject knowledge through continuing self-education.[12] A converse emphasis would now seem indicated.

Although subject knowledge, particularly of a broad "survey" nature, is essential for effective reader service, librarians should study more intently the organizing function of librarianship: how the collection is organized for use and how this organization can, or cannot, be employed to help the patron.

In most libraries, the constructors of the catalog do not interpret it to the patron, while librarians, who may often be unaware of principles embodied in cataloging and classification decisions, are expected to explain and utilize these decisions. It is difficult to conceive of any professional function in a library, thought of as a service institution, being isolated from the patron whom the library exists to serve. Such, however, seems often in practice to be true of the technical services, notably cataloging and classification.

The library might well have a "collection organization advisor" who would aid and instruct staff and patrons in the meaning and effective utilization of all approaches, bibliographical and bibliothecal, to the collection, with special reference to shelf classification and subject headings. He would be a "general specialist," commanding an overview of all means of bibliographical and bibliothecal access to all materials in the library, rather than providing specialist bibliographical guidance (perhaps to materials in other libraries)

and indicating suggested reading in specific subject areas.
The latter two duties would still devolve on the reference or
reader services "major" who would also determine the type
of information required to solve the patron's problem.

Implications for research parallel those for practice.
Integration of the bibliographical-bibliothecal approach in library school courses would mean a willingness to improve
the teaching of cataloging and classification, and to restruc-
ture the curriculum. Some courses as now constituted might
be retained as "controls" so that comparative evaluation of
acquired skills could be made. Follow-up surveys of alumni
practitioners would be needed.

As Taube[13] indicated, the value of use studies may be
very limited. However, such research will doubtless continue in some form and provide suggestive data. (A proposed
experiment is outlined below.) Continuous "feedback" from
the patron is essential, though its interpretation may be uncertain. In general, though, it would seem more desirable
to work within the frame of present acquisition and classification practices in an effort to make these as effective as
possible in attaining determined goals of patron service for
recreational and serious reading.

The possibility of advanced theoretical research on the
direct shelf approach and on "browsing" would thus not seem
promising if confined to traditional study of patron behavior
at the shelves. As Richmond[14] suggested, fundamental research is desirable on the mental associations of the patron
while using the classificatory approach to library materials.
Such research would be more likely pursued by specialists
in nonlibrary disciplines, e.g., neuro-physiology and the
psychology of learning. Results might be of considerable
importance for librarians.

A more immediate research possibility for librarians
--with due concession to Taube--would be a study of patron
choice of materials in situations "completely" controlled as
to collection content and where the choices would be instan-
taneously and accurately recorded. Such research might be
facilitated by a known computerized store of information
from which the patron at a console could retrieve desired information. The computerized store would attempt to simu-
late the contents and organization of an open-shelf collection.
This effort would expand on the Cranfield Research Project[15]
methodology. "Browsing" in a collection arranged in various

ways for patron use would be tested.   Swanson and Intrex[16]
also implied such a possibility.   Feedback on the "relevance"
of retrieved information would be essential.

A great--perhaps not insuperable--methodological ob-
stacle to such research would be the artificiality of totally
controlled computer stores and of assigned tasks.   An alternative, less mechanized and perhaps more realistic, would
be to accept the concept of the "core" or foundation collection for a patron type, e. g., freshmen studying humanities.
With the collection constant, various "guiding" methods and
schemes of broader or closer classification could be evaluated in relation to the direct shelf approach and browsing.
For some tests the card catalog might not be made available.
The tasks would be coordinated with the assignments of the
instructor who would grade the results with special attention
to the inclusion of relevant material.

Computers could aid in further application of the questionnaire approach.   A parametric statistical sampling of the
library profession would be attempted.   A relatively small
stratified random sample, perhaps personally interviewed,
might be adequate.   The questionnaire or interview schedule
would cover the more difficult problems suggested by this
study's analysis.   Statements would be constructed in correlated pairs or sets, and exhaustive correlation analysis
would be performed by computer.   Efforts at such correlation by this study suggested the intricacies of a type of analysis which might be more effective if done by statistical con-
sultants with sophisticated computer facilities.   "Voting behavior analysis" would be applied to opinions on problems of
the direct shelf approach in relation to an array of assumed
relevant factors.

In conclusion, the rationale for various specific means
of organizing open-shelf collections does not seem to rest on
a convincing theoretical justification.   The major practical
implications for libraries of all types would appear to be increasing reliance on standardized collections classified by
general available classification schemes, and continuing de-
emphasis of close shelf classification as a subject revelatory
device.   Such developments are not necessarily advocated by
this study, but are listed as probable.   They need not be inconsistent with current recommendations that the librarian
reassert his educational and social role.   Some of the foregoing implications for practice might facilitate such a reas-
sertion.

Notes

1. Minnie Earl Sears, List of Subject Headings, ed. by
   Barbara Marietta Westby (9th ed.; New York: Wilson,
   1965); U.S., Library of Congress, Subject Cataloging
   Division, Subject Headings Used in the Dictionary
   Catalogs of the Library of Congress (7th ed.; Wash-
   ington, 1966).

2. Annette L. Hoage, "Patron Use of the L.C. Classification," Library Resources and Technical Services,
   VI (Summer, 1962), 247-49; Maurice F. Tauber,
   "Review of the Use of the Library of Congress Classification," in Institute on the Use of the Library of
   Congress Classification, New York, 1966, Proceedings, ed. by Richard H. Schimmelpfeng and C. Donald Cook (Chicago: American Library Assn., 1968),
   p. 1-17.

3. Ernest A. Savage, Manual of Book Classification and
   Display for Public Libraries (London: Allen and
   Unwin, 1946).

4. Harvard University, Library, Widener Library Shelflist,
   No. 1- (Cambridge: Harvard University Library,
   1965-); Richard DeGennaro, "A Computer Produced
   Shelf List," College and Research Libraries, XXVI
   (July, 1965), 311-15, 353.

5. American Book Publishing Record, 1960-   (New York:
   Bowker, 1960-   ).

6. U.S., Library of Congress, Subject Cataloging Division,
   Catalog; Books: Subjects, 1950-   (Washington,
   1950-   ).

7. Lowell A. Martin, Library Response to Urban Change:
   A Study of the Chicago Public Library (Chicago:
   American Library Assn., 1969). His "The Changes
   Ahead," Library Journal, XCIII (February 15, 1968),
   711-16, summarized the conclusions.

8. Louis Shores, Robert T. Jordan, and John Harvey, eds.,
   The Library-College: Contributions for American
   Higher Education at the Jamestown College Workshop,
   1965 (Philadelphia: Drexel Press, 1966).

9.   "ACRL Academic Status Committee Proposes Standards for Librarians," College and Research Libraries News, No. 9 (October, 1970), 271.

10. Roger C. Greer and Douglas L. Zweizig, "An Overview of Present Selection Courses in American Library Schools," in Conference on Library School Teaching Methods: Courses in the Selection of Adult Materials, University of Illinois, 1968, Proceedings, ed. by Larry Earl Bone (Urbana: University of Illinois, Graduate School of Library Service, 1969), p. 12-20.

11. Frank A. Lundy, Kathryn R. Renfro, and Esther M. Shubert, "The Dual Assignment: Cataloging and Reference: A Four-Year Review of Cataloging in the Divisional Plan," Library Resources and Technical Services, III (Summer, 1959), 167-88.

12. Grace Osgood Kelley, "The Classification of Books in Retrospect and Prospect: A Tool and a Discipline," in Chicago, University, Graduate Library School, Library Institute, The Acquisition and Cataloging of Books; Papers Presented before the Library Insitute at the University of Chicago, July 29 to August 9, 1940, ed. by William M. Randall (Chicago: University of Chicago Press, 1940), p. 163-86.   See also her "Subject Approach to Books: An Adventure in Curriculum," Catalogers' and Classifiers' Yearbook, II (1930), 9-23.

13. Mortimer Taube, "An Evaluation of 'Use Studies' of Scientific Information," in Emerging Solutions for Mechanizing the Storage and Retrieval of Information, Vol. V of his Studies in Coordinate Indexing (Washington: Documentation, Inc., 1959), p. 46-71.

14. Phyllis A. Richmond, Transformation and Organization of Information Content: Aspects of Recent Research in the Art and Science of Classification (Copenhagen: Danish Centre for Documentation, 1965) (Pamphlet)

15. Cyril W. Cleverdon, Report on the Testing and Analysis of an Investigation into the Comparative Efficiency of Indexing Systems (Cranfield, Engl., 1962).

16. Don R. Swanson, "Dialogues with a Catalogue," in Chi-

cago, University, Graduate Library School, Library
Conference, Library Catalogs: Changing Dimensions;
the Twenty-eighth Annual Conference of the Graduate
Library School, August 5-7, 1963, ed. by Ruth
French Strout (Chicago: University of Chicago Press,
1964), p. 113-25; Planning Conference on Information
Transfer Experiments, Woods Hole, Mass., 1965,
Intrex: Report, ed. by Carl F.J. Overhage and R.
Joyce Harman (Cambridge, Mass.: M.I.T. Press,
1965). Intrex was a five-year experimental projec-
tion of J.C.R. Licklider, Libraries of the Future
(Cambridge, Mass.: M.I.T. Press, 1965).

SELECTED BIBLIOGRAPHY OF CITED WORKS

Part I: Books and Parts of Books

NOTE: Complete imprint data will be found under the main
entry for the source of the analyzed part.

A. L. A. Catalog, 1926:   An Annotated Basic List of 10,000
Books.   Ed. by Isabella M. Cooper.   Chicago: American
Library Assn., 1926.

American Book Publishing Record (BPR), 1960- .   New
York: Bowker, 1960- .

American Library Association.   A Survey of Libraries in the
United States.   4 vols.   Chicago, 1926-27.
      Often cited as the Committee of Five Report.

            .   Cataloging and Classification Section.   Catalog Use
Study: Director's Report by Sidney L. Jackson.   Ed. by
Vaclav Mostecky.   Chicago, 1958.
      Often cited as the Jackson Catalog Use Study.

            .   Committee for Purchase and Arrangement of "A. L.
A." Library.   "Introduction."   In U. S. Bureau of Education.
Catalog of "A. L. A." Library.

Angell, Richard S.   "On the Future of the Library of Congress Classification."   In International Study Conference
on Classification Research, 2d Elsinore, Denmark, Classification Research: Proceedings.

Ash, Lee.   Yale's Selective Book Retirement Program.
Hamden, Conn.:   Shoe String Press, 1963.

Bar-Hillel, Yehoshua.   Some Theoretical Aspects of the
Mechanization of Literature Searching.   U. S. Office of
Naval Research.   Technical Report No. 3.   Washington,
1960

Berelson, Bernard.   The Library's Public: A Report of the

Public Library Inquiry. New York: Columbia University Press, 1949.

Bergen, Dan, and Duryea, E.D., eds. Libraries and the College Climate of Learning. Syracuse, N.Y.: Program in Higher Education of the School of Education and the School of Library Science, Syracuse University, 1966.

Bibliographical Planning Committee of Philadelphia. A Faculty Survey of the University of Pennsylvania Libraries. Philadelphia: University of Pennsylvania Press, 1940.

Bliss, Henry Evelyn. The Organization of Knowledge and the System of the Sciences. New York: Holt, 1929.

_____. The Organization of Knowledge in Libraries; and the Subject-Approach to Books. 2d ed., rev. and partly rewritten. New York: Wilson, 1939.

_____. A System of Bibliographic Classification. 2d ed. rev. New York: Wilson, 1936.

Bostwick, Arthur E. The American Public Library. 4th ed., rev. and enl. New York: Appleton, 1929.

Bourne, Charles P. Methods of Information Handling. New York: Wiley, 1963.

Bovey, Robert L., and Mullick, Satinder Kumar. "Section IV." In Johns Hopkins University. Progress Report on an Operations Research and Systems Engineering Study of a University Library.

Branscomb, Harvie B. Teaching with Books: A Study of College Libraries. Chicago: Assn. of American Colleges and American Library Assn., 1940.

Broadfield, A. The Philosophy of Classification. London: Grafton, 1946.

Brunet, Jacques Charles. Manuel du libraire et de l'amateur de livres. 9 vols. 5 éd. originale entièrement refondue et augm. d'un tiers. Paris: Didot, 1860-80. First edition 1810.

Buck, Paul H. Libraries and Universities. Cambridge: Belknap Press of Harvard University Press, 1964.

Bundy, Mary Lee. Metropolitan Public Library Users: A Report of a Survey of Adult Use in the Maryland Baltimore - Washington Metropolitan Area. College Park: University of Maryland School of Library and Information Services, 1968.

Cannons, Harry George Turner. Bibliography of Library Economy, from 1876 to 1920. Chicago: American Library Assn., 1927.

Carter, Mary, and Bonk, Wallace. Building Library Collections. New York: Scarecrow Press, 1959.

Chicago. University. Graduate Library School. Requirements Study for Future Catalogs; Progress Report No. 2. Chicago, 1968.

_____. Library Conference. Bibliographic Organization; Papers Presented before the Fifteenth Annual Conference of the Graduate Library School, July 24-29, 1950. Ed. by Jesse H. Shera and Margaret E. Egan. Chicago: University of Chicago Press, 1951.

_____. Library Conference. Library Catalogs: Changing Dimensions; the Twenty-eighth Annual Conference of the Graduate Library School, August 5-7, 1963. Ed. by Ruth French Strout. Chicago: University of Chicago Press, 1964.

_____. Library Institute. The Acquisition and Cataloging of Books; Papers Presented before the Library Institute at the University of Chicago, July 29 to August 9, 1940. Ed. by William M. Randall. Chicago: University of Chicago Press, 1940.

Clapp, Verner W. The Future of the Research Library. Urbana: University of Illinois Press, 1964.

Cleverdon, Cyril W. Report on the Testing and Analysis of an Investigation into the Comparative Efficiency of Indexing Systems. Cranfield, Engl., 1962.
     Often cited as the Cleverdon Report or the Cranfield Report.

Coates, Eric J. Subject Catalogues: Headings and Structure. London: Library Assn., 1960.

Columbia University. President's Committee on the Educational Future of the University. Subcommittee on the University Libraries. The Columbia University Libraries; a Report on Present and Future Needs, Prepared for the President's Committee on the Educational Future of the University by the Subcommittee on the University Libraries. Maurice F. Tauber, Chairman, C. Donald Cook and Richard H. Logsdon. New York: Columbia University Press, 1958.

Commission on the Humanities. Report of the Commission on the Humanities. New York: American Council of Learned Societies, 1964.

Committee on College Reading. Good Reading. Ed. by J. Sherwood Weber. 35th ed. New York: New American Library, 1969.

Conference on Library School Teaching Methods: Courses in the Selection of Adult Materials, University of Illinois, 1968. Proceedings. Ed. by Larry Earl Bone. Urbana: University of Illinois, Graduate School of Library Service, 1969.

Cooper, William S. "The Potential Usefulness of Catalog Access Points Other than Author, Title and Subject." In Chicago. University. Graduate Library School. Requirements Study for Future Catalogs; Progress Report No. 2.

Courtney, Winifred F. The Reader's Adviser. 2 vols., 11th ed. New York: Bowker, 1968-69.

Custer, Benjamin A. "Editor's Introduction." In Melvil Dewey. Dewey Decimal Classification and Relative Index. 17th ed.

Cutter, Charles Ammi. Expansive Classification; Part I: The First Six Classifications. Boston: The Author, 1891-93.

_____. "Library Catalogues." In U.S. Bureau of Education. Public Libraries in the United States of America.

_____. Rules for a Dictionary Catalog. 4th ed., rewritten. Washington: Govt. Print. Off., 1904.
The 1876 edition was Part II of U.S. Bureau of Education. Public Libraries in the United States of America.

Dana, John Cotton. A Library Primer. 5th rev. ed. Chicago: Library Bureau, 1910.

Davia, Richard A., and Bailey, Catherine A. Bibliography of Use Studies. Philadelphia: Graduate School of Library Science, Drexel Institute of Technology, 1964.

Dewey, Harry. An Introduction to Library Cataloging and Classification. 4th ed., rev. and enl. Madison, Wis.: Capital Press, 1957.

Dewey, Melvil. "Catalogues and Cataloguing." In U. S. Bureau of Education. Public Libraries in the United States of America.

_____. Decimal Classification and Relativ Index for Arranging, Cataloging, and Indexing Public and Private Libraries and Pamphlets, Clippings, Notes, Scrapbooks, Index Rerums, etc. 2d ed., rev. and greatly enl. Boston: Library Bureau, 1885.

_____. Dewey Decimal Classification and Relative Index. 2 vols. 17th ed. Lake Placid Club, N. Y.: Forest Press, 1965.

_____. "Editorial Preface." In U. S. Library of Congress. A. L. A. Catalog.

Ditzion, Sidney Herbert. Arsenals of a Democratic Culture: A Social History of the American Public Library Movement in New England and the Middle States from 1850 to 1900. Chicago: American Library Assn., 1947.

Downs, Robert B. Resources of New York City Libraries, a Survey of Facilities for Advanced Study and Research. Chicago: American Library Assn., 1942.

Dunkin, Paul S. Cataloging U. S. A. Chicago: American Library Association, 1969.

Durkheim, Émile, and Mauss, Marcel. Primitive Classification. Tr. by Rodney Needham. Chicago: University of Chicago Press, 1963.

Eaton, Thelma. Cataloging and Classification: An Introductory Manual. 4th ed. Ann Arbor, Mich.: Edwards Brothers, 1967.

_____. Classification in Theory and Practice: A Collection of Papers. Champaign, Ill.: Illini Union Bookstore, 1957.

_____. "Epitaph to a Dead Classification." In her Classification in Theory and Practice.

Ellsworth, Ralph E. Planning the College and University Library Building: A Book for Campus Planners and Architects. 2d ed. Boulder, Colo.: Pruett Press, 1968.

Encyclopaedia of Librarianship. Ed. by Thomas Landau. 3d rev. ed. New York: Hafner, 1966.

Evans, Arthur Burke Agard. "Documentation." In Encyclopaedia of Librarianship.

Foskett, D. J. Classification and Indexing in the Social Sciences. London: Butterworths, 1963.

Franklin, Benjamin. Autobiography. The Works of Benjamin Franklin. Ed. by John Bigelow. Vol. I. New York: Putnam, 1904.

Frarey, Carlyle J. Subject Headings. Vol. I, Pt. 2 of The State of the Library Art. 1960.

Fussler, Herman H. "The Problems of Physical Accessibility." In Chicago. University. Graduate Library School. Library Conference. Bibliographic Organization.

_____, and Simon, Julian L. Patterns in the Use of Books in Large Research Libraries. Chicago: University of Chicago Library, 1961.
A reedited version with unchanged conclusions appeared in 1969.

Gore, Daniel. Bibliography for Beginners. New York: Appleton-Century-Crofts, 1968.

Grässe, Johann Georg Theodor. Trésor de livres rares et précieux. 7 vols. Dresden: Kuntze, 1859-69.

Great Books of the Western World and the Great Ideas. Ed. by Robert M. Hutchins and Mortimer J. Adler. 54 vols. Chicago: Encyclopaedia Britannica, 1952.

Greer, Roger C., and Zweizig, Douglas L. "An Overview
    of Present Selection Courses in American Library Schools."
    In Conference on Library School Teaching Methods: Courses
    in the Selection of Adult Materials, University of Illinois,
    1968. Proceedings.

Haines, Helen E. Living with Books: The Art of Book Se-
    lection. 2d ed. New York: Columbia University Press,
    1950.

Harris, William Torrey. "Letter of Transmittal." In U.S.
    Bureau of Education. Catalog of "A.L.A." Library.

The Harvard Classics. Ed. by Charles W. Eliot. 50 vols.
    New York: Collier, 1909.

Harvard University. Lamont Library. Catalogue. Prep.
    by Philip J. McNiff and members of the Library staff.
    Cambridge: Harvard University Press, 1953.

_____. Library. Widener Library Shelflist, No. 1-   .
    Cambridge: Harvard University Library, 1965-   .

Institute on the Subject Analysis of Library Materials, Co-
    lumbia University. The Subject Analysis of Library Ma-
    terials; Papers Presented at an Institute, June 24-28,
    1952. Ed. by Maurice F. Tauber. New York: School
    of Library Service, Columbia University, 1953.

Institute on the Use of the Library of Congress Classification,
    New York, 1966. Proceedings. Ed. by Richard H.
    Schimmelpfeng and C. Donald Cook. Chicago: American
    Library Assn., 1968.

International Conference on Scientific Information, Washing-
    ton, D.C., 1958. Proceedings. 2 vols. Washington:
    National Academy of Sciences and National Research Coun-
    cil, 1959.
        Often cited as PICSI.

International Research Associates, Inc. Access to Public
    Libraries: A Research Project Prepared for the Library
    Administration Division, American Library Association.
    Chicago: American Library Assn., 1963.

International Study Conference on Classification Research,
    2d, Elsinore, Denmark. Classification Research: Pro-

ceedings. Ed. by Pauline Atherton. Copenhagen: Munks-gaard, 1965.

Jevons, W. Stanley. The Principles of Science; a Treatise on Logic and Scientific Method. 2d ed. London: Macmillan, 1877.

Jewett, Charles Coffin. Notices of Public Libraries in the United States of America; Printed by Order of Congress, as an Appendix to the Fourth Annual Report of the Board of Regents of the Smithsonian Institution. Washington: Printed for the House of Representatives, 1851.

_____. On the Construction of Catalogues of Libraries and of a General Catalogue, and Their Publication by Means of Separate Stereotype Titles. With Rules and Examples. Washington: Smithsonian Institution, 1852.
A 2d ed. appeared in 1853. The 1852 version also had appeared as part of the 1851 Fifth Annual Report of the Board of Regents of the Smithsonian Institution.

Joeckel, Carleton Bruns. The Government of the American Public Library. Chicago: University of Chicago Press, 1935.

Johns Hopkins University. Progress Report on an Operations Research and Systems Engineering Study of a University Library. Baltimore, 1963.

Johnson, Pamela Hansford. On Iniquity: Some Personal Reflections Arising out of the Moors Murder Trial. New York: Scribner, 1967.

Jolley, Leonard M. The Principles of Cataloguing. New York: Philosophical Library, 1961.

Jordan, Robert T. Tomorrow's Library: Direct Access and Delivery. New York: Bowker, 1970.

Kelley, Grace Osgood. The Classification of Books: An Inquiry into Its Usefulness to the Reader. New York: Wilson, 1937.

_____. "The Classification of Books in Retrospect and in Prospect: A Tool and a Discipline." In Chicago. University. Graduate Library School. Library Institute. The Acquisition and Cataloging of Books.

Kephart, Horace. "Classification." In U.S. Bureau of Education. Report of the Commissioner for Education for 1892-93.

King, Gilbert W. Automation and the Library of Congress; Report of a Survey Sponsored by the Council on Library Resources, Inc. Submitted by Gilbert W. King, Chairman, and others. Washington: Library of Congress, 1964.
  Often cited as the King Report.

Knapp, Patricia B. The Monteith College Library Experiment. New York: Scarecrow Press, 1966.

LaMontagne, Leo E. American Library Classification, with Special Reference to the Library of Congress. Hamden, Conn.: Shoe String Press, 1961.

Leigh, Robert D. The Public Library in the United States: The General Report of the Public Library Inquiry. New York: Columbia University Press, 1950.

Library Surveys. Ed. by Maurice F. Tauber and Irlene Roemer Stephens. New York: Columbia University Press, 1967.

Licklider, J.C.R. Libraries of the Future. Cambridge, Mass.: M.I.T. Press, 1965.

Little, George T. "School and College Libraries." In U.S. Bureau of Education. Report of the Commissioner for Education for 1892-93.

Lovejoy, Arthur Oncken. The Great Chain of Being: A Study of the History of an Idea. The William James Lectures Delivered at Harvard University, 1933. Cambridge: Harvard University Press, 1936.

Lowndes, William Thomas. Bibliographer's Manual of English Literature. 6 vols. New ed. rev., corr., and enl. by H.G. Bohn. London: Bell, 1858-64.

Lyle, Guy R. "An Exploration into the Origins and Evolution of the Library Survey." In Library Surveys.

McNiff, Philip J. "Introduction." In Harvard University. Lamont Library. Catalogue.

Mann, Margaret. Introduction to Cataloging and the Classification of Books. 2d ed. Chicago: American Library
Assn., 1943.

Martin, Lowell A. Library Response to Urban Change: A
Study of the Chicago Public Library. Chicago: American
Library Assn., 1969.

Mathews, William. "Professorships of Books and Reading."
In U. S. Bureau of Education. Public Libraries in the
United States of America.

Menzel, Herbert. "The Information Needs of Current Scientific Research." In Chicago. University. Graduate
Library School. Library Conference. Library Catalogs: Changing Dimensions.

_____. "Planned and Unplanned Scientific Communica-
tion." In International Conference on Scientific Information, Washington, D. C., 1958. Proceedings.

Merrill, William Stetson. Code for Classifiers: Principles
Governing the Consistent Placing of Books in a System of
Classification. 2d ed. Chicago: American Library
Assn., 1939.

Metcalf, Keyes D. Report on the Harvard University Library: A Study of Present and Prospective Problems.
Cambridge: Harvard University Library, 1955.

Metcalfe, John. Information Indexing and Subject Cataloging:
Alphabetical, Classified, Coordinate, Mechanical. New
York: Scarecrow Press, 1957.

_____. Subject Classifying and Indexing of Libraries and
Literature. New York: Scarecrow Press, 1959.

Morse, Philip M. Library Effectiveness: A Systems Approach. Cambridge, Mass.: M. I. T. Press, 1968.

Needham, C. D. Organizing Knowledge in Libraries: An Introduction to Classification and Cataloguing. London:
Deutsch, 1964.

Needham, Rodney. "Introduction." In Émile Durkheim and
Marcel Mauss. Primitive Classification.

Norris, Dorothy May. A History of Cataloguing and Cataloguing Methods, 1100-1850; with an Introductory Survey of Ancient Times. London: Grafton, 1939.

Palmer, Bernard Ira. Itself an Education: Six Lectures on Classification. London: Library Assn., 1962.

Perkins, F.B., and Mathews, William. "Professorships of Books and Reading." In U.S. Bureau of Education. Public Libraries in the United States of America.

Pettee, Julia C. Subject Headings: The History and Theory of the Alphabetical Subject Approach to Books. New York: Wilson, 1946.

Piternick, George. "Duplicate Catalogs in University Libraries." In Chicago. University. Graduate Library School. Library Conference. Library Catalogs: Changing Dimensions.

Planning Conference on Information Transfer Experiments, Woods Hole, Mass., 1965. Intrex: Report. Ed. by Carl F.J. Overhage and R. Joyce Harman. Cambridge, Mass.: M.I.T. Press, 1965.

Princeton University. Julian Street Library. The Julian Street Library: A Preliminary List of Titles. Comp. by Warren B. Kuhn. New York: Bowker, 1966.

Problems in Library Classification: Dewey 17 and Conversion. Ed. by Theodore Samore. New York: Bowker, 1968.

Public Library Association. Subcommittee on Standards for Children's Service. Standards for Children's Services in Public Libraries. Chicago: American Library Assn., 1964.

Ranganathan, S.R. Colon Classification. 6th ed., reprinted with amendments. New York: Asia Publishing House, 1963.

_____. "Colon Classification and Its Approach to Documentation." In Chicago. University. Library Conference. Bibliographic Organization.

_____. Elements of Library Classification. 3d ed. New

York: Asia Publishing House, 1962.

_____. Prolegomena to Library Classification. 3d ed.
New York: Asia Publishing House, 1967.

_____. Theory of Library Catalogue. Madras: Madras
Library Assn., 1938.

Reichmann, Felix. "The Catalog in European Libraries."
In Chicago. University. Graduate Library School. Library Conference. Library Catalogs: Changing Dimensions.

Richardson, Ernest Cushing. Classification, Theoretical and
Practical; Together with an Appendix Containing an Essay
towards a Bibliographical History of Systems of Classification. 3d ed. New York: Wilson, 1930.

Rider, Fremont. Rider's International Classification for the
Arrangement of Books on the Shelves of General Libraries.
Prelim. ed. Middletown, Conn.: The Author, 1961.

_____. The Scholar and the Future of the Research Li-
brary: A Problem and Its Solution. New York: Hadham
Press, 1944.

Rigby, Malcolm. "Browsability in Modern Information Retrieval Systems: The Quest for Information." In Symposium on Education for Information Science, Airlie House,
1965. Proceedings.

_____, and Rigby, Marian K. "Cost Analysis of Bibliog-
raphies or Bibliographic Services." In International Conference on Scientific Information, Washington, D.C.,
1958, Proceedings.

Robinson, Otis H. "College Library Administration." In
U.S. Bureau of Education. Public Libraries in the United
States of America.

_____. "Titles of Books." In U.S. Bureau of Education.
Public Libraries in the United States of America.

Rothstein, Samuel. The Development of Reference Services
through Academic Traditions, Public Library Practice and
Special Librarianship. Chicago: Assn. of College and
Reference Libraries, 1955.

Samore, Theodore. "Summary and Analysis." In Problems
    in Library Classification: Dewey 17 and Conversion.

Savage, Ernest A. Manual of Book Classification and Dis-
    play for Public Libraries. London: Allen and Unwin,
    1946.

Sayers, W. C. Berwick. Canons of Classification Applied to
    "The Subject," "The Expansive," "The Decimal" and "The
    Library of Congress" Classifications. White Plains, N.Y.:
    Wilson, 1916.

_____. An Introduction to Library Classification, Theoret-
    ical, Historical and Practical, with Readings, Exercises
    and Examination Papers. 7th ed. London: Grafton, 1946.

Schneider, Georg. Theory and History of Bibliography. Tr.
    by Ralph R. Shaw. New York: Scarecrow Press, 1961.

Sears, Minnie Earl. List of Subject Headings. Ed. by Bar-
    bara Marietta Westby. 9th ed. New York: Wilson,
    1965.

Shaw, Charles B. A List of Books for College Libraries.
    Chicago: American Library Assn., 1931.

_____. A List of Books for College Libraries, 1931-38.
    Chicago: American Library Assn., 1940.

Sheehy, Eugene P. Guide to Reference Books, Eighth Edi-
    tion, by Constance M. Winchell; First Supplement, 1965-
    1966. Chicago: American Library Assn., 1968.

_____. _____; Second Supplement, 1967-1968. Chi-
    cago: American Library Assn., 1970.

Shera, Jesse H. "Classification as the Basis of Bibliograph-
    ic Organization." In Chicago. University. Graduate Li-
    brary School. Library Conference. Bibliographic Organi-
    zation.

_____. "Classification: Current Functions and Applica-
    tions to the Subject Analysis of Library Materials." In
    Institute on the Subject Analysis of Library Materials,
    Columbia University. The Subject Analysis of Library Ma-
    terials.

_____. Foundations of the Public Library: The Origins of the Public Library Movement in New England, 1629-1855. Chicago: University of Chicago Press, 1949.

_____, and Egan, Margaret E. The Classified Catalog: Basic Principles and Practices. Chicago: American Library Assn., 1956.

Shores, Louis; Jordan, Robert T.; and Harvey, John, eds. The Library-College: Contributions for American Higher Education at the Jamestown College Workshop, 1965. Philadelphia: Drexel Press, 1966.

Sonnenschein, William Swann. Best Books: A Reader's Guide and Literary Reference Book, Being a Contribution towards Systematic Bibliography. 6 vols. 3d ed., entirely rewritten. London: Routledge, 1910-35. First edition 1887.

Spofford, Ainsworth Rand. A Book for All Readers; Designed As an Aid to the Collection, Use, and Preservation of Books and the Formation of Public and Private Libraries. 3d ed., rev. New York: Putnam, 1905.

_____. "Library Bibliography." In U.S. Bureau of Education. Public Libraries in the United States of America.

Standard Catalog for Public Libraries, 4th Ed. 1958: A Classified and Annotated List of 7610 Non-fiction Books Recommended for Public and College Libraries, with a Full Analytical Index. Comp. by Dorothy H. West and Estelle A. Fidell. New York: Wilson, 1959.

The State of the Library Art. Ed. by Ralph R. Shaw. 5 vols. New Brunswick, N.J.: Graduate School of Library Service, Rutgers University, 1960-61.

Stevens, Rolland E. Characteristics of Subject Literatures. Chicago: Assn. of College and Reference Libraries, 1953.

Swanson, Don R. "Acknowledgement." In Chicago. University. Graduate Library School. Requirements Study for Future Catalogs; Progress Report No. 2.

_____. "Dialogues with a Catalogue." In Chicago. University. Graduate Library School. Library Conference. Library Catalogs: Changing Dimensions.

Symposium on Education for Information Science, Airlie
House, 1965. Proceedings. Ed. by Laurence B. Heil-
prin, Barbara E. Markuson, and Frederick L. Goodman.
Washington: Spartan Books, 1965.

Taube, Mortimer. "An Evaluation of 'Use Studies' of Scientific Information." In Emerging Solutions for Mechanizing the Storage and Retrieval of Information. Vol. V of
his Studies in Coordinate Indexing. 1959.

_____, and associates. Studies in Coordinate Indexing.
6 vols. Washington: Documentation, Inc., 1953-59.

Tauber, Maurice F. Louis Round Wilson: Librarian and
Administrator. New York: Columbia University Press,
1967.

_____. "Review of the Use of the Library of Congress
Classification." In Institute on the Use of the Library of
Congress Classification, New York, 1966. Proceedings.

_____, and Wise, Edith. Classification Systems. Vol. I,
Pt. 3 of The State of the Library Art. 1961.

Ulveling, Ralph. "Foreword." In Mary Carter and Wallace
Bonk. Building Library Collections. New York: Scarecrow Press, 1959.
    Cited by Roger C. Greer and Douglas L. Zweizig.
    "An Overview of Present Selection Courses in Amer-
    ican Library Schools." Q. v.

U.S. Bureau of Education. Catalog of "A.L.A." Library:
5000 Volumes for a Popular Library Selected by the American Library Association and Shown at the World's Columbian Exposition. Washington: Govt. Print. Off., 1893.

_____. Public Libraries in the United States of America;
Their History, Condition, and Management; Special Report; Part I. Washington: Govt. Print. Off., 1876.
    Part II was Cutter's Rules for a Dictionary Catalog.

_____. Report of the Commissioner for Education for 1892-93. 2 vols. Washington: Govt. Print. Off., 1895.

U. S. Library of Congress. A. L. A. Catalog: 8,000 Volumes for a Popular Library, with Notes. Ed. by Melvil Dewey. Washington: Govt. Print. Off., 1904.

_____. Annual Report of the Librarian of Congress for the Fiscal Year Ending June 30, 1961. Washington, 1962.

_____. Subject Cataloging Division. Catalog; Books: Subjects, 1950- . Washington, 1950- .

_____. _____. Subject Headings Used in the Dictionary Catalogs of the Library of Congress. Ed. by Marguerite V. Quattlebaum. 7th ed. Washington: Govt. Print. Off., 1966.

U. S. National Advisory Commission on Libraries. Library Services for the Nation's Needs: Toward Fulfillment of a National Policy. Bethesda, Md.: ERIC Document Reproduction Service, 1968.

U. S. Office of Education. Library Services Branch. Library Science Dissertations: 1925-60: An Annotated Bibliography of Doctoral Studies. Comp. by Nathan M. Cohen, Barbara Denison, and Jessie C. Boehlert. Washington: Govt. Print. Off., 1963.

_____. Statistics of Public Libraries Serving Communities with at Least 25,000 Inhabitants, 1965- . Washington: Govt. Print. Off., 1968- .

Vaughan, Delores K. "Memorability of Book Characteristics: An Experimental Study." In Chicago. University. Graduate Library School. Requirements Study for Future Catalogs; Progress Report No. 2.

Voigt, Melvin J., and Treyz, Joseph H. Books for College Libraries. Chicago: American Library Assn., 1967.

Waples, Douglas. Investigating Library Problems. Chicago: University of Chicago Press, 1939.

Warner Library ... Ed. by John W. Cunliffe and Ashley H. Thorndike. 30 vols. New York: Warner Library Company, 1917.
    First edition 1896-97 had title: Library of the World's Best Literature.

Warren, S. R., and Clark, S. N. "General Statistics of All Public Libraries in the United States." In U. S. Bureau of Education. Public Libraries in the United States of America.

_____, and _____. "Introduction." Ibid.

Watt, Robert. Bibliotheca Britannica; or, A General Index to British and Foreign Literature. 4 vols. Edinburgh: Constable, 1824.

Weber, David C. "The Changing Character of the Catalog in America." In Chicago. University. Graduate Library School. Library Conference. Library Catalogs: Changing Dimensions.

Wilson, Louis Round. "Foreword." In Carleton Bruns Joeckel. The Government of the American Public Library. Chicago: University of Chicago Press, 1935.

_____. The Geography of Reading: A Study of the Distribution and Status of Libraries in the United States. Chicago: American Library Assn. and University of Chicago Press, 1938.

_____, and Tauber, Maurice F. The University Library: The Organization, Administration, and Functions of Academic Libraries. 2d ed. New York: Columbia University Press, 1956.

Winchell, Constance M. Guide to Reference Books. 8th ed. Chicago: American Library Assn., 1967.
    For supplements, see Sheehy, Eugene P.

Winsor, Justin. "Library Buildings." In U. S. Bureau of Education. Public Libraries in the United States of America.

_____. "Reading in Popular Libraries." Ibid.

Woodruff, Edwin H. "Some Present Tendencies in University Libraries." (A paper read before the International Congress of Librarians at Chicago, July 14, 1893.) Quoted by George T. Little. "School and College Libraries." Q. v.

Part II: Journal Articles

"ACRL Academic Status Committee Proposes Standards for
    Librarians." College and Research Libraries News, No.
    9 (October, 1970), 269-72.

Akers, Susan Grey. "To What Extent Do the Students of the
    Liberal-Arts Colleges Use the Bibliographic Items Given
    on the Catalog Card?" Library Quarterly, I (October,
    1931), 394-408.

"American and British Open Access." Anonymous letter to
    the editor. Library World, X (1907-08), 46-47.

American Library Association. Adult Services Division.
    "Library Services--A Bill of Rights for Adults." Library
    Journal, XCIV (August, 1969), 2745-46.
        The preliminary draft version.

_____. Classification Committee. "Report, May 15,
    1964: Statement on Types of Classification Available to
    New Academic Libraries." Library Resources and Tech-
    nical Services, IX (Winter, 1965), 104-11.

"Analysis of Book-Stack Use." U.S. Library of Congress
    Information Bulletin, XIX (July 25, 1960), 435-36.

Ansteinsson, John. "Dilemmas of Classification." Library
    Quarterly, IV (April, 1934), 136-47.

Beals, Ralph Albert. "Education for Librarianship." Li-
    brary Quarterly, XVII (October, 1947), 296-305.

Berry, John III. "The New Constituency." Library Journal,
    XCIV (August, 1969), 2725-39.

"Birkdaler." Letter to the editor on "Open Access." Li-
    brary World, XI (1906-07), 76.

Brodman, Estelle. "Choosing Physiology Journals." Bul-
    letin of the Medical Library Association, XXXII (October,
    1944), 479-83.

Celoria, Francis. "The Archaeology of Serendip." Library
    Journal, XCIV (May 1, 1969), 1846-48.

416   Access to Library Collections

"Choice Opening Day Collection." Choice: Books for College Libraries, IV, special supplement (June, 1967).

Clapp, Verner W., and Jordan, Robert T. "Quantitative
Criteria for Adequacy of Academic Library Collections."
College and Research Libraries, XXVI (September, 1965),
371-80

Clay, Sam. "Open-Stack Study." Letter to the editor. Library Journal, XCIV (October 1, 1969), 3378, 3381.

Cutter, Charles Ammi. "Classification on the Shelves; with
Some Account of the New Scheme Prepared for the Boston
Athenaeum." Library Journal, IV (July-August, 1879),
234-43.

_____. "Close Classification, with Special Reference to
Messrs. Perkins, Schwartz, and Dewey." Library Journal, XI (July, 1886), 180-84.

DeGennaro, Richard. "A Computer Produced Shelf List."
College and Research Libraries, XXVI (July, 1965), 311-
15, 353.

Dewey, Melvil. "Arrangement on the Shelves." Library
Journal, IV (April 30, June 30; 1879), 117-20, 191-94.

_____. "The Decimal Classification, a Reply to the
'Duet.'" Library Journal, XI (April, 1886), 100-06.

_____. "Decimal Classification Beginnings." Library
Journal (February 15, 1920), 151-54.

Dix, William S. "On the Arrangement of Books." College
and Research Libraries, XXV (March, 1964), 85-90.

Downs, Robert B. "Leading American Library Collections."
Library Quarterly, XII (July, 1942), 457-73.

_____. "Research in Problems of Resources." Library
Trends, IV (October, 1957), 147-59.

Dubester, Henry J. "Stack Use of a Research Library."
(Review of "A Pilot Study of the Use of the Stacks of the
Library of Congress," by Saul Herner.) American Li-
brary Association Bulletin, LV (November, 1961), 891-93.

Dunkin, Paul S. "Catalog Use Study by Sidney L. Jackson."
Library Quarterly, XXIX (April, 1959), 140-42.

Editorial note. The Booklist, LXVI (November 15, 1969),
353.

Editorial note. Choice: Books for College Libraries, IV,
special supplement (June, 1967), 1.

Editor's footnote. Library Journal, XI (March, 1886), 74.

Editor's note. Library World, XI (1906-07), 76.

Farradane, J. E. L. "Psychology of Classification." Journal
of Documentation, XI (December, 1955), 187-201.

_____. "Relational Indexing and Classification in the
Light of Recent Experimental Work in Psychology." Information Storage and Retrieval, I, No. 1 (1963), 3-11.

Foskett, D. J. "The Classification Research Group, 1952-
1962." Libri, XII, No. 2 (1962), 127-38.

Gaines, Ervin J. "Zenith or Nadir?" (Review of Metropolitan Public Library Users, by Mary Lee Bundy.) Library
Journal, XCIV (May 1, 1969), 1849.

Harris, Willaim Torrey. "The Function of the Library and
the School in Education." Library Journal, XV (December, 1890), 27-33.

Herzberg, Joseph G. "Libraries Going Underground As Colleges Seek Book Space." New York Times, March 25,
1968.

Hoage, Annette L. "Patron Use of the L. C. Classification."
Library Resources and Technical Services, VI (Summer,
1962), 247-49.

Hosmer, James K. "On Browsing by a Book-Worm." Library Journal, XV (December, 1890), 33-37.

Hulme, E. Wyndham. "Principles of Book Classification."
Library Association Record, XIII (1911), 354-58, 389-94,
444-49; XIV (1912), 39-46, 174-81, 216-21.

Jackson, Sidney L. Review of Requirements Study for Future

Catalogs; Progress Report No. 2, by University of Chicago, Graduate Library School. Library Journal, CXIII
(October 1, 1968), 3525-26.

Kelley, Grace Osgood. "The Democratic Function of Public
Libraries." Library Quarterly, IV (January, 1934), 1-15.

_____. Review of The Organization of Knowledge in Li-
braries; and the Subject-Approach to Books, by Henry
Evelyn Bliss. Library Quarterly, IV (December, 1934),
665-68.

_____. "Subject Approach to Books: An Adventure in
Curriculum." Catalogers' and Classifiers' Yearbook, II
(1930), 9-23.

Lacy, Dan. "The Dissemination of Print." Wilson Library
Bulletin, XXXVII (September, 1963), 54-64.

Lundy, Frank A., Renfro, Kathryn R., and Shubert, Esther
M. "The Dual Assignment: Cataloging and Reference:
A Four-Year Review of Cataloging in the Divisional Plan."
Library Resources and Technical Services, III (Summer,
1959), 167-88.

Lyster, T. W. "Observations on Shelf-Classification." Library Association Record, II (1900), 399-409.

Martel, Charles. "Classification: A Brief Conspectus of
Present-Day Library Practice." Library Journal, XXXVI
(1911), 411-16.

Martin, Lowell A. "The Changes Ahead." Library Journal,
XCIII (February 15, 1968), 711-16.

Mills, Elizabeth. "The Separate Undergraduate Library."
College and Research Libraries, XXIX (March, 1968),
144-56.

Morse, Philip M. "Search Theory and Browsing." Library
Quarterly, XL (October, 1970), 391-408.

Moss, R. "Categories and Relations: Origins of Two Classification Theories." American Documentation, XV (October, 1964), 296-301.

Myres, J. N. L. "The Bodleian Library: Organization, Administration, Functions." Library World, LXII (April, 1961), 225-29.

Orne, Jerrold. "The Place of the Library in the Evolution of Graduate Work." College and Research Libraries, XXX (January, 1969), 25-31.

Perkins, F. B., and Schwartz, Jacob. "The Dui-Decimal Classification and the 'Relativ Index.' " Library Journal, XI (February, 1886), 37-43.

Piaget, Jean. "Genetic Epistemology." Columbia Forum, XII (Fall, 1969), 4-11.

Prevost, Marie Louise. "An Approach to Theory and Method in General Subject Heading." Library Quarterly, XVI (April, 1946), 140-51.

_____. "Classification of Books." (Review of The Classification of Books: An Inquiry into Its Usefulness to the Reader, by Grace Osgood Kelley.) Library Journal, LXIII (January 15, 1938), 69.

Rider, Fremont. "Old Classifications--and the Excuse for New Ones." Library Journal, XXXV (September, 1910), 387-96.

Rutzen, Ruth. "Shelving for Readers." Library Journal, LXXVII (March 15, 1952), 478-82.

Stevens, Rolland E. "The Study of the Research Use of Libraries." Library Quarterly, XXVI (January, 1956), 41-51.

Swank, Raynard. "Organization of Library Materials for Research in English Literature." Library Quarterly, XV (January, 1945), 49-74.

_____. "Subject Catalogs, Classifications, or Bibliographies? A Review of Critical Discussions, 1876-1942." Library Quarterly, XIV (October, 1944), 316-32.

Swanson, Don R. "The Evidence Underlying the Cranfield Results." Library Quarterly, XXXV (January, 1965), 1-20.

Tapley-Soper, H. "My Opinion of 'Open Access.' " Library World, X (1907-08), 243-45.

Tauber, Maurice F., ed. "Centralization and Decentralization in Academic Libraries: A Symposium." College and
Research Libraries, XXII (September, 1961), 327-40ff.

University Microfilms, Ann Arbor, Michigan, a Xerox Company. Advertisement. Library Journal, XCIV (June 15,
1969), 2430.

Vinton, F. "Shall Borrowers Go to the Shelves?" Library
Journal, XI (March, 1886), 74.

Wagman, Frederick H. "The Undergraduate Library of the
University of Michigan." College and Research Libraries,
XX (May, 1959), 179-88.

Wiley, Edwin. "Some Sidelights on Classification." Library
Journal, XLIV (June, 1919), 288-93; 359-64.

Part III: Dissertations, Pamphlets,
Unpublished Reports, Letters

Bowen, Alice. "Non-recorded Use of Books and Browsing in
the Stacks of a Research Library." Unpublished Master's
dissertation, University of Chicago, 1961.

Detroit Public Library. Home Reading Services. The Reader Interest Classification in the Detroit Public Library.
Detroit, 1955. (Pamphlet)

Gosnell, Charles Francis. "The Rate of Obsolescence in
College Library Book Collections as Determined by an
Analysis of Three Select Lists of Books for College Libraries." Unpublished Ph.D. dissertation, New York University, 1943.

Harvard University Library. Guide to Lamont Library.
Cambridge, 1968. (Pamphlet)

Henshaw, Marie M. Personal letter.

Herner, Saul. "A Pilot Study of the Use of the Stacks of
the Library of Congress." Washington: Herner, 1960.
(Typewritten)

Hoage, Annette L. "The Library of Congress Classification
in the United States: A Survey of Opinions and Practices,

Statement (Check appropriate heading)	Agree	Unde-cided	Do not agree

library profession among the
users of the library. _____ _____ _____

3. The chief value of close
shelf classification lies in
its use by the librarian for
teaching and by the patron
for learning. _____ _____ _____

4. Close relative shelf classification is necessary for
effective direct shelf ap-
proach to subject materials. _____ _____ _____

5. Some of the limitations of
shelf classification (e. g.,
linearity, books not on the
shelves at time of search,
separate shelving sequences)
make relative shelf classification basically undependable as a primary approach
to subject materials in the
library. _____ _____ _____

6. Close classification on the
shelves, because it places
too few books under any one
subject division, is less
suitable for the direct shelf
approach than for closed
stacks. _____ _____ _____

7. Close shelf classification is
as useful and feasible for
small libraries as it is for
large libraries. _____ _____ _____

8. Shelf classification has much
greater value as a locational
device, i. e., getting the book
once you know the call number, than as a systematic
subject approach. _____ _____ _____

Statement (Check appropriate heading)	Agree	Unde-cided	Do not Agree
9. Subject headings in the public catalog are more useful to the patron than shelf classification.	___	___	___
10. Close classification notation is simple enough for the average patron to follow successfully on the shelves.	___	___	___
11. Although close shelf classification may not be justified by its cost, it is cheaper for libraries now using it to continue rather than discard it.	___	___	___

IV. Direct Shelf Approach (Open-Shelf Access):

Its Suitability in Various Libraries

Statement (Check appropriate heading)	Agree	Unde-cided	Do not Agree
1. Open-shelf access is generally desirable in all libraries.	___	___	___
2. Maintaining open-shelf access is a significant educational responsibility of libraries.	___	___	___
3. The direct shelf approach is of value primarily as a means to create for the reader or student a structured learning situation.	___	___	___
4. The value of open-shelf access is primarily conditioned by the quality and appropriateness of the library's collection.	___	___	___

Statement (Check appropriate heading)	Agree	Unde-cided	Do not Agree

5. Public libraries cannot serve their readers adequately without offering open-shelf access. ___ ___ ___

6. School libraries (elementary through high school) cannot fulfill their function adequately without open access. ___ ___ ___

7. The smaller the library, the more valuable is open-shelf access. ___ ___ ___

8. Direct shelf approach is more useful in a specialized or university departmental collection with a homogeneous clientele than in mixed collections with different types of readers. ___ ___ ___

9. Open-shelf access is more needed in university or research libraries than in general undergraduate libraries. ___ ___ ___

10. Reserved book collections and assigned reading lists make largely unnecessary open-shelf access in college libraries. ___ ___ ___

11. Open-shelf access is more needed for use of books than for serials. ___ ___ ___

12. Open-shelf access is more needed by readers in the humanities than in the sciences. ___ ___ ___

13. Open-shelf access is more needed by readers in the social sciences than in the

428 Access to Library Collections

Statement (Check appropriate heading)	Agree	Unde-cided	Do not Agree
biological and physical sciences.	___	___	___
14. Direct shelf approach is most valuable in collections for beginning students where the books are basic or "core" titles.	___	___	___
15. The validity of the direct shelf approach lessens as research in the discipline relies more on topical subjects and less on personal names and distinctive titles for access to information.	___	___	___
16. Adequate catalogs, bibliographies and, when available, reference assistance, would make open-shelf access in large academic libraries largely unnecessary.	___	___	___
17. The more advanced the student or researcher in academic libraries, the less need for open-shelf access.	___	___	___
18. A reader whose early experience has been with the Dewey classification will not be able to use effectively a collection classified by L. C.	___	___	___
19. Provision of direct shelf approach for readers is not in itself a valid reason for close classification on shelves in general academic and research libraries.	___	___	___

V.   Direct Shelf Approach (Open-Shelf Access):

The Role of "Browsing" and Related Activities

By "browsing" is meant the inspection of books on
shelves to select appropriate or desirable material for research or recreational use.   It usually involves at least a
cursory inspection of the contents.

		Agree	Unde-cided	Do not Agree
Statement (Check appropriate heading)				
1.	All readers should be encour-aged to browse.	____	____	____
2.	Browsing provides a valuable learning experience.	____	____	____
3.	Shelf classification is nec-essary for non-recreational browsing.	____	____	____
4.	Close classification on shelves is necessary for non-recreational browsing.	____	____	____
5.	The greater limits imposed on browsing by acquisition policy and by classification, the more valuable browsing will be.	____	____	____
6.	Dewey classification aids browsing.	____	____	____
7.	L. C. classification hinders browsing.	____	____	____
8.	The possible physical diffi-culties encountered in brows-ing (e.g., bad lighting, high or low shelves, lack of work-ing space, effort in lifting and replacing books) make browsing in most large aca-demic collections an unde-			

	Unde-	Do not
Statement (Check appropriate heading)	Agree	cided	Agree

sirable procedure from the
standpoint of most users.

9. In a large general academic
    collection, browsing is likely
    to be wasteful for most stu-
    dents because they will spend
    too much time on inconsequen-
    tial titles.

10. Browsing is essential for aca-
    demic research above the be-
    ginner's level.

11. A major value of browsing is
    the possibility of "serendip-
    ity," i.e., "making desirable
    but unsought-for discoveries."

12. The possibility of "serendip-
    ity" is much greater in a li-
    brary with relative shelf clas-
    sification.

13. Nothing can be accomplished
    by browsing in a general re-
    search collection that could
    not be done more easily and
    efficiently through the use of
    the library catalog and other
    bibliographical tools.

14. "Browsing" is not a suffi-
    ciently precise term to char-
    acterize serious research, so
    its use should be limited to
    describing recreational, non-
    research activities in "brows-
    ing" collections or their
    equivalent.

INDEX

A.L.A. Catalog: 1893, 149-50, 151, 156, 161; 1904, 150-51;
  1926, 150
A.L.A. Membership Directory, 230
Academic status for librarians, 390
Access to Library Collections (Hyman): assumptions, 10;
  conclusions for practice, 388-93; conclusions for research,
  393-94; library types coverage, 11; methodology, 3-5,
  11-12, 61-62, 65-66; motivation, 10
Access to Public Libraries (International Research Associates,
  Inc.), 97
Acquisition policy: direct shelf approach and browsing in relation to, 131, 141, 152-61, 292-94, 329-32, 371, 373-77;
  educational goals, 370-71; library school courses, 374,
  391
Adams, James Truslow: "New History," 74
Akers, Susan Grey: college catalog use study, 33-34
American Book Publishing Record (BPR), 390
American Library Association: book lists and buying guides,
  149-52; Catalog Use Study (Jackson Catalog Use Study),
  9, 34-38; "Library Services--A Bill of Rights for Adults,"
  97-98; Standards, 142; "Statement on Types of Classification Available to New Academic Libraries," 8, 55, 65,
  332, 335; Survey of Libraries in the United States (Com-
  mittee of Five Report), 79, 82, 85, 93-94
American Library Directory, 230
Angell, Richard S.: Library of Congress shelf classification,
  53-55; open-shelf core collection, 64-65, 142
Annual Report of the Librarian of Congress, 1960-61, 24
Ansteinsson, John: Jespersen on classifying, 365
"Archaeology of Serendip" (Celoria), 126-28, 133-34
Aristotelian logic: categories, 189; library classification
  use, 181, 190, 204-05; "Porphyry's Tree," 181, 204-05;
  true order, 362
Arsenals of a Democratic Culture (Ditzion), 74
Ash, Lee: Yale book retirement program, 141
Assigned reading lists: effects in college libraries, 300-01
Association of College and Research Libraries (ACRL): edu-
  cational role of librarian, 390
Astor Library Catalog, 148, 160

431

Audio-visual materials: direct shelf approach relation, 382
Auto-didacticism: direct shelf approach, 99-100
Automation and the Library of Congress (King Report), 54

Bacon, Francis: classification scheme, 364
Bar-Hillel, Yehoshua: data- vs. reference-providing, 71
    note 81, 131
"Basic Canon of Helpful Sequence" (Ranganathan), 189
Beals, Ralph: learned profession definition, 143; public li-
    brary aims, 74; teaching of book selection, 374
Beard, Charles Austin: "New History," 74
Berelson, Bernard: public library clientele, 96-97, 98
"Best books" lists and collections, 159-61, 391
Best Books (Sonnenschein), 159
Bibliographic Classification (Bliss): notation, 210; practicali-
    ty, 187
Bibliographic (indirect) access: complementary role, 388,
    392; desirability, 342-45, 361, 377-78; future, 381-82
Bibliography of Use Studies (Davis and Bailey), 9, 24, 31
Bibliotheca Universalis (Gesner), 148
Billings Classification, 243
Biological Abstracts, 134
Biological sciences: direct shelf approach, 304-05
"Birkdaler": direct shelf approach advocacy, 77-78
Bliss, Henry Evelyn: Bibliographic Classification, 187, 210;
    classification importance, 216-17, 258, 361, 368, 372;
    classification principles, 4, 176, 188, 190, 194, 202,
    217, 363, 364-65, 367; classification schemes critique,
    187, 216; close classification, 195-96; Dewey Decimal
    Classification, 178-79, 210; direct shelf approach descrip-
    tion, 126, 130; Expansive Classification, 177; mnemonics,
    212; on Jevons, 187-88, 205; on Kelley, 201, 206; subject
    headings, 206-07, 370;
        criticism by: Broadfield, 188, 204; Dunkin, 176;
        Kelley, 188-89; Metcalfe, 182, 188; Shera, 364
Bodleian Library, 154, 172-73
Book for All Readers (Spofford), 87
Book lists and buying guides: normative role, 373
Book selection: American public libraries study, 93-94;
    criteria, 146-47
Booklist (A.L.A.), 151-52
Books for College Libraries (Voigt and Treyz), 152, 157-59
Books for disadvantaged, 98-99, 385 note 39
Boston Athenaeum: Catalog, 148, 160; close classification,
    192-93
Boston Public Library: classified catalogs, 148
Bostwick, Arthur E.: close classification critique, 195, 198,

263; direct shelf approach advocacy, 75-76, 79, 83, 124, 128, 294; educational role of libraries, 86-87; notation, 214; novel reading, 145-46
Bourne, Charles P.: computer browsing, 116, 118
Bowen, Alice (Mrs. Carroll G.): non-recorded use of books and browsing, 43-46, 63-64, 141
Bradford, S. C.: close classification, 201-02
Branscomb, Harvie B.: college library direct shelf approach, 12
British Museum Library: classified catalog opposition, 173; Panizzi's "Rules," 172; reference collection, 80; Select Committee, 172
British National Bibliography (BNB), 206, 271
Broad vs. close classification, 247-49, 371-72. See also Close classification; Close shelf classification
Broadfield, A.: classification logic, 181, 363; classification study benefit, 5; evolutionary order critique, 177, 204; on Bliss, 188, 204; on Richardson, 184, 204; on Sayers, 204; "Porphyry's Tree," 181, 204-05
Brodman, Estelle: citation analysis critique, 9
Brooklyn College Library: direct shelf approach, 302-03
Brown, James Duff: direct shelf approach advocacy, 79
Browsability: information retrieval criterion, 116; functional definition, 131
Browsing: acquisition and classification in relation to, 131, 159-61, 329-32, 376, 377; aids and restrictions to, 56; bibliographic (indirect) access relation, 43, 54, 342-45, 377-78; Dewey Decimal Classification, 8, 55, 332-34; direct shelf approach relation, 8, 25-26, 53, 128-30, 320-21, 324-25, 342-43, 345, 348-54, 376-80; documentalist use, 14 note 11, 376, 386 note 44; documentary frequency analysis of, 22-26, 378; educational value, 113-14, 116-17, 118, 125-26, 325-26, 376-77; encouragement of, 320-21, 324-25, 376, 377; equivocal activity role, 54, 111-12, 113, 119-21, 336-38; etymology, 17-18, 23-24, 379; "grazing" relation, 18-20; Library of Congress Classification, 8, 55, 334-35; non-recreational function, 326-29, 376; physical difficulties, 335-36; research function, 42-43, 114-18, 121, 125-26, 338-40, 345-49, 376, 378-79; serendipity, 43, 110, 118, 128, 133-34, 340, 362, 376, 377, 380; shelf classification defense, 8, 9; typology, 30-31, 126-31. See also Non-recorded use of books; Specific and non-specific book searches
    definitions: dictionary, 18-21; functional, 128-31, 362, 368, 379-80; multi-level, 8-9, 110-14, 126-28; preliminary, 11, 110; "tight core and loose core use," 31, 41

research on: amount of, 56, 118; catalog use study relation, 37, 50-52; diary approach, 41-44; limitations, 57-58; nonrecorded use study approach, 41, 52; operations research and systems engineering approach, 9, 47-50; proposals, 393-94; search theory approach, 52; stack use study approach, 38-39, 41-44; theoretical approach, 61; use value criteria application, 9, 31, 41, 57-58. See also names of individual studies and their authors

Collection evaluation criteria, 142
"Collection organization advisor," 392-93
College and university libraries: browsing, 335-40; close classification, 312-13, 371; direct shelf approach, 307-11, 312-13; Library of Congress Classification vs. Dewey Decimal Classification, 389
College libraries: direct shelf approach, 83-85, 300-01, 338
Colon Classification (Ranganathan), 100, 194, 198, 209
Columbia University Libraries survey, 142, 171
Commission on the Humanities: direct shelf approach advocacy, 117
Committee of Five Report (Survey of Libraries in the United States) (A.L.A.), 79, 82, 85, 93-94
Committee on College Reading, 160
Compact storage, 41-42
Computerized library access, 382
"Congress for Change," 99
Cooper, William S.: non-standard book information, 51
Core collection, 142, 305-06, 370-71
Courtney, Winifred F.: normative bibliography, 160
Cranfield Project (Cleverdon), 46, 55, 393
Custer, Benjamin A.: classification role, 216; Dewey Decimal Classification description, 180-81, 197; Reader Interest Classification critique, 194
Cutter, Charles Ammi: "bad" books, 159; Boston Athenaeum classification, 192; Boston Public Library classified catalogs, 148; browsing advocacy, 20, 379; catalog notes, 146-47; classification principles, 4, 184-85; close shelf classification defense, 81, 190-92, 203, 263, 265; convenience of public, 3, 6 note 2; direct shelf approach advocacy, 8, 112, 123, 128, 130; evolutionary order, 101, 176-77; Expansive Classification, 176, 192-93; shelf arrangement, 112-13; shelf classification, 171, 176; shelf policy 80-81, 250, 357; subject headings, 203, 206, 207, 370

Dana, John Cotton: Library Primer, 87; public library role, 78-79, 80, 87
Davis, Richard A., and Bailey, Catherine A.: Bibliography of Use Studies, 9, 24; browsing study citations, 9, 24, 31; use study defense, 33; use study typology, 32
"Decimal Classification Beginnings" (Dewey), 89
DeGennaro, Richard: Harvard shelf list, 118
Departmental academic libraries, 82, 160
Detroit Public Library: Reader Interest Classification, 194-95

Dewey, Harry: direct shelf approach advocacy, 115
Dewey, Melvil: A. L. A. Catalog (1904), 150-51; close classification advocacy, 263; direct shelf approach implementation, 76, 122, 130, 170; educational role of libraries, 89;
practical library classification, 4, 177-78; relative index,
179
Dewey Decimal Classification: 14th ed., 179-80, 195, 371-
72; 15th ed., 198, 371-72; 17th ed., 180-81, 194, 197;
abridged edition, 372, 389; browsability, 8, 55, 332-34;
classified catalog relation, 180; close classification, 81,
190-92, 195, 197, 199, 203, 263, 371-72; conversion to
Library of Congress Classification, 243-46; direct shelf
approach, 88-89, 217; educational goal, 89; evolutionary
order lack, 178; Library of Congress Classification relation, 2, 175, 243-46, 249, 311-12, 389; mnemonics, 212;
notation, 210, 211-12; notation on Library of Congress
cards, 193, 360-61, 372, 382; political and social origins,
88-89, 217; practicality, 177-79; public libraries, 242; reclassification, 175-76; "subject-index illusion," 178-79
Dictionary catalog, 172, 240, 242
Direct access. See Direct shelf approach (open-shelf access)
"Direct access" (home delivery), 382
Direct shelf approach (open-shelf access): advanced study and
research roles, 310-11; advocacy, 48, 75, 77-81, 83-85,
90, 123-26, 128, 171; American and British rise, 73, 79;
books vs. serials, 301-03; British public libraries, 77-79;
browsing relation, 8, 25-26, 128-29, 320-21, 324-25, 376-
80; catalog-use relation, 34, 35-37; close shelf classification, 312-13, 371; collection quality, 292-94, 371; descriptions, 122-28; desirability, 286, 288-89, 370; Dewey-ex-
perienced patrons in Library of Congress -classed collections, 311-12; educational responsibility, 289, 291, 370-71,
377; educational value, 80, 83-85, 99-100; humanities vs.
sciences, 303-04; opposition, 75-77, 80; replacement in
academic libraries, 307-10; research proposals, 394; research ramifications, 2-3; safeguarded type, 78; shelf classification, 73, 170; social and political claims, 85-90;
social vs. biological and physical sciences, 304-05; structured learning situation, 291-92; surveys, 79; topical subjects vs. names, 306-07; validity of concept, 380-82;
   suitability in various types of libraries: college, 300-
   01; core collections, 305-06; general analysis and
   interpretation of responses on, 370-76; public, 294-
   95; school, 295-96; small, 296-97; special, 297-299;
   statistical relationships of responses on, 313-18;
   university and research, 299-300
"Directory of the Association of American Library Schools,"
230

Disarray and pilferage in stacks, 75-79, 113
Ditzion, Sidney Herbert: "good" reading, 86; public library purpose, 74, 88
Divided catalog, 240, 242
Dix, William S.: shelf classification advocacy, 53
Documentary analysis: implications, 388-94; methodology, 11-12
Documentation: browsing relation, 115, 376, 386 note 44; Universal Decimal Classification role, 389
Downs, Robert B.: acquisition departments, 374; collection evaluations, 142, 374
Dual-classified collections, 244-46
Dubester, Henry J.: Library of Congress stacks study critique, 9, 39-40, 63
Dunkin, Paul S.: catalog use studies critique, 9, 11, 33; close classification critique, 196-97; Cutter's catalog notes, 147, 165 note 27; Cutter's "Objects," 139 note 51; Dewey Decimal and Library of Congress Classification comparison, 175; Jackson Catalog Use Study review, 35, 37-38; mnemonics, 212; opposition to Richardson and Bliss metaphysics, 176; shelf classification as locational device, 175
Durkheim, Émile: classification, 4, 362; libraries, 73-74; sociology of knowledge, 364
Durkheim, Émile, and Mauss, Marcel: social origin of classification, 366-67

Eaton, Thelma: close classification roles, 195, 198; Dewey Decimal Classification, 179-80, 195, 198, 371-72
Educational role of librarian, 87-88, 97, 390, 394
Edwards, Edward: book classification study, 182
Eliot, Charles W.: "best books" collection, 159
Ellsworth, Ralph E.: browsing rooms, 119-20
Encyclopaedia of Librarianship, 115
Entropy of bibliographic system, 25, 66 note 7
Epistemology: classification element, 362-63
"Epitaph to a Dead Classification" (Eaton), 198
Evans, Arthur Burke Agard: research browsing, 115
Evolutionary theory: role in classification, 101, 176-77, 178, 186-87, 203-04
"Exploration into the Origins and Evolution of the Library Survey" (Lyle), 91
Expressive notation: 210-13, 270, 360
Expansive Classification (Cutter): Bliss critique, 177; close classification, 195; evolutionary order, 176-77; respondent use, 243, 245; structure, 192-93

Facet analysis, 189
Faculty status for librarians, 390
Farradane, J. E. L.: psychological classification, 365, 384 note 23
Fellows, Dorcas: close classification uses, 372, 389
"Five Fundamental Categories" (Ranganathan), 189
"Five Laws of the Library Science" (Ranganathan), 3, 189
Fixed location: direct shelf approach relation, 171-72, 382; random access relation, 133; revival, 7, 14 note 7, 39, 246-47, 343-44
Folger Shakespeare Library, 286
Foskett, D. J.: research browsing, 115-16
Franklin, Benjamin: subscription libraries, 86
Frarey, Carlyle J.: catalog use studies review, 9, 11, 33; subject headings review, 31
Frick Art Reference Library, 298
"Function of the Library and the School in Education" (Harris), 89-90
Fussler, Herman H.: library storage policy, 142
Fussler, Herman H., and Simon, Julian L.: acquisitions influence, 141; book use in research libraries, 41-43, 63; browsing study, 9, 31, 43, 57-58, 63; serendipity, 43, 63

Gaines, Ervin J.: public library users, 98
Genetic epistemology, 365, 384 note 24
Geography of Reading (Wilson), 95-96
Gesner, Konrad: normative catalogs, 148
Gladstone, William Ewart: direct shelf approach advocacy, 123
Good Reading (Committee on College Reading), 160
Gore, Daniel: college library browsing, 118
Gosnell, Charles Francis: weeding criteria, 141
Government of the American Public Library (Joeckel), 95
Grässe, Johann Georg Theodor: normative bibliography, 160
"Grazing": relation to "browsing," 18-20, 130-31, 133, 379
"Great American Library Dream" (Kelley), 60
Great Books of the Western World and the Great Ideas (Hutchins), 159
Great Chain of Being (Lovejoy), 101, 202, 362, 375
Greer, Roger C., and Zweizig, Douglas L.: acquisition role, 374, 386 note 40
Guiding: library application, 389

Haines, Helen E.: normative bibliography, 160
Handbuch der Bibliographie (Schneider), 175
Harris, William Torrey: A. L. A. Catalog (1893), 149-50;

classification scheme, 90; novel reading, 144; public li-
brary's role, 89-90; seminar teaching, 81-82
Harvard Business School Classification, 243
Harvard Classics (Eliot), 159
Harvard University Libraries: departmentalization, 82. See
also Lamont Library; Widener Library
Heisenberg, Werner: indeterminancy principle, 57
Henshaw, Marie M.: browsing definition, 111
Herner, Saul: core collection, 142; Library of Congress
stacks use study, 38-41; shelf classification as locational
device, 63, 214, 266
Hierarchical classification: Aristotelian origin, 181; Dewey
Decimal Classification, 180-81; evolutionary order, 203-
04; "Great Chain of Being," 202; metaphysics, 181-84;
Platonic origin, 181, 362-63; social origin, 366-67
"Higher Browsing" (Celoria), 126-28
Hoage, Annette L.: patron instruction need, 311, 319 note
3, 389, 395 note 2; patron use of Library of Congress
Classification study, 46-47; shelf classification as loca-
tional device, 63, 64, 214-15, 266
Hosmer, James K.: browsing by scholars, 30-31, 62, 126;
"browsing" metaphor, 22, 23-24, 378; open-shelf core
collections, 39, 65, 80
Hulme, E.Wyndham: "true order" opposition, 101, 182
Humanities: direct shelf approach, 303-04
Hutchins, Robert M.: "best books" collection, 159
Hyman, Richard J. See Access to Library Collections

Indirect access. See Bibliographic (indirect) access
Integrative levels theory, 104
Intrex: relation to browsing, 117, 394

Jackson, Sidney L.: Catalog Use Study, 9, 34-38; direct
shelf approach research proposal, 9, 50, 51-52; Require-
ments Study for Future Catalogs review, 50; subject head-
ings, 50-51
James, Thomas: undergraduate library proposal, 154
James, William: classification function, 364-65
Jast, Louis Stanley: direct shelf approach advocacy, 79
Jespersen, Jens Otto Harry: classification faculty, 365
Jevons, W.Stanley: library classification logic, 187-88, 205,
363, 383 note 12
Jewett, Charles Coffin: centralized cataloging, 91; mid-cen-
tury survey, 91; usefulness criterion, 3
Joeckel, Carleton Bruns: regional library service, 95
Johns Hopkins University: Progress Report, 9, 47-50, 62;
seminar teaching, 81

Johnson, Pamela Hansford: effects of reading, 164 note 22
Johnston, Edward William: classification scheme, 90
Jolley, Leonard M.: American shelf classification, 175; on Pettee, 205
Jordan, Robert T.: "direct access" (home delivery), 382
Julian Street Library Catalog (Princeton), 156

Kelley, Grace Osgood: browsing typology, 114; Classification of Books, 58-61, 198, 201, 216; education for librarians, 392; on Bliss, 188-89, 217; public library aims, 380-81; subject headings effectiveness, 65, 206, 207, 267, 360, 370, 392
Kephart, Horace: classification survey, 93; notation, 208-09
King Report (Automation and the Library of Congress), 54
Knapp, Patricia B.: college library browsing, 120-21, 160, 369; Library-College, 82
Kyle, Barbara: "dowsing" vs. "browsing," 55

Lacy, Dan: books for disadvantaged, 98-99, 385 note 39
Lamont Library (Harvard): Catalogue, 154, 156, 158; direct shelf approach, 153-54, 155, 299, 371
LaMontagne, Leo E.: Dewey Decimal Classification, 180; Expansive Classification, 176; Harris classification, 90
Leyh, Georg: classified catalog role, 174
Librarians: educational role, 87-88, 97, 390, 394
Libraries. See individual types, e.g., Small libraries; Undergraduate libraries
"Library Catalogues" (Cutter), 148
Library-College, 82, 84-85, 120, 276, 390
Library Effectiveness: A Systems Approach (Morse), 52
Library of Congress: Catalog, 148; Catalog; Books: Subjects, 390; catalog cards, 91, 193, 360-61, 372, 382; cataloger role, 344; "closed-stacks" library, 277; "special" library, 238, 294; stacks use study, 9, 38, 142, 214; Subject Headings Used in the Dictionary Catalogs, 389
Library of Congress Classification: academic libraries, 242, 389; browsability, 8, 55, 334-35; close classification, 195, 249; conversion to, 243-46; Dewey Decimal Classification comparison, 2, 175, 212, 249, 311-12, 389; future, 54; mnemonics, 212; patron use, 46-47, 214-15, 311-12
Library Primer (Dana), 87
Library respondents: size influence on responses, 282, 284, 358-59; size statistics, 236, 238
Library school curricula, 390-92, 393
Library Science Dissertations: 1925-1960 (U.S. Office of Education), 24

"Library Services--A Bill of Rights for Adults" (A. L. A.), 97-98
Library Services Acts, 88
Library Services for the Nation's Needs (U. S. National Advisory Commission on Libraries), 91-92, 93
Library surveys: Access to Public Libraries, 97; Geography of Reading, 95-96; Government of the American Public Library, 95; Jewett mid-century survey, 91; Kephart classification survey, 93, 208-09; Library Response to Urban Change, 97, 370, 373, 390, 395 note 7; Library Services for the Nation's Needs, 91-92, 93; Library's Public, 96-97, 98; Metropolitan Public Library Users, 98; Public Libraries in the United States of America, 87-88, 91-93, 142-43; Public Library in the United States, 96-97; Public Library Inquiry, 96; Steiner shelf policy survey, 79; Survey of Libraries in the United States (Committee of Five Report), 79, 82, 85, 93-94; relation to libraries' educational and social roles, 90-99
Library system centers, 234-35
Library's Public (Berelson), 96-97, 98
Linearity in classification, 200-05
List of Books for College Libraries (Shaw), 152, 153, 157, 161
Little, George T.: college library direct shelf approach, 83, 338; departmental collections, 82; undergraduate collections, 154-55, 338
Living with Books (Haines), 160
"Loose core and tight core browsing-use," 31, 41
Lovejoy, Arthur Oncken: classification, 4, 362; Great Chain of Being, 101, 202, 362
Lowndes, William Thomas: normative bibliography, 160
Lundy, Frank A.: technical and reader services relation, 391
Lyle, Guy R.: library surveys overview, 91
Lyster, T. W.: shelf classification in direct shelf approach, 73, 124, 141

Main classes, 368-69
Mann, Margaret: subject headings vs. classification terms, 206
Martel, Charles: direct shelf approach value, 124
Martin, Lowell A.: librarians as teachers, 97, 370, 373, 390, 395 note 7
Marx, Karl: effects of library reading, 86
Mathews, William: art of reading, 21; browsing opposition, 111-12; college library shelf policy, 76-77; professorships

442

of books and reading, 77, 146, 160
MEDLARS (U. K.): serendipity class definition, 133-34
Menzel, Herbert: research browsing, 55, 116
Merrill, William Stetson: classifiers' code, 93
Merton, Robert K.: serendipity definition, 134
Metcalf, Keyes D.: Harvard library departmentalization, 82
Metcalfe, John: chain indexing, 206; classification schemes
    critique, 181-84, 218, 369, 385 note 32; Dewey's index,
    179; Dewey's mnemonics, 212; notation, 212-13; on Bliss,
    188; on Kelley, 198; on Ranganathan, 3, 190; on Richard-
    son, 184; on Shera, 171, 364; specification critique, 198,
    201-02, 375-76; subject headings, 267
Metropolitan Public Library Users (Bundy), 98
Michigan, University of, Undergraduate Library: description,
    120, 155-56; influence, 158
Micro Thought: depth classification, 194
Microfilms: browsability, 117
Mills, Elizabeth: undergraduate library history, 120, 155
Minute classification. See Close classification
Mnemonics: value in classification, 212-14
Modal respondent characteristics: geographical distribution,
    356-57; influence on responses, 358; reclassification ex-
    perience, 357; shelf policy, 357; summary, 356-59
Morris, William, and Morris, Mary: "browsing" vs. "graz-
    ing, " 19-20
Morse, Philip: search theory and browsing, 52
Moss, R.: facet analysis critique, 189
Mostecky, Vaclav: college library browsing, 37

National Lending Library for Science and Technology (London),
    301
National Library of Medicine Classification (NLM), 243
Nebraska, University of, Library: cataloging-reference as-
    signment, 391
Needham, C.D.: expressive notation critique, 213; linearity
    problem, 200-01; Reader Interest Classification, 194-95;
    Tottenham (England) Public Library subject bays, 117
Needham, Rodney: Durkheim and Mauss classification theory,
    367
New York, College of the City of, Library, 187
New York Mercantile Library Catalog, 148
New York Public Library, Donnell Branch: direct shelf ap-
    proach, 298
New York Public Library, Reference Department: broad clas-
    sification policy, 312; fixed location policy, 14 note 7,
    343-44; "public" library role, 294; shelf policy, 294, 312;
    "special" library role, 238

Peabody Institute (Baltimore) Catalogue, 160
Penakes (Callimachus), 172
Pennsylvania, University of, Libraries: faculty self-survey,
    142
Perkins, F. B., and Mathews, William: professorships of
    books and reading, 146, 160
Perkins, F. B. and Schwartz, Jacob: close classification
    critique, 81, 190-92, 195, 198, 203
Pettee, Julia C.:   dictionary catalog history, 172; subject
    headings value, 205-06, 267, 360
Philadelphia, Free Library of: direct shelf approach, 78,
    79
Philadelphia, Library Company of, Catalog, 148
Philadelphia, Mercantile Library of, Catalog, 148
Physical sciences: direct shelf approach, 304-05
Piaget, Jean: classification, 4, 362; genetic epistemology,
    365, 384 note 24
Pilferage and disarray in stacks, 75-79, 113
"Pilot Study of the Use of the Stacks of the Library of Con-
    gress" (Herner), 9, 39-40, 63
Piternick, George: university departmental library catalogs,
    82
"Place of the Library in the Evolution of Graduate Work"
    (Orne), 303, 316 note 2
"Planned and Unplanned Communication" (Menzel), 55
Plato: respondent's serendipity citation, 362
Platonic realism: hierarchical classification relation, 101,
    181, 362-63, 367, 375, 391
Pomeroy, Jesse: effects of novel reading, 145
Popper, Karl R.:   respondent's serendipity citation, 362
"Porphyry's Tree," 181, 182, 204-05
Prevost, Marie: Kelley study review, 60, 201; library's
    public, 356
Primitive Classification (Durkheim and Mauss), 366-67
Princeton College Library: shelf policy, 76-77, 80
Princeton University, Julian Street Library, Catalog, 156
Printed catalogs: early European, 148; 19th-century Amer-
    ican, 148; normative role, 148, 373
"Professorships of Books and Reading" (Perkins and Mathews),
    77, 111, 146
Progress Report on an Operations Research and Systems En-
    gineering Study of a University Library (Johns Hopkins),
    9, 47-50, 62
Prolegomena to Library Classification (Ranganathan), 118
"Proposed Standards for Librarians" (ACRL), 390
Psychology: classification element, 363-65
Public libraries: American origins, 73-75, 88; direct shelf

approach, 77-79, 294-95; educational role, 80, 86-99, 380-81; mail order catalogs, 382; social role, 90-99, 380-81

Public Libraries in the United States of America (U.S. Bureau of Education), 87-88, 91-93, 142-43. See also separately indexed parts

Public Library Inquiry, 96

Putnam, Herbert: public library direct shelf approach, 79

Questionnaire analysis: conclusions for practice, 388-93; conclusions for research, 393-94

Questionnaire respondents: selection criteria, 230-32

Questionnaire responses: editing and tallying procedures, 252-53; statistical measurements of relationship: III:1-11, 278-84; IV:1-19, 313-18, 372; V:1-14, 349-54; all responses, 358-59. See also Chi-square test; Coefficient of contingency

Questionnaire statements: derivation and wording, 252; "Documentary Analysis" citations: III:1, 102, 190, 218; III:3, 102, 200; III:4, 65, 200; III:5, 63, 65; III:6, 200; III:7, 200; III:8, 63, 64; III:9, 65, 207; III:10, 64, 200, 214; III:11, 200; IV:1, 26, 62, 102; IV:2, 26, 89, 102, 134, 161; IV:3, 135, 161; IV:4, 20, 135, 161; IV:5, 87, 102; IV:6, 102; IV:8, 64, 82; IV:9, 64; IV:10, 161-62; IV:11, 64; IV:12, 62; IV:13, 62, 64; IV:14, 65, 162; IV:15, 62; IV:16, 65, 207; IV:17, 64; V:1, 26, 62, 121; V:2, 26, 135; V:5, 20, 135, 162; V:6, 65; V:7, 65; V:8, 63; V:9, 162; V:10, 64, 135; V:11, 63, 135; V:12, 135; V:13, 63, 64, 207; V:14, 22, 121, 135 (For all statements discussed in "Questionnaire Analysis," refer to "Contents," p. v-vi.)

"Random": definitions, 132

"Random access": definition, 133

"Random examination": relation to browsing, 11, 110, 131-33

Random sampling: biological sense, 132; relation to respondent selection, 230-31, 235

Ranganathan, S.R.: "Basic Canon of Helpful Sequence," 189; browsing advocacy, 118; chain indexing, 206; classification definitions, 362, 364, 365, 383 note 7; classification importance, 100-01, 171, 258, 361, 368, 372; classification schemes critique, 216; close classification, 194, 197-98, 202; direct shelf approach, 90; facet analysis, 189; "Five Laws of the Library Science," 3, 97, 189; Metcalfe on, 3, 182, 190, 201-02; Micro Thought, 194; notation, 209,

211, 211; subject headings theory, 206
"Rapid Selector" (Shaw), 116
Reader Interest Classification, 194-95, 332
Reader services: relation to technical services, 391-92
Reader's Adviser (Courtney), 160
"Reading in Popular Libraries" (Winsor), 143-44
Recall and relevance ratios, 55
Reclassification: modal respondent characteristic, 357; policy recommendations, 388-89; respondent experience, 244-46
Recorded use of books: studies of relation to browsing use, 41-42, 44, 45, 48-49, 50, 52. See also Non-recorded use of books
Referential classification (Whitehead), 364, 383 note 13
Regional library service, 95
Registrum Librorum Angliae, 148
Reichmann, Felix: European classified catalogs, 173; European shelf classification, 173-74; subject-bibliography research, 207
Relational Classification (Farradane), 365, 384 note 23
Relative shelf classification. See Shelf classification
Relative shelf location: respondent policy, 246-47. See also Fixed location; Shelf classification
Relevance and recall ratios, 55
Report of the Commission on the Humanities, 85
Republic (Plato): allegory of the cave, 363, 383 note 10; respondent's serendipity citation, 362
Requirements Study for Future Catalogs (Chicago, University of, Graduate Library School), 50-52
Research libraries: close classification, 312-13, 371; direct shelf approach, 299-300, 312-13, 371
Reserved book collections: effects in college libraries, 300-01
Respondent characteristics: classification systems, 242-44; close classification, 247-49; geographical distribution, 232; institutional types, 233-36; library sizes, 236-38, 282, 284, 358-59; library types, 236-38; professional functions, 232-33, 358; public catalogs, 240-42; reclassification, 244-46; relative shelf location, 246-47; shelf policy, 249-51; subject collections, 238-40;
    relation to type of response: by library size, 282, 284, 358-59; by professional function, 358. See also Tables 1, 12, 13, 15, 17, 18, 20, 21, 23, 24, 26
Review media, 373
"Review of the Use of the Library of Congress Classification (Tauber), 266, 284, 311, 319 note 3, 395 note 2

Ribbon arrangement of fiction, 145-46
Richardson, Ernest Cushing: browsing benefits, 113-14, 379; classification importance, 216, 372; classification laws, 184; direct shelf approach advocacy, 124-26, 130; evolutionary order, 101, 186-87, 204; metaphysics, 176, 367; Platonic beliefs, 101, 363; practical classification, 183-84; shelf classification, 171; true order of sciences, 182
Richmond, Phylis A.: browsing typology, 110-111; classification research proposals, 11, 61, 393
Rider, Fremont: close classification, 198-99; collection growth projection, 236; notation, 210; shelf classification, 171-72
Rider's International Classification, 198-99, 210
Rigby, Malcolm: browsing typology, 14 note 11, 56, 116-17
Rigby, Malcolm, and Rigby, Marian K.: entropy of bibliographic system, 25, 66 note 7
Robinson, Otis H.: college library acquisition policy, 146; college library shelf policy, 83-85, 338; didactic catalog, 147-48
Rothstein, Samuel: American public library history, 74-75; reference service origins, 92-93
Rules for a Dictionary Catalog (Cutter), 3, 6 note 2, 146-47, 206
Rullmann, F.: librarian training, 91
Russell, Bertrand: Aristotelian categories, 189

Safeguarded open access, 78
St. Louis Mercantile Library: classification scheme, 90
Samore, Theodore: browsing impracticality, 121, 122
San Francisco, Mercantile Library Association of, Catalog, 148
Savage, Ernest A.: close classification 196; direct shelf approach advocacy, 79; guiding, 389; notation, 213; temporary grouping of books, 194
Sayers, W. C. Berwick: A. L. A. Catalog notes, 151; classification definition, 364; classification importance, 216; Dewey Decimal Classification, 178; direct shelf approach advocacy, 123; evolutionary order, 101, 186-87, 203-04; Expansive Classification, 176-77; mnemonics, 212; notation, 208, 210-12, 270, 360; on Hulme and Edwards, 182; on Jevons, 205; on Kelley, 201; practical classification, 4, 185-86; reclassification, 275
Schlesinger, Arthur M.: "New History," 74
Schneider, Georg: library classification, 175, 193
School libraries: direct shelf approach, 295-96; respondents, 234-35
Schwartz, Jacob: classified catalog application, 112

Sciences: direct shelf approach, 303-04
"Search Theory and Browsing" (Morse), 52
Sears List of Subject Headings, 389
Selection policy. See Acquisition policy
Seminar teaching, 81-82
Serendipity: browsing justification, 340, 376, 377, 380;
  browsing result, 43, 110, 118, 128, 362; definitions, 133-
  34; Library-College objective, 276; shelf classification
  role, 341-42, 376, 377
Serials: direct shelf approach, 301-03
Shaw, Charles B.: college library book list, 152, 153, 157
Shaw, Ralph R.: "Rapid Selector," 116; state-of-the-library-
  art review, 31
Shelf access policy. See Shelf policy (open or closed
  shelves)
Shelf classification: acquisition policy relation, 374-75; advocacy, 53-55, 123-24, 170-72, 176; browsing relation,
  8, 9; catalog relation, 122, 124; description, 7; direct
  shelf approach relation, 8, 170, 275-78; European attitudes, 170-76; limitations, 7, 58-60, 203, 261-63; locational device, 46, 175, 214-15, 266-67, 360, 382, 388;
  maintenance problems, 7-8; non-recreational browsing
  relation, 326-27, 376; practical aims, 176-90; prestige
  effect, 257-59; revelatory role, 256-57, 372; serendipity
  relation, 341-42, 376, 377. See also Close shelf classification
Shelf classification with relative location. See Shelf classification
Shelf-level: effect on browsing, 42, 45
Shelf list: Michigan, University of, Undergraduate Library,
  156; public use proposal, 390; Widener Library (Harvard),
  118, 157, 343, 389, 390
"Shelflisting Section of the Library of Congress" (Tauber),
  170-71, 381
Shelf order: alphabetical sub-arrangement, 112-13; position
  vis-à-vis notation, 215-16
Shelf policy (open or closed shelves): Committee of Five Report, 85; respondent characteristic, 249-51, 357; Steiner
  survey, 79
Shera, Jesse H.: classification hierarchy critique, 364;
  classified catalog advocacy, 361; Durkheim influence, 73-
  74, 364, 366; public library origins, 73-75; public library
  social effects, 85-86; referential classification advocacy,
  364, 383 note 13; shelf classification critique, 171, 364
Shores, Louis: Library-College, 82
Small libraries: close shelf classification, 264-65; direct
  shelf approach, 296-97

Smithsonian Institution Catalog, 148

Tapley-Soper, H.: British direct shelf approach, 80
Taube, Mortimer: use studies critique, 9, 11, 33, 61, 380,
   393
Tauber, Maurice F.: academic library departmentalization,
   82; classification systems review, 31; patron instruction
   in Library of Congress Classification, 311, 319 note 3,
   389, 395 note 2; respondent library size influence, 284;
   shelf classification defense, 170-71, 266, 381; survey of
   Columbia University Libraries, 142; survey of faculty on
   shelf classification, 9; survey of library of Congress shelf-
   listing section, 170-71, 381
Teaching with Books (Branscomb), 12
Technical services: relation to reader services, 391-92
Temporary grouping of books, 194
Thompson, C. Seymour: "good reading" belief, 74-75, 86
Three Princes of Serendip (Walpole), 133
"Tight core and loose core browsing-use," 31, 41
Timaeus (Plato), 101
"To What Extent Do the Students of the Liberal-Arts Colleges
   Use the Bibliographic Items Given on the Catalog Card?"
   (Akers), 33-34
Tottenham (England) Public Library: subject bays, 117
Topical subject research: relation to direct shelf approach,
   306-07
"True order": relation to shelf classification, 256-57

Undergraduate libraries: Bodleian proposal, 154; direct shelf
   approach, 299-300; history, 155; Julian Street (Princeton),
   156; Lamont (Harvard), 153-54, 155; Michigan, University
   of, 155-56; requirements, 154-55
U.S. National Advisory Commission on Libraries, 91-92, 93
U.S. Office of Education, Library Services Branch: library
   science dissertations bibliography, 24, 31
U.S. Superintendent of Documents Classification, 243
Universal Decimal Classification (UDC): close classification,
   198; documentation use proposal, 389; respondent use,
   243; specification in relation to classification, 198
University libraries: direct shelf approach, 299-300
Use and user studies: case study proposal, 47; defense, 33;
   evaluation, 61, 393; goals, 9; quantitative studies of subject literatures, 32; relation to this study, 61-62
Usefulness: research criterion, 3, 170

Van Hoesen, Henry Bartlett: critique of Richardson classification, 183-84
Vaughan, Delores K.: catalog use studies, 51-52
Vinton, F.: college library direct shelf approach opposition,
   76-77, 80

Voigt, Melvin J., and Treyz, Joseph H.: college book list, 152, 157-59
Voting behavior analysis, 321, 394

Wagman, Frederick H.: Michigan, University of, Undergraduate Library, 120, 155-56
Walpole, Horace: "serendipity" origin, 133
Ward, Lester F.: order of nature, 188
Warren, S. R., and Clark, S. N.: conflicting opinions survey, 143; librarian training, 91; public library definition, 92; public library educational role, 87-88; public library statistics, 142-43
Watt, Robert: normative bibliography, 160
Weber, David C.: machine browsability, 117-18
Weeding: criteria, 141
Whitehead, Alfred North: referential classification, 364, 383 note 13
Who's Who in Library Service, 230
Widener Library Shelflist (Harvard), 118, 157, 343, 389, 390
Wiley, Edwin: mnemonics critique, 213-14
Wilson (H. W.) Co.: normative bibliographies, 152
Wilson, Louis Round: academic collection criteria, 142; Geography of Reading, 95-96; sociological research, 94-95
Winchell, Constance: 19th-century catalogs, 160
Winsor, Justin: direct shelf approach opposition, 76; novel reading, 143-44
Woodruff, Edwin H.: university departmental libraries, 160

"Xerox College Library Program," 161

Yale's Selective Book Retirement Program (Ash), 141